AF371954

OLETHA DeVANE
spectrum of light and spirit

OLETHA DeVANE

spectrum

**Edited by Lowery Stokes Sims
and Symmes Gardner**

With contributions by Leslie King-Hammond,
Christopher Kojzar, Serubiri Moses, and Tadia Rice

of light *and spirit*

Center for Art, Design, and Visual Culture
University of Maryland, Baltimore County

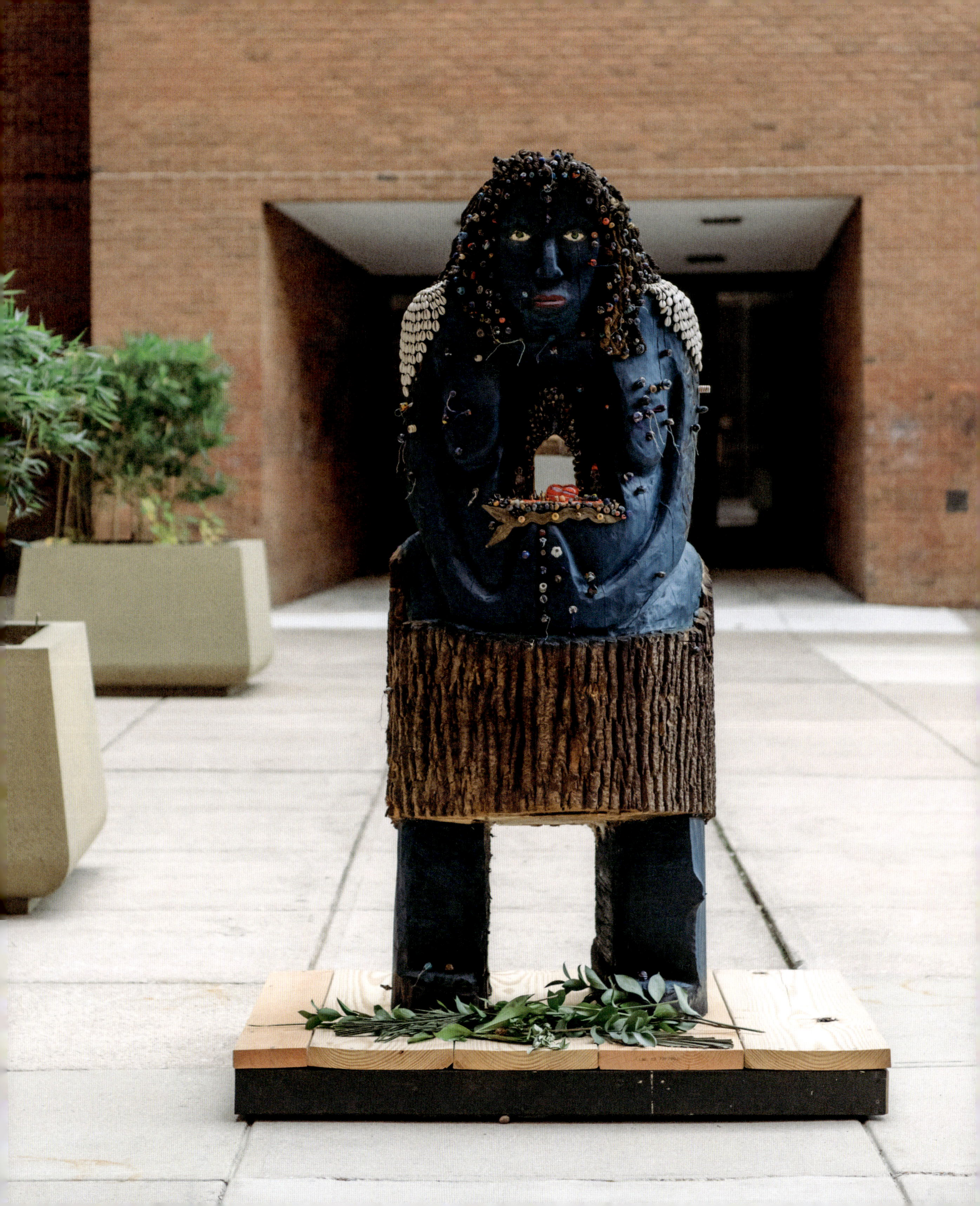

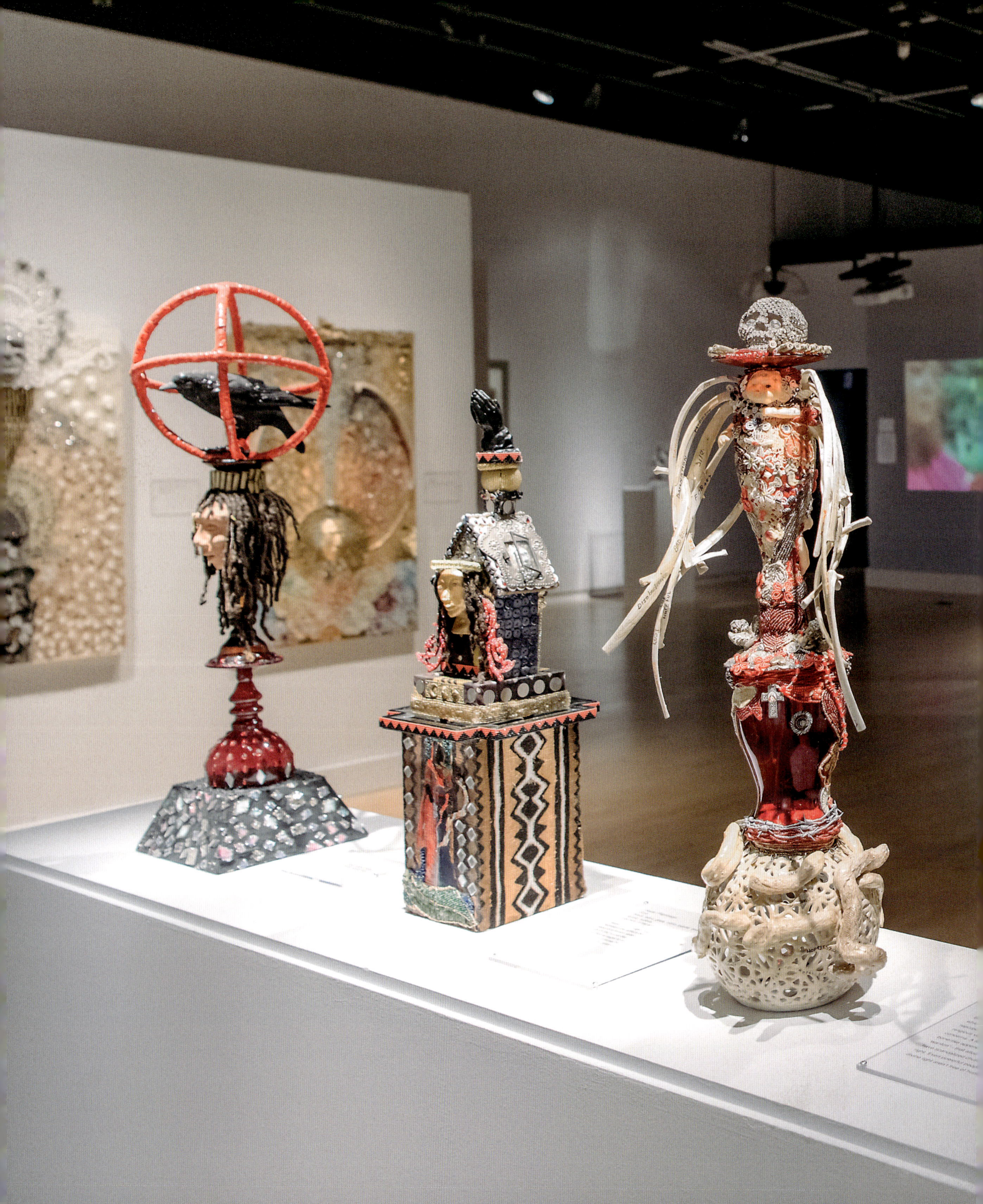

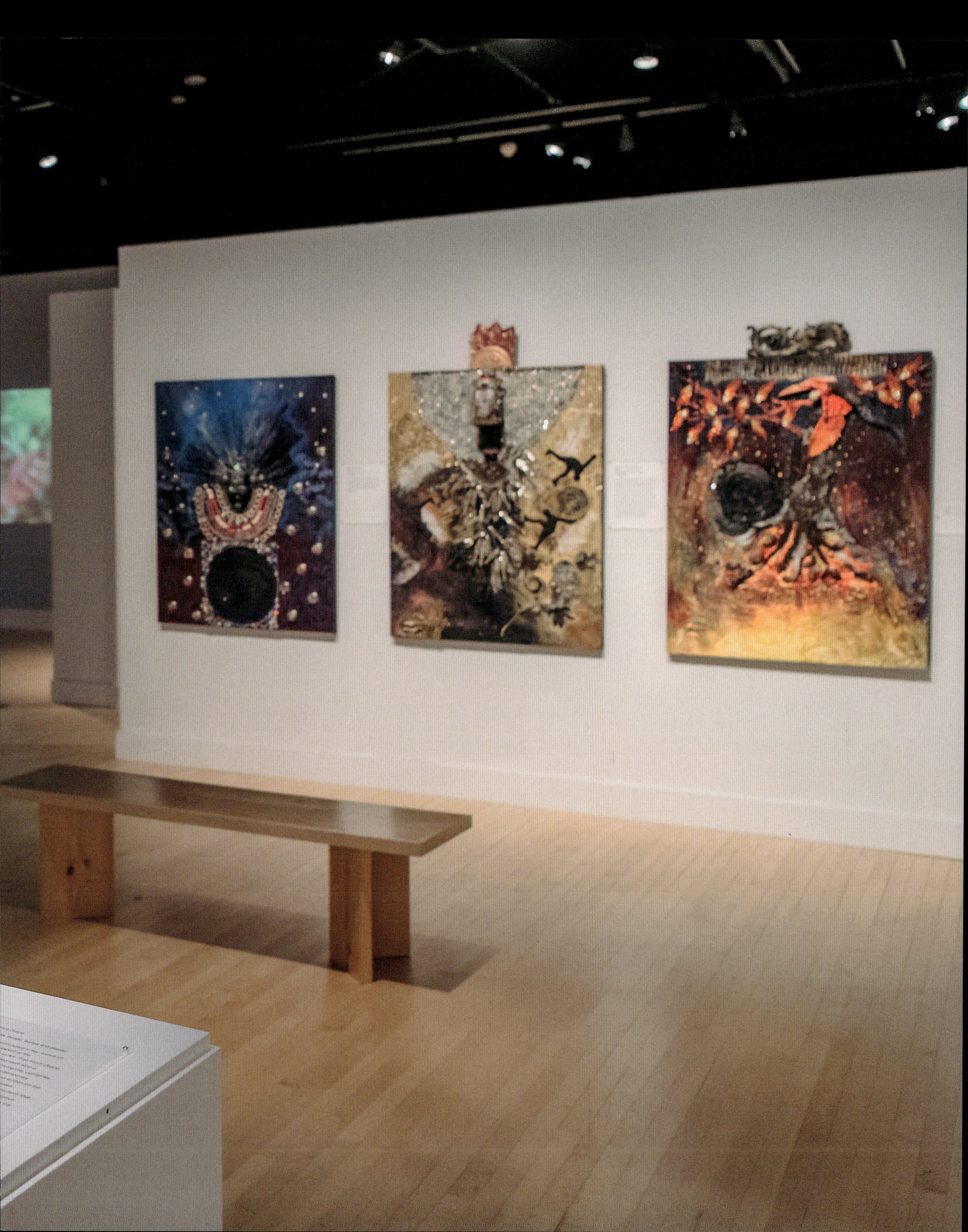

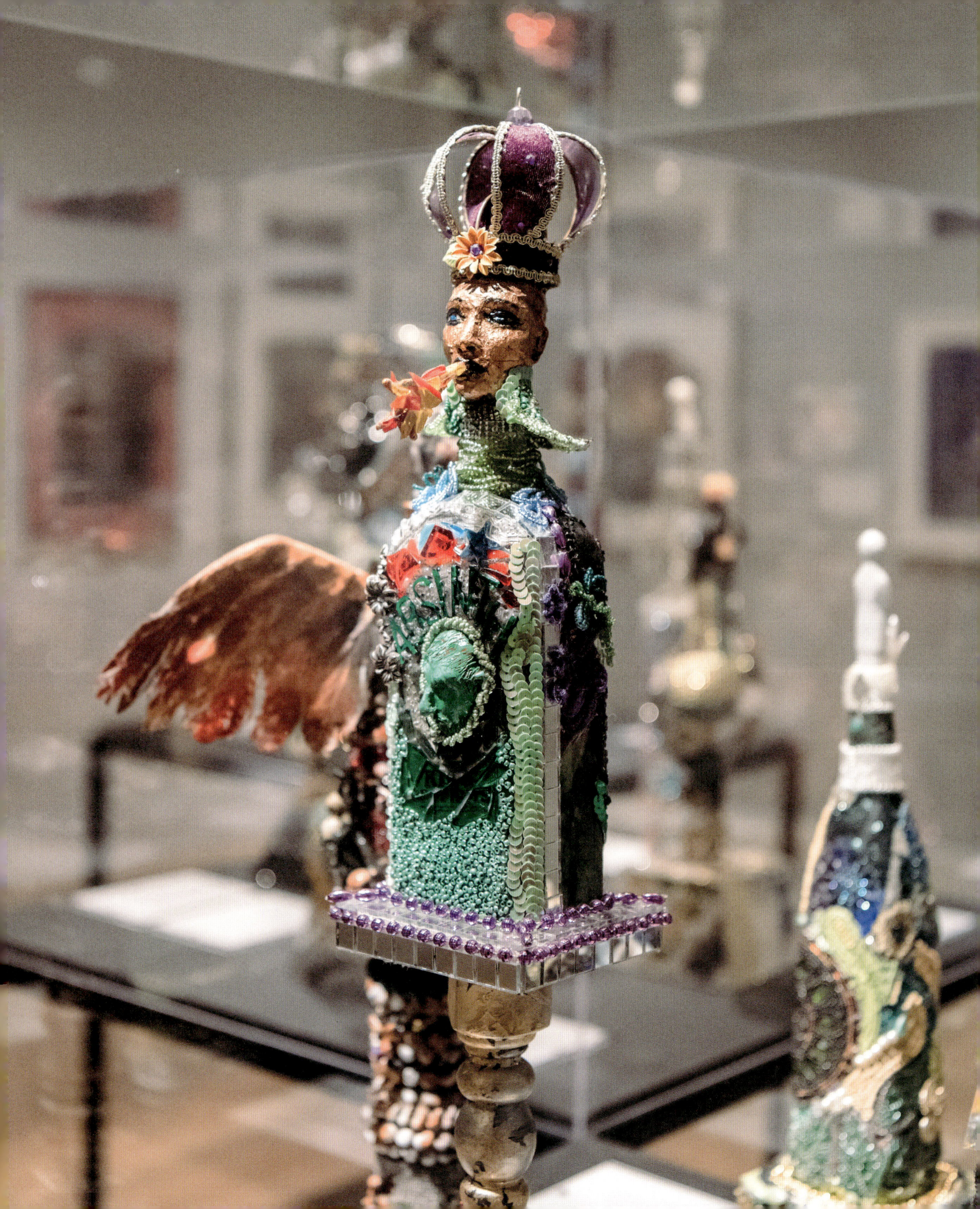

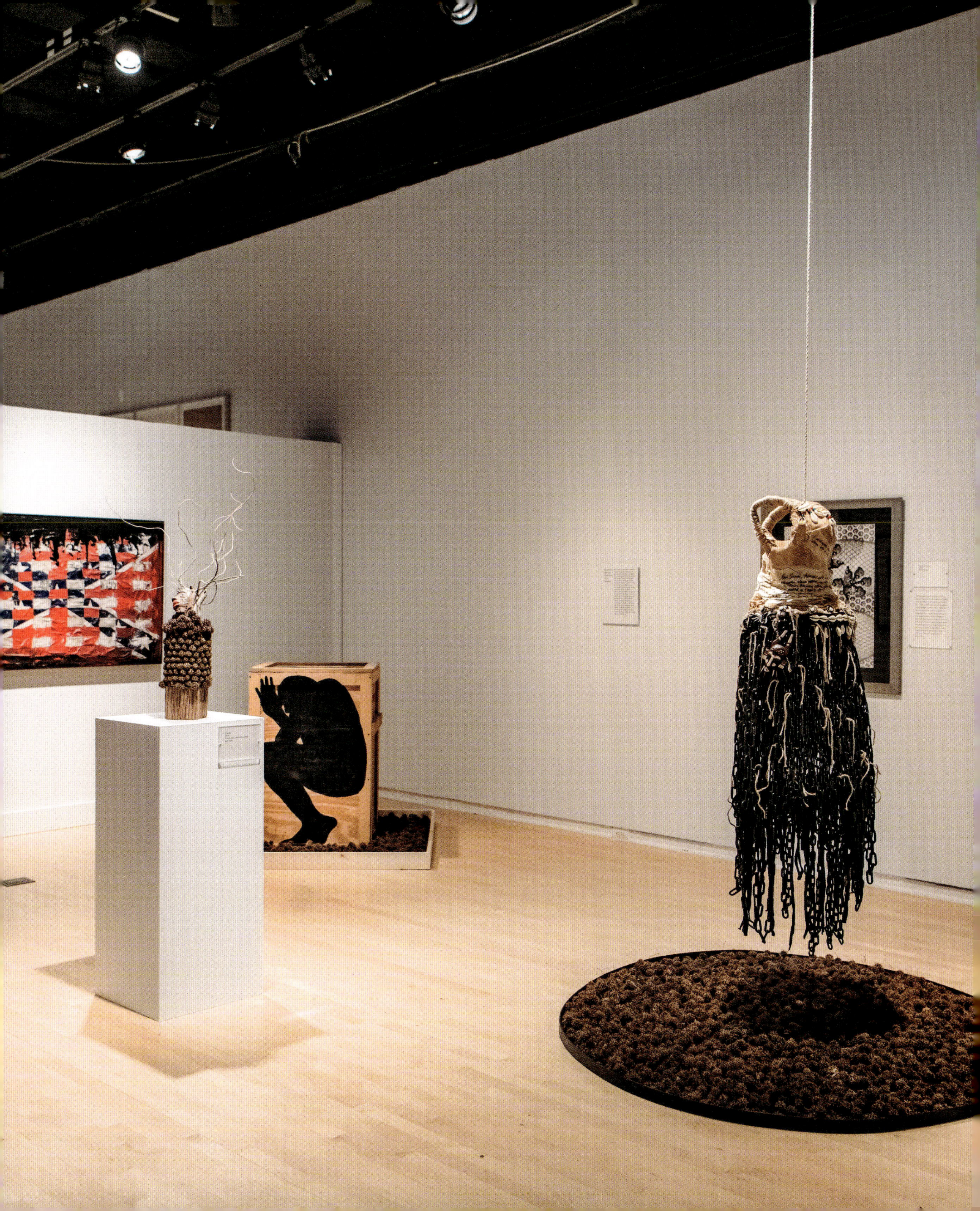

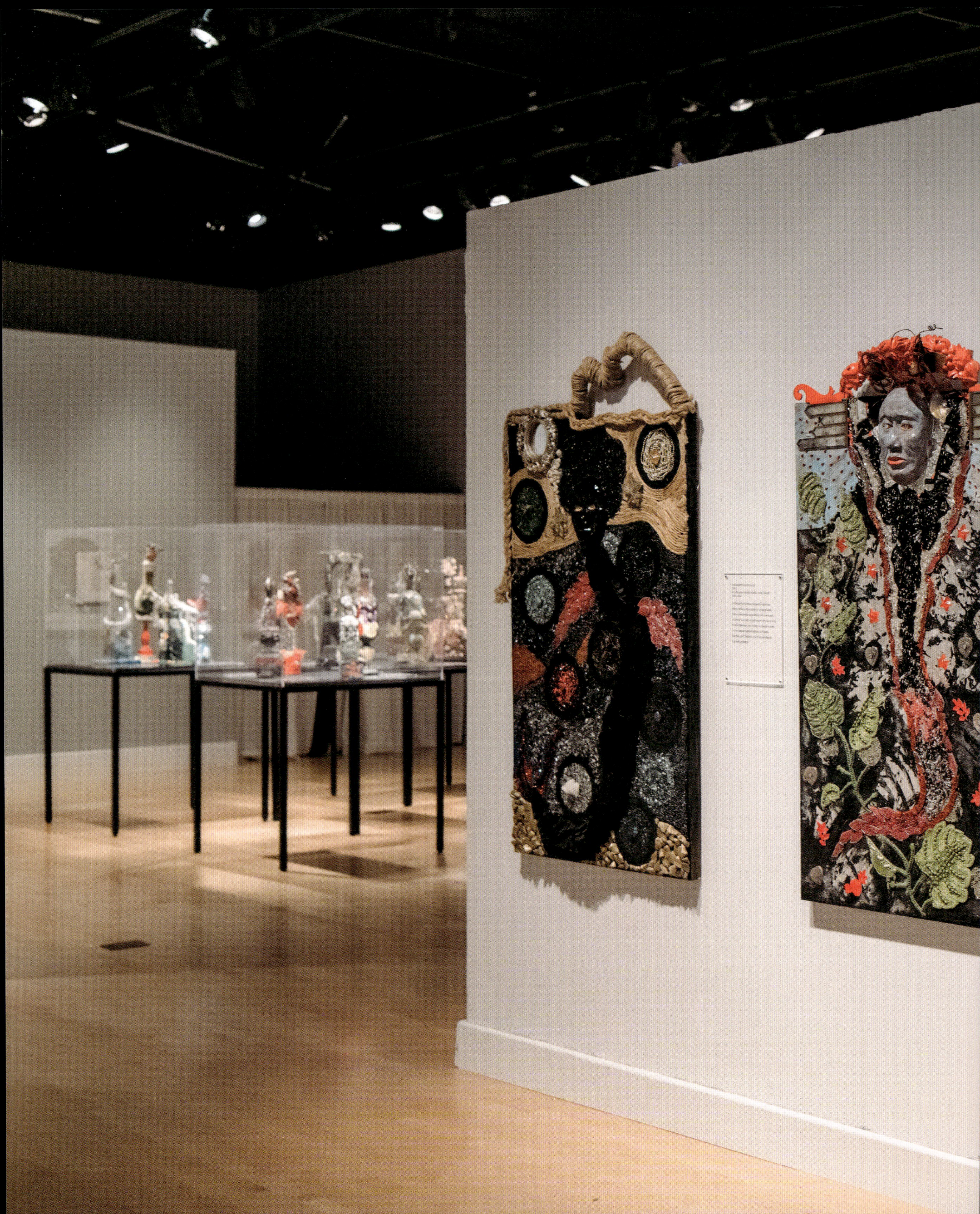

"No one can walk your path for you."

This sentiment was shared by Nichole Kojzar on October 6, 2022, as she drove a nail through the hole of a colorful speckled bead and into the foot of a humanoid figure carved from a tree trunk, painted blue, and ornamented with rope, carvings, beads, and an embedded mirror. Kojzar is one of dozens of people who have participated so far in Oletha DeVane's community engagement artwork *N'Kisi Woman–Universal N'Kisi* (pp. 4, 188–189, 194), a 2021–2022 project made to be presented in the public amphitheater of the University of Maryland, Baltimore County (UMBC) Fine Arts Building.

N'Kisi was made of a tree that previously grew outside the artist's home. From working the wood with a chainsaw alongside her late husband, Peter Kojzar, to facilitating activities related to her exhibition at the Center for Art, Design, and Visual Culture (CADVC), DeVane developed this material into a powerful catalyst for assembling diverse publics in temporary communities. Placed just steps outside the doors of CADVC, *N'Kisi* extended the exhibition footprint of *Oletha DeVane: Spectrum of Light and Spirit* to a more open and public arena. Periodic activation events invited audiences to add beads to the surface of the sculpture and to share thoughts, wishes, and reflections—accompanied by DeVane and guest facilitators, including her daughter, Nichole, whose wisdom opens this commentary. Over the course of three months in fall of 2022, these offerings ranged from expressions of grief to expressions of joy—among them tributes to women in Iran, where anti-government protests have been very active for eight weeks at the time of this writing; vulnerable memorial reflections about deceased family and friends; and a description of the River Nsiki in Nigeria offered by Gloria Chuku, Chair of Africana Studies at UMBC. In common, these offerings all shared an attentive audience brought together in a spirit of community.

P. 4
N'Kisi Woman–Universal N'Kisi installed in the amphitheater at UMBC. The sculpture features beads that have been hammered into its surface during one of the community interventions that occurred on October 6, 8, and 29, 2022.

PP. 6–7
View of the entrance of the exhibition featuring *Avatar* paintings, and in the foreground from left to right: *Genesis, Healer (Pilgrimage),* and *Fall from Grace.*

P. 8
Installation of the *Spirit Sculptures* with *Absinthe* in the foreground.

P. 9
View of gallery installation with *Henry "Box" Brown* in the distance, *Escape* on the pedestal, and *Hagar's Dress in her Exile* on the right.

OPPOSITE
Installation view with the *Spirit Sculptures* at the left and on the wall at the right: *Mamawata's Earth Song* and *Dumballa.*

Photos: Marlayna Demond.

The exhibition documented in this catalogue was organized by Lowery Stokes Sims in thematic arrangements that illustrate Oletha DeVane's vast artistic practice. DeVane's work represents decades of artistic creation responding to history and contemporary issues in diverse media. The work invites wonder over its beauty, fascination with its rich cultural references, and directed attention to the difficult histories that it chronicles. Though no one else can walk DeVane's path, we are far richer for her invitation to accompany her on it, even in temporary assembly.

We are grateful to Oletha DeVane and Lowery Stokes Sims for conceiving a magnificent exhibition. Tadia Rice's collaborative work made an important contribution to this presentation. We thank Joyce J. Scott and two anonymous donors for their support of this volume. The Maryland State Arts Council, Baltimore County Commission on the Arts and Sciences, CAHSS Dean's Office, and Dave Farace and the McDonogh School all contributed to the exhibition production and public programs. Thanks are also due to collaborators on the work in this exhibition, which include Efia Dalili, Wayne Dixon, Tim McFadden, Camille Ollivierre, and Soledad Salamé and Sol Print Studios. We also acknowledge the involvement and support of Emily Sollenberger, Virginia Anderson, Jessica Bell Brown, Christopher Kojzar, Nichole Kojzar, Olivia Surratt, and Dorothy DeVane.

At CADVC, special thanks are owed to the core team of Sandra Abbott; Janet Magruder; Mitchell Noah; and Besan Khamis, who joined the team as a substantive contributor to the exhibition production. We are grateful to our expanded team on this exhibition, who included Brian Jones, Sadaf Rehman, and Amy Teschner. We also thank our supporters in the broader university whose efforts contributed to our exhibition and its related programs; these colleagues include Amy Barnes, Jessica Berman, Lee Boot, Lynn Cazabon, Jared Christensen, Gloria Chuku, Marlayna Demond, Joel Dewyer, Felipe Filomeno, Courtney Hobson, Preminda Jacob, Brian Jones, Stephanie Lazarus, Christine Mallinson, Denise Meringolo, Kimberly R. Moffitt, Tom Moore, Cael Mulcahy, Beth Saunders, Greg Simmons, James Smalls, Karl Steiner, and Christopher Tkacik. Symmes Gardner, former Executive Director of CADVC, was key to the initiation of this project, and generously continued his relationship with the exhibition in the role of Executive Editor of this volume.

Finally, CADVC relies on the enthusiastic and brilliant involvement of our undergraduate and graduate student team, who make our center all that it is, which is far more than can be expressed in this short acknowledgment!

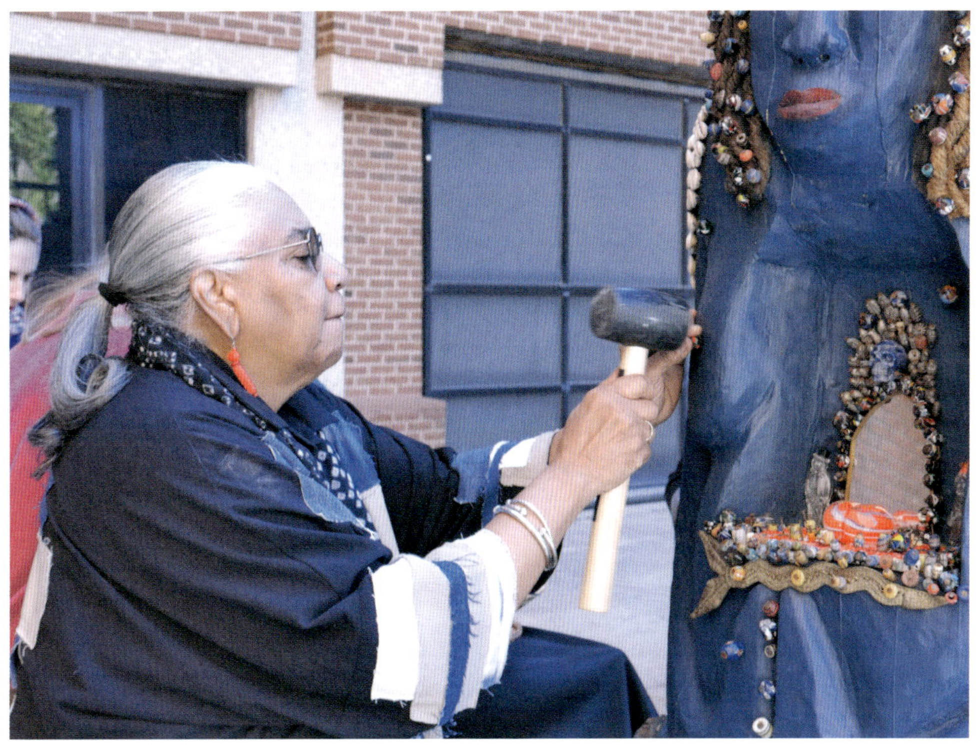

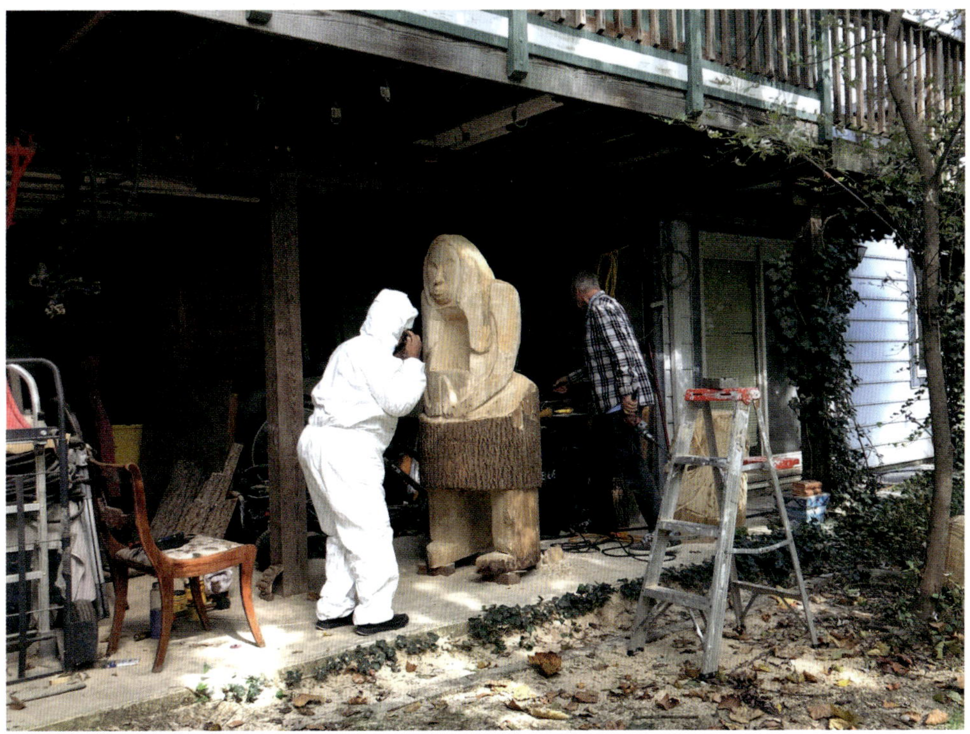

TOP
Leslie King-Hammond hammering
the beads onto the surface of
N'Kisi while expressing wishes and
intentions. Photo: Rassaan
Hammond.

BOTTOM
Oletha DeVane and Peter Kojzar
working on *N'Kisi*. Photo: Camille
Ollivierre.

We thank Madeline Arbutus, Tirell Bethel, Julia Chang, Favor Ekeagwu, Perry Gotis, Piper Haught, Aymen Haq, Camille Hu, Chris Hutton, Ahlam Khamis, Levi Lewis, Ghazal Mojtahedi, Adedamilola Olateru-Olagbegi, Sarah Rashid, Deborah Shenge, Mariia Usova, and Jae Vargas. And we look forward to the continued convergences of our many paths.

Rebecca Uchill

Director, Center for Art, Design, and Visual Culture, UMBC

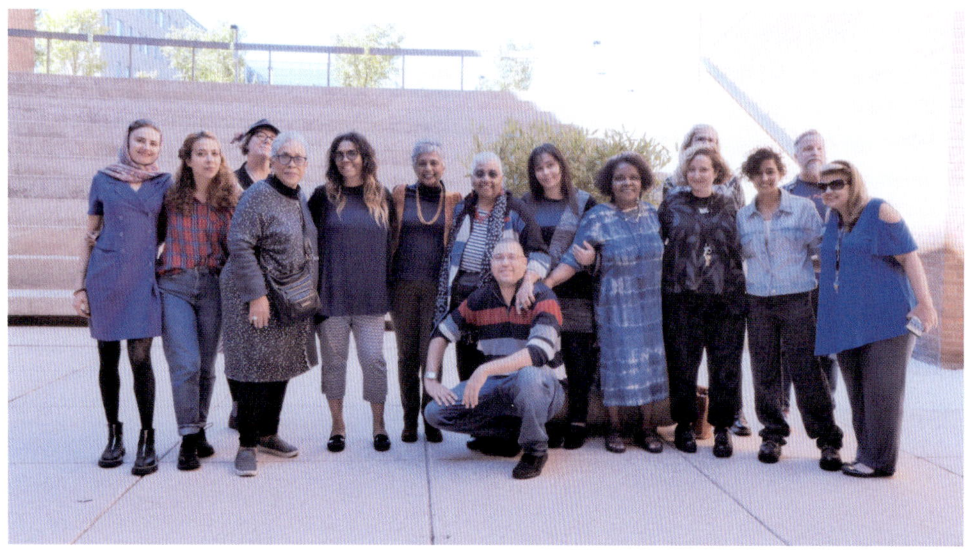

Group photograph during *N'Kisi* activation event. Photo: Rassaan Hammond.

In the spring of 2019, I attended a public programming event dedicated to Oletha DeVane's installation *Traces of the Spirit* at the Baltimore Museum of Art. Housed inside the original springhouse of a Revolutionary-era estate previously situated on what are now the grounds of the museum, the installation offered visitors a respite from the traditional museum experience. Dramatic lighting highlighted vividly encrusted totem-oriented sculptures that served as a combination of complex altar pieces and votive offerings. The experience was transformative.

I knew then that the Center for Art, Design, and Visual Culture (CADVC) needed to work with Oletha DeVane and allow her to reinterpret our space with her unique vision and understanding of the human condition. Fortunately for us, she said yes.

In envisioning the initial conception of *Oletha DeVane: Spectrum of Light and Spirit*, I would like to thank the artist first and foremost. Her unwavering commitment to the project permitted CADVC to cast a wide net regarding works to be included in the exhibition as well as thematic concerns to be addressed. Oletha's astute selection of Lowery Stokes Sims to serve as the chief curator of the exhibition also proved to be a brilliant idea. What she and Lowery have created is an incredible summation of over five decades of work in a wide variety of mediums.

Regarding the exhibition catalogue that accompanies *Oletha DeVane: Spectrum of Light and Spirit*, CADVC owes a debt of gratitude to Joyce J. Scott and two anonymous donors for their support of this publication. Their support was instrumental in allowing this exhibition project to enjoy having a print publication that not only sufficiently documents the exhibition's individual artworks and installation at CADVC but also contains a range of critical analysis of the artist's work.

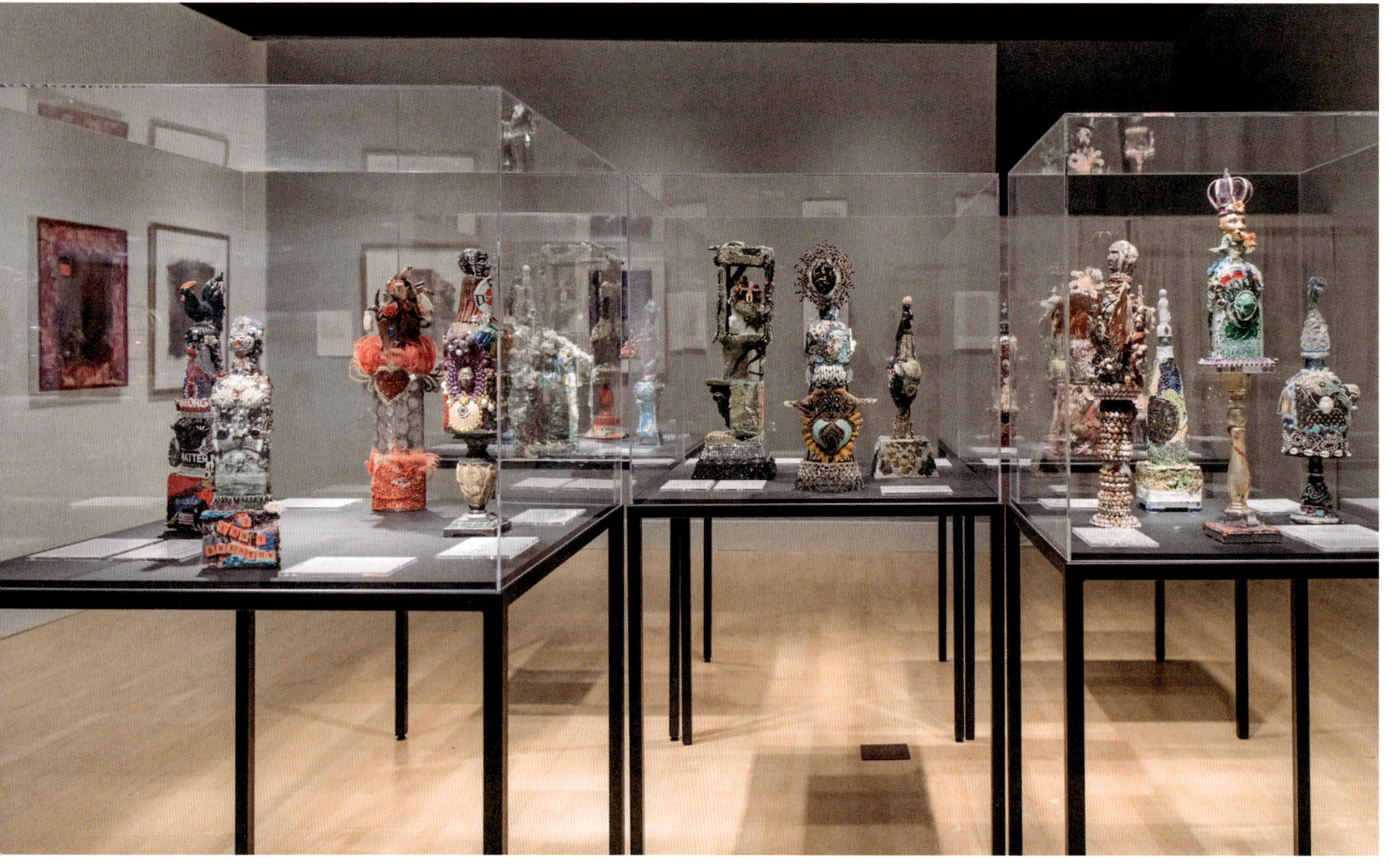

The publication has also been served extremely well by the following individuals who have contributed essays on the artist, as well those who have supervised the catalogue's design and organization of its content and imagery.

Essayists Lowery Stokes Sims, Serubiri Moses, Leslie King-Hammond, and Christopher Kojzar have all deeply broadened our understanding in a multitude of ways regarding Oletha DeVane's historical references and influences, artistic processes and methodologies, and philosophical underpinnings. Taken together, they offer a rich aggregate of Oletha DeVane's vision as an artist and her studio practice.

The catalogue design owes its particular brilliance to A. Mattson Gallagher. Coming highly recommended by Guenet Abraham, his former graphic design professor at UMBC, Mattson has designed a book that is extremely accessible in delivering a cogent overview of Oletha's wide body of visual work. Within this achievement, he also vividly conveys the sumptuous quality of color and materials the artist uses in the creation of these stunning and visceral works. As editor, James Gibbons has again successfully supervised the overall editing of the essays and related text in a masterful way. Amy Teschner assisted with proofreading in the later stages of the publication.

In photographing individual works and documenting the installation of the exhibition, a number of photographers have provided their expertise and talents. These include Mitro Hood, Michael Koryta, Dan Meyers, Rassaan Hammond (Greeneye Media), Linda Day Clark, Tadia Rice, Oletha DeVane, Camille Ollivierre, and Marlayna Demond.

We also owe particular thanks to Virginia Anderson, Department Head of American Painting & Sculpture and Decorative Arts, and Jessica Novak, Director of Content Strategy and Publications, from the Baltimore Museum of Art, for arranging the publication rights for reprinting Leslie King-Hammond's essay "The Essence of Being Lies Within Ordinary, Useful/less Stuff, and Tangible Things," which was previously featured in the BMA's 2019 catalogue *Oletha DeVane: Traces of the Spirit*.

At UMBC, praise goes to incoming President Valerie Sheares Ashby, former President Freeman Hrabowski, Provost Philip Rous, and Dean Kimberly Moffitt of the College of Art, Humanities and Social Sciences for their continued support of CADVC and its programming initiatives. Finally, special thanks and appreciation goes to CADVC's Director, Rebecca Uchill, and the staff of CADVC, Sandra Abbott, Janet Magruder, and Mitchell Noah, for their professionalism and expertise in bringing the exhibition to fruition.

Oletha DeVane: Spectrum of Light and Spirit is above all a noteworthy exhibition. Both incisive and beautiful, it challenges us to be better individuals while offering glimpses of transformation and redemption.

Symmes Gardner
Executive Editor

An Artist's Statement

Oletha DeVane

I BELIEVE OUR MYSTERIOUS ORIGIN IS COMMON GROUND in which the universe encourages human action toward the betterment of humankind. Art provides an avenue to explore issues of faith, human frailty, and spirituality.

After visiting Haiti, I seriously began to work on a series of *Spirit Sculptures* meant to occupy an altar-like setting as a concept to harness blessings and healing. The wall panels are mixed-media assemblages in which I started by using acrylic paint and reflective materials and by covering surfaces with fabric, sequins, beads, and objects to create a kind of visual narrative with found materials. I'm interested in the idiosyncratic ways that materials convey meaning and the conceptual framework they offer. The sculptures and panels are manipulated to reflect and receive light. Each piece represents a totemic spirit sculpture or panel collaged with beads, wood, mirrors, plastic figurines, sequins, fabric, and hand-sculpted heads. Snakes, mermaids, saints, and birds are all effigies found in a variety of global cultures. Sometimes I incorporate the figure as a liminal entity connecting us to a more magical and perhaps empowered state of existence. As with many sacred objects, I want the work to live outside of our current day-to-day experience; it is intended to evoke the possibilities of spiritual connection and transformation, memory and loss, celebration and mourning.

My work is informed by an evolving worldview of cultures from an African American perspective that migrated to the Americas in memory of those enslaved. It is the history of beliefs meant to serve as both a sacred ode and a spiritual manifesto. My travels to Africa, Haiti, the Caribbean, the Middle East, and the Far East inform some of the imagery, and I try to translate my travel experiences into metaphorical images using symbols, found materials and, occasionally, video. The rich aesthetic traditions from Africa that have emerged in my work are contributed through color, patterns, myths, and religions.

Oletha DeVane:
Spectrum of Light and Spirit

Lowery Stokes Sims

1 Oletha DeVane, "About Me," olethadevane.com/my-story/. Accessed February 3, 2022.

2 Angela N. Carroll, "Oletha DeVane Showcases Sculptural Works in 'Traces of the Spirit' at the BMA," *Baltimore*, August 12, 2019, www.baltimoremagazine.com/section/artsentertainment/oletha-devane-showcases-sculptural-works-in-bma-exhibit-traces-of-spirit/. Accessed February 3, 2022.

3 Oletha DeVane, conversation with the author, January 21, 2022.

OLETHA DEVANE IS A WAYFINDER AND A STORYTELLER. Over the last five decades, as she has traveled in Asia, Africa, and the Caribbean, she has been inspired by the stories and characters she encounters, "unlock[ing] the secrets to the oldest stories and creat[ing] new ones."[1] Her aesthetic impulses are driven by what critic and curator Angela Carroll describes as "anti-colonial liberation efforts, Juneteenth, the legacy of her father, and humanity's tireless existentialism."[2] In her explorations of identity, tradition, and ritual, however, she does not shirk from considerations of human frailty and the trauma of facing mortality, a trauma that is exacerbated by lost dreams and potential, urban violence, and the plight of the incarcerated, specifically women. These conditions of human existence, DeVane believes, can be mitigated by immersing oneself in the creative realm,[3] and she has navigated that realm herself in a variety of media: prints, paintings, assemblages, sculpture, installations, and videos.

The 1980s and '90s:
Wayfinding: Negotiating Beauty and Horror

4 Virginia M. G. Anderson, "In Conversation with Oletha DeVane," in *Oletha DeVane: Traces of the Spirit*, ed. Virginia M. G. Anderson, exh. cat. (Baltimore: Baltimore Museum of Art, 2019), 32.

> *Painting got to be very restrictive … so I became interested in what I could add into the process.… Once I painted something I'd always want to add materials or more paint.*[4]

To date we have seen Oletha DeVane's artistic creation only in bits and spurts. *Oletha DeVane: Spectrum of Light and Spirit* offers the first opportunity to see the scope and dimensions of her work as they have unfolded throughout her career. DeVane is probably best known for work she has designated *Spirit Sculptures*, which reveal her penchant for working as a multimedia artist. This, she states, "has always been a way that I've looked at life and at art making."[5] Built in and around ordinary bottles, found ceramic elements, or constructed containers, these sculptures are transformed by the application of sequins, beads, clay and wood elements, fabric, shells, resin, wire, glass, porcelain, even bullet casings. This aspect of DeVane's oeuvre indicates her consistent interest in the idiosyncratic ways that materials convey meaning.

But DeVane's artistic roots lie in the prodigious body of paintings, drawings, and prints that she produced in the 1980s and 1990s. *Untitled*, a composition from the early 1980s, dominated by a brushy black oval area, transversed by two flanking white lines intersecting at the bottom of the composition, seems in tune with Minimalist aesthetics. We begin to see DeVane's penchant for existential explorations in *Doorway to Nowhere* (1980s, p. 78), where an unseen figure casts a long shadow out of a brightly lit, ornately appointed doorway. The shadow indicates that the figure is about to arrive in our space, emerging from a portal of possibility. *Ode to Pre-Existence* (1998, p. 79) and *Life Pulse* (2010, p. 127) evoke the cyclical nature of existence. The heads swathed in layers of space and fabric in the 2000 series *Veils* (*I*, *II*, *III*, and *IV*, pp. 82–83), all executed in Van Dyke process[6] and acrylic on fabric, seem to have a geographic and cultural specificity, but more specifically they allude to concepts of our singularity and oneness as human beings. Their mysterious miens personify the search for the ineffable essence of creativity.[7]

DeVane's work in the early 2000s also includes a number of still-life paintings with gigantic and elaborately detailed florals that frame vignettes of figures navigating inset landscapes (*On the Hill*, 2003, p. 111) or present incongruous views of cascading airplanes, frontline newspaper headlines, and fragments of flags (*Wish*, 2003, p. 113). The subject of these works is more explicitly explored in *Through the Gates of Babylon* (p. 87), a lithograph executed the same year. It features collaged images of veiled women, a swathed warrior, and a desert landscape, along with newspaper texts about the invasion of Iraq in 2003 by troops from the United States, the United Kingdom, Australia, and Poland. The title of this print refers to the Ishtar Gate from the ancient city of Babylon, built in 575 BCE. Old and new collide and coexist in this image.

This ability to juxtapose beauty and horror, personal reflection and the exorable, is paradigmatic of her life creation of a multiracial familial unit—an African American, Southern, Czech creolization. It is also paradigmatic of her personal philosophy and spiritual path. While she may have a personal

5 Ibid.

6 "Van Dyke brown is a printing process named after Anthony van Dyck. It involves coating a canvas with ferric ammonium citrate, tartaric acid, and silver nitrate, then exposing it to ultraviolet light. The canvas can be washed with water, and hypo to keep the solutions in place." "Van Dyke brown (printing)," *Wikipedia*, en.wikipedia.org/wiki /Van_Dyke_brown_(printing). Accessed May 22, 2022.

7 DeVane, conversation with the author, January 21, 2022.

spiritual practice, she has noted that "in terms of looking at religion itself, it's about how we as human beings are on this incredible search…. It doesn't mean that any one practice is wrong, it just means that we are all, as a world community, on different paths of searching for that ultimate spiritual essence."[8] Consequently we can find in her oeuvre an image of the ancestral home of the father of the Bahá'í faith's founder, or a rendering of a spirit house in Thailand discarded on the side of the road (*Thai Spirit House*, 2013, pp. 120–121), or a statue of the Virgin Mary as a *Saint for My City* (p. 34).

Thai Spirit House is an example of DeVane's frequent collaborations with Baltimore-based artists Soledad Salamé and Michael Koryta at their non-profit, Sol Print Studios. She was introduced to Salamé when she and artist Joyce J. Scott collaborated on several prints. According to DeVane, working in the studio "changed my perception of what printmaking can be," as the residency there, "offers international and regional artists a professional creative experience that encouraged experimentation in the warmth of [Salamé and Koryta's] home."[9] For her part Salamé has remarked on DeVane's "intuitive and expressive freedom to her work and our workshops." Furthermore, "Her openness to exploration of possibilities is evidenced in her fearless approach to both technical and aesthetic challenges. Her solutions often surprised and enlightened me and fellow workshop participants."[10]

All these ideas and explorations are already manifest in DeVane's large scale artist's book *Sacred Geometry* (2001, pp. 88–97), which features poetry by DeVane's collaborator the Washington, DC–based educator Donna Denizé. This project was created in response to an invitation from then director, Cindy Kelly, to engage the Garrett Collection in the library at Evergreen, a house museum and library that is part of Johns Hopkins University Museums. DeVane has explained:

> The book is inspired from many sources … although my purpose in structuring the book using the circle, triangle, and the square was to explore their cosmological symbolism. In West African cosmic thought, the circular motion or spiral constitutes the human soul in a cycle of life that has no end.[11]

With titles such as *Dante*, *Fire Tablet*, *Boccacio*, *fire next time*, *the universe within*, *Rumor*, and *Florence poem*, the collaged, painted, printed, and calligraphed pages take the viewer on a journey through time and place through the lens of legendary Italian sagas and Black American legend James Baldwin.

8 Carroll, "DeVane Showcases Sculptural Works."

9 Oletha DeVane, email to the author, July 9, 2022.

10 Soledad Salamé, email to Oletha DeVane, July 8, 2022.

11 "An Artist's Invitation to Closing Reception at Evergreen House," McDonogh School website, https://www.mcdonogh.org /about/news-photos/news/stories /2008/an-artist-s-invitation-to -closing-reception-at-evergreen -house/. Accessed May 21, 2021.

DeVane chose "two books about explorations and journeys, *The Discovered Lands of Virginia* by Thomas Hariot and a letter, *The Discovered Islands*, by Christopher Columbus,"[12] as her points of departure. The choices were not gratuitous:

> Both presented complex ironies about colonialism and the exotic or mythic illustrations of indigenous peoples. I decided to use the "metaphorical" journey of the soul as the idea for the mixed media painted pages of the book. The poetry reflects a trip to Italy, where Donna and I met to discuss the art and architecture.[13]

Heroes and She-Roes: Those Who Have Prevailed

> *I search for ways to infuse the works with symbols of identity and mythology. The paintings, sculptures, videos, and prints are rooted in cultural histories, myths, or personal stories.*[14]

As the 2000s progressed, DeVane came into her own artistically in terms of subject matter and ways of working. What becomes evident is that there are a number of stories and events that have come to have a significance for her. She explores them often in series that span years, finding new nuances and possibilities in each iteration. DeVane defies chronology, but we can always find the way, the straight line, the path through her creative process.

Given her strong attachment to Maryland[15] it is not surprising that DeVane has chosen as her subjects the tragedy of lynching in Maryland and the consummate Maryland heroine Harriet Tubman, as well as Henry "Box" Brown of North Carolina and the biblical heroine Hagar—all of whom had to find their way out of adversity in life into the world. DeVane's 2005 video and installation *Witness*, a meditation on lynchings in the state of Maryland, "was commissioned by the Reginald F. Lewis Museum of Maryland History and Culture to document Maryland's history of lynching. It was a yearlong project which began in 2004."[16] This somber production includes a recitation of the names of lynching victims and the counties in which they died, set against a view of flowing water. For this piece, as seen in the related prints she produced on the subject (pp. 84–85), DeVane conducted meticulous research, gathering information and images from the National Archives in Washington, DC; Baltimore's *The Afro-American* newspaper; and Maryland Public Television. She also consulted with the prominent civil rights

12 Ibid.

13 Ibid.
14 See "Oletha DeVane's Portfolio," *Baker Artist Portfolios*, https://bakerartist.org/portfolios/oletha-devane. Accessed May 29, 2022.
15 Anderson, "In Conversation with Oletha DeVane," in *Oletha DeVane: Traces of the Spirit*, 38.
16 Ibid.

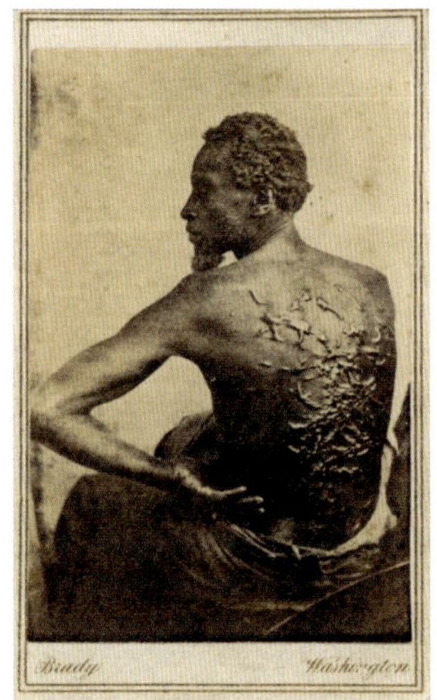

Fig. 1
Peter (formerly identified as "Gordon") at the Baton Rouge Union Camp, March 1863. Photographers: William D. McPherson and Mr. Oliver, New Orleans. National Portrait Gallery, Smithsonian Institution. Source: Wikimedia Commons.

17 Ibid.

18 Ibid.

19 "Taken at face value, the 'drinking gourd' refers to the hollowed-out gourd used by slaves (and other rural Americans) as a water dipper. But here it is used as a code name for the Big Dipper star formation, which points to Polaris, the Pole Star, and due North…. These directions then enabled fleeing slaves to make their way north from Mobile, Alabama to the Ohio River and freedom." Joel Bresler, "Follow the Drinking Gourd: A Cultural History," www.followthedrinkinggourd.org. Accessed May 24, 2022.

20 See Erin Blakemore, "The Shocking Photo of 'Whipped Peter' that Made Slavery's Brutality Impossible to Deny," *History Channel*, February 7, 2019, updated May 11, 2021, www.history.com/news/whipped-peter-slavery-photo-scourged-back-real-story-civil-war. Accessed May 18, 2022.

21 See Carrie Mae Weems, "From Here I Saw What Happened and I Cried, 1995–1996, 33 toned prints," website of Carrie Mae Weems, carriemaeweems.net/galleries/from-here.html. Accessed May 30, 2022.

22 Oletha DeVane, email to the author, May 24, 2022.

attorney and Maryland author Sherrilyn Ifill, cousin to the late journalist Gwen Ifill and recently under consideration by President Joseph Biden for nomination to the Supreme Court.[17] DeVane notes that her goal in *Witness* was "to convey loss."

> My father used to talk about it…. I knew, historically, how devastating it was for families and especially to think about where it happened, who it happened to. The idea that there was that oppressive lack of voice in one's life and the fact my father would have to leave his home [in North Carolina] was real…. *Witness* hearkened back to conversations with him about what it meant to be a Black man coming from the South.[18]

DeVane revisits the horrors faced by African Americans during slavery in a group of images from 2009 and 2010 that feature a back with scarification marks. They draw us into the ambiguity that such images can provoke in the viewer. On the one hand, scarification is documented in nineteenth-century photographs of the backs of enslaved individuals who had been whipped—images that were instrumental in bringing home the brutality of slavery to a larger public. On the other hand, as seen in *Out of Africa (Scarification Series)* (p. 124), and *Out of Africa: from beauty to pain* (p. 127), scarification also alludes to practices of modifying the body as performed in Africa to designate relationships to specific communities, to signify life status, and even to be a form of beautification. The 2011 version, *Tattoo (Scarification Series)* (p. 128), suggests further the now-pervasive contemporary fad among people of all races for radical body modifications that include tattooing and branding. The unexpected association of this image with two images from the *Harriet Tubman* series—*Star Map* (p. 125) and *Drinking Gourd* (p. 126, both 2010)—symbolizes, respectively, the use of the heavens as a means of finding a direction toward freedom and encoded escape instructions in a folk song used by individuals involved in the Underground Railroad.[19]

DeVane's approach to this type of imagery is distinct from that of her contemporary, the artist Carrie Mae Weems, who has deployed, in several of her photographic appropriations including *From Here I Saw What Happened and I Cried* (1995–1996), the now familiar 1863 photograph by McPherson and Oliver of the enslaved man Peter (fig. 1),[20] showing his scarred back.[21] DeVane has revealed that it is her own back that we see in her prints.[22] This provides a specific immediacy to the imagery, creating an empathetic connection to a fate that might very well have been suffered by one of her own ancestors. This image also attains contemporary currency in its resonance with an image of an asylum-seeker in Cairo, whose scarred back reminds us that the realities of slavery exist in the twenty-first century.[23]

Of course, there were stories of heroic escapes from the hell of slavery. One such tale provided the inspiration for DeVane's 2015 installation *Henry "Box" Brown* (pp. 134–135). The motif of wayfinding in escape encapsulated in this work is balanced by the reality of those who could not escape or escaped only by enduring unconscionable hardship. Harriet Jacobs (1813–1897) might have shut herself away for seven years to evade the unwanted advances of her enslaver, but Henry "Box" Brown (1815/16–1897) resolved to escape from slavery and enlisted the help of a free Black man and a white slaveowner, who conspired to ship him in a box to Philadelphia, which arrived there in March 1849 and was accepted by a leader of the Pennsylvania Anti-Slavery Society.[24]

DeVane's depiction of this saga includes a figure in a fetal position painted in black on the side of a crate, which sits in a square area filled with sweet gum burrs. On the wall hangs a version of the American flag overpainted with the cross bars of the Confederate flag. The sweet gum pods frequently occur in DeVane's work—sometimes literally, sometimes pictorially. As Kate Clifford Larson writes in her biography of Harriet Tubman, *Bound for the Promised Land*,[25] the seedpods of the sweet gum tree (common in the forests of Maryland's Eastern Shore) "litter the forest floor, sometimes inches deep, nature's bed of nails." On the one hand, enslaved African Americans used these seedpods to make medicine with an aromatically therapeutic fragrance; as a folk treatment, they were employed to heal wounds and dysentery. On the other, the seedpods would "pierce the calloused, unprotected feet of terrified runaway slaves. The sweet gum tree, therefore, would be among the first barriers on the road to freedom."[26]

Tubman (ca. 1822–1913) herself features prominently as a subject in DeVane's work, as seen in a series of solar etchings from 2017 and 2019—*Minty* (p. 165), *Eliza* (pp. 162–163), and *Harriet the Raven* (p. 118). DeVane adapts a previously unknown photograph of the freedom fighter taken in 1868 (fig. 2) that came to the world's attention in 2017 and caused a flurry of interest on the art market. It was eventually acquired by the National Museum of African American History and Culture.[27] Tubman was born into slavery in Dorchester, Maryland. Ordinarily her life would probably have passed unremarked save in the collective memory of descendants or of witnesses to her heroic actions. But Tubman distinguished herself not only by escaping

23 See "Egypt: Forced Returns of Eritrean Asylum Seekers," *Human Rights Watch*, January 17, 2022, www.hrw.org/news/2022/01/27/egypt-forced-returns-eritrean-asylum-seekers. Accessed May 18, 2022.

24 This summary account of Brown's life is based on the entry on Brown in *Encyclopedia Virginia*, encyclopediavirginia.org/entries/brown-henry-box-1815-or-1816-1897/. Accessed March 25, 2022.

25 Kate Clifford Larson, *Bound for the Promised Land: Harriet Tubman: Portrait of an American Hero* (London: Oneworld Publications, 2004).

26 The source of this information and the quotations from Larson can be found on DeVane's *Baker Artist Portfolio* page. Accessed May 10, 2022.

27 See Allison Keyes, "A Previously Unknown Portrait of Tubman Goes on View," *Smithsonian Magazine*, March 26, 2019, www.smithsonianmag.com/.../previously-unknown-portrait-abolitionist-harriet-tubman-young-woman-goes-view-180971796/. Accessed May 28, 2022.

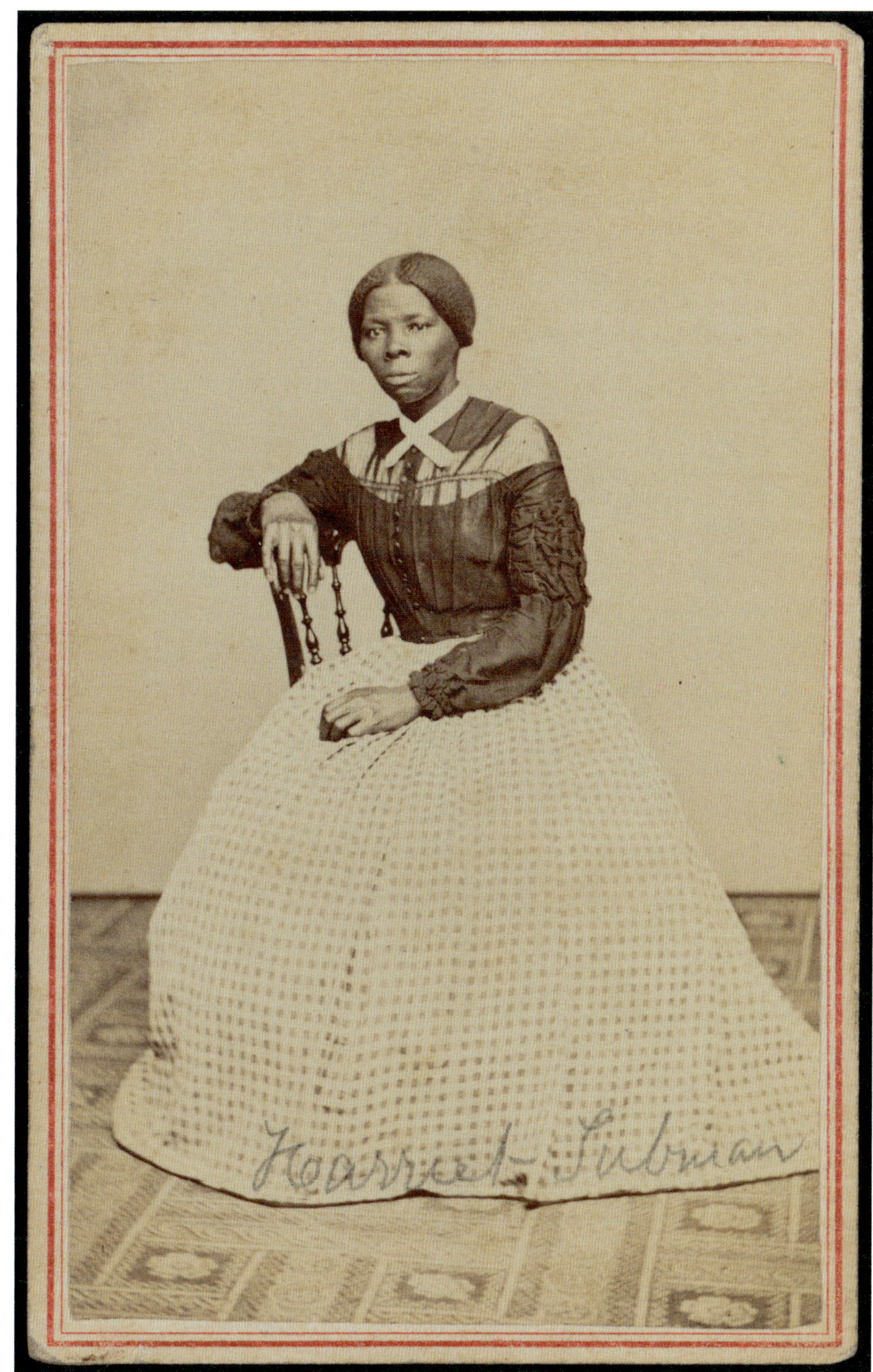

Fig. 2
Portrait of Harriet Tubman by Benjamin F. Powelson, Auburn, New York, 1868 or 1869. Albumen print on card mount. Collection of the Library of Congress and the National Museum of African American History & Culture. Reproduction # LC-DIG-ppmsca-54230.

to freedom in Philadelphia but also by having the guts and audacity to go back to Maryland to bring out her family and hundreds of other African Americans to freedom. Tubman's nom de guerre was, appropriately enough, "Moses." Wanted posters for her capture mention her as "Minta," which is the source of the title of DeVane's aforementioned print. "Minta" is short for "Araminta," the name she was given at birth. It is not known exactly when she changed her name to Harriet—after her mother—but the change probably occurred around the time she planned her escape. Tubman then went on to work for the Union army during the Civil War as a cook, a nurse, and eventually as a scout and spy, becoming the first woman to lead an expedition in the war.

In the 1868 photograph, Tubman is seen "wearing a pleated, buttoned blouse with ruffles at her forearms and wrists, and a flowing [lattice-print] skirt."[28] She is seated at an angle with her right arm resting atop the edge of a lathed-back chair. In her adaptations of this image for her print, DeVane eliminates the chair and situates Tubman variously against a large doily halo (*Minty*) or in a triangular space flanked by gigantic leaves and topped with sweet gum seedpods (*Eliza*). This name change is unexpected and may very well be a reference by DeVane to Eliza Baptiste, who with her husband, Ezekiel, hosted Tubman on their farm in Newberry Township, Pennsylvania. The Baptistes had the distinction of being among the few Black landowners in the area and were noted locally for their skillful regeneration of the land and for the produce on the farmland they owned. [29]

In *Harriet the Raven*, Tubman sits in a miasma of leaves, sweet gum pods, and ravens. These birds—which DeVane considers to be personal guiding spirits—symbolize the oracle, the intelligence, courage, and singularity in pursuit as represented by Tubman. Additionally, they serve as the focal point for prints and paintings on the theme of release and escape—such as *Call to Freedom* (2012, p. 119) and *Migration* (2012, p. 45). They fly in various formations with an abandon that is exhilarating.

Given DeVane's considerations of the stories of Henry "Box" Brown and Harriet Tubman, it is probably no surprise that the biblical figure Hagar would have caught her attention. *Hagar's Dress in Her Exile* (2013, p. 138) deals with the Egyptian slave who was the handmaiden of Sarah, the wife of Abraham in the Old Testament. Her son, Ishmael, was commonly believed to have been the progenitor of the Arab peoples. Here Hagar is represented by a dress form assembled from chains, rope and burlap, hemp, cowrie shells, and chains over an infrastructure of wire, fabric, and some plaster. In

28 Ibid.

29 Scott Mingus, "Meet the Underground Railroad Conductors Who Hosted Harriet Tubman in Central PA," *York Daily Record*, October 29, 2019, www.ydr.com/in-depth/news/2019/10/29/harriet-tubman-underground-railroad-eliza-ezekiel-baptiste-central-pa/3863180002/. Accessed May 28, 2022.

some versions of this installation a pathway to the suspended form is covered with spiky "sweet gum balls," which were to be walked on barefoot by viewers seeking to get closer to the dress. As DeVane reminds us, the story of Hagar resonates with generations of Black women who have struggled to hold their families together, and in the Harriet Tubman story, people walked across fields of sweet gum balls when escaping enslavement via the Underground Railroad. The story of Hagar metaphorically validates the struggle and strength to endure injustice and was particularly of interest among the stories told by African Americans in church.[30]

This use of a dress as a surrogate for a female figure can also be seen in the etchings *Sex Slave* (p. 137) and *Red Riding Hood* (p. 136) as well as the mixed-media painting/assemblage *Restavek* (p. 164), all created in 2016. The first two works are part of an exploration of the theme that DeVane calls "The Other Side of Darkness."[31] Indeed, in the context of increasing global awareness of sex trafficking, pedophilia, and the abomination of continuing mass shootings especially at schools in the United States, these works show a concern for the fate of young people, specifically girls. *Sex Slave* and *Red Riding Hood* suggest a co-tangency between fairy tales about imperiled young girls and real life.

The images of the dresses are accompanied by a band of images of snarling wolves, who represent the predators who threaten innocent lives. The threat evoked is made more explicit in a second dress, which is soiled as if to show the aftermath of an assault. That persona was not able to hide behind the copious tree in *Red Riding Hood*. These events become more personal and focused in *Restavek*. The word "restavek" is a creolization of the French "rester avec," which means "to stay with," referring to female Haitian children from rural areas sold to affluent individuals in the cities because their parents lacked sufficient food or money to support them. DeVane became aware of this custom when she traveled to Haiti to do a mural project in 2016. The expectation is that the host family will provide girls with food, shelter, and education, but in reality these girls, for the most part, are for all intents and purposes enslaved in the household that buys them.

It might be discerned from this discussion that DeVane's travels have provided inspiration for her artwork. Sometimes images come out of random, unscheduled encounters, as when she met three women in chadors in Cape Town on a trip to South Africa during the summer of 2014. She photographed them from behind, focusing on the elaborate patterns on their clothing. *Chador Flowers I* (2014, p. 130) and *Patterns (Three Women from*

Dubai) (2015, p. 131) are two of the solar etchings and digital prints that resulted from this encounter. DeVane reminisces that "our discussion led us to the changes that have engulfed the Middle East":

> The uncertainties about religious truths are so prevalent that it's a struggle to glean from the media the truth of the narratives. While all societies are going through transition, knowledge can inform our view, and talking to these women made me realize their mode of dressing offered protection. I wanted to convey the chador as a second skin that housed spirit.[32]

32 Ibid.

This notion of probing beyond appearances and our glib readings of them is certainly the theme of the video project *Dion'e: Searching for Self* (2016, p. 123). Dion'e narrates her harrowing story of being a transgender woman was who born a hermaphrodite. DeVane met Dion'e when she and Tadia Rice began collaborating on the *Beyond Bars* project in 2018 at the Women's Community Correctional Center in Kailua, Hawai`i. Dion'e had just been released from prison after having been wrongly accused, convicted, and placed in an all-male facility, where she ended up in the hospital after being repeatedly raped. She nearly lost her life but survived to tell her story. Dion'e and DeVane talked about making a video about her experience. To show her complicated transition involved in claiming her identity, DeVane filmed her in the garden space behind Rice's condominium. As we listen to Dion'e's narrative, we see her carefully making up her face, doing her hair, donning flowers and jewelry until, at last, she is the true self she feels herself to be and wants us to acknowledge. Dion'e's message at the end of the video is potent: "It not only matters where we come from, but it is also about where we're going. My message to the world is to allow no one to dim your leading light."

The *Beyond Bars* project (pp. 158–160), a transformative program for women inmates at the Women's Community Correctional Center in Kailua, Hawai`i, is also documented in this exhibition. Conceived in 2018 by Tadia Rice and DeVane, this multidisciplinary project centers on the stories, images, and performances of female inmates. The project includes brief interviews with several women and photographs of the participants, all of which are formatted as direct views, with two profiles facing left and right, respectively, so that what we see represented is the Past/Present/Future. The presentation here makes reference to Hekate/Hecate, the three-faced Greek/Roman goddess of crossroads who inspired the format of the portraits. The focus is on community outreach and partnerships with organizations to add qualitative value to the women's recovery from trauma, substance abuse, and mental health issues. In her statement about the project, Rice observes that despite the fact that at times these women's stories seem "unreal," "their stories are poignant reminders that anyone, given certain circumstances, can end up behind bars. The common thread is childhood trauma, violence, addiction, homelessness, and repeated sexual assaults." But, "Once you know them you see how it could have been you. Such life-changing circumstances can happen to the best of people, and the worst."[33]

Avatars: Incarnations and Symbol

From the Realm of Dust *is a series of works about the human condition and our relationship to realms beyond us. It's archaically framed in the religious or mythical text as origin stories.*[34]

Since 2017, DeVane has been involved in the creation of large-scale personifications, representing mythological and religious figures and entities who have come to encompass universal concepts and beliefs. We can consider them "avatars" in order to evoke the notion of an alternate identity in the digital universe, as well as the Hindu concept of the "materialization or incarnation of a deity on Earth."[35] For DeVane, as noted above, these works are "about the human condition and our relationship to realms beyond us … framed in the religious or mythical text as origin stories."[36]

The surfaces of these wall pieces feature relief elements and are festooned with paint, beads, shells, glass, wax, plastic, resin, and other substances. We can also see here signs of DeVane's progression as she gradually moves back again into engaging what can broadly be described as "painting." *Swamp Angel* (2017) is more conventionally painted (albeit with an infusion of sequins), while in an apparition of divinity in *Epiphany* (p. 175), created a year later, DeVane has meticulously modeled the face and the articulation of the wing/phalange-like forms that frame his head. Her painting technique is more "impressionistic," enhancing the dreamlike quality of the image in the delicate pinks, blues, and yellows.

Two apparitions from 2018 feature the Haitian *loas* or deities *Dumballah* and *Erzulie* (both 2018, p. 168). Both of these characters had been the subjects of *Spirit Sculptures*: *Elegba (Dumballa)* (2008) and the *Erzulie Dandor* (2017, p. 149). While the *Dumballah* in the *Avatar* version is swathed in apparel that resembles Mardi Gras finery, the *Spirit Sculpture* version reflects

---

33 Tadia Rice, Artist's Statement, 2022. See page 161 in this volume.

34 Ibid.

35 Geoffrey Parrinder, *Avatar and Incarnation: The Divine in Human Form in the World's Religions* (London: Oneworld Publishing, 1997), 19–20.

36 Oletha DeVane, conversation with the author, January 21, 2022.

the fact that in the pantheon of deities in the African-based religion of Vodou in Haiti, he takes the form of a snake and is an agent of fertility. The snake swirling around the column of shells in *Elegba (Dumballa)* reflects DeVane's notion that "the spiral constitutes the human soul in a cycle of life that has no end."[37] In a complementary way Erzulie is invoked as a symbol of female courage, desirability, and strength. She is the ideal mother, the comforter of women, and the source of desire in men. Avatar *Erzulie* seems to have a scaly, larva-like body with opulent wings—like a caterpillar in mid-metamorphosis into a butterfly. As a *Spirit Sculpture* her presence is more syncretized with Catholicism (akin to how African religions have survived in the Americas), and this entity is built by DeVane on a devotional candle—such as those found in botanicas—that is heavily beaded, and crowned with a gazebo-like form in elaborate curlicues that shelters a robin, which symbolizes new beginnings and new projects and is a sign of good things to come.[38]

With *Mamawata's Earth Song* (2019, p. 171) and *Mawumoongoddess* (2019, p. 174), DeVane explores the intersection of the aquatic and the divine,[39] and as she observed in an interview with Leah Clare Michaels, "It is common in global mythologies for there to be a connection between water and the birth/origin story of humanity."[40] In African and African diasporic lore Mami Wata is mother of oceans/water. She is sometimes associated with mermaids or sirens, who can tempt sailors off course to their demise. Her mythic story is deeply rooted in the coastline regional stories of Nigeria, Zambia, and Thailand, and thus has a more global presence. This breadth is patently evident in the collection of vernacular representations of Mami Wata that the artist has collected from Haiti, Mexico, the United States, and South Africa. Made of cloth, wood, ceramic, and glass, they are poised to dive, seduce, or serenade. But for the artist, the significance of these mementos is that they indicate how

> as a people, we traversed the waters and oceans, either because we were enslaved, or when we were moving around this world, because Africans are on every continent in every country…. The water is a major conduit for movement and our ability to be everywhere. I look at water as a spiritual element. It's the life force of the planet and something that we need to take care of.[41]

She adds: "The joy of the water is that feeling of 'buoyancy'; we are Earth-bound creatures for the most part, so to be in that element is quite different."[42]

37 See DeVane's *Baker Artist Portfolio* page.

38 See https://worldbirds.com/robin-symbolism/. Accessed May 29, 2022.

39 Leah Clare Michaels, "The Divinity of Water: An Interview with Artist Oletha DeVane," *The Debutante: The Feminist-Surrealist Arts Journal*, October 29, 2020, www.thedebutante.online/post/the-divinity-of-water-an-interview-with-artist-oletha-devane-by-leah-clare-michaels.

40 Ibid.

41 Carroll, "DeVane Showcases Sculptural Works."

42 Michaels, "The Divinity of Water."

But interestingly enough, as opposed to being presented as an aquatic entity, DeVane's Mama Wata is a confection of geo stones, plastic, nails, and paint. Here we might have more of a cautionary tale about ecological threats to water. If we compare her with the representation of Mawu (also a water-associated deity, worshipped in coastal West Africa by the Fon people): associated with the moon, and presiding over creativity, abundance, birth, and inspiration, she is presented as an awe-inspiring presence with dramatically radial/spiked head appendages, an elaborate bead necklace, and a wide-eyed glance. Her expression is comparable to the strong emotion and determination inherent in the expression of the Maori *pūkana*.

DeVane conjures a composite spirit in *Sirius–Asteria* (2000, pp. 172–173), a hybrid of the star Sirius, considered the brightest in the night sky, and the Greek goddess Asteria, whose polymorphous identity was associated with nocturnal oracles and shooting stars. This richly appointed composition shows a central figure with an elaborate astral aura, surmounted by a golden female figure. Like an out-of-body specter with a ball-like projectile emanating from his head, there spouts the caption "how we begin to that end." In *Whatever Happened to Icarus?* (2020, p. 166), the foolhardy human of Greek mythology seems almost an afterthought—seen in sequence spinning down to earth, his wings scattered, having been destroyed by the sun's heat. In DeVane's 2013 solar print *Icarus*, his fall synchronizes with the soaring of two birds/ravens who fly up to meet him in a coordinated scene of free movement. Here the scene is dominated by an awesome presence wearing a superannuated headdress, who scornfully observes Icarus's presumptuous attempts to transcend his natural state.

In Islamic lore, what is depicted in *The Lote-Tree* (2020, p. 169) marks the utmost boundary of the seventh heaven across which no one can pass except the Prophet Mohammed, who encountered it at the climax of his legendary nocturnal ascent through the seven heavens. There are also the concepts of the seven earths and seven underworlds found in many philosophical traditions. In Bahá'u'lláh's mystical writings, the "Seven Valleys" and "Four Valleys" define the wayfarer's journey toward enlightenment. DeVane continues her exploration of garden motifs and arboreal symbolism in *Garden of the Heart* (2021, pp. 176–177), a delightful confection in yellows, blues, and purples. DeVane has collaged a variety of open-work, lacy elements that suggest the floral delights of a garden. A slightly sinister dark tangle of collage dominates the center, lending a more sinister nuance to the image. On the opposite end of the spectrum, *Tree from Hell* (2021, p. 167) is a

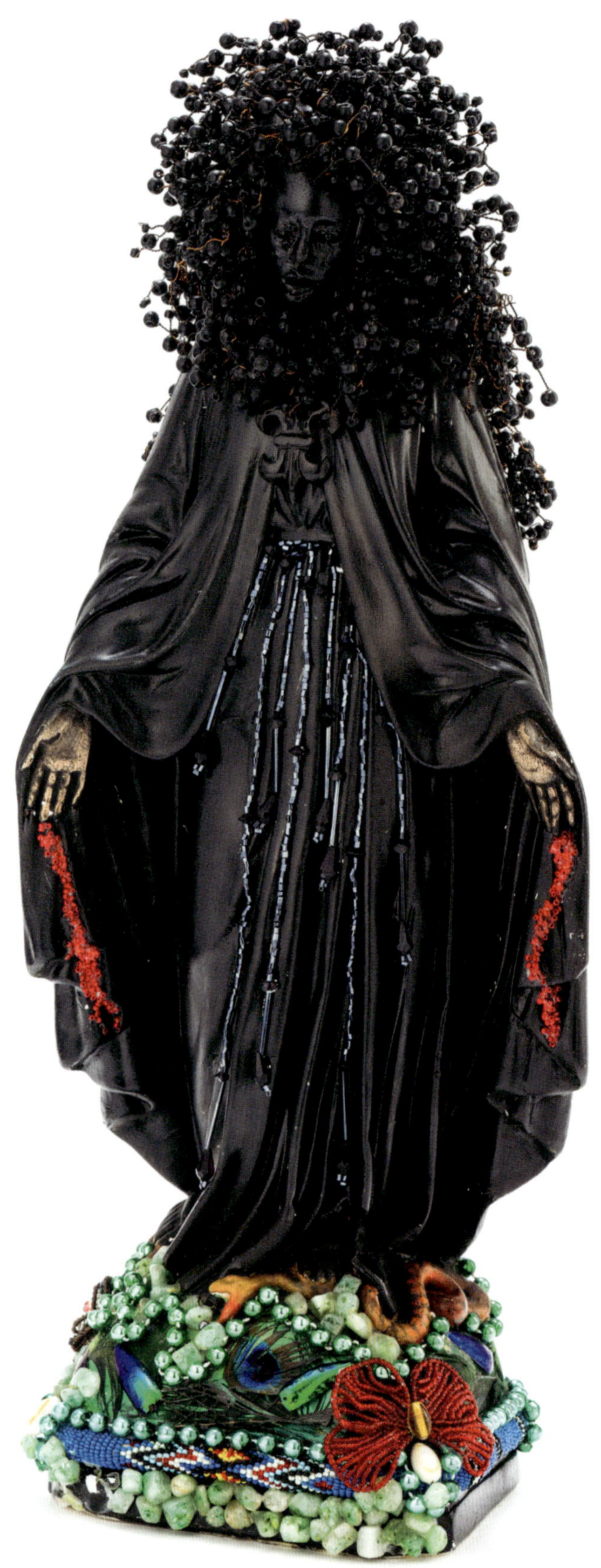

Saint for My City, 2007–2010, wood, plaster, glass, encaustic, plastic, metal, fabric, fiber, acrylic paint, hot glue, mirror, cowrie shells, bullet casings, peacock feathers

86 ⅞ × 12 ⅞ × 13 in. (220.7 × 32.7 × 33 cm). The Baltimore Museum of Art: purchase with exchange funds from the Pearlstone Family Fund and partial gift of The Andy Warhol Foundation for the Visual Arts, Inc., BMA 2020.22. Photo: Mitro Hood.

foreboding forest scene, not unlike the *Untitled* drawings (p. 86) of a figure in a similar scene from 2003 seeking a way through the mire. DeVane was working on *Tree from Hell* at the same time as *The Lote-Tree* and sees them as opposite aspects of the realm of existence.[43]

One work in DeVane's oeuvre that can been seen as a precursor to the *Avatar* series is *Saint for My City* (p. 34, 2007–2010, collection of the Baltimore Museum of Art). This sculpture presents what Angela Carroll has described as an avatar in the disguise of an "astral-Black holy figure."[44] A familiar statue of the Virgin Mary drawn from Catholic ritual has been painted black—conjuring traditions of the Black Madonna in Europe. Characteristically she is seen standing, head inclined toward the supplicant, her hands turned out in a posture of resignation and acceptance. DeVane has framed her head in an elaborate headdress/collar. The pedestal is an "embellished pillar laden with the names of immortalized African diasporic deities including Isis, Osiris, Horus, Ogun, and Dumballa. There is a large snake that coils from the base to the top where the saint stands."[45] Such power entities are evoked in this memorial to people killed in Maryland at the time, each represented by a single bullet casing.[46]

Writing about this work, Carroll suggests it is an apt symbol for the resiliency of Baltimore, where "the sacredness of the city and its inhabitants are often overlooked":[47]

> Those who live here and opt to stay here know that the city is more than its traumas. Baltimore is vibrant unbridled brilliance—charged invention and adaptation. DeVane channels that spirit of the city, its energy, and humanity through the Black saint whose outstretched arms reach towards the doorway of the small house as if beckoning saint and sinner alike to find solace in her embrace.[48]

Carroll's framing this piece within an urban context suggests a connection with the 2003 exhibition at UCLA's Fowler Museum *A Saint in the City: Sufi Arts of Urban Senegal*,[49] which focused on the urban Sufi movement inspired by the mystical teachings of Sheikh Amadou Bamba (1853–1927), who stood up to colonial French rule through passive resistance.[50] We can also think of the observation of the sculptor Nari Ward, who identifies urban space as a metaphorical space of "chance and unpredictability," where its refuse and detritus can serve as portable ambulatory elements of memorial that gain new meanings in different spaces.[51]

43   Oletha DeVane, conversation with the author, January 21, 2022.

44   Carroll, "DeVane Showcases Sculptural Works."

45   Ibid.

46   Virginia Anderson, "Artist Oletha DeVane on Materials and the Meanings They Hold," *BMA/Stories*, May 17, 2019, stories.artbma.org/oletha-devane/. Accessed May 18, 2022.

47   Carroll, "DeVane Showcases Sculptural Works."

48   Ibid.

49   See exhibition webpage at fowler.ucla.edu/exhibitions/a-saint-in-the-city-sufi-arts-of-urban-senegal/. Accessed May 18, 2022.

50   Ibid.

51   "Nari Ward on How to Make a True Portrait of New York City," *The Art Angle*, May 12, 2022, news.artnet.com/multimedia/the-art-angle-podcast-nari-ward-2114107. Accessed May 16, 2022.

I experiment with all kinds of materials … hoping to reclaim the spiritual memory that came with us as Africans to the Americas. I continue to draw upon my experiences, politics and our place in world histories.[52]

Up to this point, this discussion of Oletha DeVane's oeuvre has elucidated her philosophical approach to her life and work, highlighted the subject matter that has captivated her interest, and emphasized her particularly materialistic technique in constructing her work. All these elements have undoubtedly found their fullest realization in the *Spirit Sculptures.* As noted at the beginning of this essay, this genre can be considered DeVane's signature form.

She has described the *Spirit Sculptures* as having "emerged as a concept to harness blessings and explore the intuitive, irrational, or unconscious phenomena."[53] This body of work was inspired by a beaded Haitian bottle that DeVane acquired from her friend the artist William Rhodes.[54] These "common libation or rum bottles," transformed by the application of "sequins or beads," are "placed on altars as offerings to the *orishas*,"[55] or *loas*, the entities that in the Yoruba religious pantheon rule over various aspects of nature and life.[56] Curators Laura Roulet and Irene Hoffman would also remind us that "precedents for these sculptures can be found in African and Afro-Caribbean spiritual objects such as nkisi figures, [and] Kongo packets" and that these creative and ritual practices[57] "migrated to the deep South of the United States in the form of Bottle Trees. All share the notion of embellishing a receptacle to attract and hold the 'flash of the spirit' in scholar Robert Farris Thompson's words."[58]

In her essay in the catalogue, Leslie King-Hammond[59] analyzes DeVane's skill in manipulating materials and seeing their visual potential, which offers the artist many ways of expressing an idea through "found objects, beads, clay, glass, and other materials."[60] DeVane observes, "Although each one is different, they are linked to nature, emotions, or cultural myths…. For me, the work has evolved to have a meditative quality as I build them."[61] She finds kindred spirits in artists such as Washington, DC–based Renée Stout, who creates talismans and charms out of handmade potions, roots and herbs, found objects, bones and feathers, painted and sculptural elements, and technological components, which then convey her own narratives

52 See DeVane's *Baker Artist Portfolio* page.

53 Ibid.

54 Oletha DeVane, Artist Registry, Maryland State Arts Council website, www.msac.org/artists /oletha-devane#/o. Accessed December 12, 2018.

55 See See DeVane's *Baker Artist Portfolio* page.

56 There are many publications on orishas. For this discussion I would refer the reader to Migene Gonzalez-Wippler, *Powers of the Orishas: Santeria and the Worship of Saints* (New York: Original Publications, 1992).

57 Laura Roulet and Irene Hoffman, *Corridor: Baltimore, Maryland–Washington, DC*, exh. cat. (Washington, DC: Art Museum of the Americas, Organization of American States, 2011), unpaginated, museum.oas.org/img /exhibitions/2011-corridor /CorridorExhibitionCat_AMA.pdf.

58 Ibid.

59 Originally published as Leslie King-Hammond, "The Essence of Being Lies Within Ordinary, Useful/less Stuff, and Tangible Things," in *Oletha DeVane: Traces of the Spirit*, 5–14.

60 Oletha DeVane, "Artist's Statement," website of the artist, http://www.olethadevane.com /artist-statement.html. Accessed November 30, 2018.

61 Ibid.

62 Renée Stout, "Tales of the Conjure Woman" exhibition page on the website of the Halsey Institute of Contemporary Art, halsey.cofc.edu/main-exhibitions/tales-of-the-conjure-woman/. Accessed December 13, 2018.

63 "Vanessa German: ARThouse," *ARThouse* website, spacesarchives.org/explore/collection/environment/vanessa-german-arthouse/. Accessed December 12, 2018.

64 Ibid.

65 Jeff R. Donaldson, "AfriCobra Manifesto: Ten in Search of a Nation," *Nka: Journal of Contemporary African Art* (Spring 2012), http://391.org/wp-content/uploads/2019/01/1970-AfriCOBRA-manifesto-jeff-donaldson.pdf. Accessed May 30, 2022.

66 Ibid. AfriCobra artist Napoleon Jones-Henderson reflected on the origins of the idea of "coolade colors": "I don't remember the exact manner in which we came up with the terminology, but the colors we were dressed in and moving about through the community were the same colors as the Kool-Aid we were drinking." D. Amari Jackson, "A Life in Color: The Spirited Image Making of Napoleon Jones-Henderson," *Black Art in America* (April 2022), www.blackartinamerica.com/index.php/2022/06/01/a-life-in-color-the-spirited-image-making-of-napoleon-jones-henderson/. Accessed June 2, 2022.

about "romantic relationships, social ills, or financial woes."[62] Similarly the Pittsburgh-based collage sculptor Vanessa German achieves such embellishments through her own accumulative processes, which she sees as a means to "ward off evil," "heal broken hearts," and "bear powerful witness of the possible."[63]

While the elements that anchor DeVane's embellishments might be beverage bottles, or ceramic bric-à-brac, the finished sculptures can range in height from about 22 to 30 inches, having a variety of silhouettes that inevitably belie their origins. Carroll claims a quality of "monumentality" for these "repurposed found objects," with which DeVane "constructs monumental spiritual sites."[64] Indeed, the use of this term is apt because, experienced close-up, they are monumental in intent, monumental in theme, and monumental in impact. In 2021–2022 she began to approach the scale we associate with the monumental in her *N'Kisi* (pp. 4, 188–189, 194), a superannuated version of the art form we know as Kongo fetishes.

If the *Spirit Sculptures* can engage us in the ways DeVane's chosen materials come together to create presences that dazzle us with their visual velocity and engaging sumptuousness, it is interesting to consider here a previously unexplored pictorial relationship to the precepts set by the Afri-Cobra group in the 1970s. This is pertinent because DeVane's advisor in graduate school was the painter Nelson Stevens, a prominent figure in the Afri-Cobra group. In delineating the particular formal and technical qualities of the work of AfriCoba artists, Jeff Donaldson and Cherilyn C. Wright stress elements such as free symmetry and "repetition with change, based on African music and African movement."[65] Reflecting DeVane's concept of how her work functions in the world, they also note, "We want the work to look like the creator made it through us," so it should "shine," have a "rich luster," and feature "coolade colors for coolade images for surreal people."[66]

Although DeVane began working on the *Spirit Sculptures* around 2007, it is in *Meditation* of 2019 (p. 72) that she more specifically retains the presence of the original bottle, of a type similar to the one from Haiti given to her by William Rhodes. The beads have been applied in semicircular patterns with occasional ocular elements. The added base has layers of terrain with inlaid blossoms, and the usual stopper has been replaced with the contemplative glass figure. Incarnations of familiar mythological figures were among the earliest in this series, including *Janus* (2007, p. 100), *Songs of Orpheus* (2008), and *Kronos (Collateral)* of 2018 (p. 153). The first, characteristically two-faced, has been endowed with wings, and the second has a tangled of tendrils around his head as if to visualize his song. But with *Kronos (Collateral)* DeVane achieves a metaphorical corollary to modern stories in a powerful way.

DeVane conflates Central American celebrations of the dead—where bodies are disinterred and venerated—with ancient Greek mythology, using the story of the Titan Kronos, who devoured his own children to circumvent a prophecy that he would be deposed as ruler by his own sons. This myth casts the children as "collateral damage," the unknowing, often innocent and incidental victims in the power struggles of war, historical and contemporary alike. Surmounted by a skull (which eerily retains wisps of air), toy soldiers struggle freeform within its skeletal hands in a fall from grace reminiscent of what Michelangelo depicted in the Sistine Chapel. All this occurs beneath a table structure, on top of which are a miniature missile, tank, and plane. The base is decorated with beaded bands of blue, white, and red, and white stars on a blue background have been applied to the pyramidal phalanges that extend out from the base. It is a visual parable for our times.

As mentioned earlier in this essay, DeVane often combines and collapses the identities of established characters, navigating, as Angela Carroll observes, "belief systems from native and global communities."[67] So, the characteristics of Dumballah, the Haitian *loa* who is a benevolent father figure, can be combined with those of Elegba, the Yoruba orisha who is variously messenger, the guardian of crossroads, and trickster, in the 2008 *Elegba (Dumballah)*. *Isis/Virgin* of 2010 (pp. 106–107) illuminates how the enduring concept of the Egyptian goddess, who embodied maternity and the notion of the afterlife, survived in the minds of humans through millennia to impact Christian beliefs and practices around the veneration of the Virgin Mary. Another example, *Woman Who Married a Snake* of 2017 (p. 152), takes the form of an open-sided altar or reliquary to represent the character Ayida-Weddo—the Rainbow Serpent in Benin, and in Haitian lore, the wife of Dumballah. While the visual combination suggests an interesting continuation of the encounter between Eve and the Serpent in the Old Testament, it is, in the end, a fierce commentary on connubial relations in the extreme.

DeVane can also approach the making of commentary in more lighthearted ways. In *Consummate Consumer #1* (2016), a female figurine stands atop an ornately beaded bottle form on a fringed pedestal. Slogans affirming presumptions of quality and uniqueness swirl up the stem, and at the bottom we spy a group of grasping, grabbing gold figures. *Lifeisbutadream*

67 Angela N. Carroll, "Dark Things Matter: Oletha DeVane's The Other Side of Darkness at Project 1628," *Bmore Art*, May 10, 2017, www.bmoreart.com/2017/05/dark-things-matter.html. Accessed December 17, 2018.

(2015, p. 148) is a pink vision with a plastic Cinderella figure at the apex, presiding over a cake confection held up by blue/black male figures at the base. A cautionary feminist comment on marriage? *Spring [Sohappyitsspring]* (2018, p. 75), also features pink elements. The bottle becomes a bulbous-trunked tree with outsized flowers and sits atop a platform with a plethora of beaded flowers. A snake—a motif that, as we have seen, frequently appears in DeVane's work—curves around the trunk, adding an element of foreboding.

But the state of the world is never far from DeVane's mind. We find in this selection *Spirit Sculptures* that also memorialize political and social challenges specifically faced by Black people in America. *Samuel's Dream* (2012, Homewood Museum, Johns Hopkins University) was made when DeVane thought of a spirited young man she once met who was battling drug addiction. He was one of eight people who lost their lives in a fire in a New Orleans warehouse, where he had fallen asleep when the blaze broke out. DeVane references a passage from the book of Samuel in the Old Testment, which describes how he was called to his spiritual mission by God in a dream. For DeVane her friend, too, was called to a higher purpose through the Second Line musical parade that concluded his funeral ceremony, serving as a means to ease his passage forward.

George Floyd (Black Lives Matter) (2021, pp. 180–181) captures the global sense of horror and sorrow that erupted in 2021 as reportage on the deaths of Black men and women activated our consciousness. Prominent among the societal response was that of the Black Lives Matter movement, which had reflected the crescendo of anger and frustration that had been building over the last decade with each successive instance of human rights violations committed against Black people. In turn, *I can't Breathe* (2021, pp. 182–183, 2021), the last words of Eric Garner while he was brutally subjected to a chokehold by a New York City police officer in 2014, is a searing reminder of the persistence of that state of affairs. DeVane takes on these incessant specters of racial whiteness and violence in *Subsumed by Whiteness* (2020, p. 170), part of the *Avatar* series. Here an expressionless white head is framed by a lacy halo even as he wears a neckpiece made of bullet casings. This figure is a timely and apt metaphor for the stubborn social resistance to gun control even in the face of surge of mass shootings all over the United States in 2022. Is that a gaping wound in the composition, out of which flowers for the deceased fall?

The George Floyd sculpture suggests the type of plinth that Confederate monuments were mounted on, and names (including that of Breonna Taylor), slogans, suggestions of a flag, and other shapes function like projections that at times have replaced those monuments after they were toppled in the summer of 2021. The *I can't breathe* apparition suggests a female figure with a jeweled pin as features—creating a rather ferocious glance, and there are circles of pearls for breasts, a cross in her solar plexus. Her arms are crossed at her waist. The base has photographs of Black men, over which are applied the works, "I can't breathe," spelled out in block shapes.

A 2022 work may indicate DeVane's position with regard to these challenges. *Transcend* (pp. 184–185) is an amalgam of glass, clay, beads, metal, sequins, mirrors, and cowrie shells—materials coming together to symbolize a convergence of energy and power. Cowries refer to prosperity and fecundity, glass and mirrors reflect and attract, beads ornament, metal and sequins shine, and clay grounds all to the earth. Embroidered emblems, turquoise fragments complete the sumptuousness of the totality. As extraordinary as the *Spirit Sculpture* can get, this version is truly exemplary.

Perhaps the most personal of all these creations is *12202021* (2022, pp. 186–187), a poignant memoir of DeVane's late husband, Peter Kozjar. She writes, "This is a tribute to his gentle spirit."[68] She has collaborated with the Baltimore-based glass artist Tim McFadden to create a composite of a found Meissen German porcelain vase (Meissen is near the region where Peter grew up) and a small Czech bowl, combined with McFadden's blown glass and vines, as well as an embellished wooden base."[69] DeVane reminisces about his journey of escape from what was then Czechoslovakia by way of Germany before his arrival in the United States; his apolitical stance despite his love of talking about politics; and his dislike of computers even though he earned an MA in computer science at Johns Hopkins.[70]

> He felt more comfortable conceptualizing real-world problems, tinkering with machines, traveling and collecting bird sculptures along the way and sitting on the porch watching birds in the morning while we drank coffee. He was an avid reader, fascinated by human foibles, but endlessly curious about people.[71]

As we are now in the third decade of the twenty-first century, DeVane is expanding her creative reach through public sculptures, which are discussed in the essay by Christopher Kojzar in this catalogue. These projects continue DeVane's exploration of Black history and contributions and bring them to the consciousness of a wider audience. It might be said that *Healer*

68 Oletha DeVane, email to the author, June 1, 2022.

69 Ibid.

70 Ibid.

71 Ibid.

72 Anderson, "In Conversation with Oletha DeVane," 39.

73 Ibid.

74 Lowery Stokes Sims, "A Calling and Response," in *Oletha DeVane: Traces of the Spirit*, 22.

(Pilgrimage) of 2018 (p. 145) personifies DeVane's creative journey. The head of a seeker extends outward from one side of the house-like shrine; like the artist, this apparition is eager to receive beliefs and ideas from various cultures, which she renders in forms that actuate their potential. When asked by Virginia Anderson, who curated DeVane's 2019 installation *Traces of the Spirit* at the Baltimore Museum of Art, whether she thought the *Spirit Sculpture* series was ongoing or was now complete, DeVane responded, "Yes, it's ongoing because a lot of times, I come across material that calls for the creation of another piece."[72] Speaking to the impact of the work in that installation, DeVane noted that she hoped that viewers would come away with a sense of wonder. "I'm sure there will be questions about meaning. I hope the pieces resonate visually and that people feel the energy from which they were created."[73] As this writer noted in 2019, for DeVane, therefore, art-making is inseparable from her sense of herself, her vision of her place on this earth, and her conception of why she is here at this particular moment.[74]

Oletha DeVane's Adventurous Search for Meaning

Serubiri Moses

1 Serubiri Moses, interview with Oletha DeVane, April 2021.

IN THIS ESSAY, I pursue a close reading of artist Oletha DeVane's biography, philosophical views, and faith in dialogue with her art. I focus on her travels to Haiti, Thailand, and South Africa. I depart from my interview with DeVane[1] in close view of a passage from Zora Neale Hurston's novel *Their Eyes Were Watching God*; the art historian Julie L. McGee's theorization of syncretism; the poet and literary scholar Fred Moten's idea of Black metaphysics; the art historian Leslie King-Hammond's theorization of materiality; and the philosopher Alain L. Locke's pluralism, all with the aim of more closely examining specific events in DeVane's life in dialogue with her art. For example, I draw on DeVane's upbringing, which imbued her art with philosophical pluralism. From her mastery of American abstract painting while a student at University of Massachusetts Amherst, to her rigorous research on religious philosophy, DeVane's art speaks *loud* and clear. In this essay, my method consists of philosophical and biographical approaches. This essay considers works from the solo exhibitions *Traces of the Spirit* (2019) and *The Other Side of Darkness* (2017).

"An incredible search …"

2 Angela N. Carroll, "Oletha DeVane Showcases Sculptural Works in 'Traces of the Spirit' at the BMA," *Baltimore*, August 12, 2019, www.baltimoremagazine. com/section/artsentertainment /oletha-devane-showcases -sculptural-works-in-bma-exhibit -traces-of-spirit/.

In an interview with the art critic Angela N. Carroll, DeVane spoke about her guiding philosophy: "In terms of looking at religious practice itself, it's about how we as human beings are on this incredible search for meaning. It doesn't mean that any one practice is wrong; it just means that we are all, as a world community, on different paths of searching for that ultimate spiritual essence."[2] How might we think of DeVane as undertaking an adventurous search for meaning, perhaps one as adventurous as that taken by the novelist Zora Neale Hurston? How might we also think of DeVane's practice as going beyond the category of Black culture demarcated by the national border in the US, and moving toward the categories of continental African, cosmopolitan, and Black diaspora cultures? On the one hand, contemporary scholars grapple with the idea of a Black studies that is limited by the nation's borders,[3] but Black artists, on the other hand, have crossed those borders for at least a century.[4] Hurston, the poet Langston Hughes, and the dancer Katherine Dunham all went to Port-au-Prince, Haiti, just as James Baldwin later lived in Paris, France. It has been recorded that Paris was attractive to the earliest Black modernists such as Henry Ossawa Turner and, later, Beauford Delaney, both artists who made their homes there. Notably, in the 1950s, W. E. B. Du Bois immigrated to Ghana at the invitation of Ghanian President Kwame Nkrumah. The literary scholar Farah Griffin has argued that a dominant aspect of Black life in the early twentieth century is movement.[5] In the post-Reconstruction era, migration took place inside national US borders, from the South to the North, and then later outside the US, with Black Americans migrating across the national border to destinations in Europe and Africa. How, then, do we situate Black artists outside the US, such as in Africa? A few examples come to mind.

The artist and art historian David C. Driskell traveled to Africa in the early 1970s and produced a number of paintings following his journey, which according to Julie L. McGee resulted in a *syncretic* iconography:

> Driskell's work continually straddled Africa and America, so it is little wonder that he developed a syncretic iconography. This syncretism is most directly expressed in the bilateral faces seen in numerous works, including *Bakota Girl* (1971). Driskell, now working predominantly in collage and mixed media, often combined a spliced photograph of an African mask with a hand-rendered image, effectively splitting the head in two portions, one more clearly African, the other a more generalized Black physiognomy.[6]

McGee reflects on the "syncretism" that emerged from Driskell's journey. Though that syncretic impulse is narrated through formalist iconography such as the bilateral faces in his work, the experience of traveling to Africa, as this quote shows, created a rearticulation of Black American identity. Black artists have often said, regarding their crossing of the border, that they learned how American they were by being elsewhere. As McGee writes of Driskell: "He had always said that what he discovered in Africa was his Americanness."[7] This tendency to leave America behind only to rediscover

3 Rinaldo Walcott, "Outside in Black Studies: Reading from a Queer Place in the Diaspora," in *Black Queer Studies: A Critical Anthology*, ed. E. Patrick Johnson et al. (Durham, NC: Duke University Press, 2005), 90–105.

4 Farah Griffin (ed.), *A Stranger in the Village: Two Centuries of African American Travel Writing* (New York: Beacon Press, 1998); Tyler Stovall, *Paris Noir: African Americans in the City of Light* (Boston: Houghton Mifflin, 1996); Brent Hayes Edwards, *The Practice of Diaspora: Literature, Translation, and the Rise of Black Internationalism* (Cambridge, MA: Harvard University Press, 2009).

5 Farah Griffin, *Harlem Nocturne: Women Artists and Progressive Politics* (New York: Basic, 2013), 15–16.

6 Julie L. McGee, *David C. Driskell: Artist and Scholar* (Petaluma, CA: Pomegranate, 2006), 90–96.

7 Ibid.

8 James Baldwin, "Princes and Powers," in *The Price of the Ticket* (New York: St. Martin's, 1985).

9 Griffin, *Stranger in the Village.*

10 Moses, interview with Oletha DeVane, April 2021.

Migration, 2012, etching and silkscreen

it elsewhere is echoed in accounts by numerous Black artists and cultural figures including James Baldwin, who, as an attendee of the 1956 Congress of Black Writers and Artists in Paris, reported having the same experience in his essay "Princes and Powers."[8] Yet despite this tendency, Black artists have often learned immensely from their experiences abroad.

Locating Black artists outside the national border can be a challenge for the critic, and yet many Black artists have taken that risk. Often it brought with it some misrecognition of other Black artists in other parts of the world, something that Baldwin pointed out in his essay and Griffin has noted in travel narratives by African Americans.[9] But what can be made of Oletha DeVane's own journeys to Haiti, Thailand, and South Africa? In our interview, DeVane revealed an opposite picture of learning and sharing with the artists she met in Haiti and Thailand. She described techniques she learned from an artist producing costumes for the carnival in Jacmel, Haiti.[10] She recalled precisely how she approached the artist with a request, and that in response the Haitian artist quite openly showed her the technique. DeVane's connection to such techniques reverberates in many of her sculptures. A more concise description of this sort of instruction is that it manifests an ability to "weave" together seemingly disparate materials and to make use of iconographic design. Elsewhere, DeVane has said:

> Going to Thailand was a major experience, and so was my trip to South Africa. Those two places, for me, were incredibly visually rich. Thailand was 2014; Thailand was the inspiration for a series on "Spirit Houses"

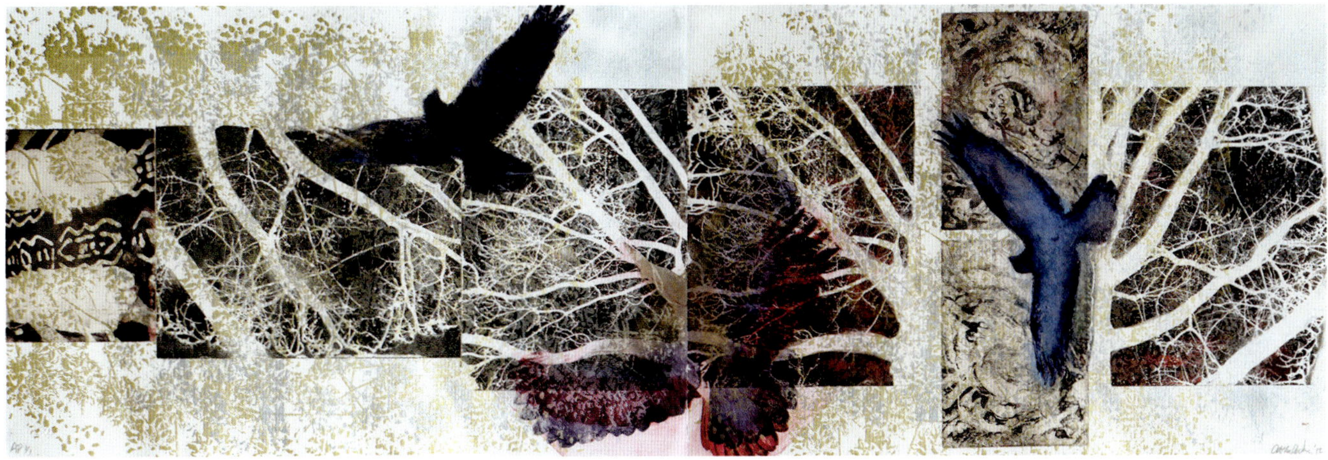

(2014), which are located near homes throughout Southeast Asia. The small, ornately carved shrines are to appease the "spirits" or "deities." In Thailand, to walk inside the Buddhist temples and view the richness of the materials and gold used was a sensual experience.[11]

This focus on materials mirrors her encounter with the costume-maker during carnival in Jacmel. Her attention to material economy is matched by her ethical view, one shaped by a search for "spiritual essence." Furthermore, DeVane has since become involved in humanitarian activities in the country following the 2010 earthquake there, including current appointments to the board of the Build Haiti Foundation.

"Right after that was the trip to South Africa with five artists to visit a former sugar plantation near Durban where the Ubuhle women created wall-like panels of landscapes using glass beads. The beading techniques they developed were stunning. We sat on the ground and watched the magic of the reflected light upon the finished panels," DeVane said.

We can say that DeVane is adventurous: that her work moves across national borders, and that she in turn becomes involved in spaces outside America, that her art is rooted in a similar vein as one finds with Driskell, Hurston, Baldwin, and others before her. And thus her work necessarily returns to a mode of movement that appeared prevalent from the 1920s to the 1960s, of Black artists taking that risk of crossing the border, at times urged by the war and by the political and/or economic situation at home. And similarly, like Driskell's, DeVane's iconography is syncretic. Departing from this dialectical form in Driskell's artwork, I look toward Alain Locke's value pluralism to situate DeVane's distinctly pluralistic attitude.

DeVane's Pluralistic Attitude and the Creative Economy

The art historian Leslie King-Hammond, following the art historian Robert Farris Thompson, wrote in the catalogue for *Traces of the Spirit* that "the bottle 'spirit forms' and the totemic sculptures in this exhibition are the result of introspection, experimentation, and African retentions. The accumulation of these disparate items transforms ordinary, so-called useful and useless stuff and unremarkable tangible things into a personalized artistic vocabulary that enables DeVane to expressively tell her stories—known, unknown, imagined—or yet to be defined … or divided."[12] *Traces of the Spirit* relied on a particular metaphysics that is likened to what Fred Moten has called

11 Virginia M. G. Anderson, ed., *Oletha DeVane: Traces of the Spirit*, exh. cat. (Baltimore: Baltimore Museum of Art, 2019), 32.

12 Leslie King-Hammond, "The Essence of Being Lies Within Ordinary, Useful/less Stuff, and Tangible Things," in *Oletha DeVane: Traces of the Spirit*, ed. Anderson, 5–14.

13 See Fred Moten, "The Case of Blackness," *Criticism* 50, no. 2 (Spring 2008): 177–218.

14 Carroll, "DeVane Showcases Sculptural Works."

15 Rowland Abiodun, "Understanding Yoruba Art and Aesthetics," *African Arts* 27, no. 3 (1994): 74.

a metaphysics of Blackness.[13] It is a metaphysics that, writes Angela Carroll, can be negated: "DeVane's work relies on contextualization beyond Western philosophies, and an openness to appreciate humanity's attempts to comprehend and encompass the immensity of god."[14] I am reminded of the Yoruba art historian Rowland Abiodun, who writes about the inescapable connection between spirit and form, thus producing a kind of physical manifestation of spirit: "Without this asé, many an appreciable artifact would fail to make a religio-aesthetic impact."[15]

I want to bring King-Hammond in dialogue with Moten in order to address what appears to me as their shared singular mission, which is to show how Black people think/act in ways that are at times misread or misunderstood as incoherent. King-Hammond's focus on materiality is perhaps due to her approach as an art historian specifically interested in the material conditions and their exceptional genealogies in the study of art. Her genealogy reveals the material conditions of Black Americans, being those descended from slavery, and reflects a creative economy that dates back a few centuries. In brief, when King-Hammond points out that DeVane's work is characterized by "useless stuff," and "unremarkable things," she brings us precisely into that creative economy that dates back centuries in America. The reader needs to escape stereotypical readings. If the *things* that DeVane works with are useless and unremarkable, what is their inherent value in art?

In contrast, Moten's work and its focus on Black metaphysics rests on the distinction between the norm and its deconstruction. For him, such a dialectic is evident not only in Black academic spaces but also in barbershops and beauty shops. The concept of Black metaphysics shows how art can become a site of Black politics. DeVane's sculptural works such as *Saint for My City* (2007–2010, p. 34) and her exhibition project on Harriet Tubman, *The Other Side of Darkness* at Project 1628 gallery, are important because they show DeVane's attention to the "social" and delineate her attunement to Black politics in the US. *Saint* shows the sociopolitical realities of present-day Baltimore. *The Other Side* accesses the memory of abolitionist Harriet Tubman, whose life intersected with Baltimore. As Carroll noted, "It is fitting then that DeVane should feature this rarely published depiction of Tubman, not as an old woman, but as a young warrior, an alert archangel perched and ready for battle."[16]

When positioned in dialogue with DeVane's art, Moten and King-Hammond show us this idea of a centuries-old material history in America and its creative economy, as well as its interconnection with social and

16 Angela N. Carroll, "Dark Things Matter: Oletha DeVane's The Other Side of Darkness at Project 1628," *Bmore Art*, May 10, 2017, www.bmoreart.com/2017/05/dark -things-matter.html.

political history. She attends to Black life in an approach that charts diverse temporal and material realities. DeVane's art is thus situated along a continuum. It connects past and present, whether from the purview of a centuries-old material history or from Black political history.

Whereas King-Hammond situates DeVane's sculptures within a tradition of *objet trouvé*, I hold that the artist's experimentation is matched only by the rigor of her study of world faiths, Baltimore's political and social history, and her philosophical views on "spiritual essence." As with Driskell's "bilateral faces" and syncretic iconography, DeVane marries global religious icons in Asia Pacific and Africa to the Christian and Hellenic icons in works such as *Saint for My City*, which includes the figure of a Black Madonna and the names of various deities graffitied on the obelisk. The use of the skeletal form, often incorporating skulls, as in *Kronos (Collateral)* (2018), resonates as much with the Haitian deity of Papa Legba and accurately recalls the iconography of skulls and bones in Haitian carnival, which she found and studied on her trips to Jacmel. The artwork is based on the notion of time and thus portrays a philosophical interpretation of the Greek "Kronos." Her frequent references to Greek literature and philosophy, such as in *Songs of Orpheus* (2008), reflect DeVane's specifically pluralistic attitude. Thus her images and icons may be reflective of Haitian and Yoruba ontologies as well as Black politics, but her work also draws equally from the philosophical traditions contained in Christian and Greek sources.

Alain Locke's Bahá'í Faith and Value Pluralism in Comparison to DeVane's Art and Faith

In a biographical note on Locke in his introduction to *The Philosophy of Alain Locke*, Leonard Harris writes that "the Baha'i belief in the ultimate spiritual unity among the plurality of religious faiths and the treatment of death as a passing into another present, instead of the traumatic ending of a condemned born sinner hoping for an uncertain redemption, were appealing to Locke." Harris goes on to write that Locke, who practiced the Bahá'í faith, had written essays on his trips to Luxor and Haifa, and these writings reflected his deep appreciation for "human and spiritual unity." These journeys beyond the national border are similar to DeVane's travels to Thailand, Haiti, and South Africa, given what she was seeking: "In terms of looking at religion itself, it's about how we as human beings are on this incredible search. It doesn't mean that any one practice is wrong, it just means that we are

17 Carroll, "DeVane Showcases Sculptural Works."

all, as a world community, on different paths of searching for that ultimate spiritual essence."[17] That sense of adventure or the search for meaning is evident in both Locke and DeVane. I find that the philosophical views of each are bonded with spiritual practice. That "spiritual unity" and "spiritual essence" are enacted through their practice as Bahà'ís.

Regarding the many aspects that may define that spiritual essence, the exhibition press release for *Traces of the Spirit* notes that DeVane "derives her inspiration from the Bahà'í Faith, Greek mythology, Yoruba religious practices, Buddhism, Haitian Vodou, and biblical references, among others." Thus, the Bahà'í faith represents an openness and an affirmative attitude toward the meeting of seemingly disparate faiths and philosophies. Further along this relation between Locke and DeVane we find a shared affirmative attitude toward Hellenic and African religions. Harris writes, "Although enamored at a young age by the lifestyle of classical Greek culture, educated at institutions offering little positive incentive to study African culture or race relations, and attracted also to the Bahà'í spirituality, Locke felt that the promotion and study of African culture and race relations were integral to his being."[18]

18 Leonard Harris, "Introduction," in *The Philosophy of Alain Locke: Harlem Renaissance and Beyond*, ed. Leonard Harris (Philadelphia: Temple University Press, 1989), 3–30.

In our interview, DeVane said that her parents were very encouraging toward her art and recalled that her family urged her to think for herself and tolerated her investigation into multiple faiths. DeVane's move toward the Bahà'í faith as a teenager reflects an awareness of the difference between one calling and another. When DeVane told me that she gravitated toward the Bahà'í faith because it encouraged the study of religious progression, her statement resonated deeply with me.[19] I also recognized the artist's move toward African art, both through the broader philosophical view of a "search for meaning" and via a Black feminist ethic that often references African, Caribbean, and African American belief systems. Here I am thinking of Baby Suggs's sermon in the "clearing" in Toni Morrison's novel *Beloved*.[20] The tableau is a return to that creative economy of a centuries-old material history in America and that of the enslaved Africans. Baby Suggs's sermon was outdoors in a "clearing," which showed how the natural environment merges with spirituality in African cultures. This Black feminist ethic is about the sharing of knowledge within spaces of intimacy and friendship.

19 Moses, interview with Oletha DeVane, April 2021.

20 Toni Morrison, *Beloved* (New York: Knopf, 2006), 115–116.

Like DeVane, Locke gravitated toward African art and did so as a way to complement rather than undermine the Hellenic basis of his formal education. This means that in his argument that Black artists should pay attention to African art, Locke saw such study to be consistent with the interest shown by earlier artists such as Henri Matisse and Pablo Picasso.[21] His arguments aren't about creating Black art that goes beyond modern Eurocentric art, but rather—and here I return to Driskell's syncretism—he encouraged Black artists to find inspiration in it and to create a pluralistic form.

Leonard Harris cites Locke, who held that "values are rooted in attitudes, not in reality and pertain to ourselves, not to the world."[22] Harris clarifies that by "values" Locke means "feelings, attitudes, beliefs, preferences, attenuations for moral principles, aesthetic objects, religious beliefs, racial and ethnic loyalties, and political persuasions."[23]

Locke was drawn to the notion of plurality because of his own study of value theory, which led him to investigate and distinguish between value systems and, going even further, to articulate a theory of what he referred to as "Black feeling."[24] The spiritual connotations of Locke's pragmatism are self-evident. Indeed, he followed the tradition of American pragmatism elaborated by William James, the philosopher who taught philosophy to both Locke and W. E. B. Du Bois at Harvard. For purposes of this essay, I use Locke's theory of Black feeling or, more directly, Black value systems to show Oletha DeVane's engagement with value pluralism.

It is important to reflect on the tolerance of a diversity of values and beliefs in such a domestic space. I am interested in how DeVane's upbringing bears on her art. Thus her formal training in American abstraction, with its roots in early to mid-twentieth century American painting, diverges from her later work in its material and spiritual excess. It is crucial to note here that DeVane is an academically trained artist, since this point is at times taken for granted. She received her BFA at the Maryland Institute College of Art in Baltimore and received her MFA at the University of Massachusetts Amherst. In our correspondence, she shared an image of an early abstract painting made shortly after she received her MFA degree, which shows her mastery of American abstract art.

Biographical readings can be troublesome given how stereotypical and questionable Black artists are at times portrayed within them. The blanket assumption that Black people couldn't make art, as the literary theorist and historian Henry Louis Gates Jr. has noted, emerged from Enlightenment ideas within continental European thought.[25] Furthermore, the South African art historian Nontobeko Ntombela has argued that there are misconceptions about premier Black women artists. In such cases, Black artists are relegated to "primitive" or "self-taught" categories. Furthermore, their

21 Alain Locke, "The Legacy of the Ancestral Arts," in *The New Negro: An Interpretation*, ed. Alain Locke (New York: Albert & Charles Boni, 1925).

22 Harris, "Introduction."

23 Ibid.

24 Ibid.

25 Henry Louis Gates Jr., *The Trials of Phillis Wheatley* (New York: Basic, 2003), 22–24.

biographies are often used to fortify these arguments, for example using the absence of written documents or the suggestion of growing up "rural" as evidence of either pathology or underdevelopment.[26] In my own research, I have pointed out how Black women artists are often portrayed in a light that is less than ideal—for example, when they are pathologized under the mantle of art criticism.[27]

Because a large part of my argument rests on the facts that make up the artist's biography, I want to be careful not to fall into these problematic historiographic pathways. I want to be careful not to place Oletha DeVane in the domain of Hegelian historiography, within which African religions are misconceived as irrational and ahistorical. I also want to avoid the unnecessary focus on naming DeVane as "the first Black woman artist" in any field or category of art-making. Rather I engage with DeVane's biography, specifically her focus on a diversity of world religions, in dialogue with ideas of diaspora that can accommodate pluralistic attitudes and diverse philosophical traditions.

DeVane's Art in Comparison to Hurston's
Their Eyes Were Watching God

Zora Neale Hurston's work enables me to put DeVane's travel itinerary in Haiti in context. In her foreword to a reissue of the novel, Edwidge Danticat points out that it was in Haiti that Hurston wrote *Their Eyes Were Watching God*.[28] To do so is important, because in viewing DeVane's work, the artist could easily be isolated from other cosmopolitan Black intellectuals who traveled from the United States to Africa, Europe, Asia Pacific, the Caribbean, and South America during the twentieth and twenty-first centuries. DeVane takes her place along this same continuum of Black cosmopolitanism, and thus her adventurousness is comparable to Hurston's. On the subject of Black modernity, the scholar Daphne LaMothe argues that Hurston embodied two positions: she was both the authority on folklore as well as the native informant, such that she inhabited a complex subjectivity when writing her novels on Black subjects.[29]

I want to focus here on the idea of the carnival in Jacmel, particularly given that it featured prominently in DeVane's travel itinerary in Haiti, according to what she said in my interview with her.[30] The recent monograph by Leah Gordon reproduces several accounts of the costumes worn during carnival.[31] These accounts are oral history interviews on the making of the

26 Nontobeko Ntombela, "A Fragile Archive: Refiguring | Rethinking | Reimagining | Representing Gladys Mgudlandlu," MA thesis, University of Witwatersrand, Johannesburg, 2014.

27 Serubiri Moses, "Counter-Imaginaries: 'Women Artists on the Move', 'Second to None', 'Like A Virgin,'" *Afterall* 47 (Spring/Summer 2019): 117–125.

28 Edwidge Danticat, "Foreword," in *Their Eyes Were Watching God* (New York: HarperCollins, 2006), xi.

29 Daphne LaMothe, "Narrative Dissonance: Conflict and Contradiction in Hurston's Caribbean Ethnography," in *Inventing the New Negro: Narrative, Culture, and Ethnography* (Philadelphia: University of Pennsylvania Press, 2008), 141–158.

30 Moses, interview with Oletha DeVane, April 2021.

31 Leah Gordon, *Kanaval* (London: Here Press, 2021), 118.

costumes, as well as on the purpose of carnival. Salnave Raphaël, one of the interviewees in Gordon's oral history, describes the role of *Lanse Kòd* or rope-throwers during carnival: "At Carnival, people like to be scared. We are the scariest. The Zél Maturin are supposed to be scary, but they're more scared of us—they worry that they'll dirty their fancy satin disguises if they touch us. Our disguises are much cheaper to make than many others—no materials, no papier-mâché, just a charcoal-and-syrup mixture."[32] Indeed, the photographs that Gordon reproduces of the *Lanse Kòd* reveal a kind of costume that is not premised on the brightly colored papier-mâché used to produce other costumes but instead reveals shiny Black bodies covered in a dense black lubricant, holding ropes and wearing horns or paper-bag masks.

Raphaël continued his account of carnival by observing, "We are making a statement about slavery and being freed from slavery—it's a celebration of our independence in 1804. The ropes we carry are the ropes that were used to bind us. We know that slaves never wore horns. But this is about the slave revolt, and we wear the horns to give us more power and to look even more scary. We're always sullen and menacing. And we never smile."[33] These reenactments, in the use of ropes and indeed in the menacing facial expressions and behavior, are based on the history of slavery on the Hispaniola island, as well as the history of the Haitian revolution that began in the 1790s. The carnival thus animates radical Black traditions of revolt and rebellion, as well as reenacts or anticipates Black freedom. In this sense, the carnival has a purpose that is rooted in cultural memory and political history.

The invocation of Africanity in DeVane's art is rooted in a similar cultural memory of what Fred Moten, following Cedric Robinson, has called the Black radical tradition in the United States.[34] Moten described that tradition as a political genealogy in the Americas, in which Black people have resisted the conditions of being of non-value. The Black radical tradition is evident in Black cultures that reorganize and inject meaning into things deemed to be without value. This reminds me of Leslie King-Hammond's reading of DeVane's art: "It is the essence of the indispensable energies of life, without which nothing can exist, that drives her to create images and objects and useless stuff and ordinary."[35]

Hurston's novel *Their Eyes Were Watching God* struck me with the idea of excess. The novel is overwhelming in its attenuations and diction, its mood and chatter, and its extravagant and flamboyant characters. The novel is a "riot" in the sense of bursting open the expectations of modern fiction. It is

32 Ibid.

33 Ibid.

34 Fred Moten, "Blackness and Nothingness: Mysticism in the Flesh," *South Atlantic Quarterly* 112, no. 4 (Fall 2013): 737–780.

35 King-Hammond, "The Essence of Being."

36 Zora Neale Hurston, *Their Eyes Were Watching God* (New York: HarperCollins, 2006), 2–3.

37 Hortense Spillers, "Formalism Comes to Harlem" in *Black, White, and in Color: Essays on American Literature and Culture* (Chicago: University of Chicago Press, 2003), 91.

38 Virginia M. G. Anderson, "In Conversation with Oletha DeVane," in *Traces of the Spirit*, 25–38.

39 King-Hammond, "The Essence of Being."

loud and chaotic when, for example, Hurston writes, "Pearl Stone opened her mouth and laughed real hard because she didn't know what else to do. She fell over Mrs. Sumpkins while she laughed. Mrs. Sumpkins snorted violently and sucked her teeth."[36] Speaking, and in this case sound and gesture, is crucial for a number of Black writers because, as the literary theorist Hortense Spillers notes, "For them, language, withheld for so long, by law, from the African-American as the origin of his human power, does *speak*."[37] The dialogue is comparable to the language used in other ethnographies such as Alex Haley's novel *Roots* (1976), drawn excessively from oral history interviews and archival research. And thus the excess at the start of *Their Eyes Were Watching God*, when we witness a Black woman returning from a funeral, is a fictional scenario that had possibly been inspired by Hurston's ethnographic note-taking in her home state of Florida. What moved me about the opening scene of Hurston's novel, and why I think it resonates with DeVane's art, was its pathbreaking language and its flair for narrative. It brought me into the sort of excess that I might encounter in the work of Black visual artists. DeVane's art, as Carroll points out, does similar things, in how its excess can be misinterpreted as "ornamentalism."

"The materials—I put together for their language. They *speak* to each other," DeVane said in an interview.[38] I interpret this quote on materials that *speak* as being similar to the loudness of Hurston's characters. There's something about DeVane's art that is *self-aware* of its own ability to speak. That self-awareness propels rather than delimits her work, pushing it toward the lush and the excessive. Her ability to speak through her art, as King-Hammond writes, is predicated in transforming seemingly useless stuff into "a personalized artistic vocabulary that enables DeVane to expressively tell her stories."[39]

Just as Hurston's work spoke so thoroughly to the urgency, genius, and intricacy of Black Southern life, I emphasize here DeVane's own attention to the political strivings that we find in urban Black life. Specifically, DeVane's work on the historical figure of abolition Harriet Tubman is self-aware of its ability to generate a conversation on history and iconography beyond the strictures set by either contemporary art or its abstract painting precedent. DeVane's Tubman is sitting in a tree and appears in a striking Day-Glo–like color purple. Tubman is alert and present. She is regal and spiritual. DeVane's art foregrounds the duality of Black creative economy and the Black radical tradition that informs it. It speaks in terms that are *loud* and errant, as a mode of the artist's deeper, adventurous search for meaning.

Bonds of Permanence: Familial Ties, Memorials, and the Public Art of Oletha DeVane

Christopher Kojzar

"FOLLOW THE SOUNDS OF THE DRUMS," I kept saying over my phone to navigate family members from the parking lot of McDonogh School to the dedication ceremony for *Memorial to Those Enslaved and Freed* (figs. 1–2). Surely for me and for them, the directive sounded out of place, even though the site of this memorial is on a campus where orphan boys once donned military uniforms, where they once beat drums to take part in military parades to signal the unchallenged affirmation of American freedom. Today's drum rhythm, however, was ecstatically unmoored from that sharp, metallic precision of military cadence that we so often equate and, in effect, marry to nation-state doctrine. Today's beats, the ones reverberating in spring's clear blue sky, were soothing if they weren't penetrating to the ears, offering an homage to a history that must be recognized as a markedly different kind of limitless being inferred from the word "freedom." Without even seeing the drummers, the rhythm held deep and low in the air, resonant and cultured, brilliant and melodic, its sound waves inducing eyes to lay vision on a new landscape—to acknowledge for the soul what is tragically beautiful, what is lost and disposed, un-truthed, what is no more but is felt in the hearts of everyone who experiences colonial transgression, even to this day.

The gathering was a modestly attended outdoor celebration, much sparser in number than the hundreds who had attended the prior ceremony on April 19. Still, the company today was no less distilled, and it was even more emotional than the gathering that splashed on the front page of the *Baltimore Sun* under the headline "'Complex Legacy': A Baltimore County Private School Considers How to Remember Those Enslaved by its Founder."

The tears began to flow from the alumna's eyes, from our eyes, as she read from the podium the tenth name and age of one of those enslaved by John McDonogh, a partial reading of the approximately two hundred names

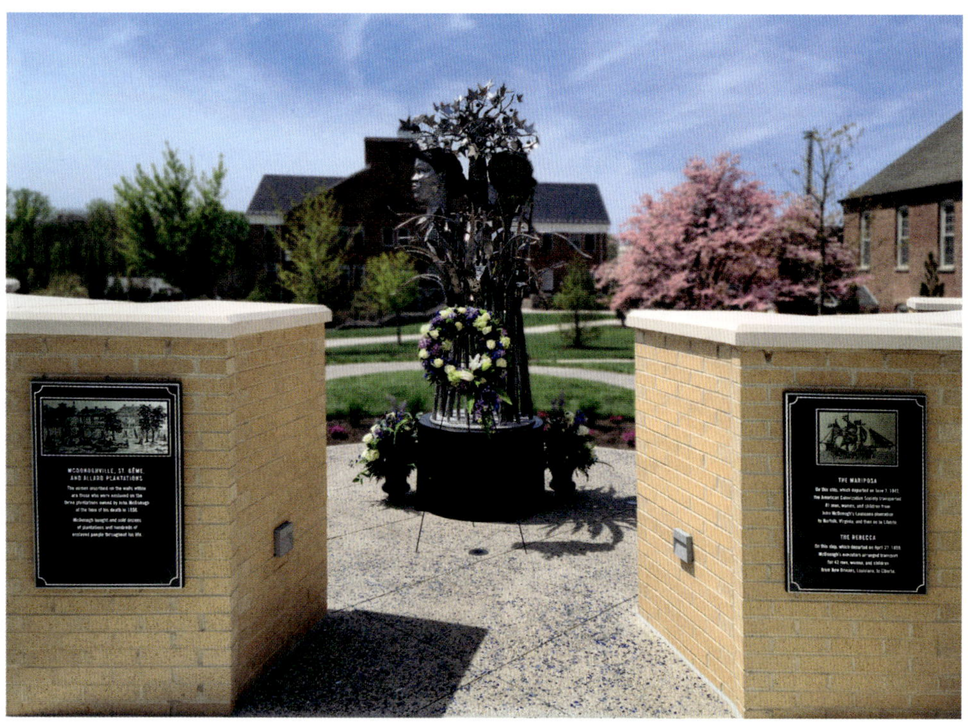

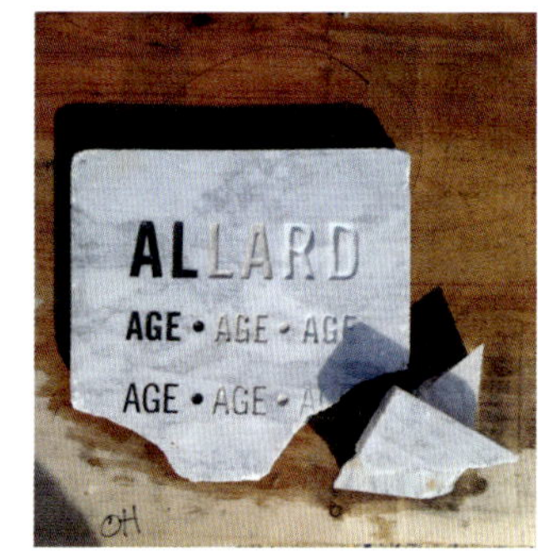

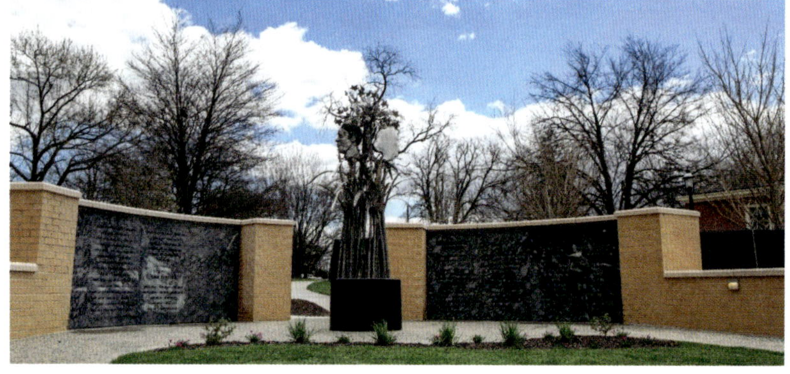

engraved on the waterfall wall (fig. 3) flanking the outdoor sculpture designed by Oletha: "ABEL, AGE 28. CAROLINE, AGE 24. PIERRE, AGE 6. HENRIETTE, AGE 3. PHILLIS, AGE 52. MOLLY, AGE 21. HARRIET, AGE 9. EMANUEL, AGE 7. GEORGE ELLIS, AGE 22. NANCY, AGE 18 MONTHS."

A percussionist draped in West African ceremonial regalia walloped a stark drumbeat after the speaker read each name, calling to the cathedral on campus to respond with successive solitaire rings of the church bell, each instrument relieving the audience of an emotional weight held for generations, held unanswered as collective muted trauma. If, in a lifetime, one

Fig. 1 TOP LEFT
View of the entrance to *Memorial to Those Enslaved and Freed*, featuring the sculpture *Ascend*. Inaugurated at the McDonogh School, Owings Mills, Maryland, April 19, 2022. Photo: Christopher Kojzar.

Fig. 2 TOP RIGHT
Detail of wall tile for *Memorial to Those Enslaved and Freed*, with the name and age of one of the slaves of John McDonogh. Photo: Christopher Kojzar.

Fig. 3 BOTTOM
View of *Memorial to Those Enslaved and Freed*, featuring the sculpture *Ascend* and the wall installation of names and ages of the slaves of John McDonogh. Photo: Dave Radford.

happens to attend an event that memorializes ancestors, especially those who were held as chattel, as property, and as bodies who unwillingly served as the founding impetus to our country's economic success, weeping gives space to never take for granted why joy must be consumed by the movements of air. For the eternal winds that blow through the trees and to birds that flutter in the fountain's outpour, as with nature, so it is in spirit we must give alms to the lives of the men, women, and children who purged the earth with their hands to create the United States of America.

John McDonogh's statue fell off its perch in New Orleans, Louisiana, during the summer of 2020, and I write "fell" because the action was only as passive as the history that erected its subject, as an accidental aside to a story, as a collapse commanded by more than just a sole individual's determination to bring it to the ground. It was conducted in a movement, performed out of unabashed humanity to let prevailing cultural winds re-solve what glory was reshaping history for the present day. Soon after media reports went out about the fallen monument in New Orleans, the school announced in a very timely fashion their efforts to reconcile with the school's past, and Oletha DeVane was elected as the artist to develop the site.

The days I worked with my mom to piece together this sculpture; the trips to Lancaster, Pennsylvania, to consult with the fabricator (figs. 4–5); the computer renderings of intricate designs for its various elements; the laughter that came from tearing apart and disposing of two large, failed models

Figs. 4–5

Views of the fabrication of *Memorial to Those Enslaved and Freed*, Lancaster, Pennsylvania. Photos: Christopher Kojzar.

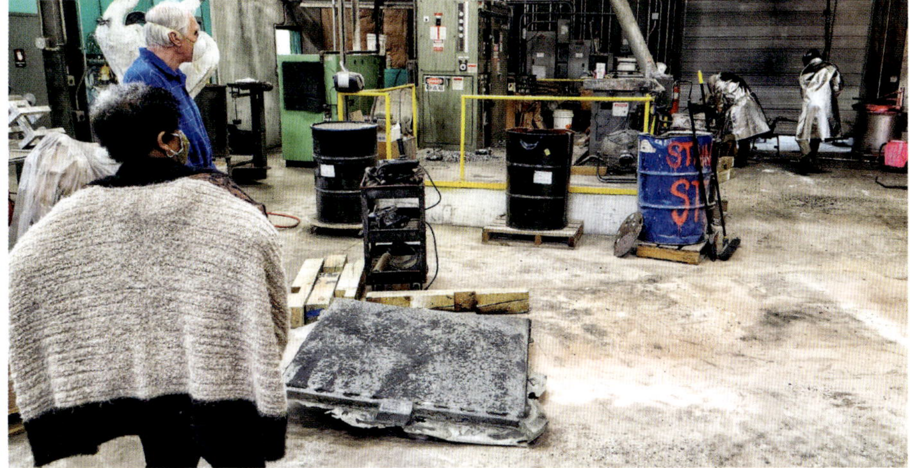
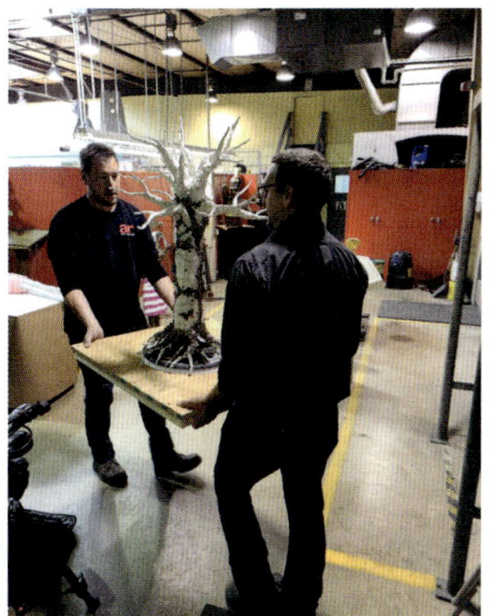

made respectively out of papier-mâché and clay; the quest to find sugarcane stalks; the critique of handmade sugarcane stalks; the draftings of plaques to represent nineteenth-century plantations and ships; the discussion of materials; the choice of lettering; the choice of coloring; the virtual remote meetings; the discovery and purchase of Africana beads at a local auction house; the countless cups of coffee; the consideration of casting butterflies; all this time spent didn't equate to the seventeen (plus) years I observed, and was in fact quite separate from, the development of *Memorial to Those Enslaved and Freed*. There is a chance that pieces like this wouldn't exist in the world without the dedication and commitment among intuitive people to challenge the norm.

After the drumbeats subsided into the noon hour and an organized alumni luncheon came to a close, my mom and I took a circuitous route back to the car by way of the memorial. The prior presence of all the attendees hadn't given me a full chance to take in the site and sculpture, and this was my first day seeing the memorial outside of piecemeal photos of its development. Light hits its lustrous metal quite differently depending on the time of day, and step-down walls flank the sculpture on each side. The walls are staggered at seated height, and we sat down to take a contemplative respite. Oletha never stopped wanting to add elements to the sculpture, once opting for the etched formations of a Presbyterian cross and a schoolbook to signal the occupations of David McDonogh as minister and Nancy McDonogh as teacher. Each individual is figured opposite one another as profiled busts sitting atop a bundle of sugarcane stalks and divided by a rendition of a sweet gum tree. As complex as the 11-foot sculpture stands, she was still deciphering ways to add to its completed design.

"I want the students to take advantage of the walls, maybe plaster some mosaics on the side." I smile and look past her to see student work installed but a few yards away, deliberately placed in the grass to encircle the memorial grounds. Perhaps made by middle schoolers or even high-school students, the 12-by-4-inch-thick mosaic blocks are set as individual mobile concrete pavers, teasing out an idea that they can last in permanence, though weathering would soon enough break apart their construction. I looked at the pavers and held within me unremarkable memories of my own childhood, in that moment accepting their designs as a part of McDonogh art culture so familiar to my memory of when my mom began her career at the school thirty years ago.

This evening's pouring rain was no less cataclysmic than the other torrential downpours that spare Marylanders of unchecked heat waves during our summers. The last time I did this drive to David Hess's home, years ago, my Subaru had total engine failure and David had to come pick me up on the side of the highway. This was a different evening, but a similar circumstance had led me to meet with David and discuss the logistics of creating artwork. This time I was accompanied by Oletha, and after weeks of deliberation, Seawall Development Firm and the Municipal Art Society of Baltimore City (a committee on which David sat) chose us to create a public artwork for the newly redesigned Lexington Market. Behind the wheel of my mom's Prius, I was driving 35 mph with rain slamming on the windshield as she and I found ourselves in the throes of a discussion about whom to choose to fabricate the work, and in an instant, prior to a shock, it was decided. We pulled over to make a phone call while the rain subsided.

Lightning struck a vehicle in front of him: he was marred by the sight, a little blinded by it even, and couldn't let go of what he had just witnessed. As anyone in their right mind that night would be, Nick Ireys just wanted to get back to a safe space, out of the rain. After spending the day working as a team member on one of David's public art pieces, Nick had been driving away from David's home in that very same downpour, and perhaps we, Oletha and I, were like passing "ships" to Nick's car somewhere along the road between the county and city. We hadn't witnessed the lightning but called Nick right after that flash jolted his car ride. In a sort of voltaic "aha" moment, Oletha made the phone call to declare our allegiance to Nick for this prospect of building a new piece for the plaza.

When time slows down in these moments, when something prophetic happens that is out of your control—like Zeus reigning down his fire to say, "Choose this man!"—you remember the metaphor you've been given. Oletha offered a bit of wonder and grace in the conversation so that she could be clear about her desire to work with Nick on the Lexington Market project. Weeks before, I had put two names in front of her: Nick's and another firm out in Virginia. The decision wasn't necessarily rocket science and was not mine to make, but it was definitely a sort of exercise in commitment, trust-building, and kinship, especially since this public artwork would be highly visible, installed in the center of Baltimore's oldest standing market. As the days and months went on, it was clear that Nick had most assuredly been the right choice.

We all have our roles in any piece headed by Oletha as the lead artist. Collaboration among artists, whether related by blood or not, isn't to be tossed aside as something easy, but it is also a mode of working that should be encouraged and ought to be more ubiquitous. One often glaring problem is that there is never enough funding when artists collaborate on a major project at the local level, especially on grant-funded initiatives: the work turns out to be more a labor of love than a prospect of achieving something unique. The deliberation to design the Robert and Rosetta public artwork felt like it lasted years, even if it actually took a few months, partly because we all had coinciding projects that we were working on individually, and at times we didn't want to leave anything by the wayside because of budget constraints and swiftly rising material costs. The site needed careful attention to precise considerations in concept and form, as well as sufficient space for education and the authentic intertwining of the historical elements marked by the plaza's narrative as the "iron neighborhood." Today, ornamental cast patterns can be found speckled throughout the city on doors, fences, spiral staircases, loft overlooks, monuments, and intricate outdoor treasures.

 After a site visit to Lexington Market among the other semifinalists, and six weeks prior to actually being selected for the commission, we got back to the studio with intentions to reach out and research what might inspire the sculpture's design. At first, the ideas were unadventurous, somewhat clichéd, and our brainstorming usually came to a dead end. "Let's do a sundial" was one idea. Or 'How about a play off 'BLM' as the initials for both 'Baltimore's Lexington Market' and 'Black Lives Matter?'" "Why not something kinetic?" or "Maybe the site just really needs some public restrooms and a hot shower?" All the prospects fell short until we made contact with Dean Krimmel at the Peale Center for Baltimore History & Architecture. He presented a series of photographs and fortuitously landed on two newspaper articles from the nineteenth century that disclosed the stories of two modest yet notable individuals who would seismically shift the idea behind "exchanging goods" in Lexington Market.

 Robert and Rosetta (2022), the public artwork and more literally the man and woman who hold those names, realizes a history of the Market that allows us to infer how it was once used and, more specifically, how these individuals had been assertively noticed on its grounds during the time of slavery (fig. 6). To contribute to the historical narrative of the site, these people are commemorated as forged metal panels intended to challenge viewers to consider what one would advertise as "value." In 1838, the *Baltimore Sun* ran an article, perhaps the only known recorded instance of a woman named Rosetta being sold by the city bailiff in the open-air market. In recognizing Rosetta and her counterpart Robert, we want to cue onlookers, in a very approachable way, to view two granite, ground flagstones etched with newspaper articles from the *Baltimore Sun* (1838) and the *American Commercial & Daily Advertiser* (1833). Robert's narrative places him under surveillance as a runaway with a fifty-dollar reward for his capture. As a way to jog its readers' memories, the news clipping states that Robert used to sell butter in the market under the auspices of Governor Howard's Waverly farm in Elkridge, Maryland.

The articles engraved on the oversized pavers mimic granite stand markers that still line the curbs in the area today. Even though the site was never truly considered a primary location for slave merchants, the conditionality to Rosetta's advertisement and the surveillance placed upon Robert would serve as residual stamps of American imperial economics. Since

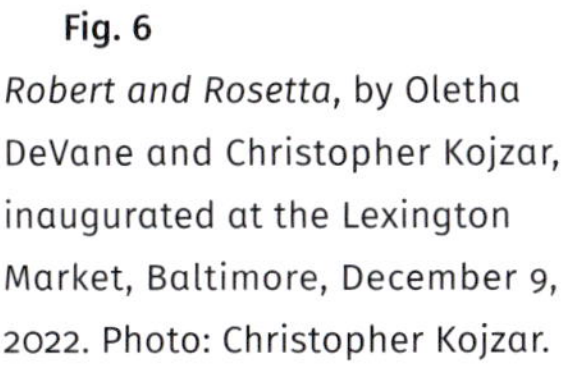

Fig. 6
Robert and Rosetta, by Oletha DeVane and Christopher Kojzar, inaugurated at the Lexington Market, Baltimore, December 9, 2022. Photo: Christopher Kojzar.

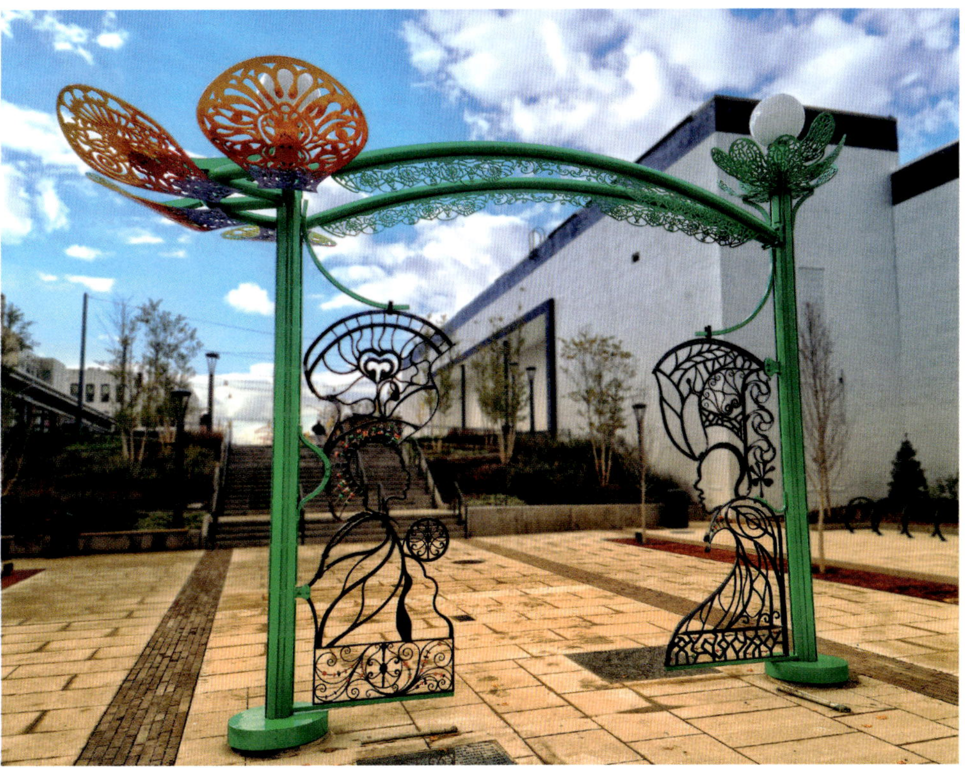

photographs were by and large coveted objects in the nineteenth century after the medium was invented in 1839, the individuals' representations are imagined as silhouettes and embellished with iron bead-like rings.

The biography of Robert and Rosetta and the motivation to focus on everyday people align with threads in both my and Oletha's separate practices, so the choice to create this work was never inconsistent. The methodology to broaden historical visibility in the realm of public art has a chance to make the subject matter emotive, more personal, perhaps even controversial, though this latter quality has never been intended. We saw a need to deepen awareness with a truth that is politicized, obscured from the naked eye, and uncovered only by our collective acknowledgement of how people were treated, how they lived.

I often think about my own family's history, how it gets diluted and obscured in white history. My great-great-great-grandfather London Welch Herring bore his namesakes from Richard Herring and John Devane, men who founded a gun factory in 1776 on the Black River north of Wilmington in what is now Sampson County, North Carolina. A plaque signpost from the North Carolina Historical Society stands near the former site of the gun factory, telling who Richard Herring and John Devane were, but accordingly (and quite commonly among these historical signposts) never mentions the Black, Indigenous, or alternate names that make up the larger story. What gets lost, and what begs for connection, is the means of finding how we claim our heritage and of reimagining why we so often have trouble deciphering our tribe, our land, or our identity. What shocked me about Robert's story is that he toiled on a farm just down the street from where I grew up. If he had been my long-lost cousin so many times removed, I'd be prouder of his resilience, prouder to carry *his* story than I would be to anyone who compelled the body of my forefather to carry an imposed surname.

July 7, 2018: Mural Project at Camp Coq, Haiti

Resilience. It is an ill-begotten term used today to imply the fallout placed upon people of African descent by way of Western imperialism, a word that seems to indicate the nonexistence of any hope and prosperity Black and Brown people might be able to attain in order to prevail, a term used to justify misfortune afflicted upon African societies, connoting, in a way, that one should be in good conscience when finding the resolve to meet a hardship that has been manufactured by centuries of oppression. For a place

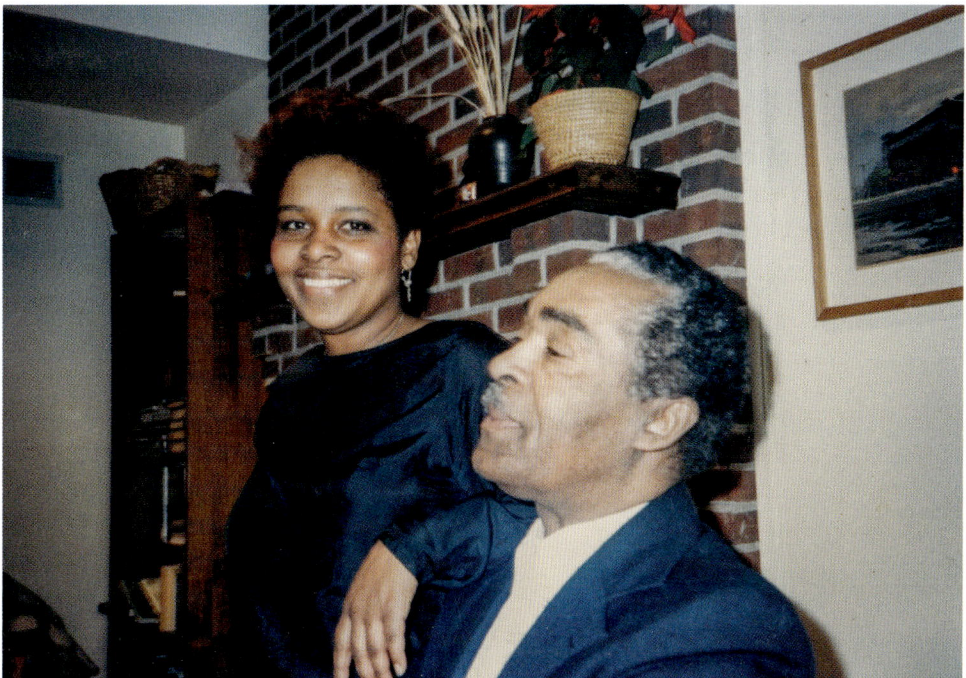

like Haiti, it's a word that permeates the media every time something challenging happens—an earthquake, a hurricane, a gas shortage, coups d'état, a presidential assassination—all taking place on a singular island confronted with two centuries of administered indebtedness to the French for its independence and autonomy.

I began taking note of the word when it rolled off the tongues of media personalities in July 2018, the first time I made my way to Haiti with my mother for her international foray into public art. While on our connecting flight from Baltimore to Florida, American Airlines canceled all outgoing departures to the island. A gas shortage had motivated the US State Department to issue a "do not travel" warning for US citizens in what was stated to be "widespread civil unrest and violent demonstrations in Haiti. Protests, tire burning, and road blockages are frequent and unpredictable."[1] The complexity of pain endured in Haiti is often coupled with internal strife and violence, and the long game for a solution is truly piecemeal, to be built brick by brick, with aid coming sporadically from intragovernmental entities and Haitians living abroad.

My mother makes a point to stand in the face of what is unknown through her guided faith and intuition, especially when it comes to finding

1 James Doubek, "Haiti's Prime Minister Resigns After Riots over Fuel Price Hike," NPR, July 15, 2018, https://www.npr.org/2018/07/15/629198841/haitis-prime-minister-resigns-after-riots-over-fuel-price-hike.

purpose in her work or challenging unconventional norms that others
may take as sacrosanct. This attitude reclaims what I imagine resilience to be
on an individual level: resilience as an unspoken term, as a purpose in faith
to guide what may seem unachievable, be it in work, life, or spirit. We made
it to the island four months later when things had apparently "calmed
down" and she was able to navigate the country in stride as she worked to in-
stall her mosaics on a wall at a school in Camp Coq.

My mother has traveled through most of the United States, most of Europe,
Southeast Asia, Africa, South America, Central America, the Caribbean,
and the Pacific Isles, but for her, Haiti is more than a destination. She had
already been there three times, and her calm determination was to use
funds from a Rubys Artist Grant (administered by The Robert W. Deutsch
Foundation) to complete a mosaic mural in the country.

    Needless to say, the journey from the airport to the inner countryside
was dynamically complicated, finding materials was a mission in itself, and
the project was constrained due to the daily logistics of maneuvering from
town to town in a country lacking sufficient infrastructure. A fifty-mile SUV
ride would take eight hours on mostly unpaved roads. We got into a minor
car accident in the packed streets of Cap-Haïtien—and no insurance information was exchanged. Roadblocks were very real, with one of our counter-
parts being held against her will while we were able to get through a gaggle
of tires surrounded by men brandishing guns. Water, scarce in the country,
is drinkable only if bottled or sealed in small plastic bags, otherwise a consumer might get violently ill for days. Conversely, the country is distinctly
beautiful, with lush rolling hills cascading high into the sky and dipping
below into warm rich waters. The people are washed by the sun, their greet-
ings and pointed awareness possessed of a cosmopolitan flair, and a street
beat that owes its characteristics to people spending most of their day outdoors. Avenues and thoroughfares were in constant movement, and children were dressed colorfully in school uniforms while adults primed their
businesses early in the morning for long shifts over the day ahead.
    Oletha goes to Haiti as part of her involvement with the Build Haiti
Foundation. This nonprofit has been raising funds and awareness for a
K–12 school that has no running water or electricity (figs. 8–10). I came to
document the mosaic project and provide a digital media workshop for
the students at the school in Camp Coq, where onlookers and students alike
took on the task of creating the mural with Oletha. The project, lasting

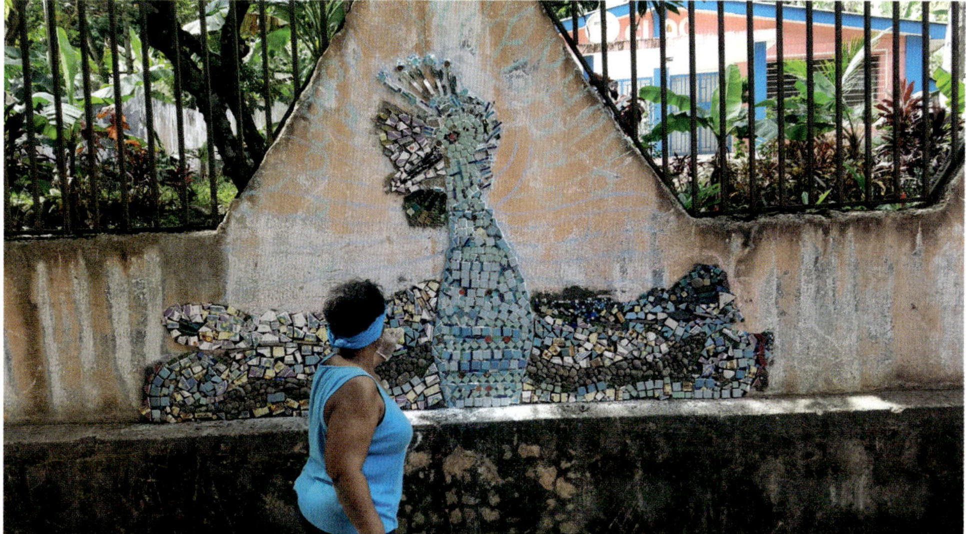

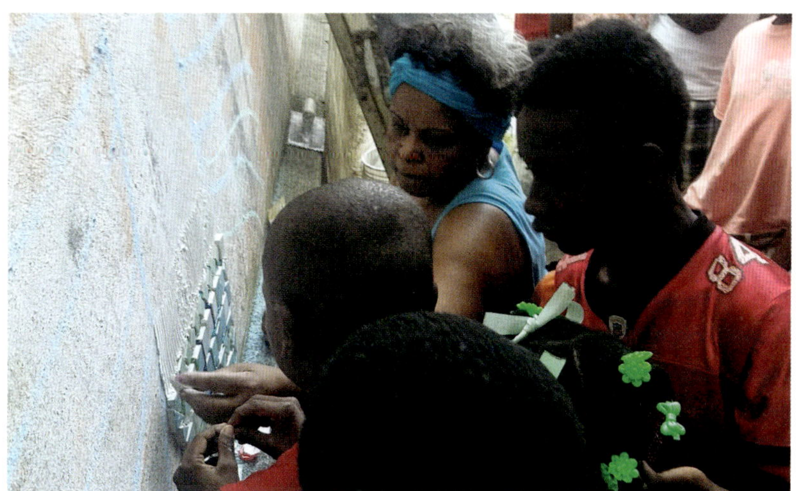

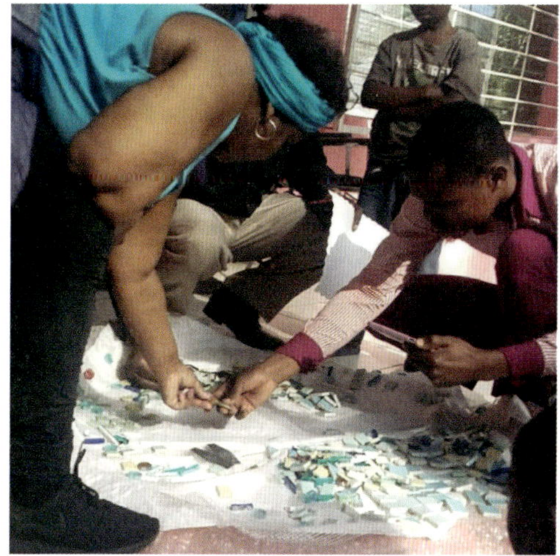

about ten days, brought many people out of their homes to watch and participate in its creation.

Oletha would often be on a ladder, receiving suggestions or bright laughter or quiet gazes. The school where we placed this mural did not have a complementary arts program and had just received their first computer donations. In the winding down of days, when we worked together with students, they wanted to show us how they cherished their territory, as they envisioned themselves to be fortunately separate from the imprint of words like *colonial*, *Western*, and *resilience*. A visible desire for beautification was evident. The Parisian architecture has been repurposed in thick concrete form yet is stylized via Caribbean colors and aesthetics. In reality, the homes and clean streets give Camp Coq its modest allure, and the surrounding countryside makes it more appealing than the metro areas of Port-au-Prince or Cap-Haïtien. The town feels like "home" in the Caribbean, separate from the associations made about the country's strife.

While there, the general attitude was to design more, make the mosaic bigger, make the project last longer, and in the short amount of time we had we could complete only a fraction of what we had envisioned. There was just not enough material, not enough connections to contractors who had supplies or time to add expertise. In its completion, the design fanned out as a peacock with ceramic blue, green, and yellow as well as colored glass tiles, adorning a pink wall that might have been there for a century. In island spirit, people considered how to build upon its design, our assent given via an agreement we made with participants after we left.

The last day in Haiti, we made our way to a small island off the coast of Cap-Haïtien on a dingy commandeered by a local who knew the waters well. The island was idyllic, and we had an hour to rest on its beach and dive into Haitian waters before the sun set. On the way back, twenty-five minutes out, I gazed at a nearby rowboat that was confidently on course to the mainland, steered by two young boys who offered me what I lacked. It was abstract, a metaphor for the skill of not just survival but of total resolution to be in a world that offers elemental alms. Their ability to move with the waves and the tides was matched by their capability to navigate without a motor. Their bodies, silhouetted behind green mountains dipping into the Caribbean, were unchastened by any need for a formal institutional coda. Their own wayfaring techniques amounted to what I never knew, maybe due to misaligned comfort, but it was something that in that moment I could not ascribe a name to. Paradisal, Regenerative, Potent, Undiscovered—or perhaps it can only be named without names.

Summer, Mid-1990s:
West Friendship Elementary School, Maryland

This is a vague recollection, not of a site or of a conviction that something existed, but of time. I remember driving to West Friendship Elementary School more than once, first to see the site prior to the installation and then afterward, to see the work installed. I don't remember if I was old enough

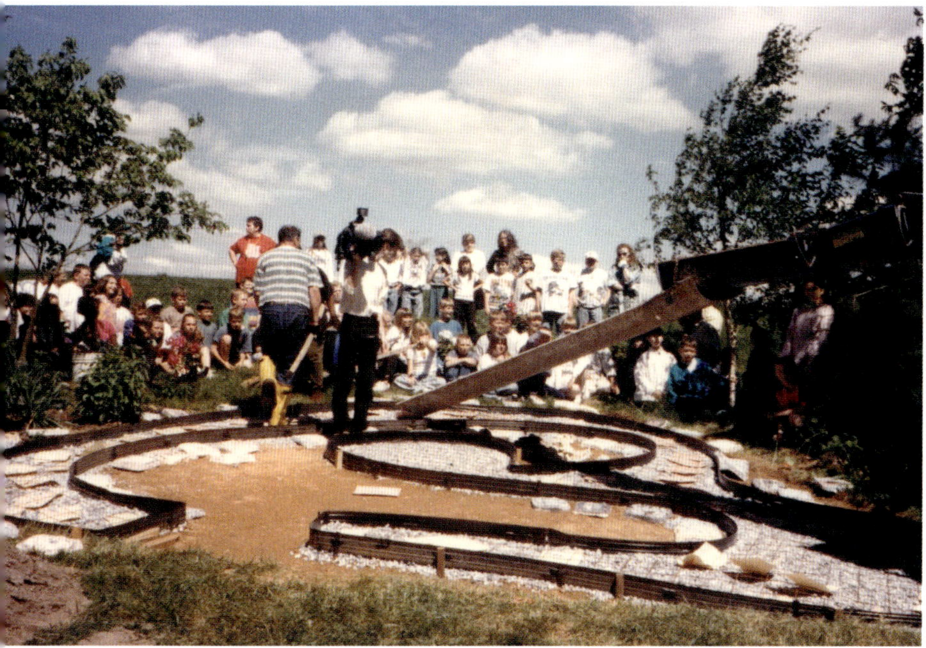

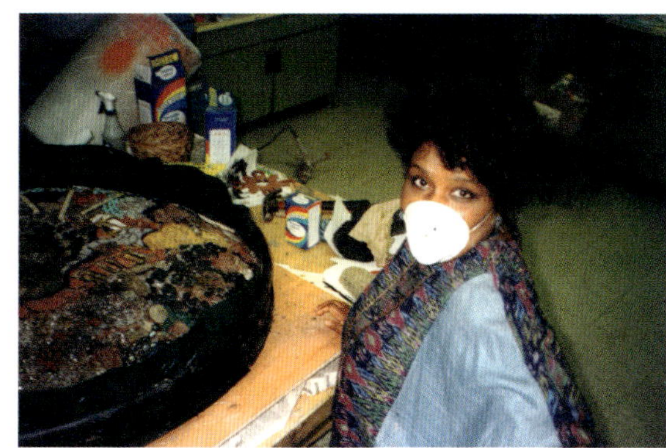

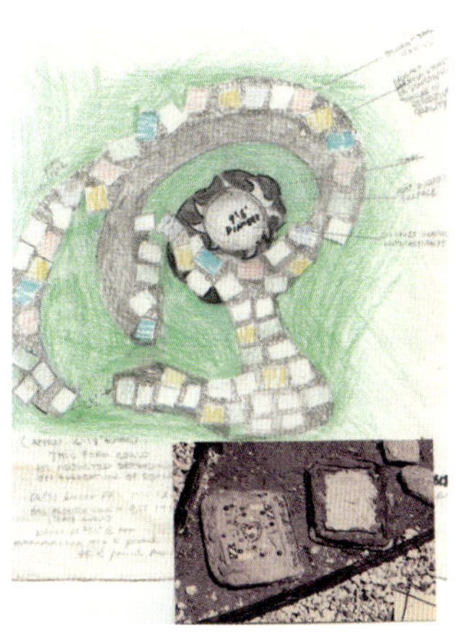

to drive, but I do recall that the piece was my mother's first public art project, a modest redesign of a garden grove at the school in Howard County,
Maryland. She had submitted a grant proposal to do this work, and every-
thing was laid at ground level. Students at McDonogh School created
mosaic patterns that my father set into concrete as 12-by-12-inch blocks.
Oletha organically positioned the blocks to flow in and out of flowerbeds,
mulch, and grass under a few newly planted trees.

Extra mosaic patterns sat around my parents' home for decades afterward, maybe even to this day. By now, however, the garden's mosaics must
have crumbled away due to the elements, the natural consequence of climate
erosion, or just from the residual upkeep involved in mulching over and
cutting into the garden every year. Oletha's West Friendship Elementary
School public art piece is likely to be no more, just a vague recollection from
those who participated in its development to those who walked past it when
the season permitted. I myself caught a glance of this public art site mainly
as a memory on that circuitous route back to *Memorial to Those Enslaved and
Freed* in 2022. When I happened upon the re-creation of these concrete
mosaic pavers on this campus, I just accepted that memory could be more
eternal, more set in permanence, than what wind, water, and light might
soon enough break apart.

The Essence of Being Lies Within Ordinary, Useful/less Stuff, and Tangible Things

Leslie King-Hammond

1 Maryland State Arts Council Artist Registry. https://www.msac .org/artists/oletha-devane#/0. Accessed December 14, 2018.

2 See W. E. B. Du Bois, *The Souls of Black Folk: Essays and Sketches* (Chicago: A.C. McClurg & Co., 1903) and Paul Gilroy, *The Black Atlantic: Modernity and Double Consciousness* (Cambridge, MA: Harvard University Press, 1993), 2.

OLETHA DEVANE has spent the better part of her artistic life with a driving need to, in her words, "understand the human condition, the uncontrolled events and our purposeful actions through whatever medium serves to tell the story."[1] It is the *essence* of the indispensable energies of life, without which nothing can exist, that drives her to create images and objects inspired by unremarkable, often useful and useless stuff and ordinary tangible things. In effect, material culture becomes the catalytic, transformative element that mediates and channels how she sees the world. Many of DeVane's queries into her art-making processes are not unlike those of an archeologist who excavates sites, seeking tangible remnants and objects to reconstruct the meanings of past lives, civilizations, and cultures.

DeVane began as a painter-printmaker—creating beautiful, often haunting imagery of dense landscapes that evoked scenarios and longings of struggle, a sense of being, place, liberation, and freedom. Her aesthetic is deeply affected by W. E. B. Du Bois's concept of "double consciousness"—living simultaneously in a Black and white world—or what Paul Gilroy has described as "the processes of cultural mutation and restless (dis)continuity"[2] given the biases of Western canons and the benign recognition of the confluences of African diasporic aesthetic practices. The bottle "spirit forms" and the totemic sculptures in this exhibition are the result of introspection, experimentation, and African retentions. The accumulation of these disparate items transforms ordinary, so-called useful and useless stuff and unremarkable tangible things into a personalized artistic vocabulary that enables DeVane to expressively tell her stories—known, unknown, imagined—or yet to be defined … or *divined*.

The life of an artist is in many ways about a very personal journey in the discovery of a sense of self in relationship to the world in which she lives. What becomes of that adventure—its discoveries, revelations, epiphanies, tragedies, and triumphs—is revealed as one seeks to find meaning from "uncontrolled events." The struggle to survive, protect, and prevail hopefully yields lessons or wisdoms from the knowledge accumulated via those experiences, which are then imparted to the creation of an artistic vision.

DeVane was born and educated in Baltimore, Maryland, earning a BFA from the Maryland Institute College of Art and later, an MFA in painting from the University of Massachusetts in Amherst. Her mother was born in Virginia, and her father was a native of North Carolina. The essential education imparted by her parents was especially significant and crucial to DeVane's aesthetic development. John Edward DeVane, her father, would regularly take walks with his family, teaching and inspiring them to engage with nature. DeVane recalls how her father was insistent that they should always search for smooth, shiny rocks, often called lucky rocks—which are harder to find than ordinary coarse rocks, common to most geographical terrains.

It is important to note that the transmission of this familial knowledge is critical to DeVane's education, in light of Gilroy's position on "cultural mutation and restless (dis)continuity," especially for African Americans in search of their ancestral heritage.[3] The fractured legacy and relentless search for the histories of African descendants is further elaborated in Christopher C. Fennell's *Crossroads and Cosmologies: Diasporas and Ethnogenesis in the New World*, in which he cites how:

> The importance of tangible cultural heritage played out in a critical way in the movement of particular African traditions across the Atlantic Ocean during the slave trade. Captive Africans were rarely able to transport the heirlooms of their tangible cultural heritage with them to the New World plantations. However, their knowledge, beliefs, and skills in performing the cultural traditions of the society from which they were abducted could be applied in locations in the Americas to create new material expressions of those legacies. European slave traders could steal their captives' tangible heirlooms, but not the intangible facets of knowledge, beliefs, and expressive skill.[4]

In the historical narratives of the lives of African American artists, too little attention has been given to the early influences of their artistic development, given the biases of Western canons of critical evaluation, which accorded no value to factors that were considered to be ordinary, common, or of mundane origins. DeVane's early life is very similar to the experiences of

3 Gilroy, The *Black Atlantic*, 2.

4 Christopher C. Fennell, *Crossroads and Cosmologies: Diasporas and Ethnogenesis in the New World* (Gainesville: University Press of Florida, 2007), 2.

Romare Bearden, who spent summers in his grandmother's garden, that gave rise to his *Conjur Woman* series. Mixed media–fiber artist Aminah Brenda Lynn Robinson's father was instrumental in educating her on which materials from nature to use in her art-making. Joyce J. Scott's mother, Elizabeth Talford Scott, used smooth rocks and pebbles, buttons, and beads in her quilts and shared rich oral family histories of African beliefs and aesthetic practices. The artistry of Betye Saar has opened the door for this type of archeological scholarship, from which many artists, including her daughters, the artists Alison and Lezley Saar, have benefited: they have an artist-mother who regularly foraged through flea markets and garage sales in search of items with unique, subtle character to augment her creations, which are loaded with cosmological and symbolic signifiers that can be traced back to African belief systems. Each of these African-descendant artists, like DeVane, has profound respect for spiritual belief systems of African origin and the inherent powers of materials and discarded objects of modest origins that once had a viable life force in their original formation and function.

The seminal research of Robert Farris Thompson (1983) and Suzanne Preston Blier (1995) explores the roots of African retentions as distinguished by the Yoruba, Kongo, Fon, and Dahomey people from West and Central Africa, who comprise significant ancestry connections to the descendant people of the African diaspora in the Americas. These cultures have inspired brilliant, vibrant aesthetic traditions and practices that use natural and ordinary materials and objects to convey complex symbolic meaning in their artistry. The impulse and inspiration to use materials and "things" with limited connotations beyond an ordinary, commonplace recognition have a revered role within the realm of African and African-diasporic culture, philosophy, and aesthetics. David Doris in his research on ordinary objects in Yoruba culture of Nigeria cites, "If the real 'power' of an object resides not in finely articulated visible form but in the accumulation of invisible essences and processes, then what is at stake is the very authority of the 'artwork' as the ultimate bearer of meaning and value."[5] DeVane is in fact a member of a very elite group, a sacred continuum of artists, in search of an understanding of an authority and agency to inform their individualized, psychic, spiritual, and aesthetic worldviews.

The principal catalyst for the emergence of DeVane's *Spirit Sculptures* was a gift she received of an ornate Haitian bottle from a fellow artist, William Rhodes. Artists throughout the African diaspora of the Americas have been actively exploring how to reclaim the aesthetic agency of their traditional

5 David T. Doris, *Vigilant Things—On Thieves, Yoruba Anti-Aesthetics, and the Strange Fates of Ordinary Objects in Nigeria* (Seattle: University of Washington Press, 2011).

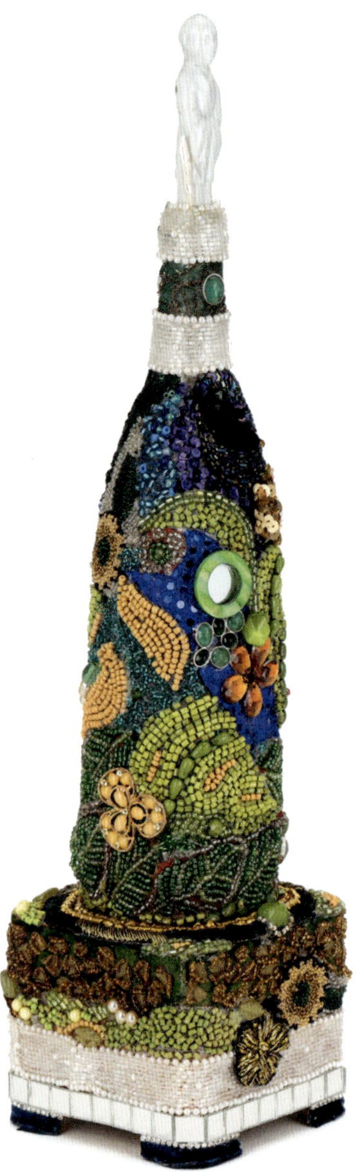

Meditation, 2019, glass, beads, porcelain, wood

African heritages in the aftermath of the horrors of the Middle Passage, slavery in the Americas, and the relentless assaults of racism into present time. These diasporic artists are continually studying, researching, and seeking ways and means to reconnect with the traditions, culture, religions, and belief systems of their motherland.

The bottle gifted to DeVane embodies characteristics reflective of similar bottles as described by Robert Farris Thompson in his seminal study *Flash of the Spirit* as:

6 Robert Farris Thompson, *Flash of the Spirit: African and Afro-American Art & Philosophy* (New York: Vintage Books, 1984), 125–126.

7 Oletha DeVane, interview by Leslie King-Hammond, Ellicott City, Maryland, November 25, 2018.

ingenious reformulations of (Kongo) *nkisi* charms, sometimes called *pacquets congo*…. The more elegant *pacquets* are wrapped in silk instead of ancestral cotton or raffia cloth; are tied with broad silk ribbons (secured with pins) instead of cord; are adorned with sequins as well as beads; and sometimes crowned with plumes made of metallic cloth instead of actual feathers.[6]

These charms are containers—usually constructed from old bottles—that become a body or vessel to house a spirit, into which "medicines" are inserted to create protections from evil or to stimulate the presence of the "flash of the spirit." Rhodes's gift initiated a period of deep contemplation and artistic inspiration for DeVane, inspiring her sculptural series.

The surfaces of the bottles, vessels, containers, and totems of DeVane's sculptures are always festooned and riddled—literally, figuratively, and symbolically—with clustered embellishments and layered elements of ordinary, mundane, sometimes even boring materials that by themselves would be simply unremarkable. Within DeVane's psyche: combined with her technical prowess for assemblage, she *remembers* and *reimagines* found, cast-off materials. These works are conceived by the technique of bricolage with which she leverages the use of available materials. Those materials fuel and load her sculptures with symbolic signifiers of intangible and often uncontrollable, inexplicable forces, which include the crucial dynamics of being human and coexisting with otherworldly beings. She explains how "the *Spirit Sculptures* emerged as a concept to harness blessings and explore the intuitive, irrational, or unconscious phenomena."[7] DeVane's artistic vision radiates the presence of life forces in the world, in present time or beyond to otherworldly spaces where gods, spirits, and ancestors reside. In *Songs of Orpheus* (2008), for example, a bottle form is covered with a beaded netting, with dangling beads at the neck and the base of the sculpture. A clay head is affixed to the top facing upward, as Orpheus sings his rapturous songs to otherworldly gods. Sprouting from the head is a wired, beaded headdress alluding to the harmonic and arresting sounds of his songs. The cumulative effect of combining fragmented objects that still embody energies from a functional past life transforms her sculptures into icons of power, authority, and beauty.

Using found elements as the infrastructure for the *Spirit Sculptures* became the catalyst to create much needed new "monuments," or guardian figures for sites in need of protection. *Saint for My City* (2007–2010, p. 34) is a totemic guardian structure designed with a colorful mixed-media assemblage of glass, beads, ceramic, acrylic, plaster, and bullet casings, made to protect Baltimore, where she was born. At the top, a "saint" stands watch to ward off negative elements that need constant monitoring in the contentiousness of the times in which we live. In *Gemini* (2018, p. 144), the sculptural elements become more complex. The bottle form is placed on a base that is ornamented with decorative pins; on top of the bottle is positioned a crowned, Janus-like pairing of heads that face in opposite directions. They project an attitude of vigilance and hyperawareness to disruptive behaviors and social or political discord. In addition, and even more importantly, they seem to see into the two worlds of the living and the afterworld.

DeVane's own artistic vision has been stimulated and excited by the inventiveness and potential applications of using colorful, shiny materials and recycled glass bottles. Her curiosity has been further stimulated by several trips to Haiti to work on a series of mural projects with local communities. While in Haiti, she was able to observe a wide range of ritual objects similar to the bottle she received, and to learn from Haitians about their religious, spiritual, and aesthetic practices. The ethical and moral implications of these objects allowed DeVane to address her personal and intellectual issues of social, political, and spiritual concerns through her deft and nuanced application of beads, sequins, small plastic figures, snakes, figurative charms, insects, wire, glitter, fabric, enamels, ceramic tiles, glass, pearls, and fibers to the bottle forms. *Spring* (2018, p. 75), for example, becomes a virtuoso statement of the abundance of beauty in nature through DeVane's use of antique beaded flower components. The physical disposition of DeVane's sculptural installation transforms spaces like The Baltimore Museum of Art's Spring House, where her work was installed in the summer of 2019, into sanctified, spiritualized spaces of beauty, tranquility, and meditation. The resonances of traditional African religion and philosophy play a powerful role in the works of artists throughout the African diaspora.

Popular colonialist and contemporary practices have resisted the possibilities of contemporary aesthetic retentions of African belief systems and practices. However, the innovative creations of descendant artists affirm philosopher John Mbiti's belief that "Africans are notoriously religious, and each people has its own religious system with a set of beliefs and practices."[8] Within each system of belief that has emerged in the African diaspora, objects, instruments, and ensembles were continually made by skilled makers and artisans to help guide, educate, mediate, protect, heal, celebrate, and

8　John Mbiti, *African Religions and Philosophy* (Garden City, New York: Doubleday, 1970), 1.

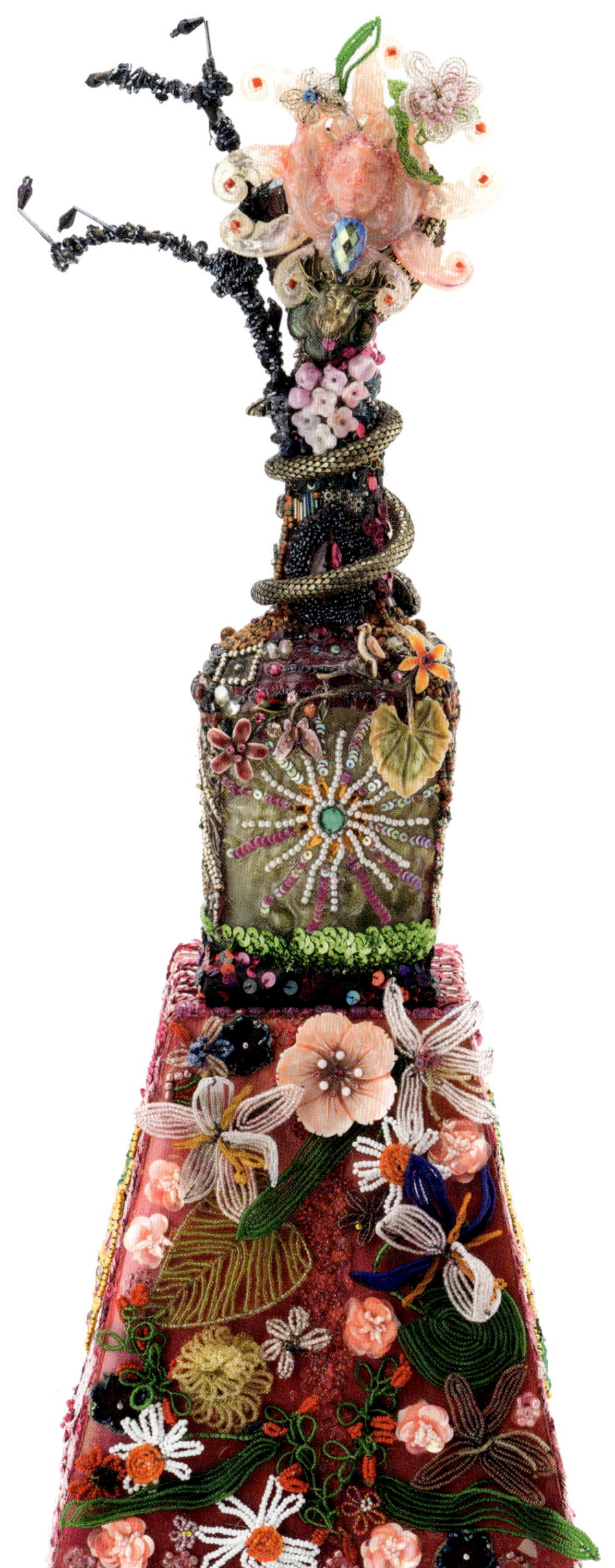

Spring [Sohappyitsspring],
2018, glass, wood, metal,
glass beads, plastic, metal
wire, sequins, fabric

commemorate all aspects of earthly life and otherworldly spheres. Oletha DeVane is a member of this growing legion of elite enlightened artists and makers, committed to creating powerful, spiritualized creations that deal with the human condition and ponder the nature of otherworldly states of being that address the realm of spirits, gods, and ancestors.

The aesthetics of Amalia Amaki, Xenobia Bailey, Romare Bearden, Willie Birch, Chakaia Booker, Mark Bradford, Nick Cave, Sonya Clark, Loring Cornish, Mel Edwards, Joan Gaither, Vanessa German, Victor Harris, Maren Hassinger, Senga Nengudi, William Rhodes, Aminah Brenda Lynne Robinson, Elizabeth Talford Scott, Joyce J. Scott, Adejoke Tugbiyele, Jack Whitten, Fred Wilson, and so many other artists, are committed to the active reclamation of knowledge essential to the legacy of an African descendancy and heritage. In recognition of this demonstrative course of artistic reclamation, Harvard scholar Jacob K. Olupona has observed:

> While African traditional religions are engaged in a battle for their lives on the African continent, they and their sister African diaspora religions are thriving elsewhere in the world—particularly in the Americas and in Europe.... Over the centuries, they have in many cases developed into traditions that have broad appeal not only to their inheritors but also to a broad range of Black, mixed-race, and white peoples.[9]

Pursuing agency and authenticity has been an arduous mission for artists of African descent. They struggle constantly against Western assumptions that assert the inferiority of Black identity, and that doubt the authenticity of an aesthetic specific to a psychic, spiritual, and intellectual space of Blackness. Oletha DeVane and her peers continue to redefine, visually articulate, and expand an artistic terrain that now prioritizes a space for this uniquely American genre in the lexicon of art history. Poet Elizabeth Alexander queries the nature of "the Black interior" as "the great hopeful space of African American creativity." She further explains, "I see it as inner space in which Black artists have found selves that go far, far beyond the limited expectations and definition of what Black is, isn't, or should be."[10] Oletha DeVane is at the forefront of this journey, transforming ordinary, useful and useless, tangible things into compellingly complex and iconic works of beauty, empowerment, healing, and protection from events and actions beyond our control.

9 Jacob K. Olupona, *African Religions—A Very Short Introduction* (New York: Oxford University Press, 2014), 107.

10 Elizabeth Alexander, The *Black Interior* (Saint Paul: Graywolf Press, 2004), 5.

artworks

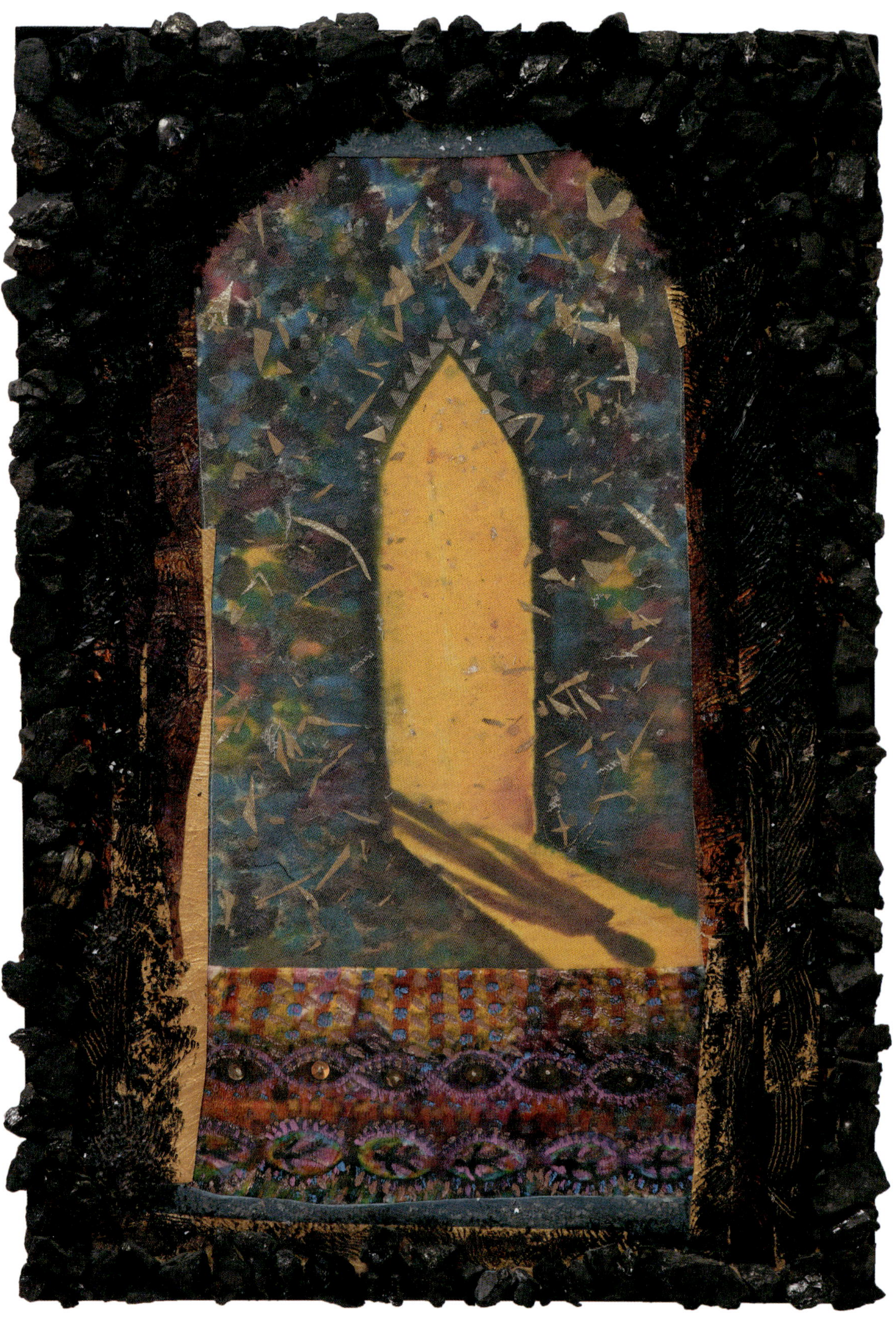

Doorway to Nowhere, 1980s,
acrylic, charcoal on paper

Ode to Pre-Existence, 1998,
acrylic, pastels

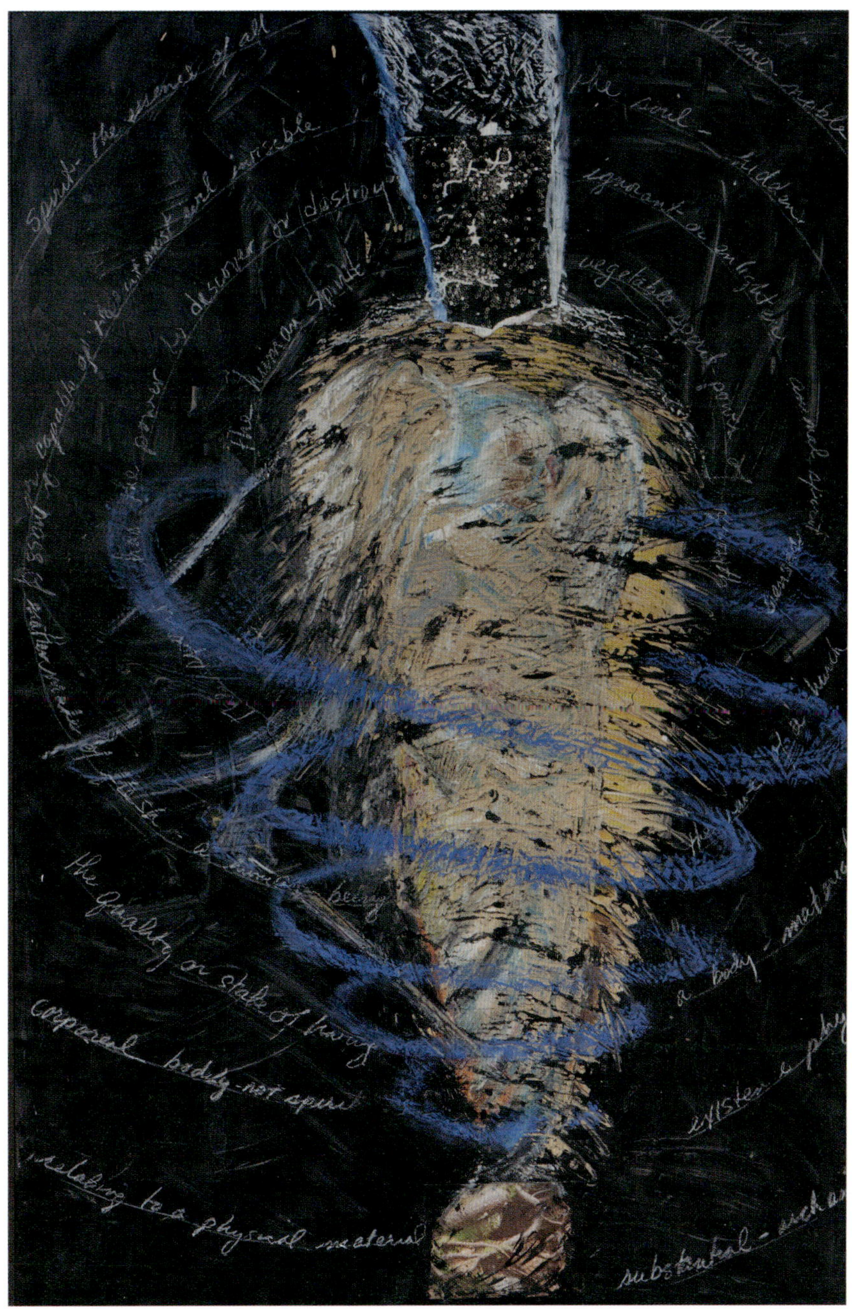

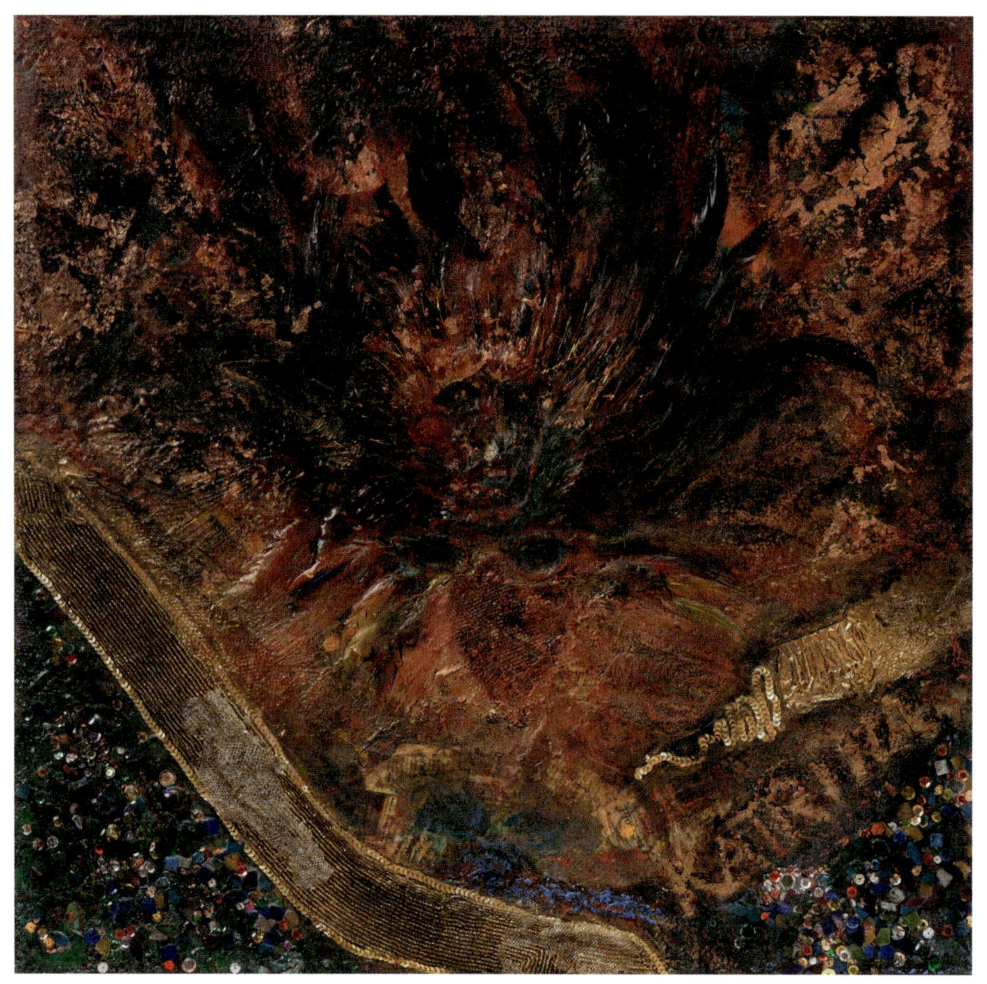

Spirits II, 2000, acrylic,
feathers, fabric, beads

OPPOSITE
Roses, 2000, acrylic
on canvas, Collection
of Dorothy DeVane

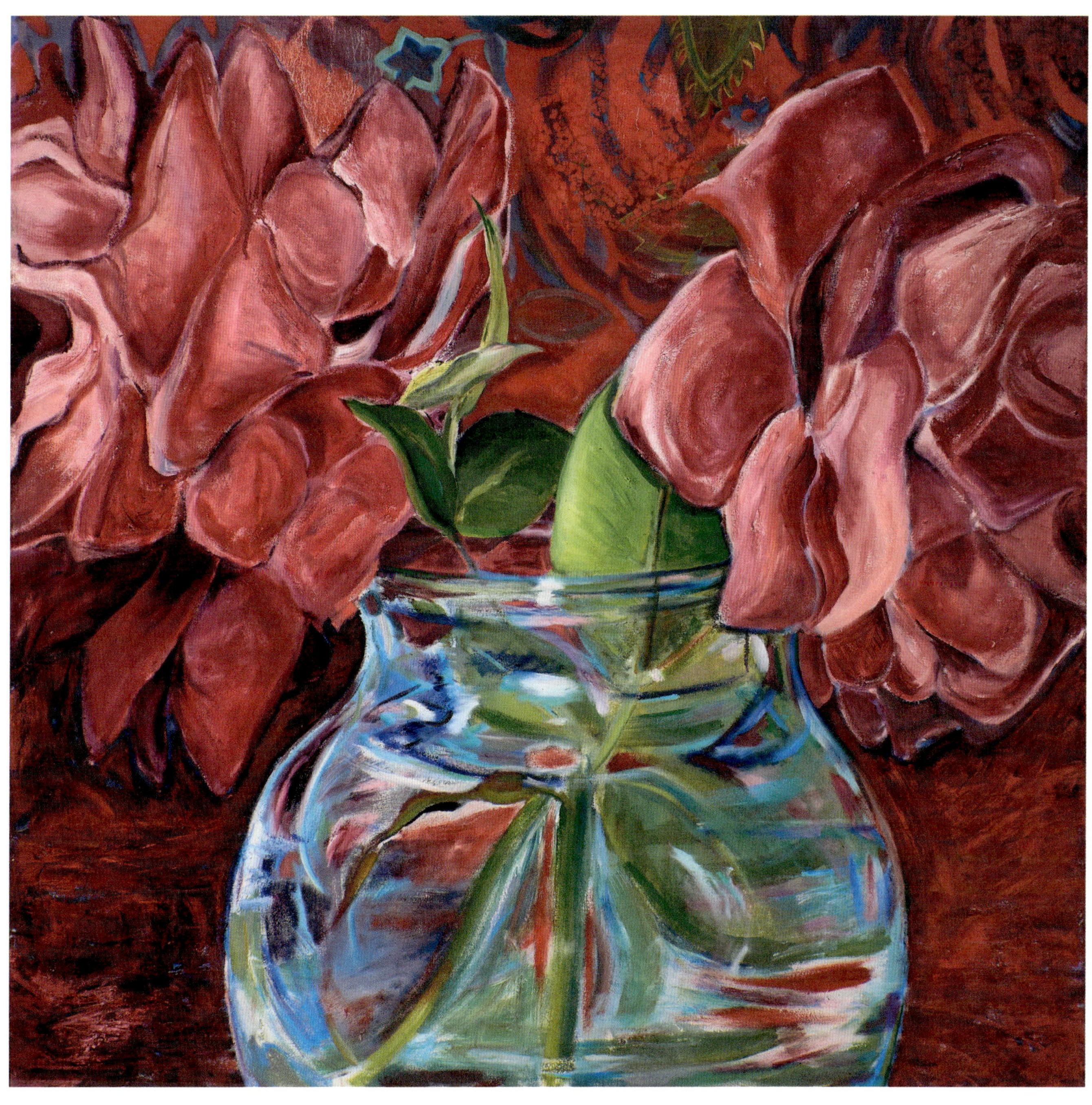

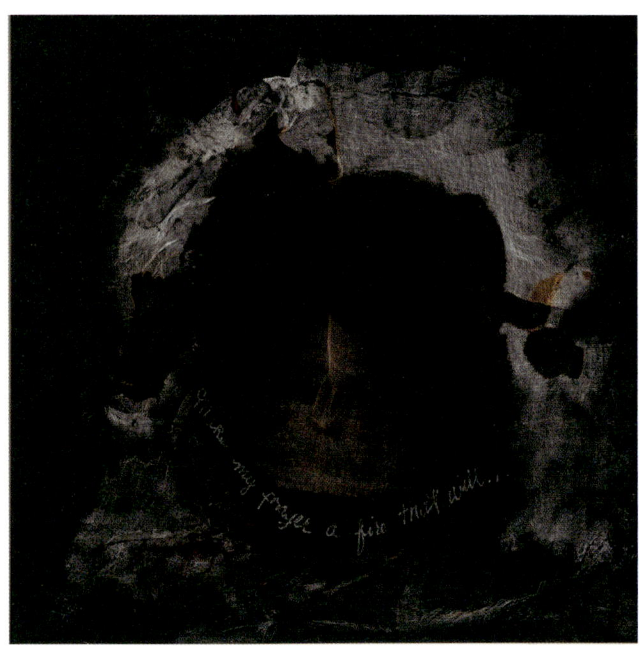

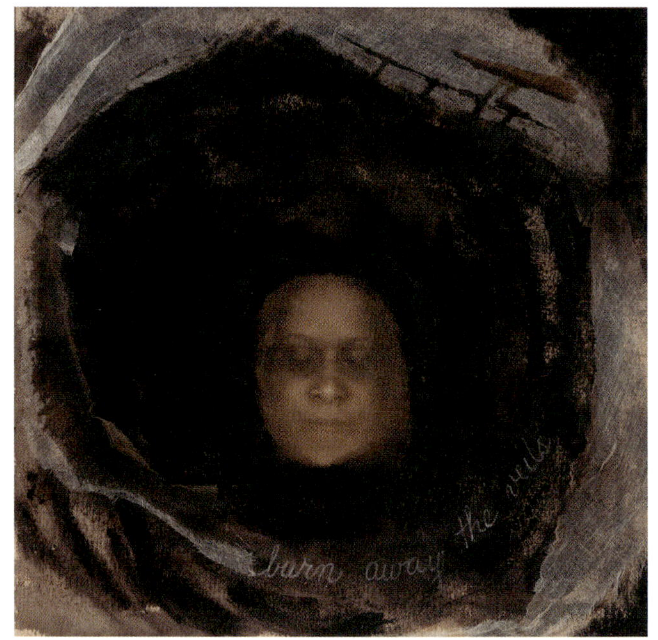

Veil I, 2000, Van Dyke process, fabric, acrylic

Veil II, 2000, Van Dyke process, fabric, acrylic

Veil III, 2000, Van Dyke process, fabric, acrylic

Veil IV, 2000, Van Dyke process, fabric, acrylic

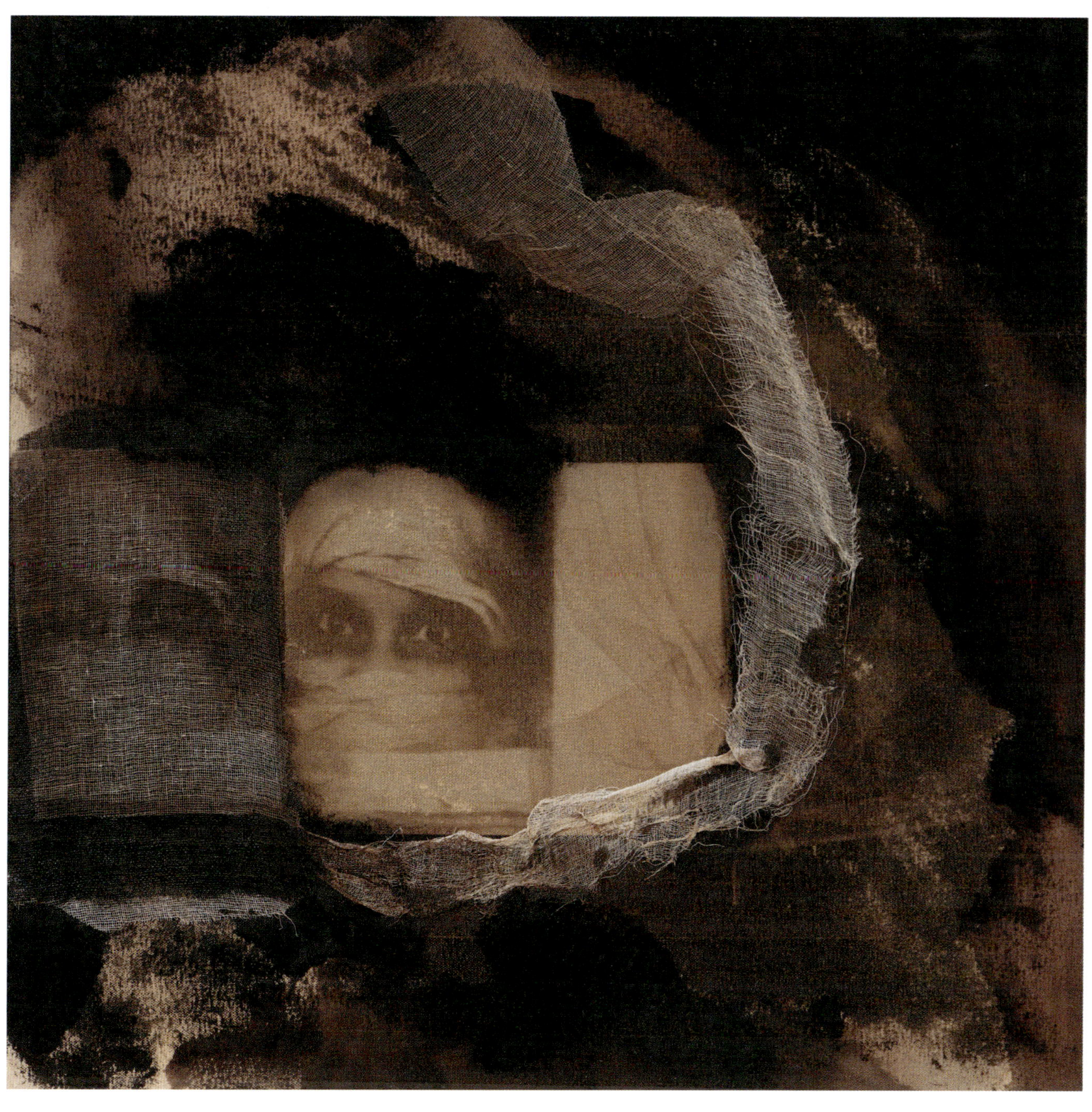

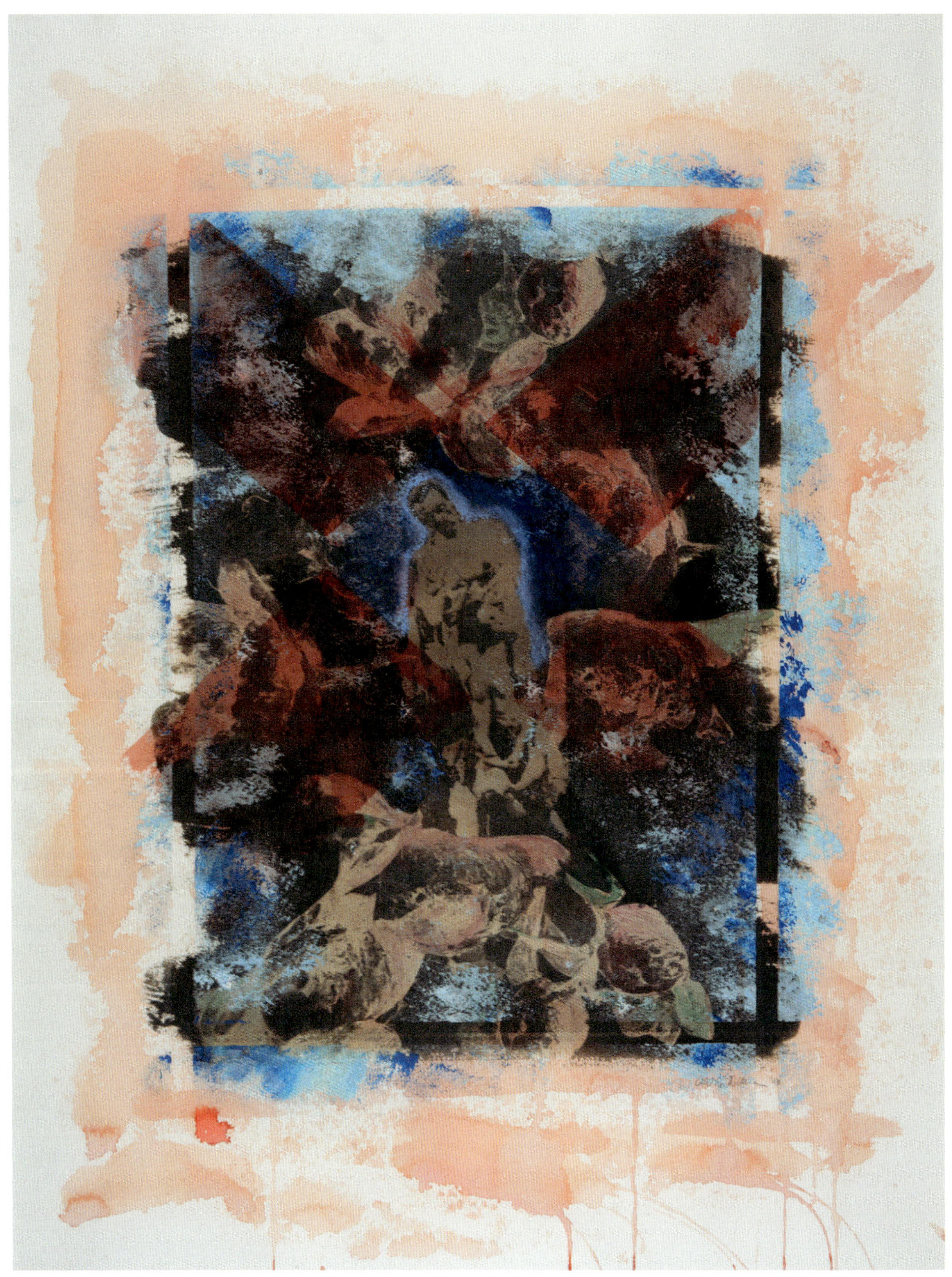

Witness I, 2003, acrylic,
watercolor and solar
etching

Witness II, 2003, acrylic,
watercolor and solar
etching

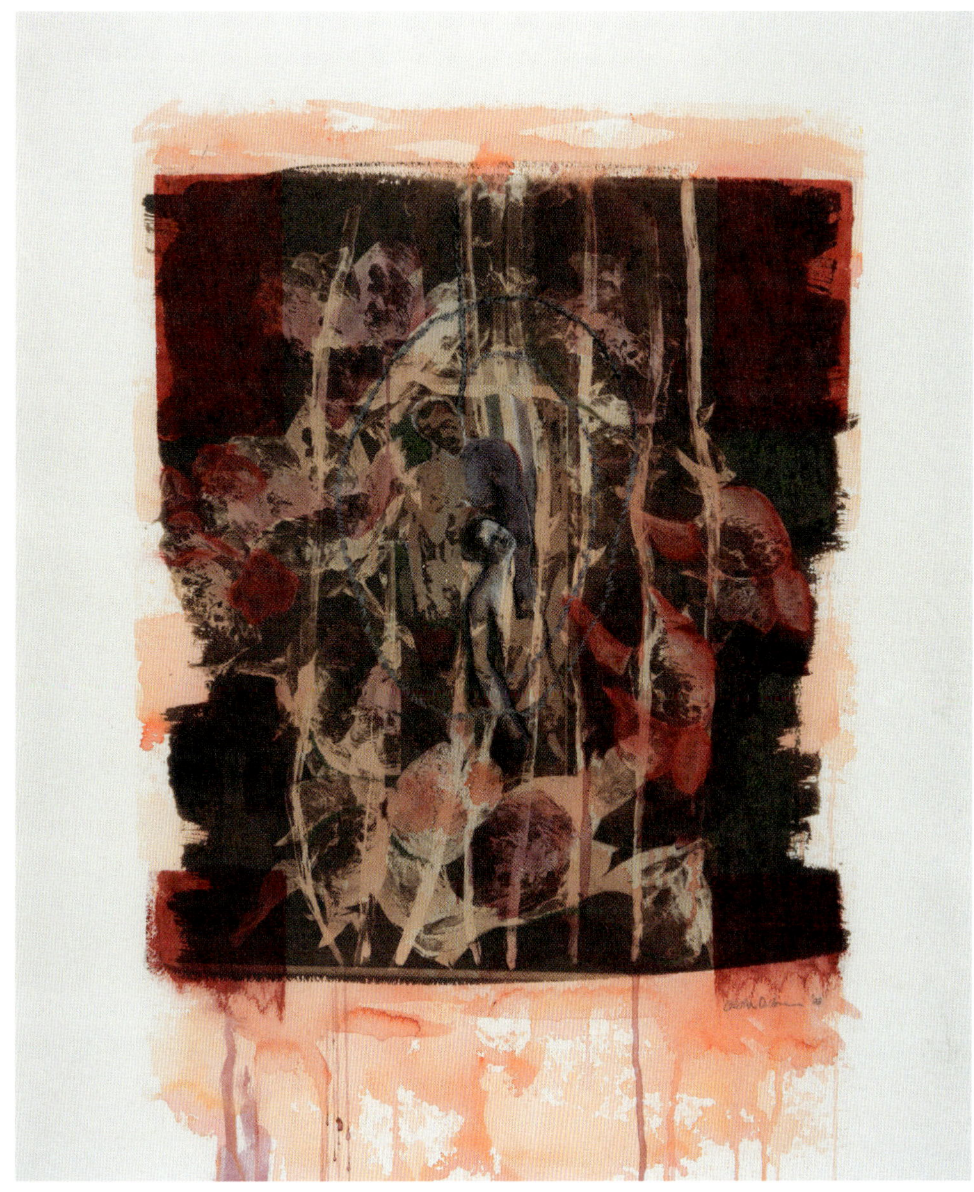

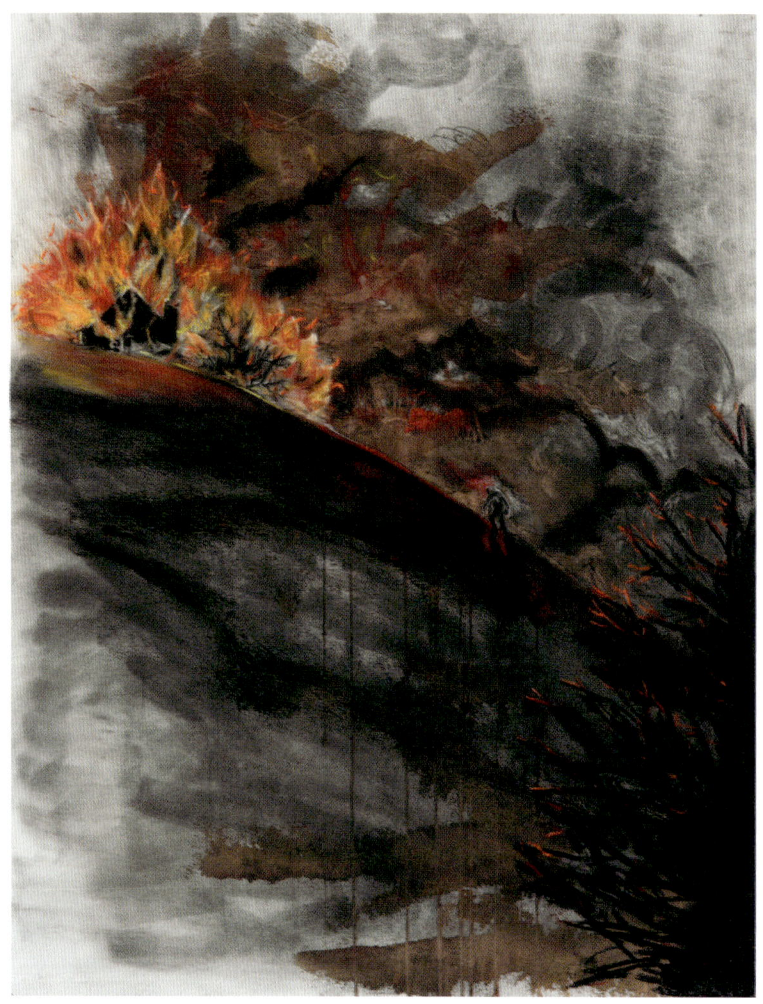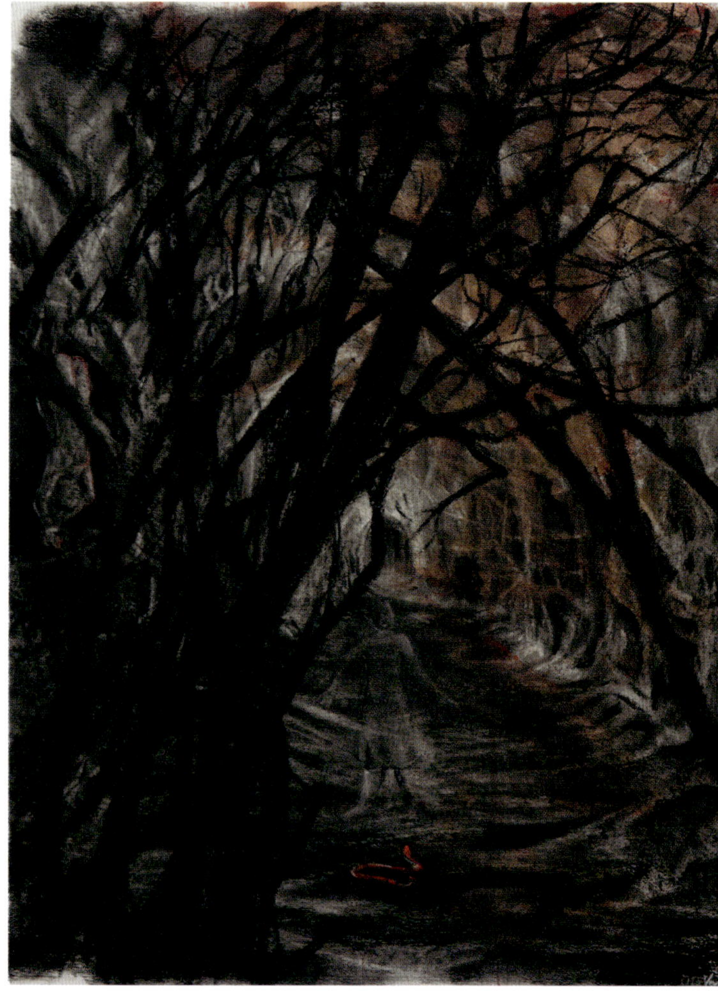

**Untitled [figure climbing hill
towards fire and figure with
red snake]**, 2003, charcoal and
pastel on paper; diptych

OPPOSITE
Through the Gates of Babylon,
2003, lithograph

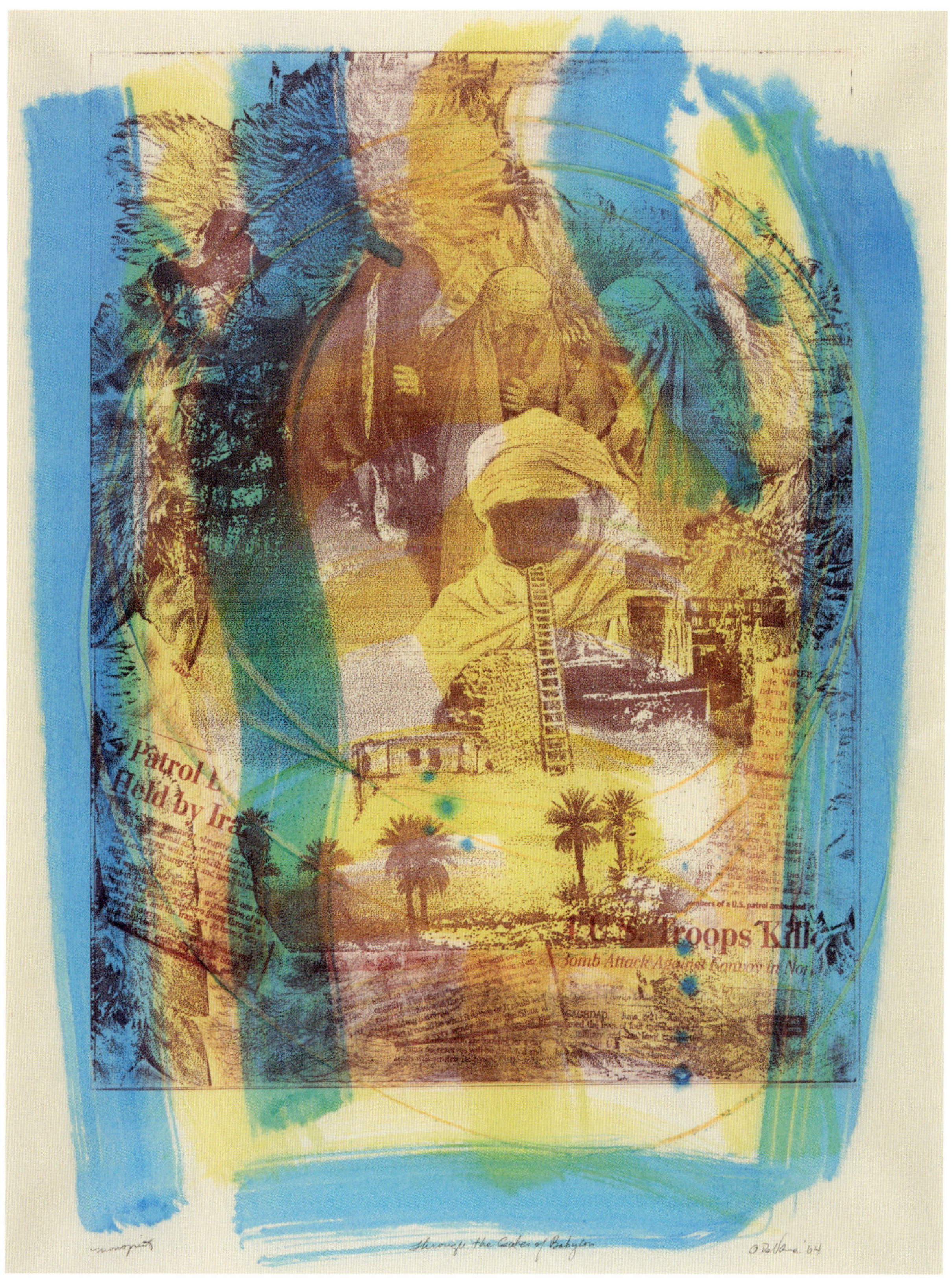
Patrol
held by Ira
U. S. Troops Kill
Bomb Attack Against Convoy in No
through the Gates of Babylon

Sacred Geometry [collabora-
tion with Donna Denizé],
2001, mixed media, 9 double
folios

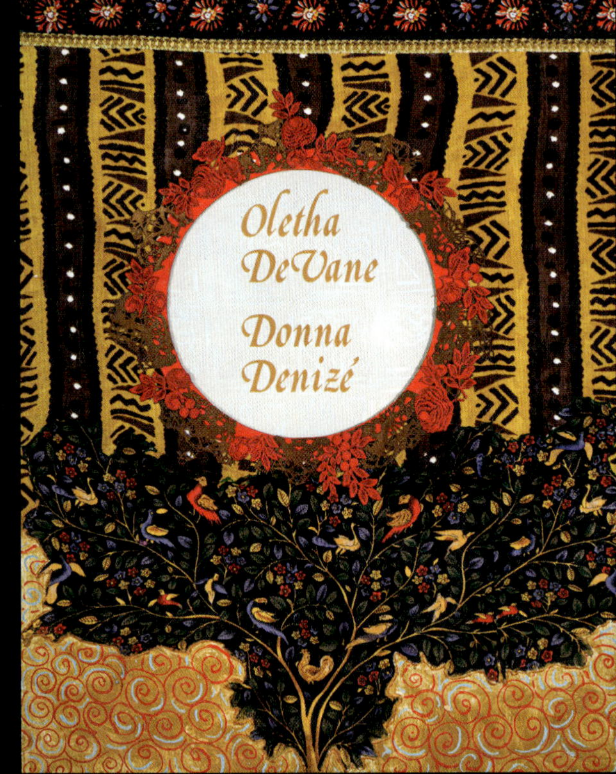

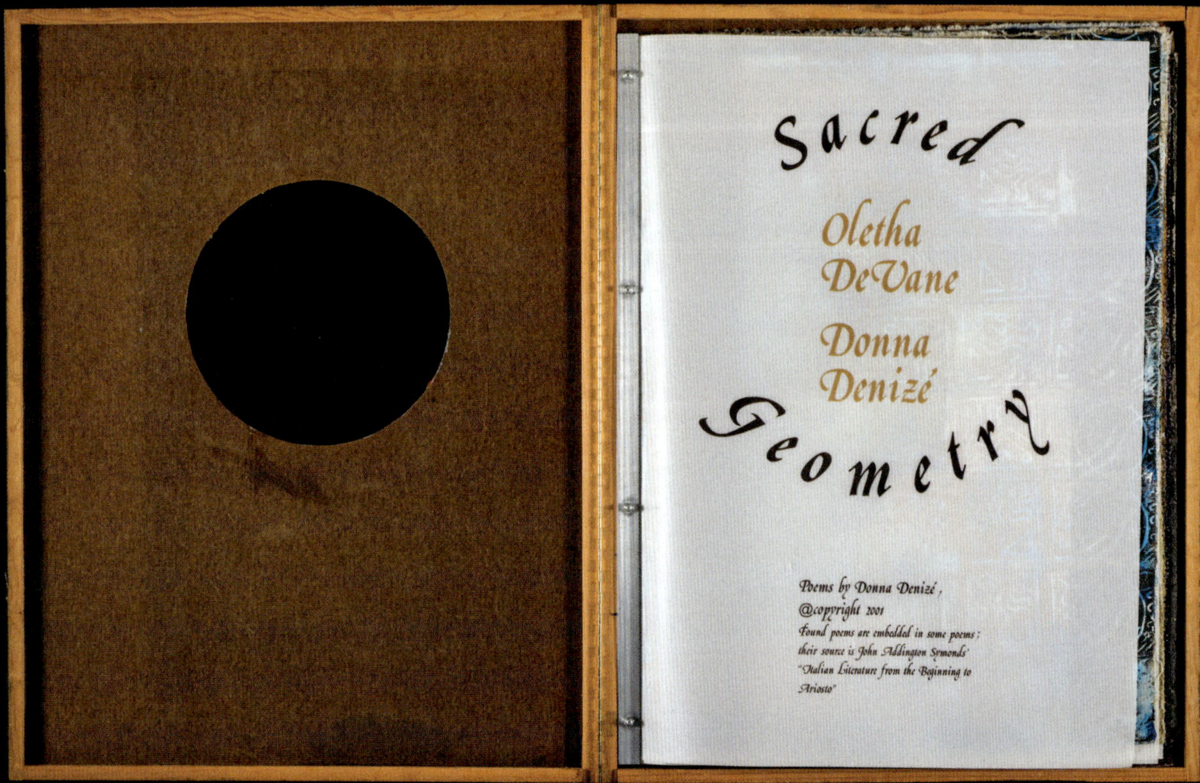

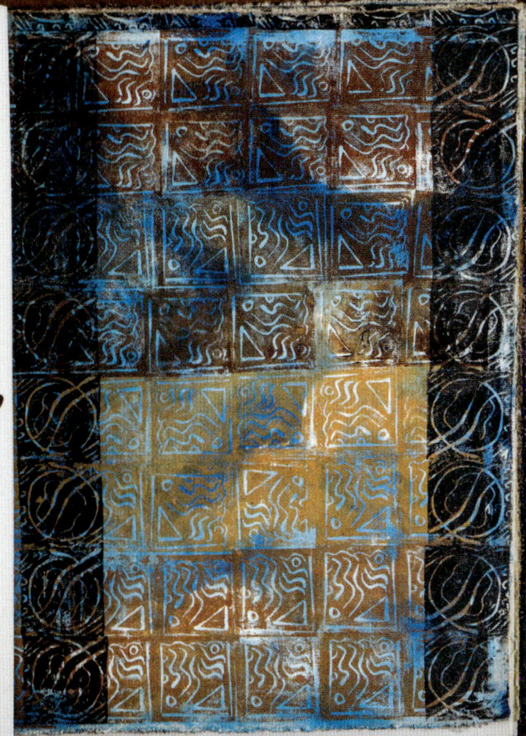

Sacred Geometry

Oletha DeVane

Donna Denizé

Poems by Donna Denizé,
©copyright 2001
found poems are embodied in some poems;
their source is John Addington Symonds'
"Italian Literature from the Beginning to
Ariosto"

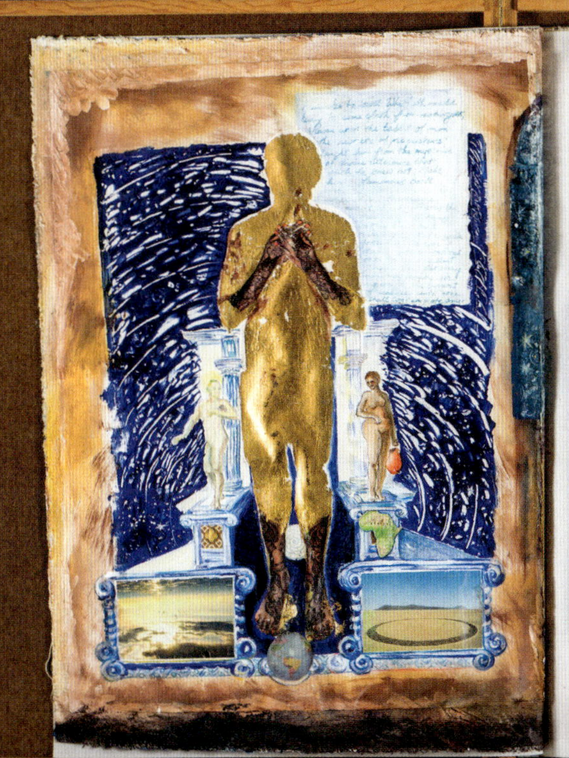

Dante

Whatever Dante knew, he wrote
    Of inspiration that made him poet of divine
Love, like a man seeking silver and finding
    Gold. In the words of a book, a gentle
Lady with adoring eyes and a sweetness
    Destroying all, Dante pursued one line, held
One hand through labyrinths of love
    where the first full blossom of
Beauty is song, and the Spirit of life,
    indwelling in heart's
Secret chambers, Writer,
    From the highlands of devotion,
Attending to a vision of life beyond
    The tomb-symbols for another reality,
which alone give life on earth its
    value, as shadows before the sun.

*

We need not doubt the fidelity of
Manners or daily conversation,
a transparent language, always
Lucid, smooth and fluent, the hearts
Of lovers who understand the dialogue
Of dawn, are words, alone addressing
themselves to us and life as gods.

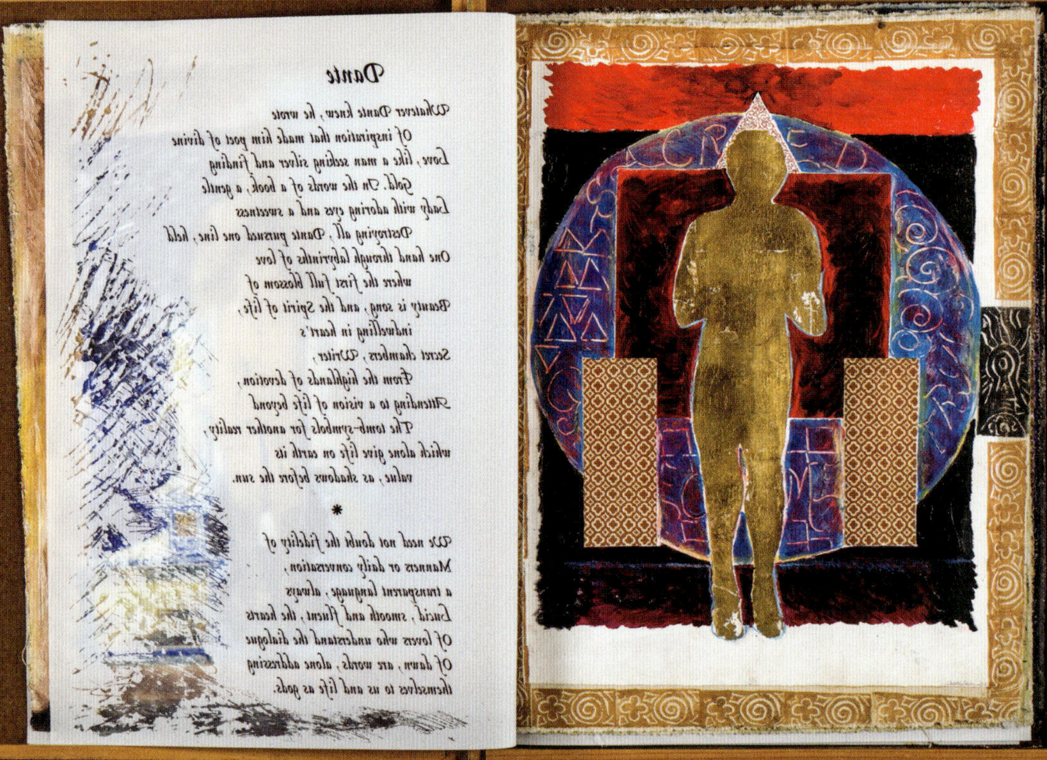

Dante

Whatever Dante knew, he wrote
Of inspiration that made him poet of divine
Love, like a man seeking silver and finding
Gold. In the words of a book, a gentle
Lady with adoring eyes and a sweetness
Destroying all, Dante pursued one line, held
One hand through labyrinths of love
where the first full blossom of
Beauty is song, and the Spirit of life,
indwelling in heart's
Secret chambers, Writer,
From the highlands of devotion,
Attending to a vision of life beyond
The tomb-symbols for another reality,
which alone give life on earth its
value, as shadows before the sun.

*

We need not doubt the fidelity of
Manners or daily conversation,
a transparent language, always
Lucid, smooth and fluent, the hearts
Of lovers who understand the dialogue
Of dawn, are words, alone addressing
themselves to us and life as gods.

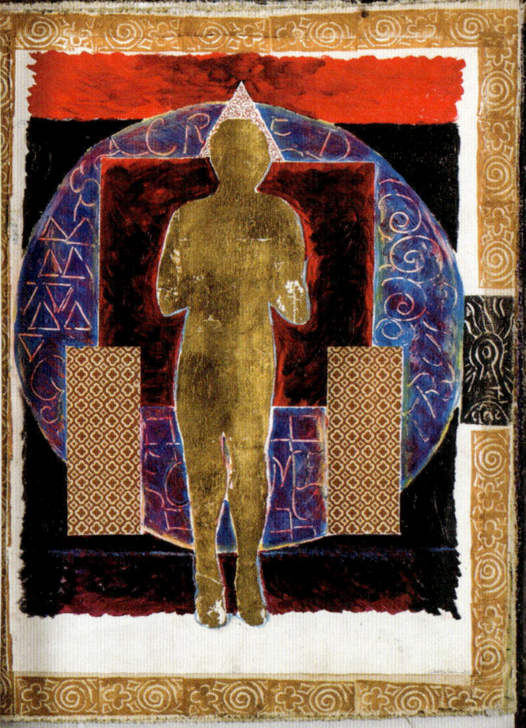

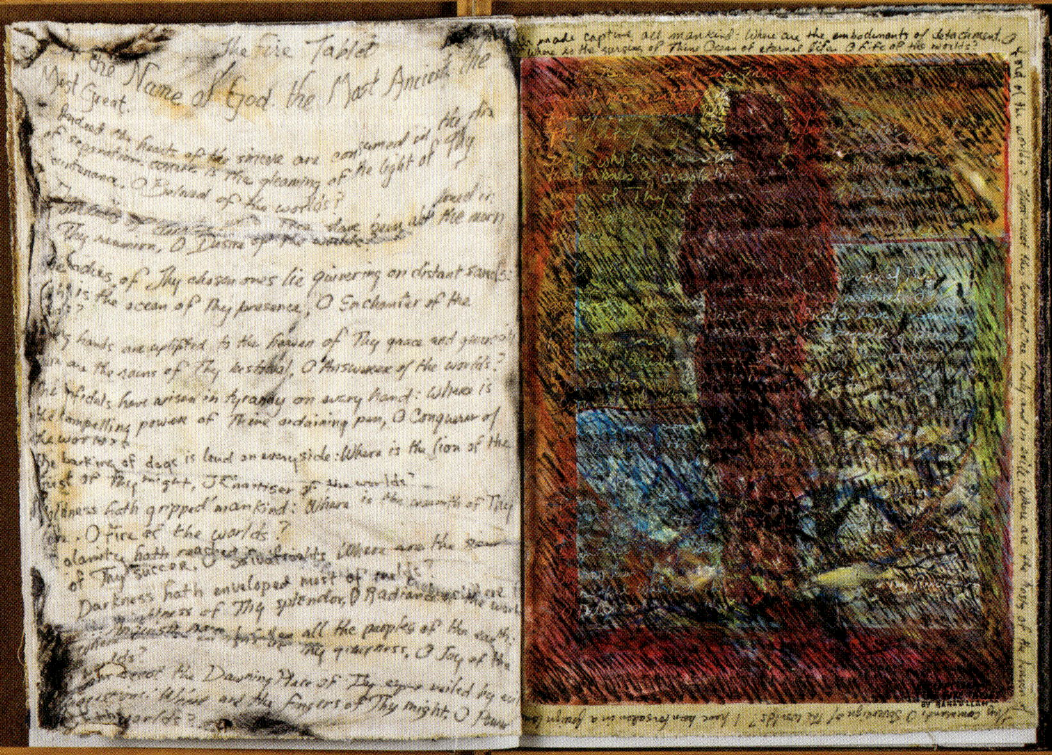

The Fire Tablet

In the Name of God, the Most Ancient, the Most Great.

Indeed the hearts of the sincere are consumed in the fire of separation: Where is the gleaming of the light of Thy Countenance, O Beloved of the worlds?

Thy near ones have been abandoned in darkness: Where is the shining of the morn of Thy reunion, O Desire of the worlds?

The bodies of Thy chosen ones lie quivering on distant sands: Where is the ocean of Thy presence, O Enchanter of the worlds?

The hands of supplication are uplifted to the heaven of Thy grace and generosity: Where are the rains of Thy bestowal, O Answerer of the worlds?

The infidels have arisen in tyranny on every hand: Where is the compelling power of Thine ordaining pen, O Conqueror of the worlds?

The barking of dogs is loud on every side: Where is the lion of the forest of Thy might, O Chastiser of the worlds?

Coldness hath gripped mankind: Where is the warmth of Thy love, O Fire of the worlds?

Calamity hath reached its height: Where are the signs of Thy succor, O Salvation of the worlds?

Darkness hath enveloped most of the peoples: Where is the brightness of Thy splendor, O Radiance of the worlds?

Ignorance hath become a snare for all the peoples of the earth: Where are the embodiments of knowledge of Thy greatness, O Joy of the worlds?

Thou dost behold the Dawning Place of Thy signs veiled by evil suggestions: Where are the fingers of Thy might, O Power of the worlds?

...made captive, all mankind: Where are the embodiments of detachment, O Where is the surging of Thine Ocean of eternal life? O Life of the worlds?

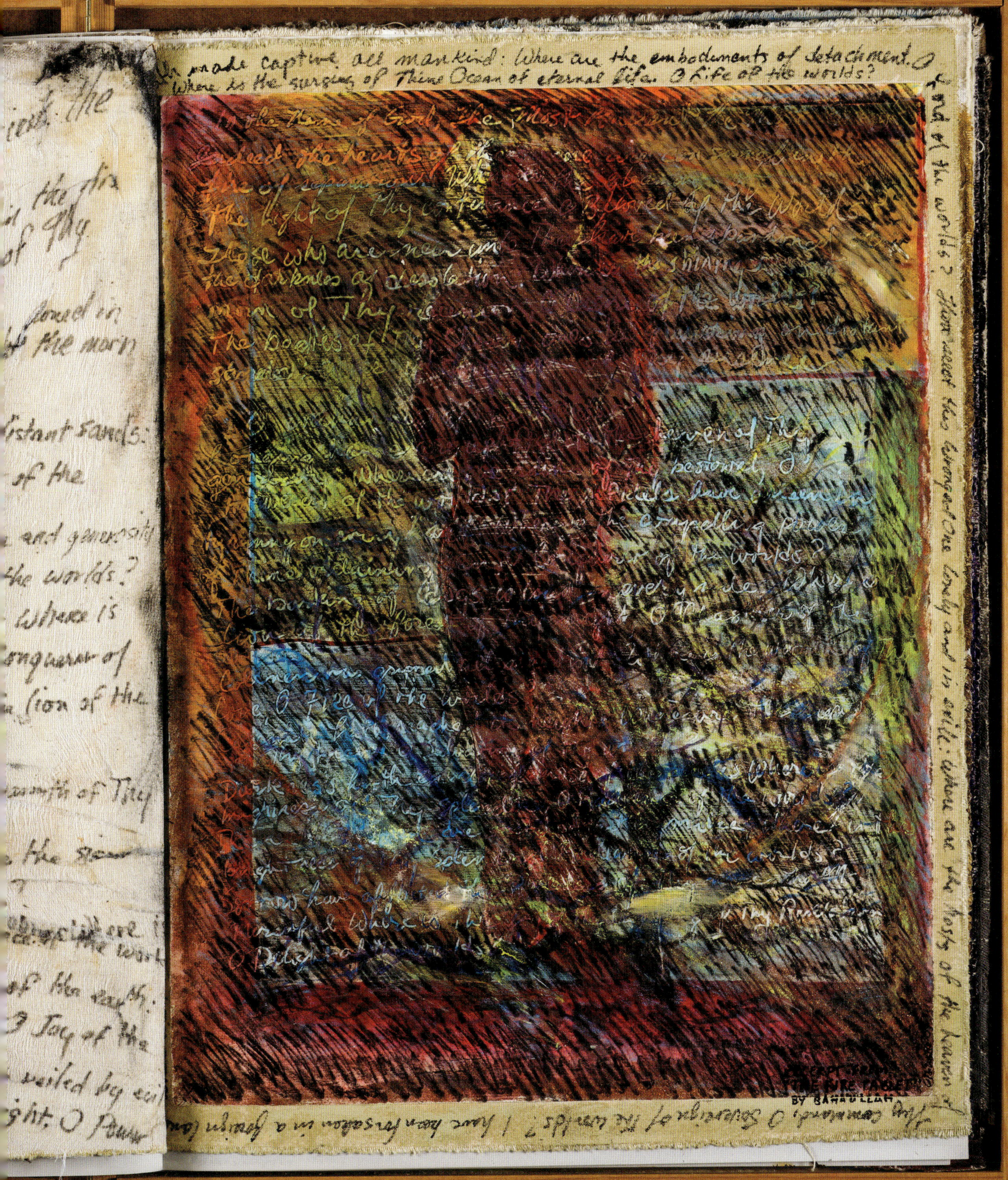
EXCERPTED FROM
THE FIRE TABLET
BY BAHÁ'U'LLÁH

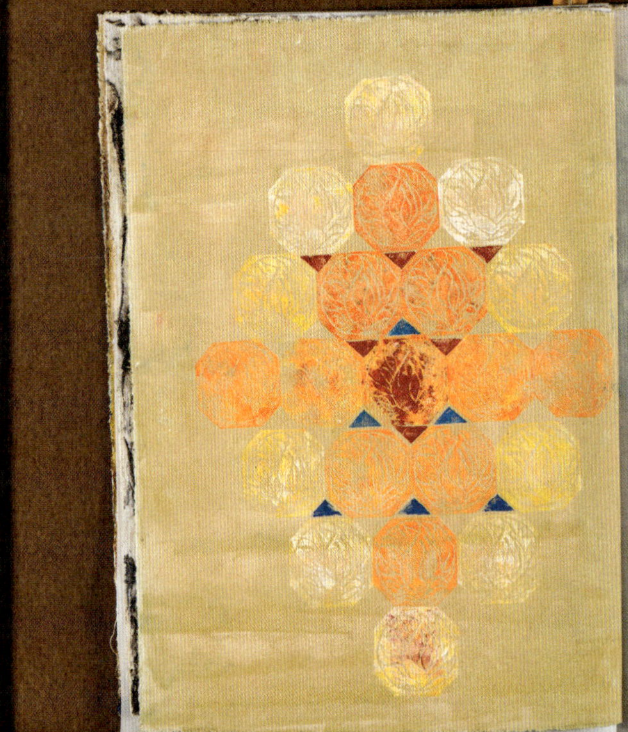

BOccacio

His: Earthly Songs, Paradise sounding
in his ears, Singer of the living, of
        the universe as a single point within
Ones breast, and the tale, a map
        where the whole is surveyed–the
disappointed
        Monk, Francesca's episode, a discourse
        On gentle birth, those with contempt
for the common folk
or Poetry. His
        a study, not a finished picture
but inexhaustible details, like
Rhetoric to drama,
        his dreams capturing our gaze, our brief,
        pregnant touches of fancy, illness
And despair. Poet singing
the tragic love of a young man
        and a nun, or hero shepherd–
his argument, position, or thought,
        designs as geometrical as a church by Brunelleschi,
        and passion, beauty, ache, the
simple, human outline sung
        In "the art of lies" walking within dark places,
        And truth beneath "a veil of fables."

BOccacio

His: Earthly Songs, Paradise sounding
in his ears, Singer of the living, of
        the universe as a single point within
Ones breast, and the tale, a map
        where the whole is surveyed–the
disappointed
        Monk, Francesca's episode, a discourse
        On gentle birth, those with contempt
for the common folk
or Poetry. His
        a study, not a finished picture
but inexhaustible details, like
Rhetoric to drama,
        his dreams capturing our gaze, our brief,
        pregnant touches of fancy, illness
And despair. Poet singing
the tragic love of a young man
        and a nun, or hero shepherd–
his argument, position, or thought,
        designs as geometrical as a church by Brunelleschi,
        and passion, beauty, ache, the
simple, human outline sung
        In "the art of lies" walking within dark places,
        And truth beneath "a veil of fables."

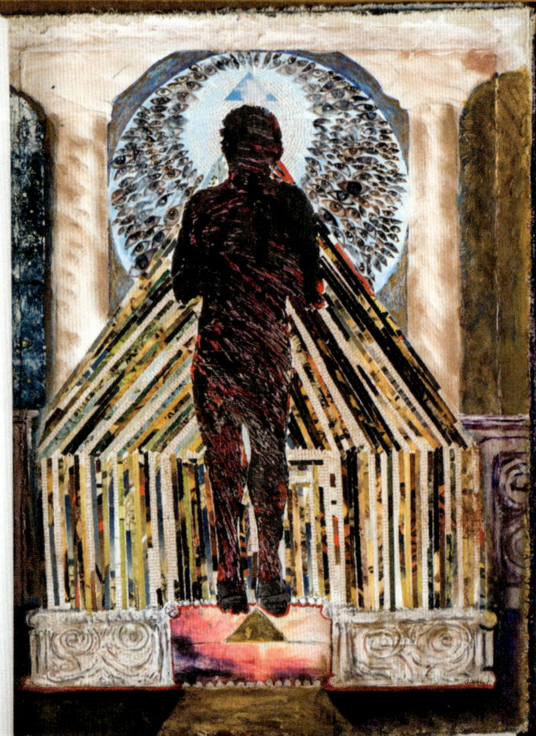

To Petrarch: Another Earthly Conflict

When the moon holds sway, and the sun
sleeps in a mystical veil of a thousand

Paradises, a poet knows offerings should be
Made to good fires and warm

Chambers: the fountains flow,
Beyond Glory, love, fortune

And the poet, resigned
to Nirvana or beatitude, finds

the poem unsuccessful,
obsolete, an art

beyond its scope, for in this
night, one cannot

pour Wine, new
and divine, into old bottles.

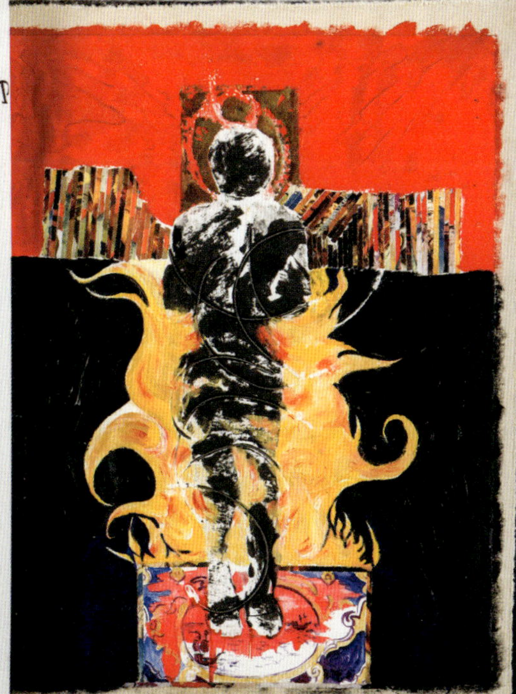

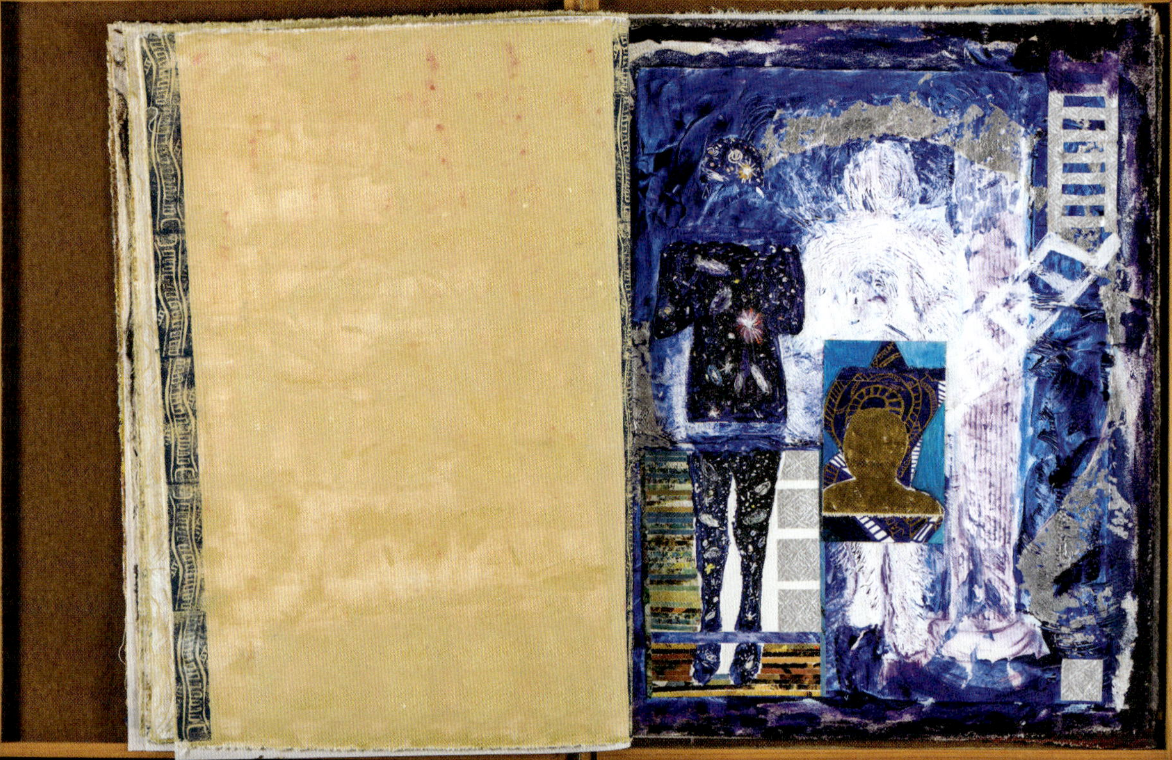

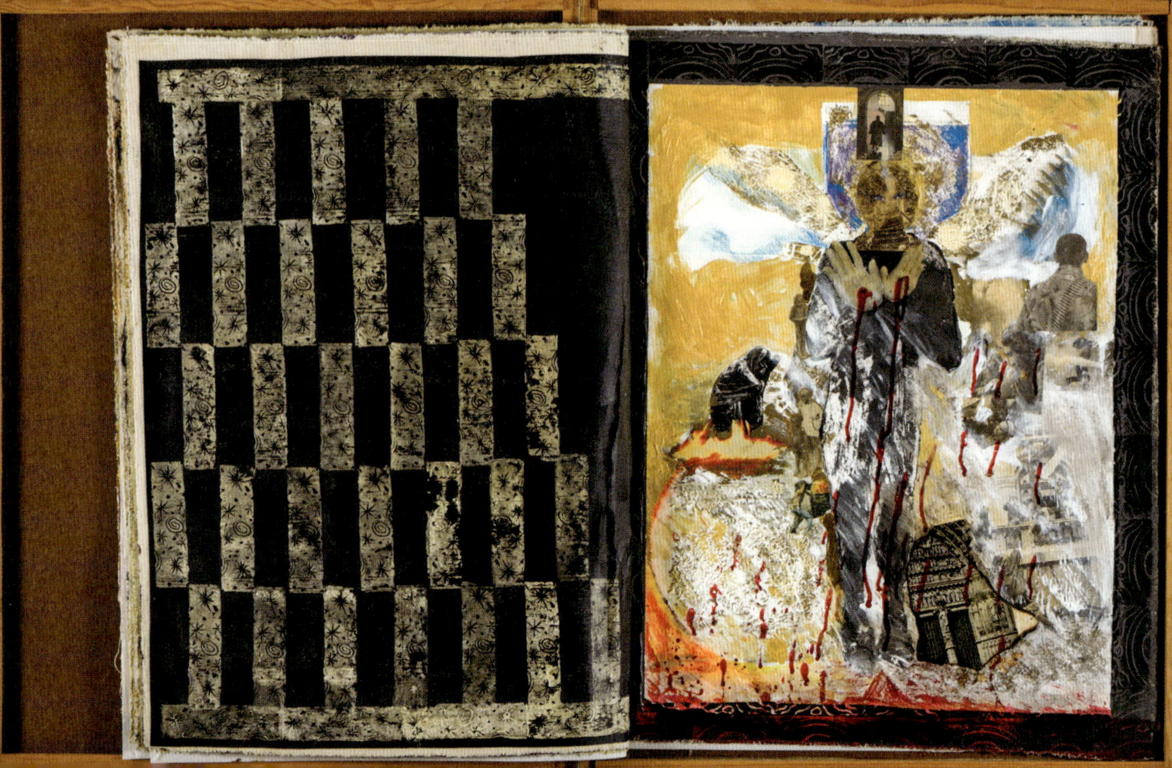

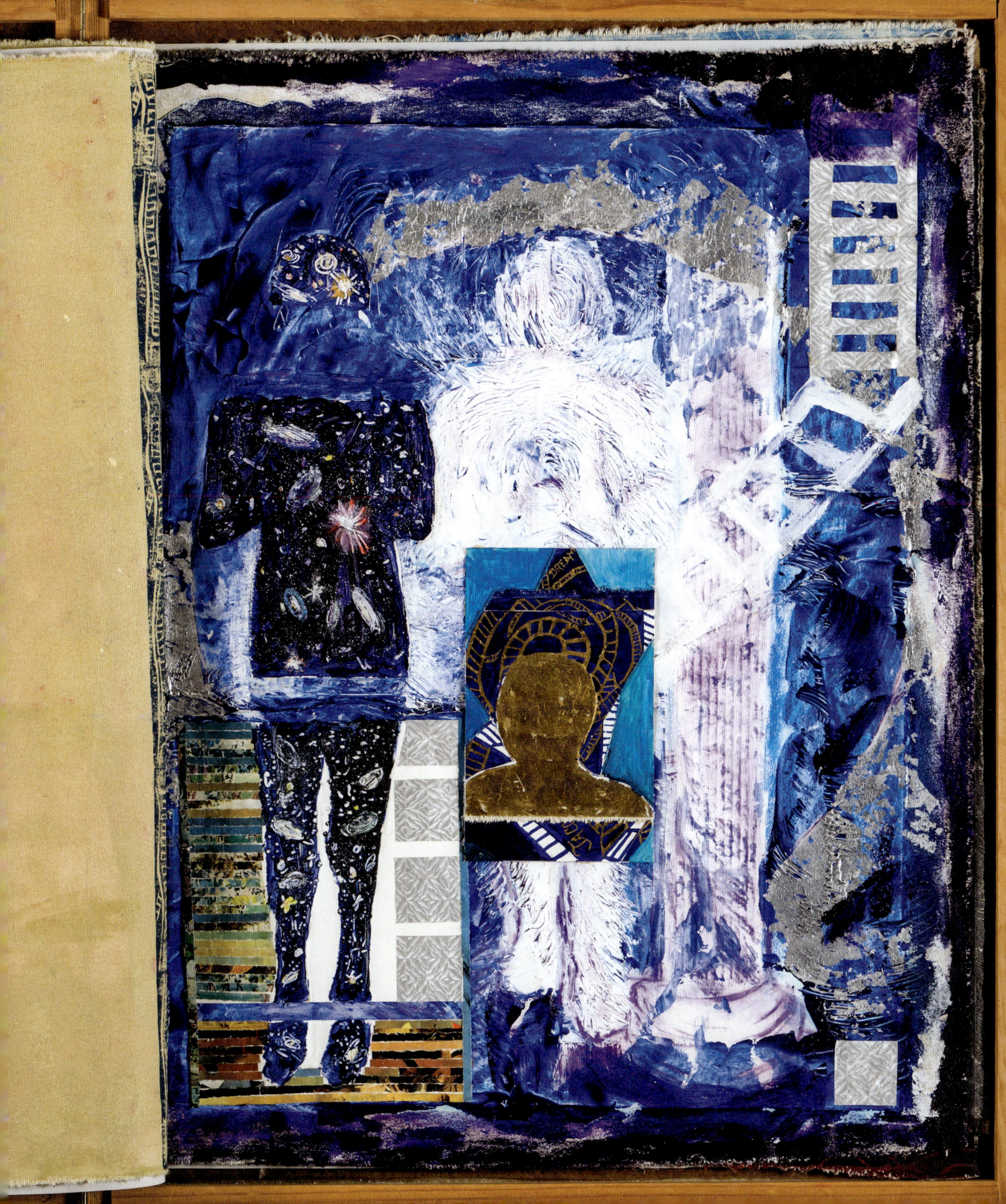

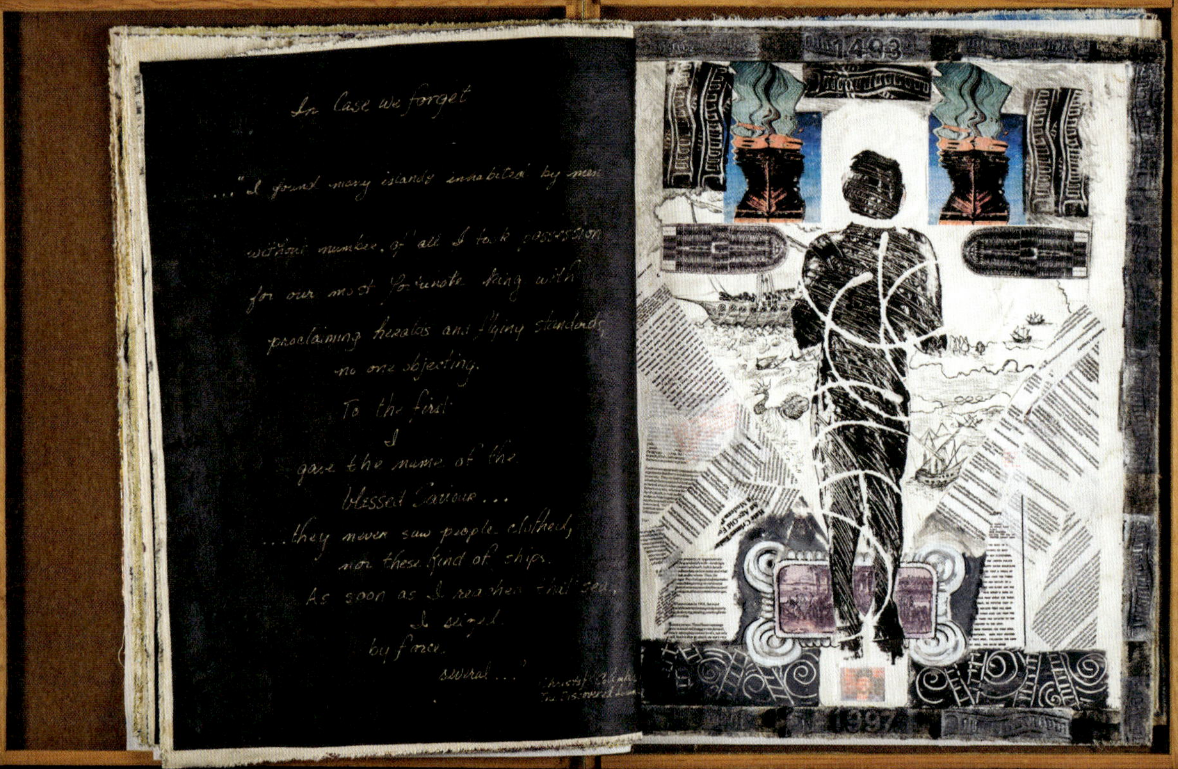

In case we forget

... "I found many islands inhabited by men without number, of all I took possession for our most Fortunate King with proclaiming heralds and flying standards no one objecting. To the first I gave the name of the Blessed Saviour... ...they never saw people clothed, nor these kind of ships. As soon as I reached that sea, I seized by force. several..."

— Christof. Columbus, who discovered...

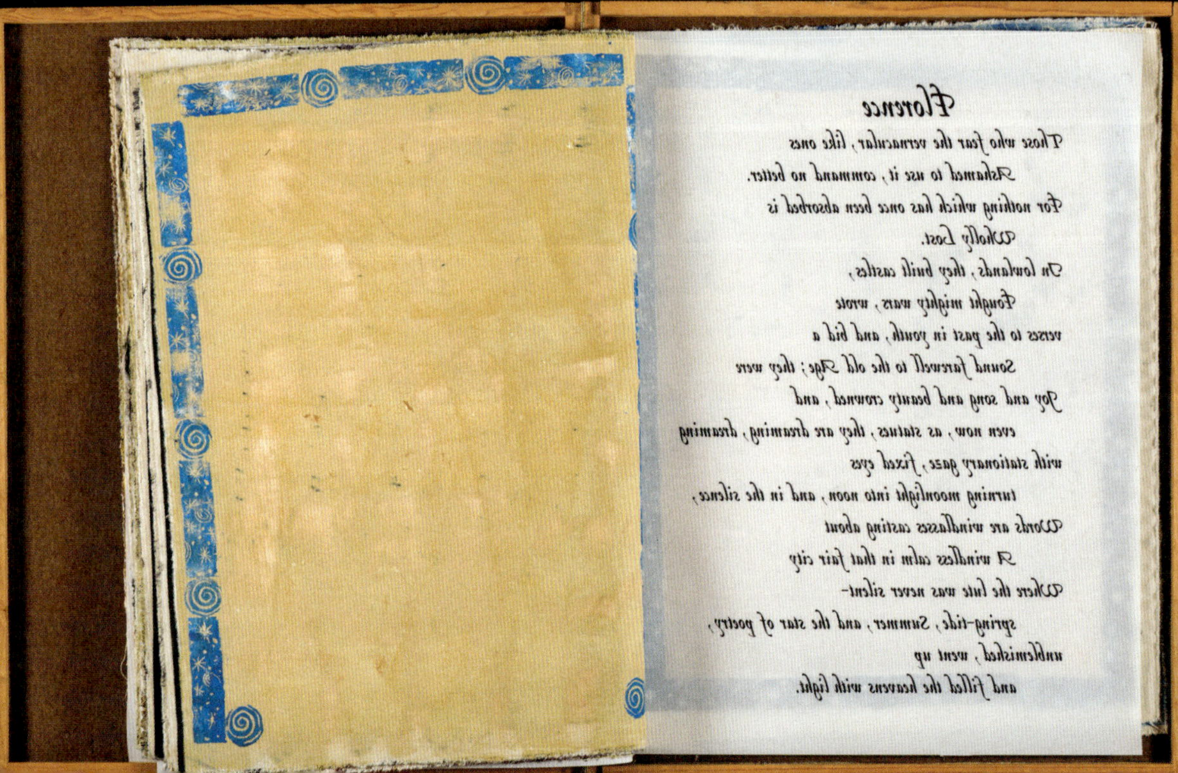

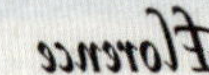

Florence

Those who fear the vernacular, like ones
Ashamed to use it, command no better.
For nothing which has once been absorbed is
Wholly lost.
In lowlands, they built castles,
Fought mighty wars, wrote
verses to the past in youth, and bid a
Sound farewell to the old Age; they were
Joy and song and beauty crowned, and
even now, as statues, they are dreaming, dreaming
with stationary gaze. Fixed eyes
turning moonlight into noon, and in the silence,
Words are windlasses casting about
A windless calm in that fair city
Where the lute was never silent—
spring-tide, Summer, and the star of poetry,
unblemished, went up
and filled the heavens with light.

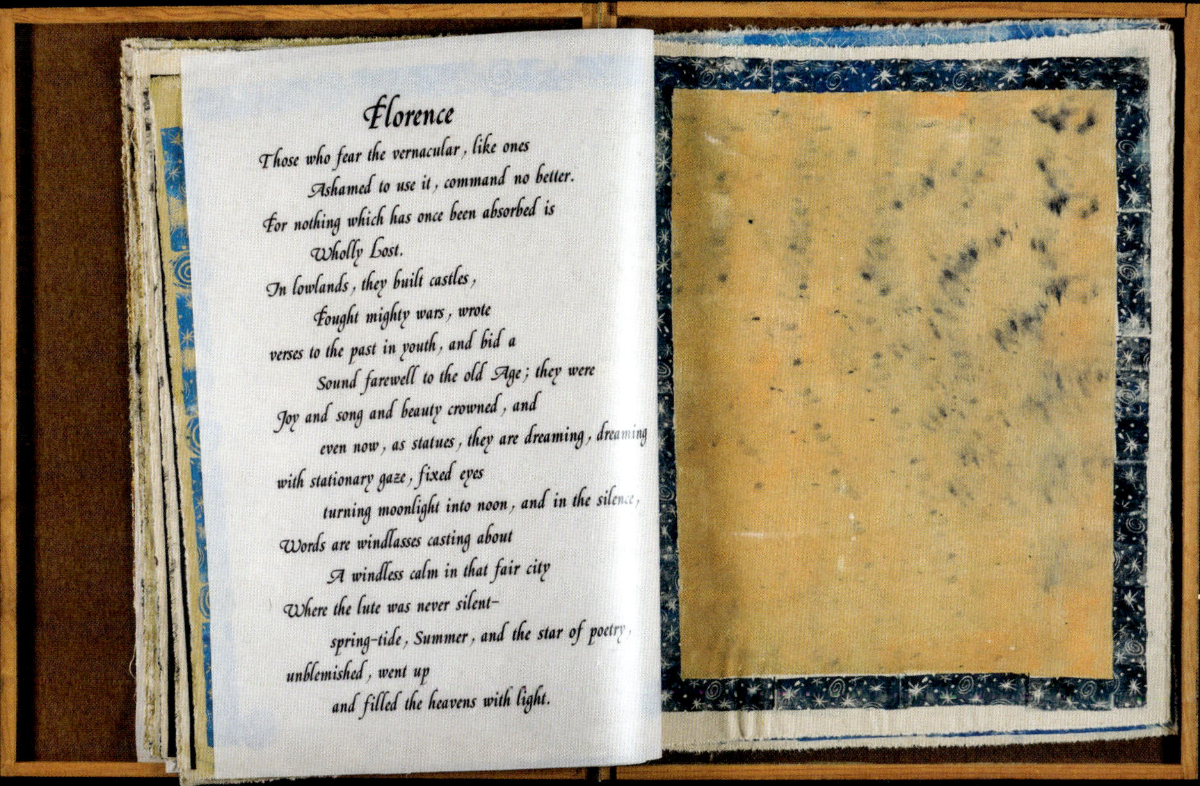

Florence

Those who fear the vernacular, like ones
    Ashamed to use it, command no better.
For nothing which has once been absorbed is
    Wholly Lost.
In lowlands, they built castles,
    Fought mighty wars, wrote
verses to the past in youth, and bid a
    Sound farewell to the old Age; they were
Joy and song and beauty crowned, and
    even now, as statues, they are dreaming, dreaming
with stationary gaze, fixed eyes
    turning moonlight into noon, and in the silence,
Words are windlasses casting about
    A windless calm in that fair city
Where the lute was never silent—
    spring-tide, Summer, and the star of poetry,
unblemished, went up
    and filled the heavens with light.

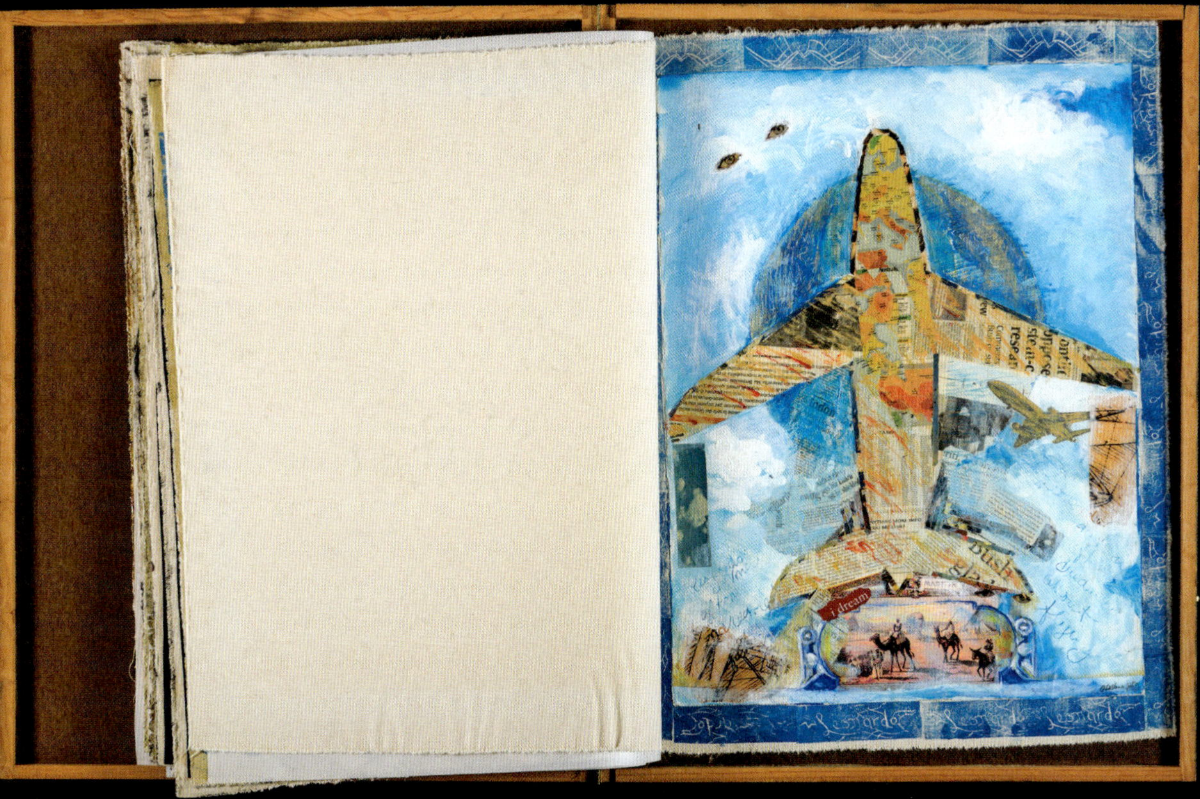

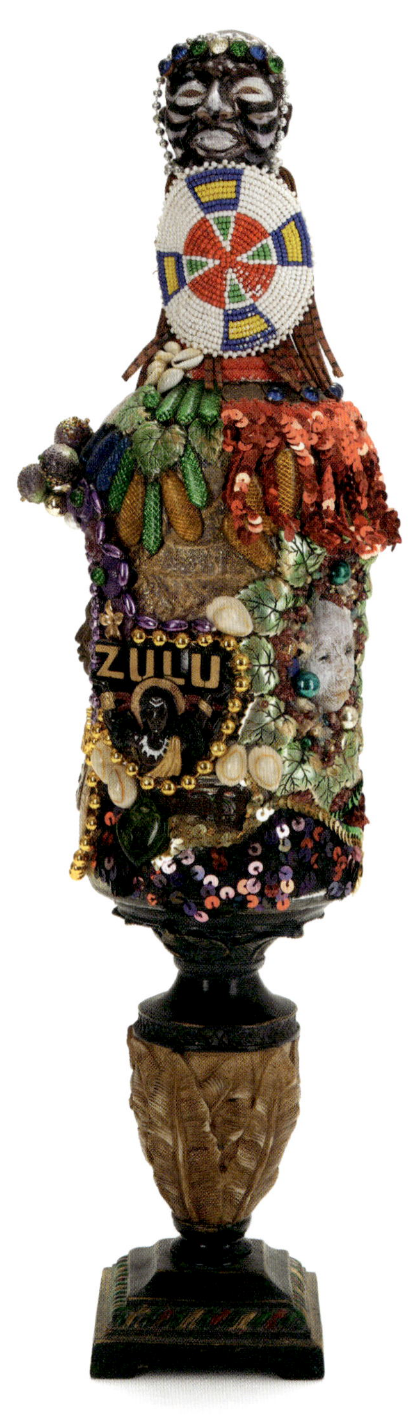

Zulu, 2007, sequins, beads,
glass, clay, acrylic, wood

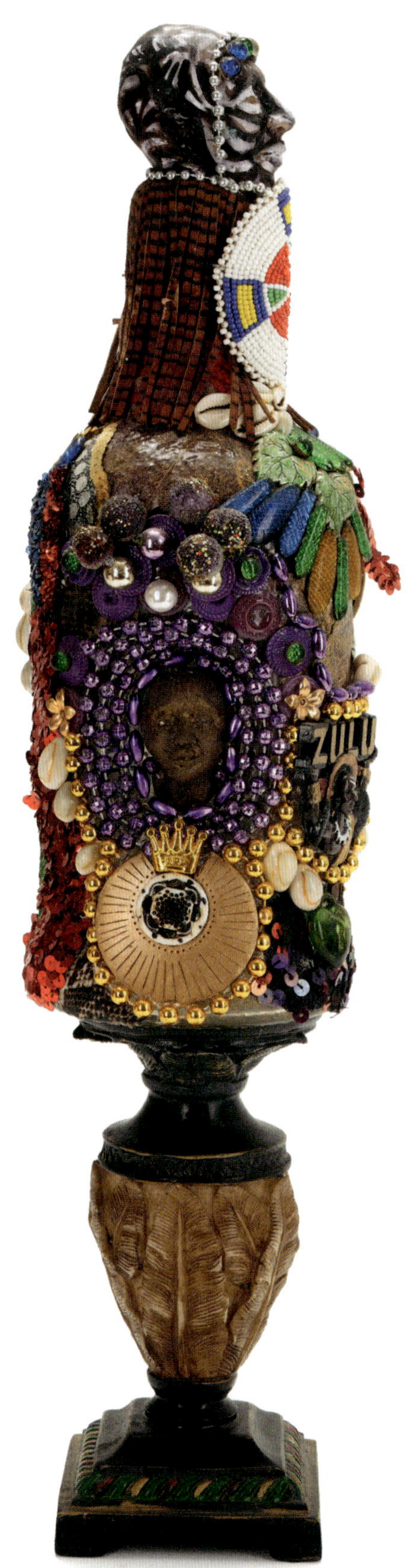

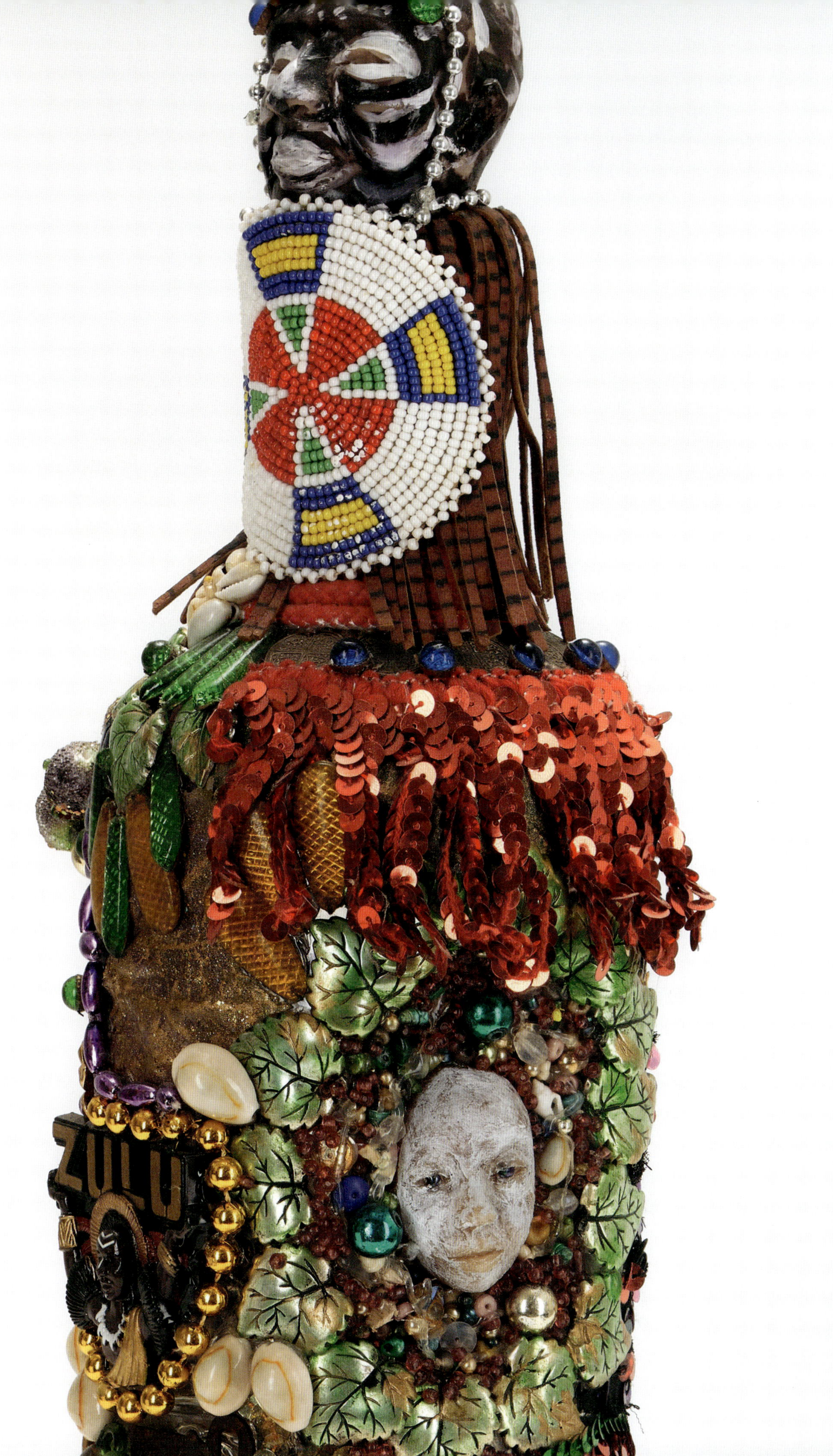

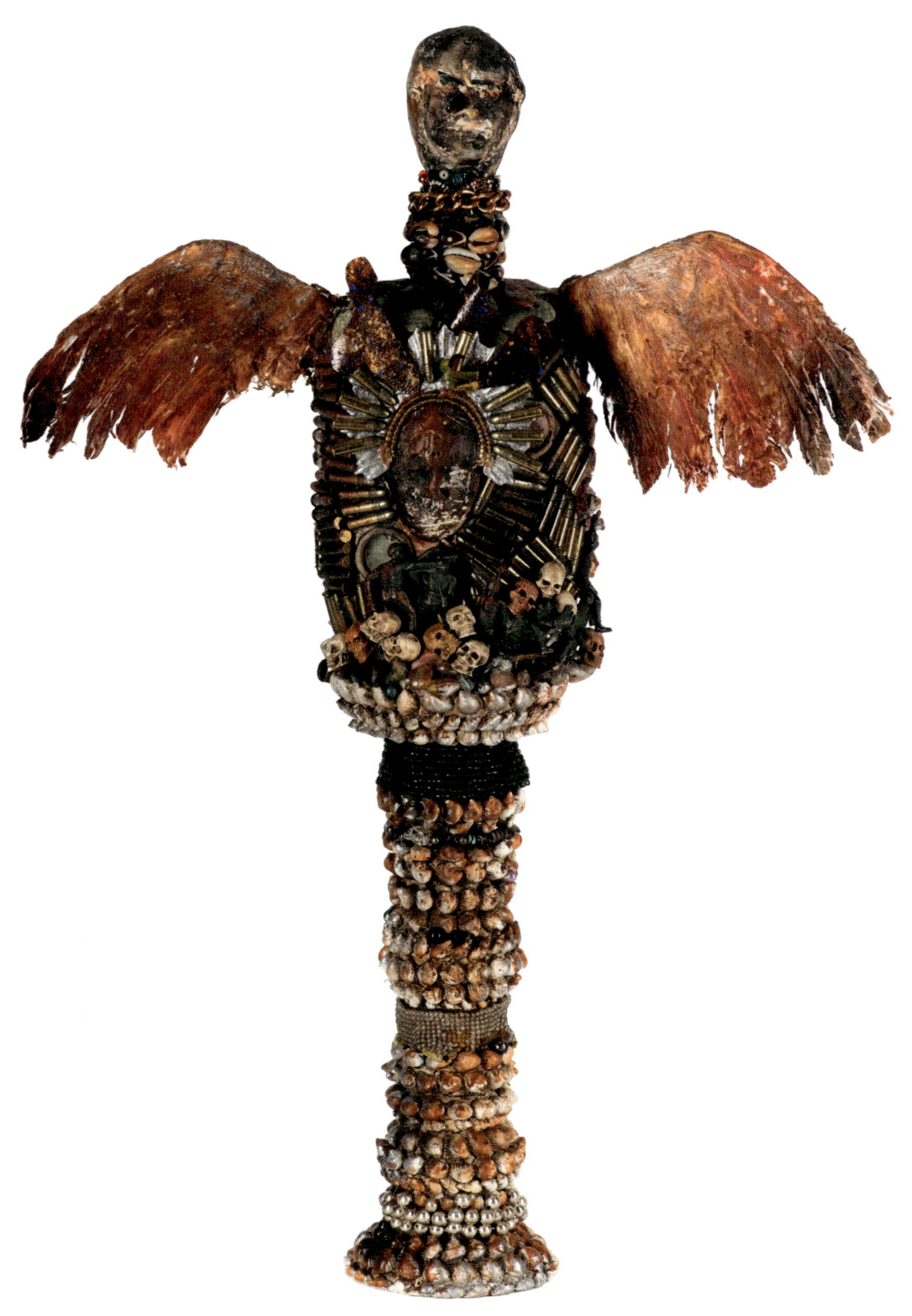

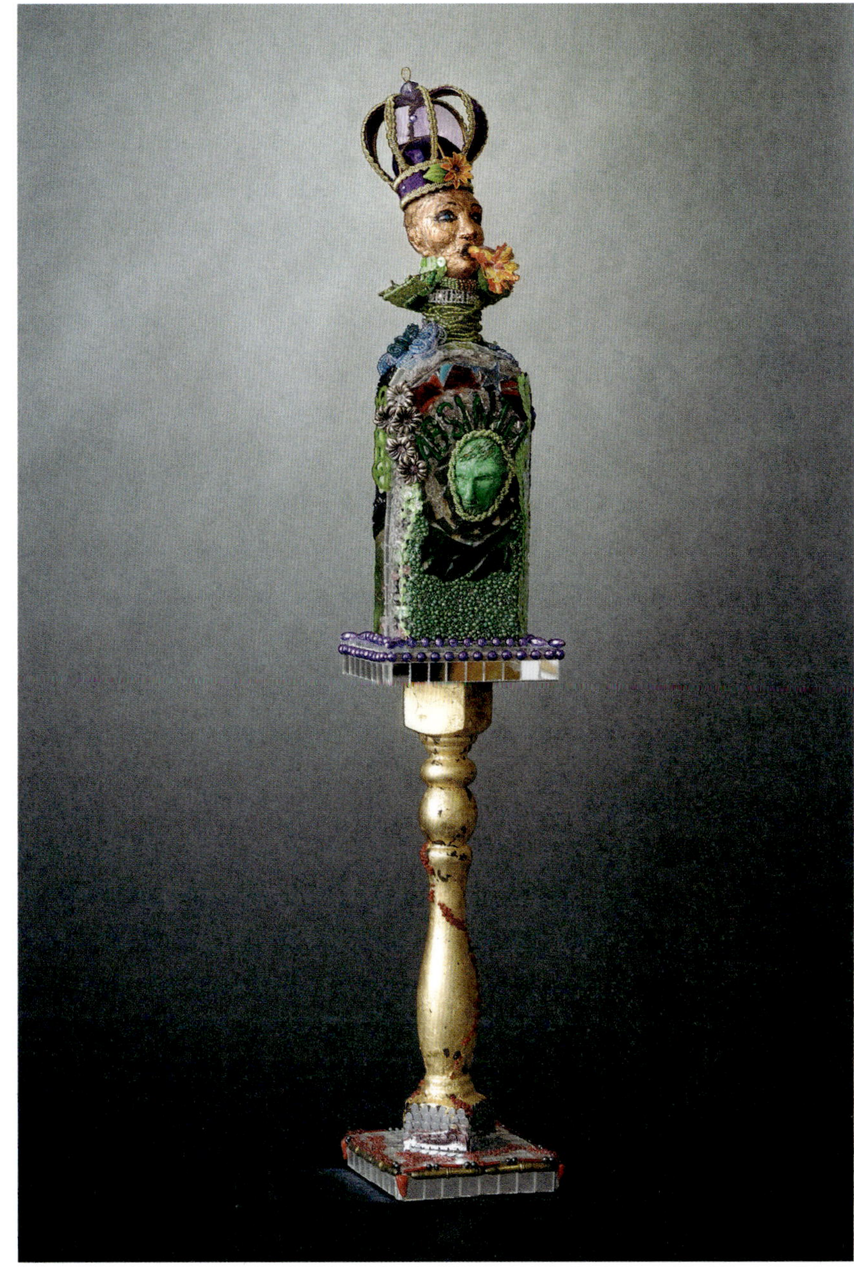

Janus, 2007, clay, glass, shell, features, bullet casings

Absinthe, 2009, nails, shells, beads, fish bones, glass, painted clay, toy soldiers, wood, paint, twine, encaustic

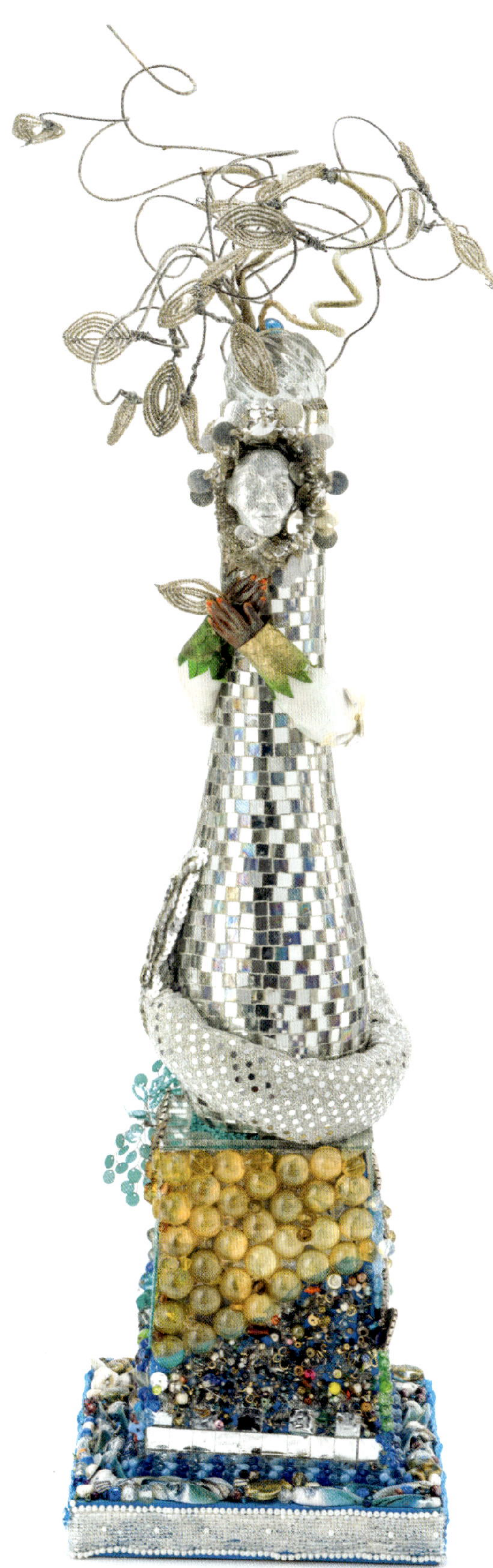

Siren (Mami Wata), 2011, glass, metal, shells, beads, clay, string, metal wire, silver fabric

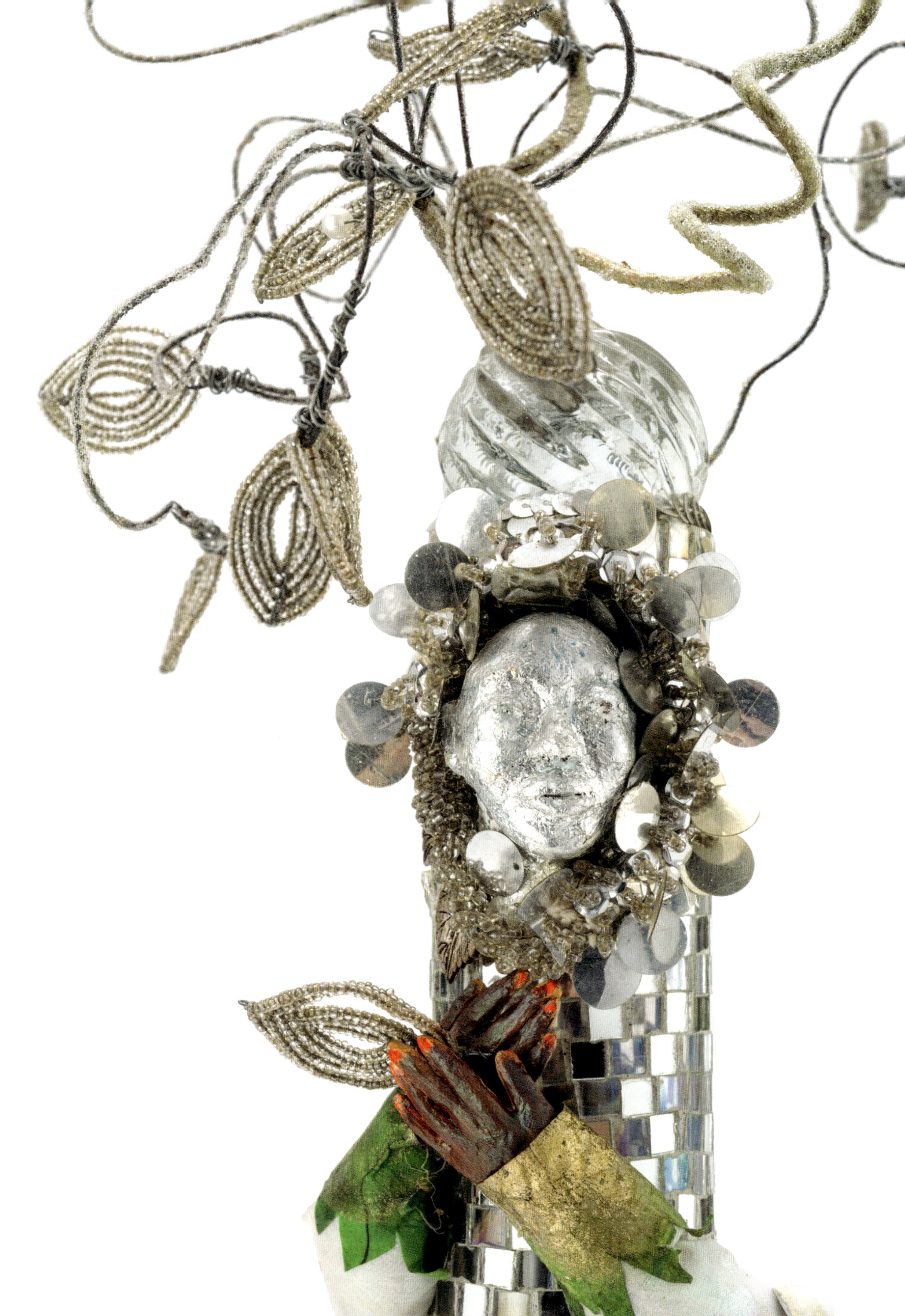

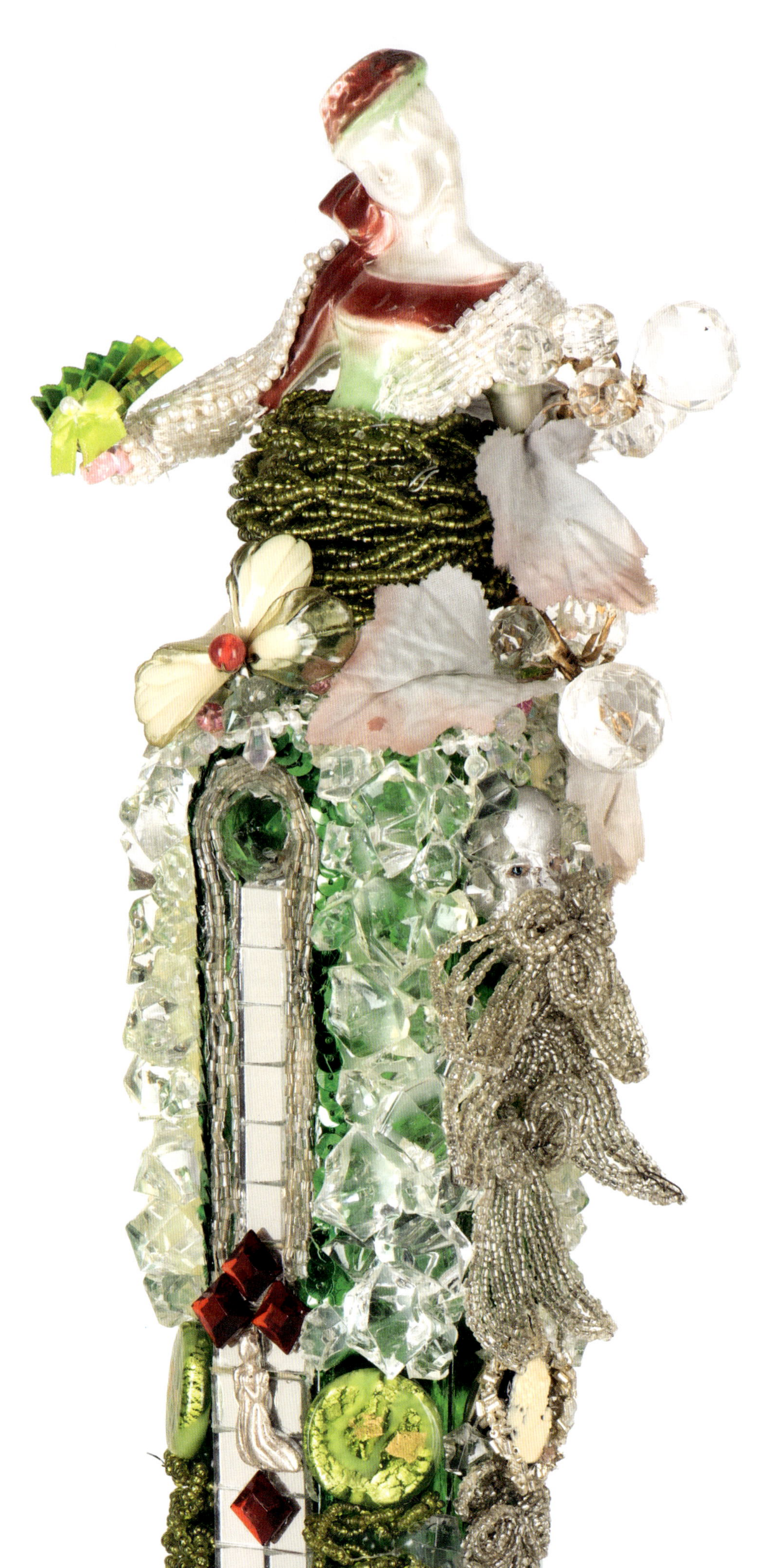

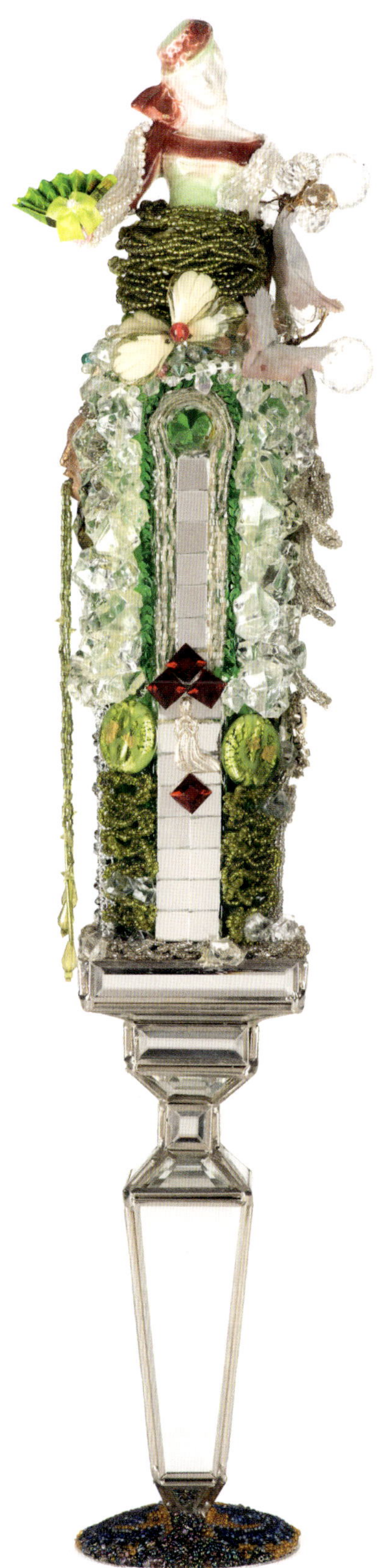

A Lady of Means, 2010, glass,
beads, ceramic

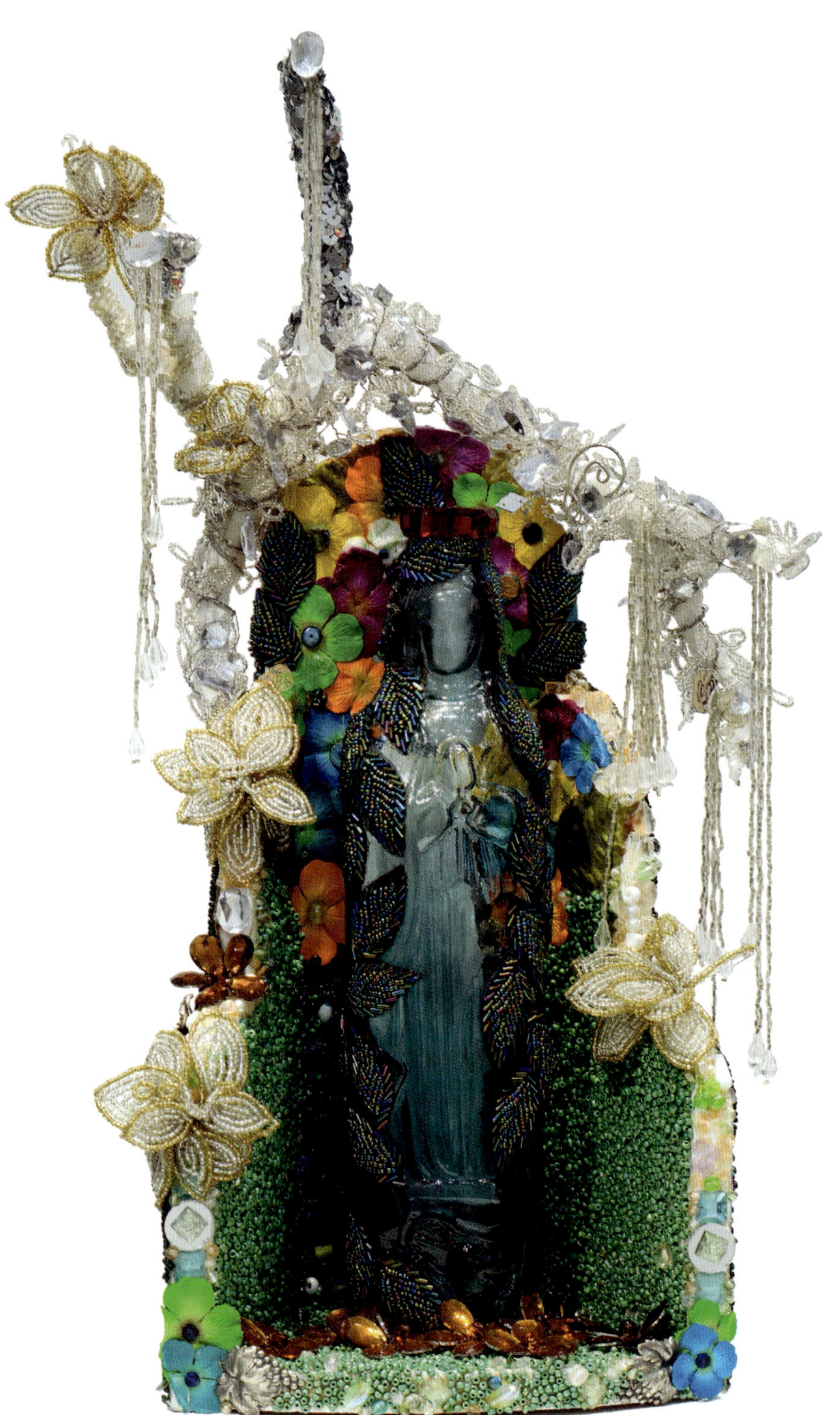

Isis/Virgin, 2010, wood, beads, fabric, glass, metal

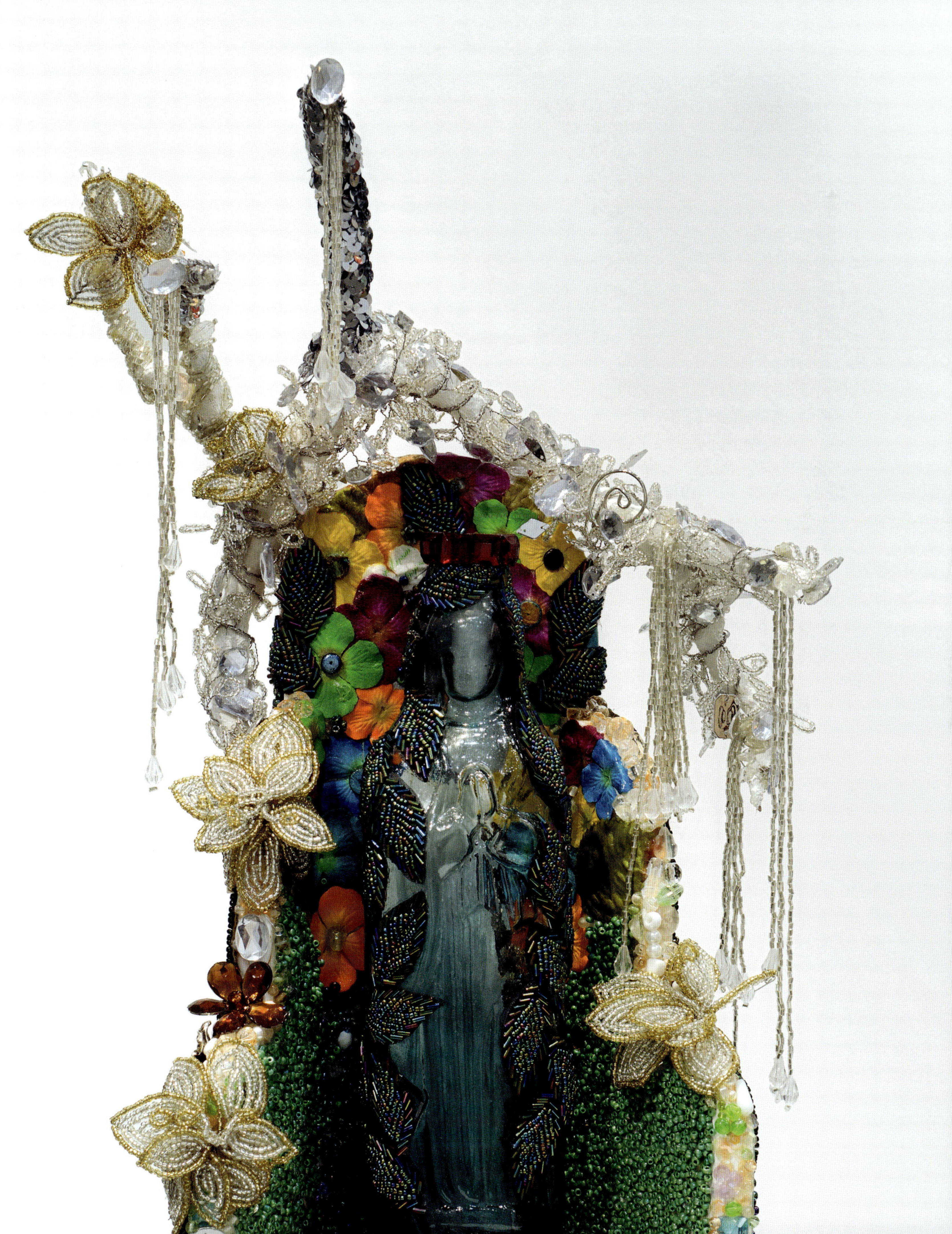

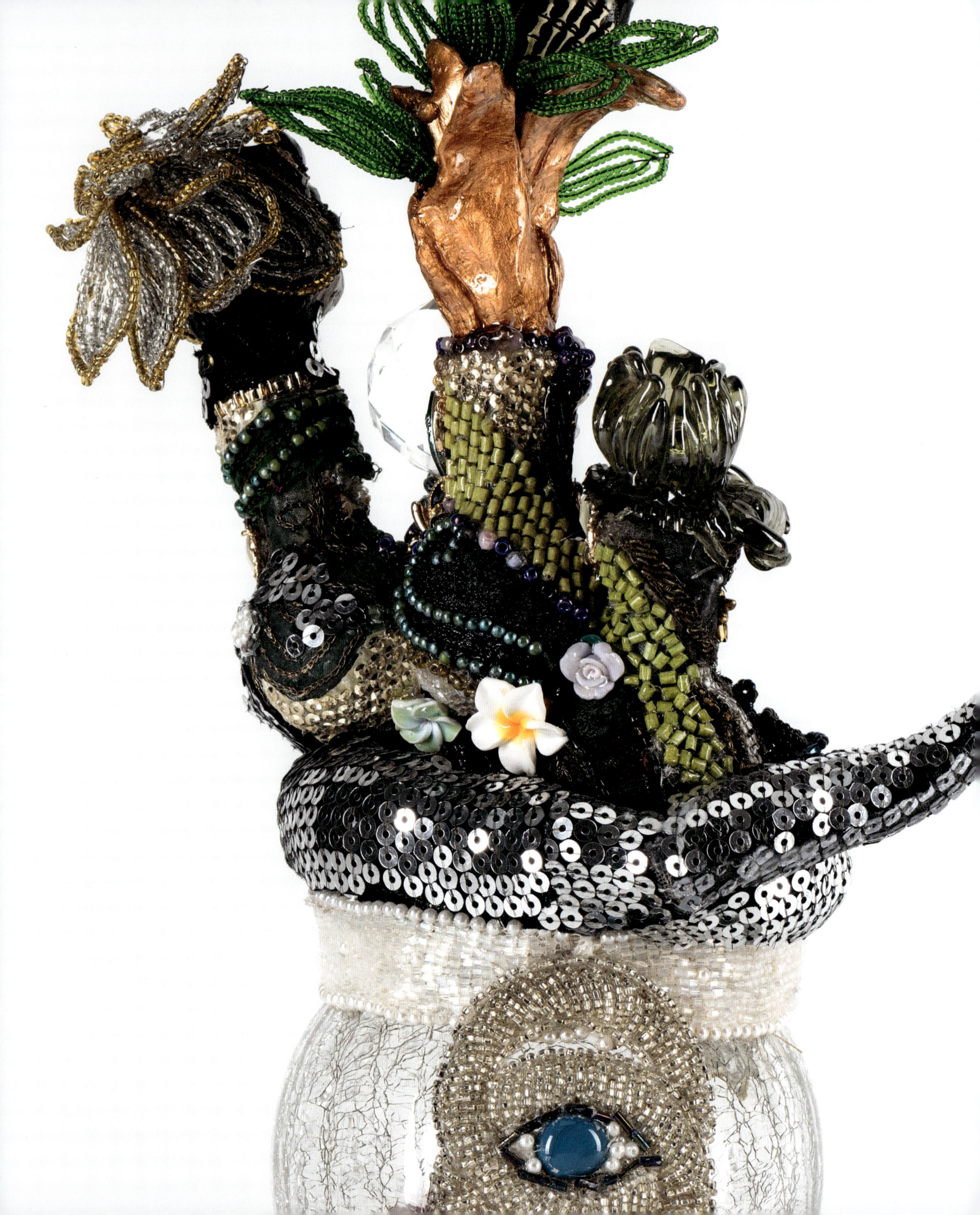

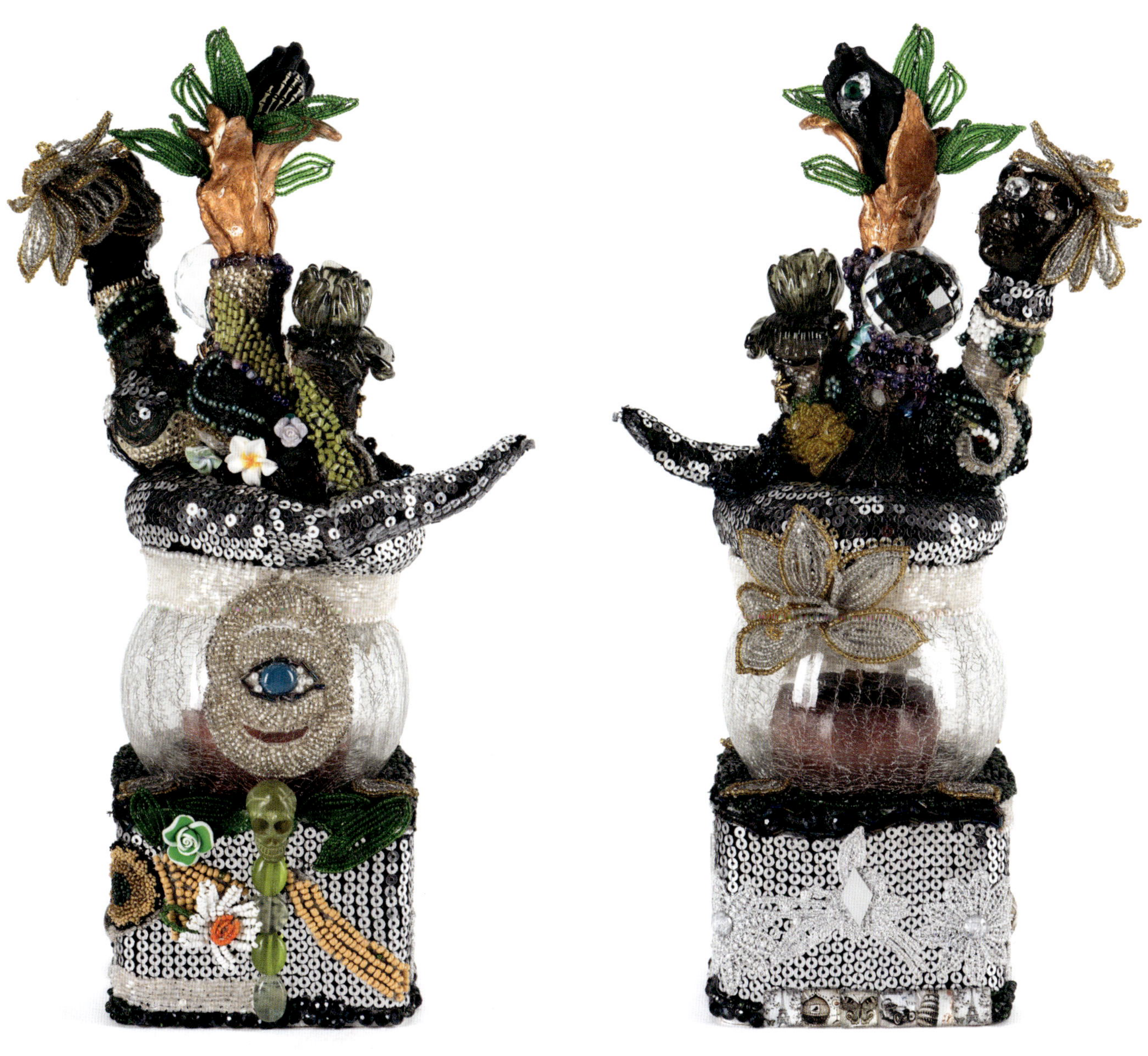

Garden, 2019, glass, sequins, beads, clay

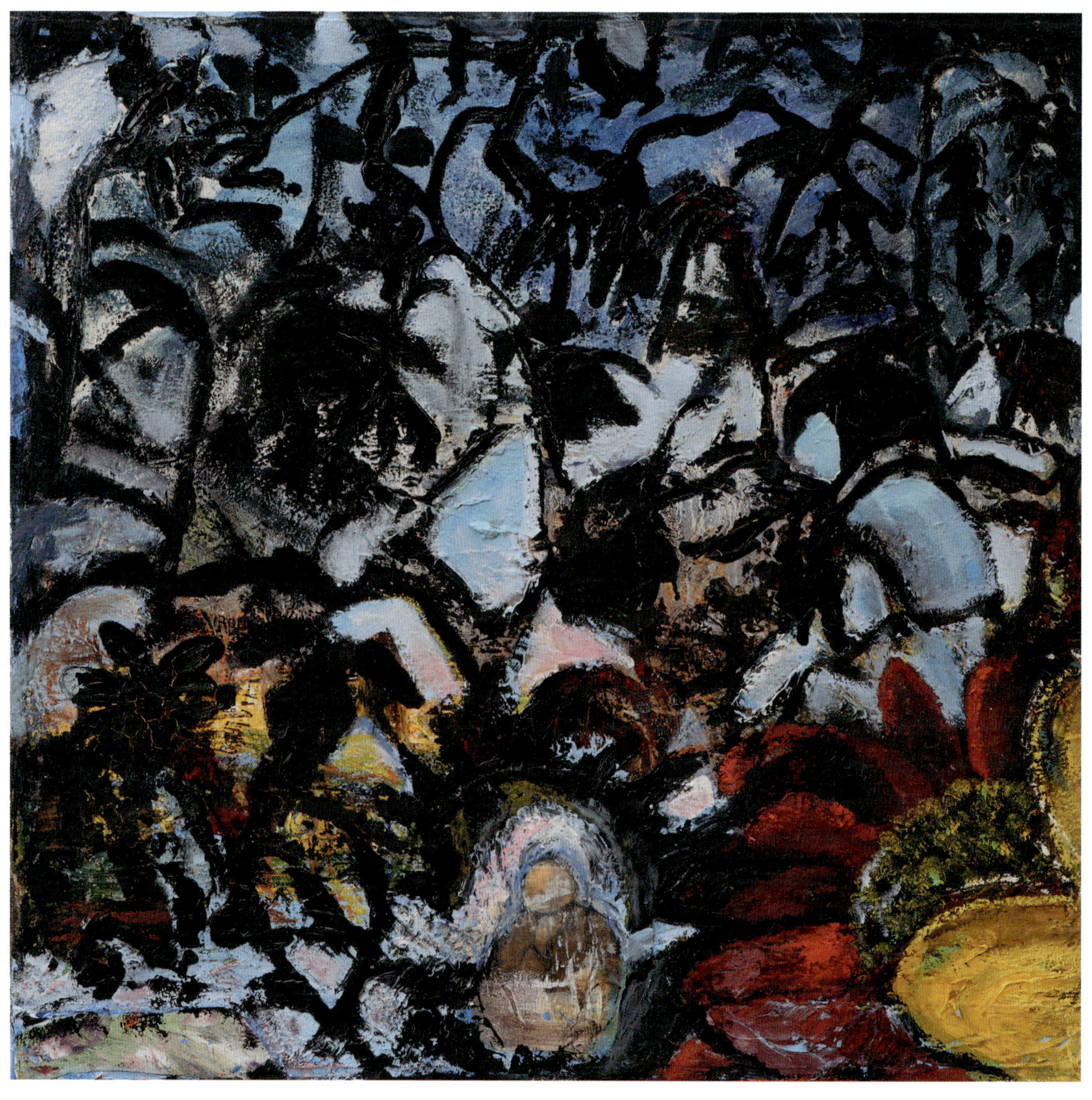

Mourning, 2003, acrylic
and oil on canvas

On the Hill, 2003, acrylic
and oil on canvas

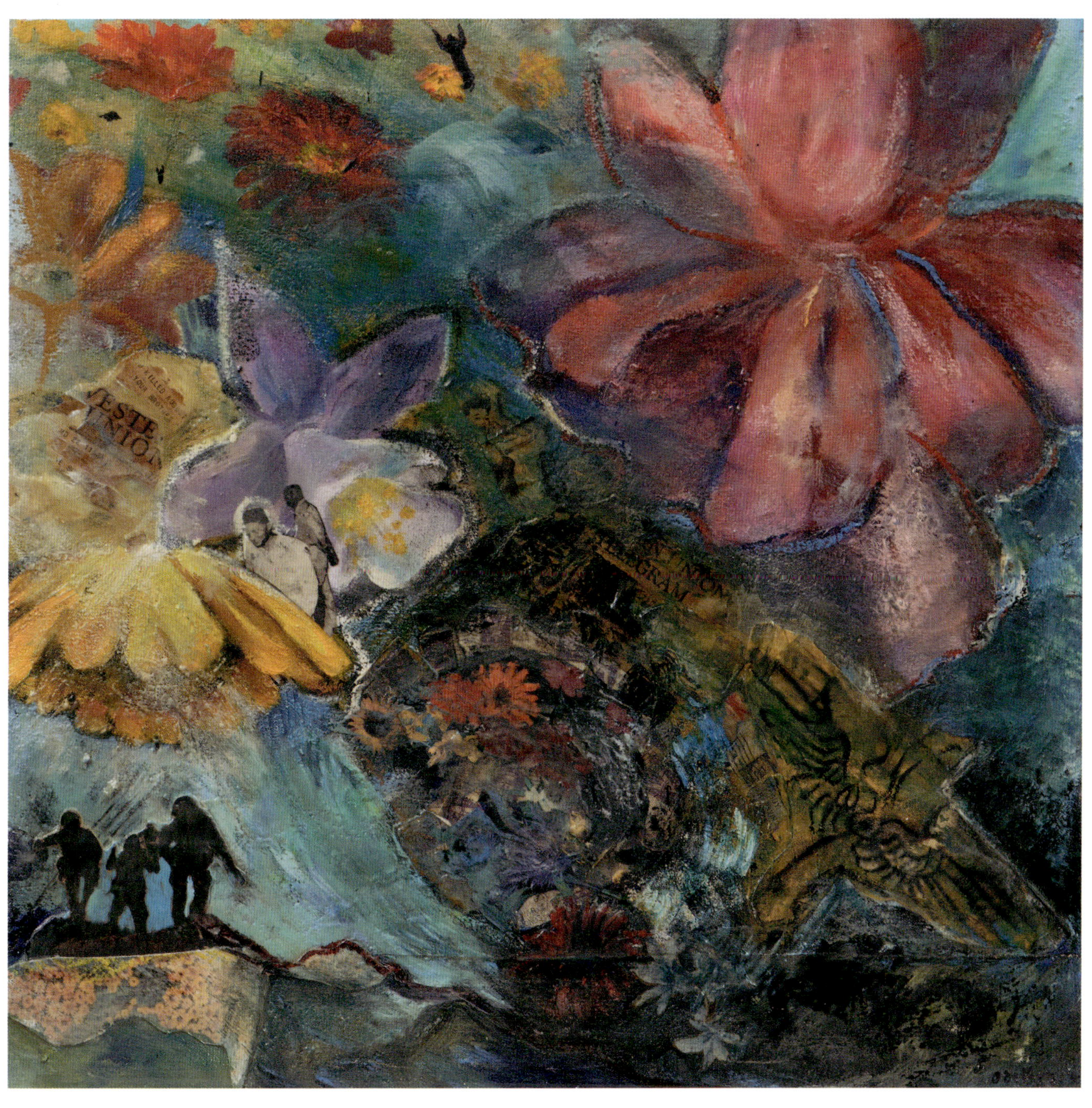

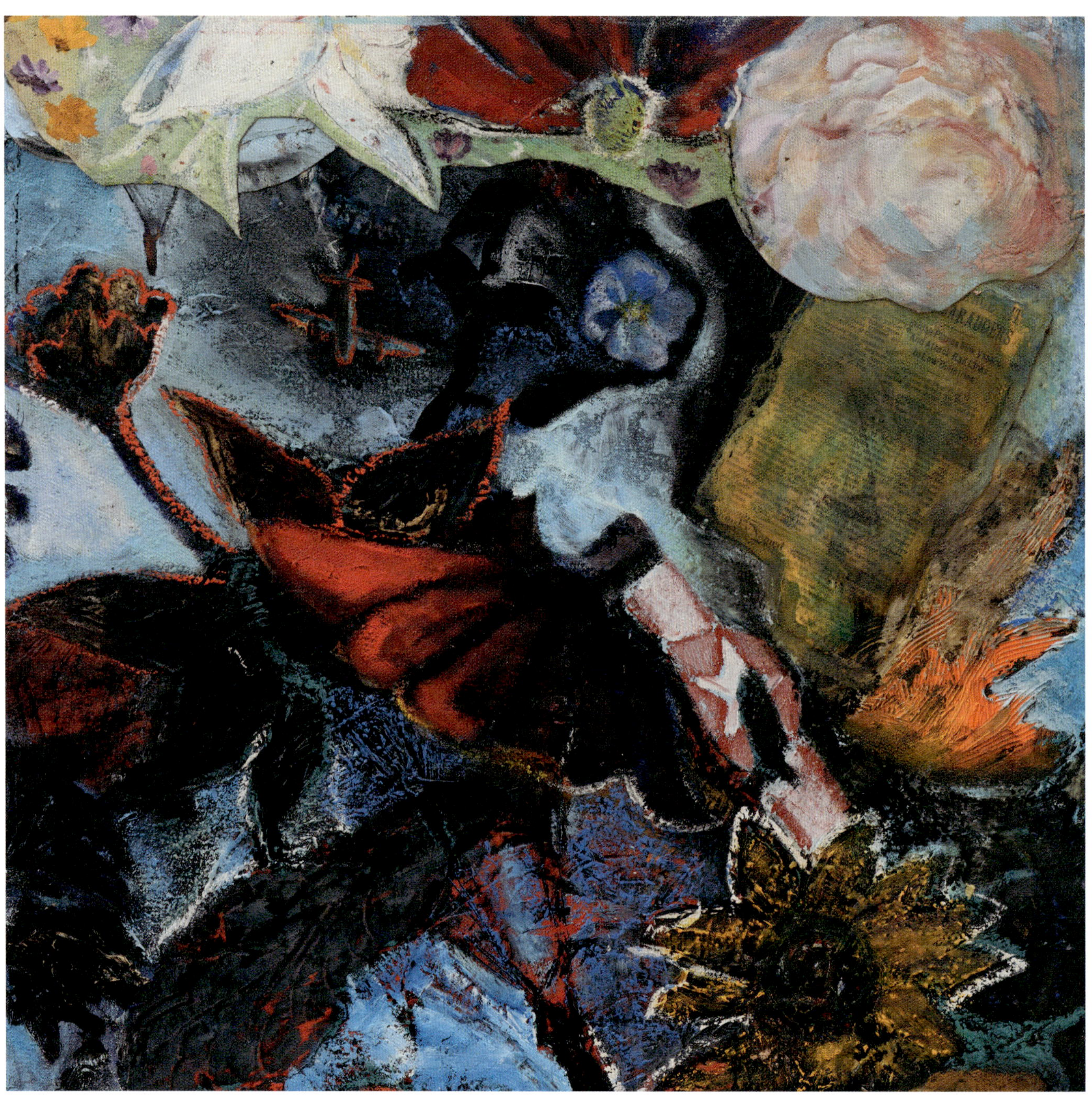

Red Tails (Tuskegee Airman Series), 2003, acrylic and oil on canvas

Wish, 2003, acrylic and oil on canvas

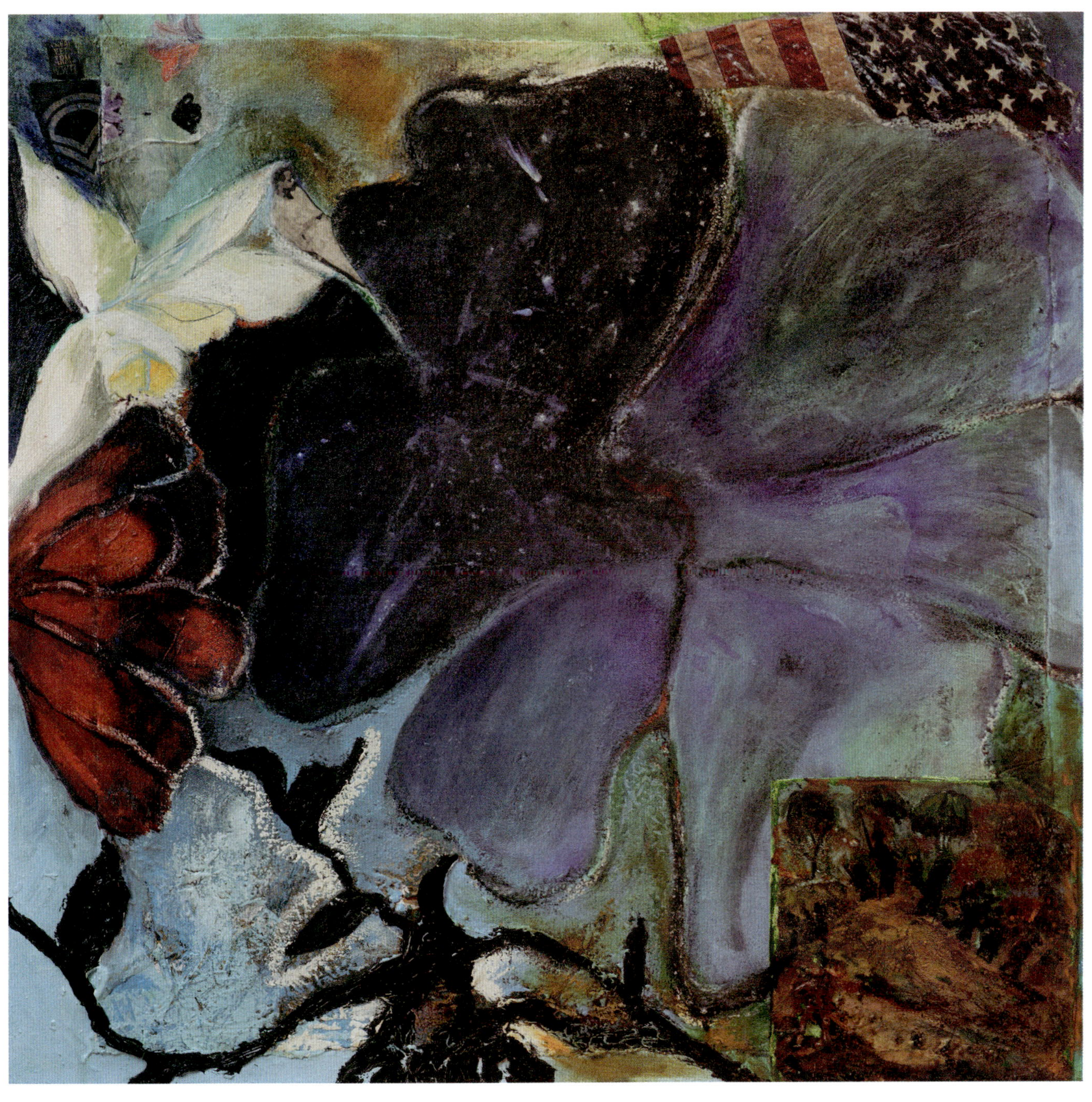

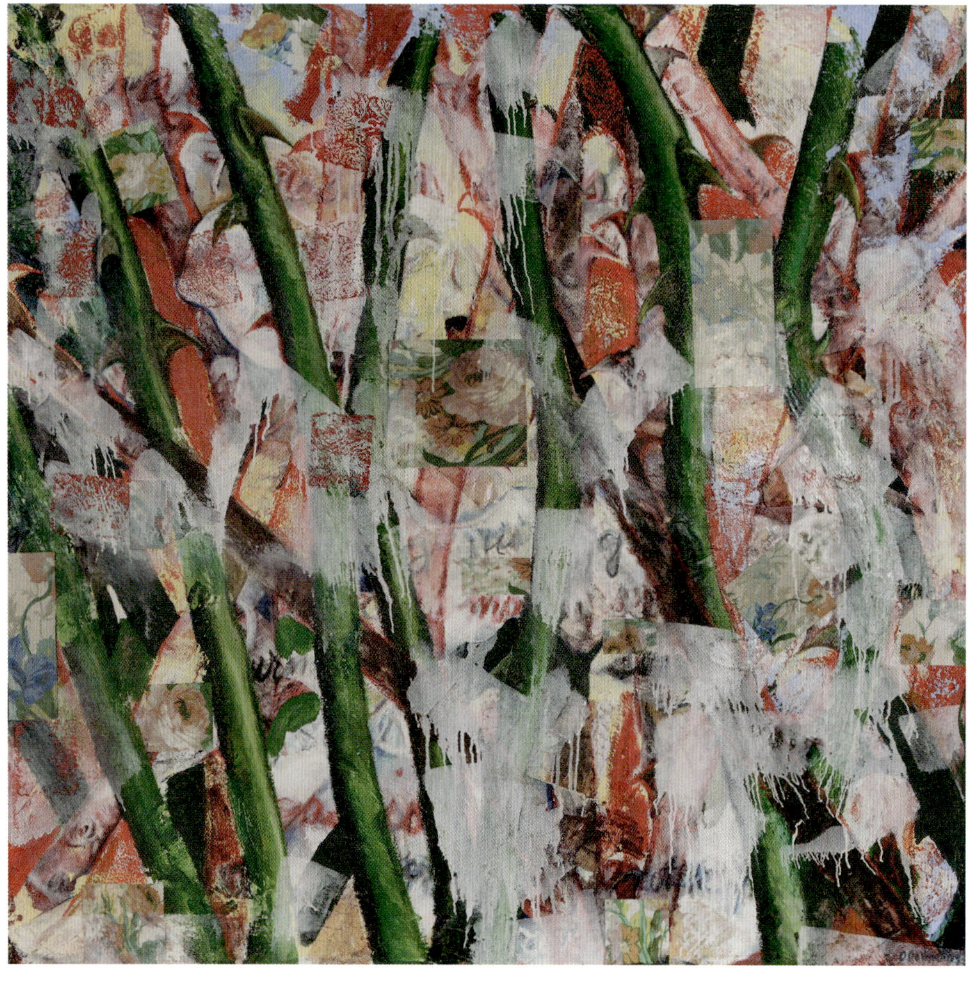

Love Letter, 2004, acrylic, oil,
and paper on canvas

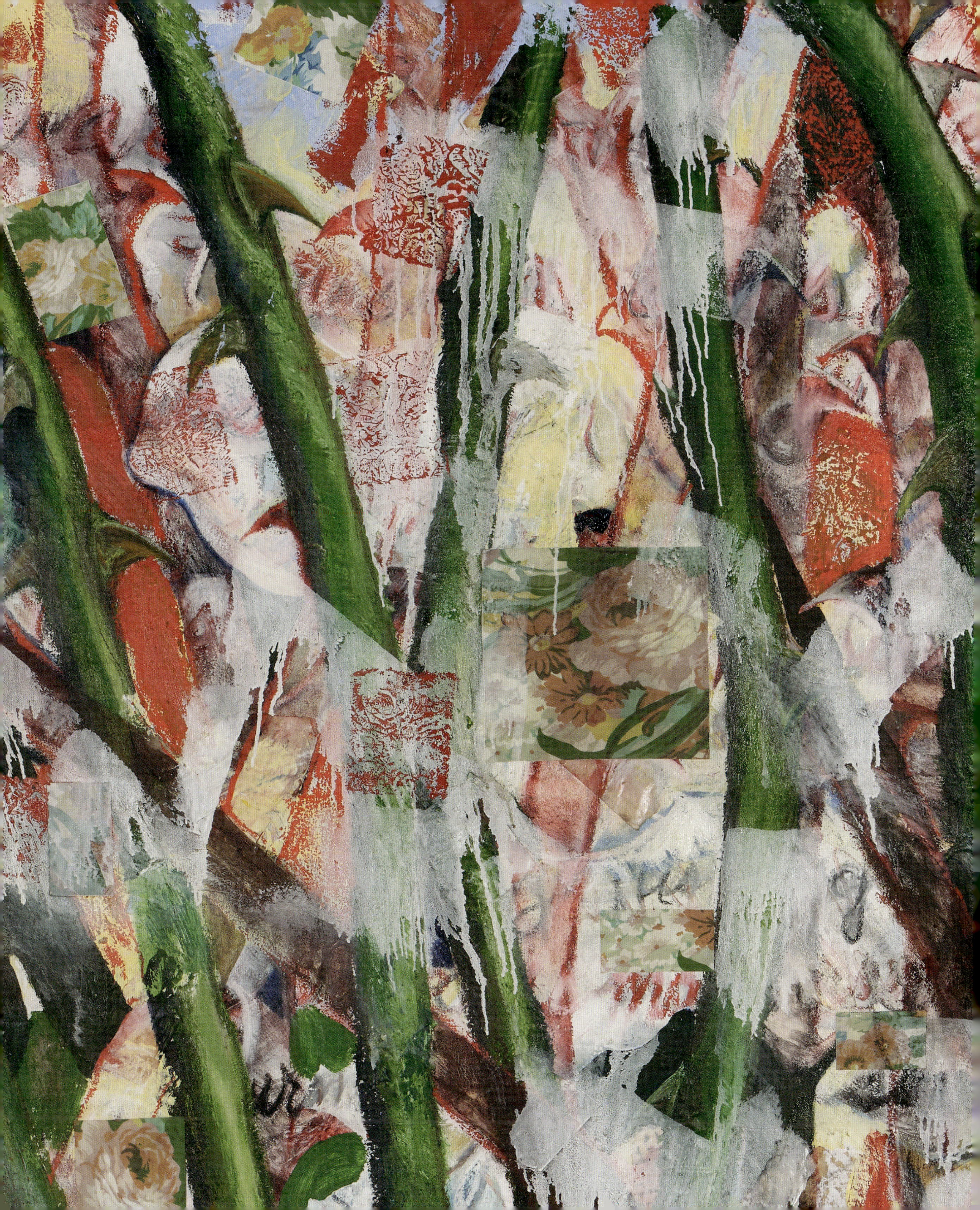

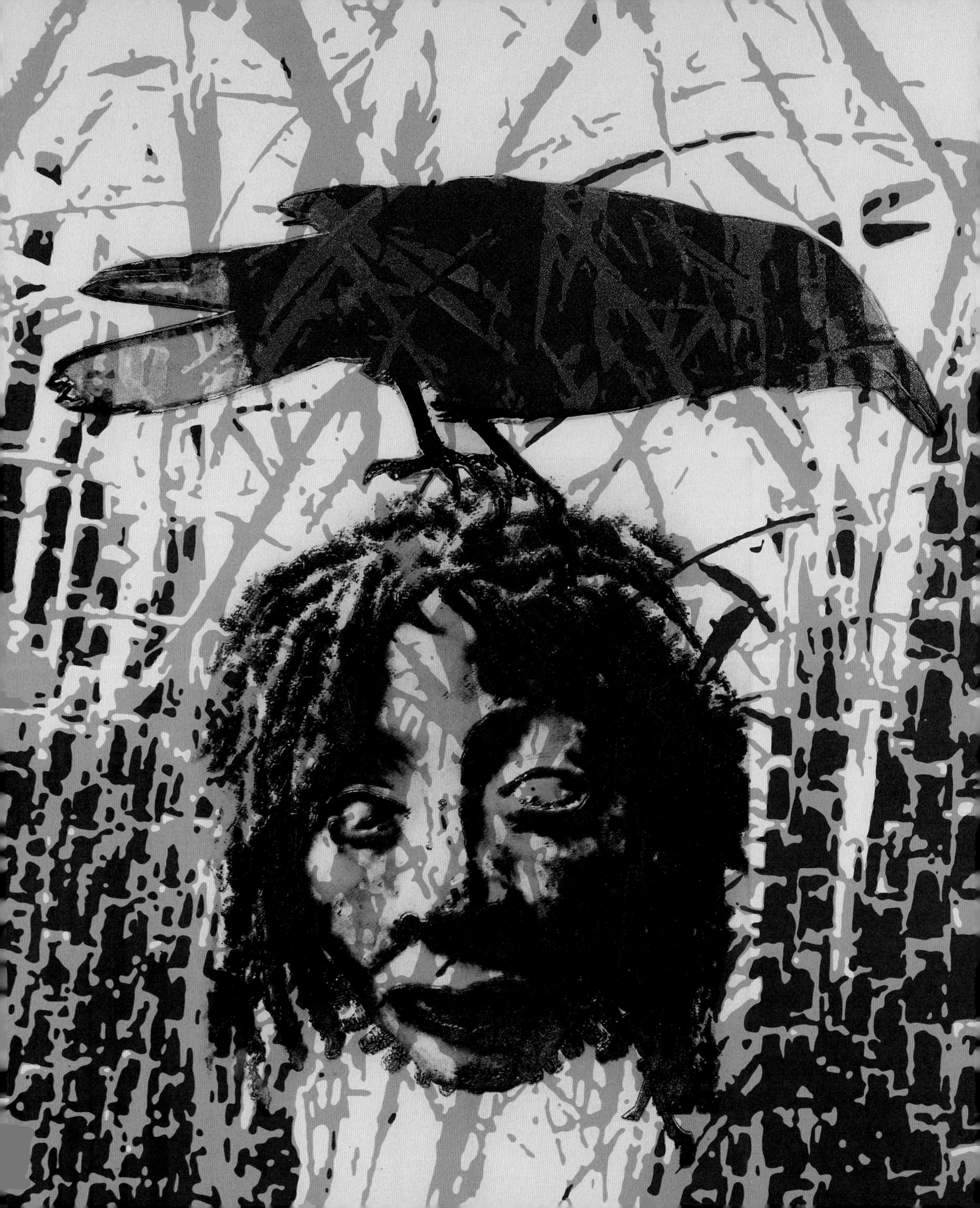

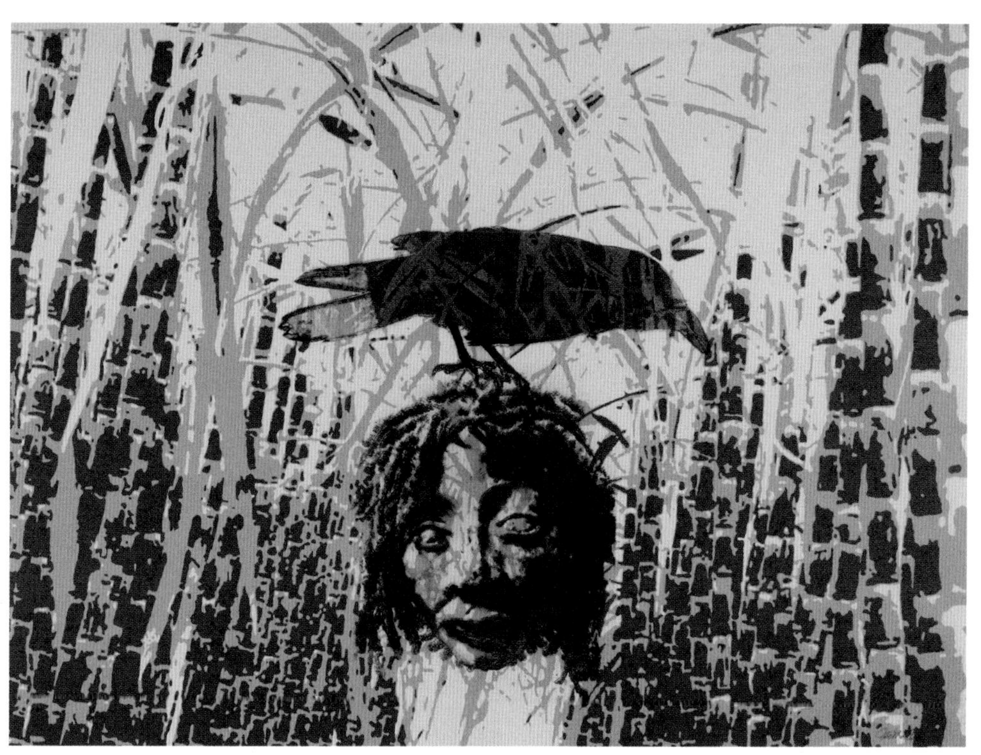

Sugarcane Blues, 2020,
solar and digital
etching on Rives paper

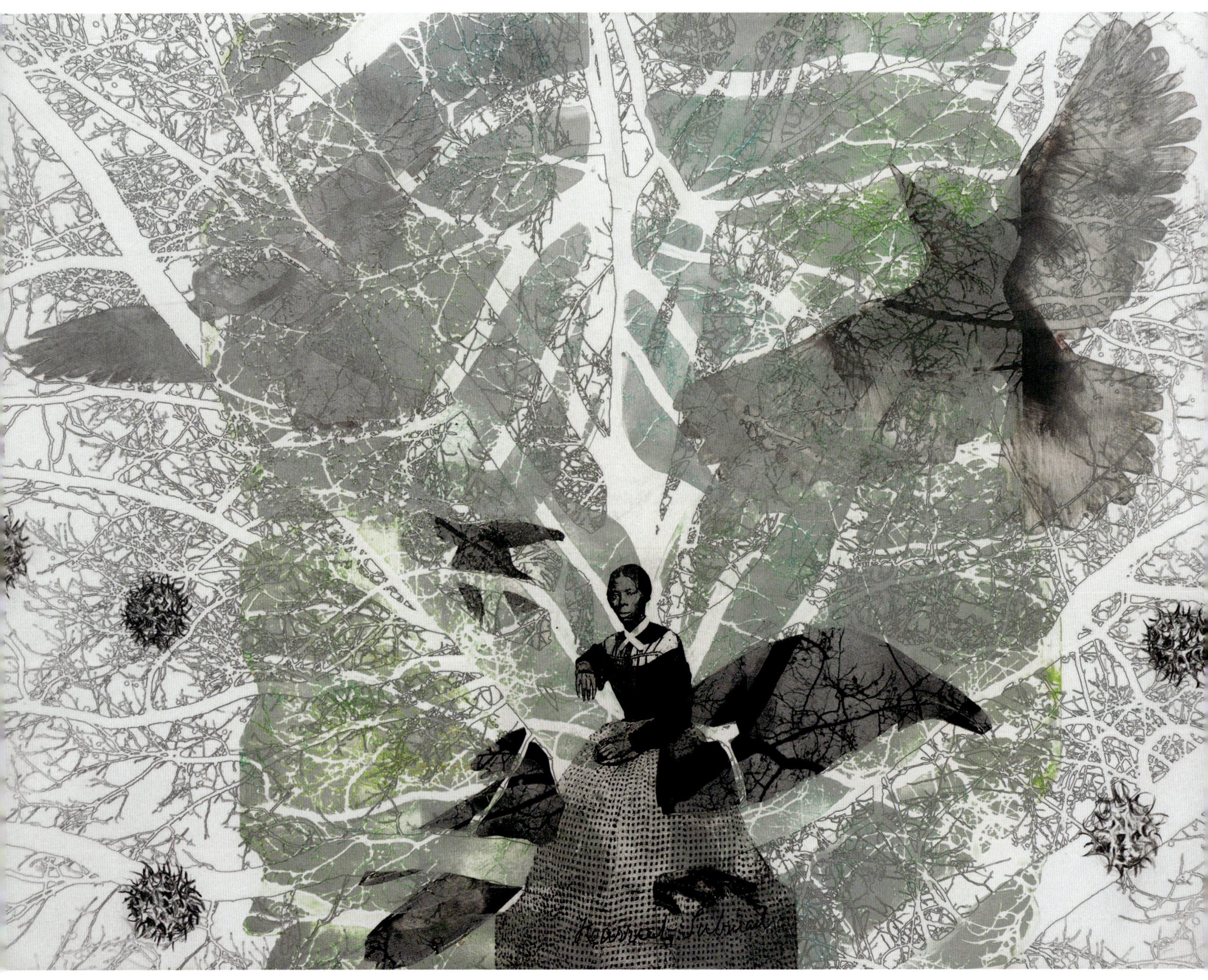

Harriet the Raven, 2019,
digital media, solar etching,
and graphite on paper

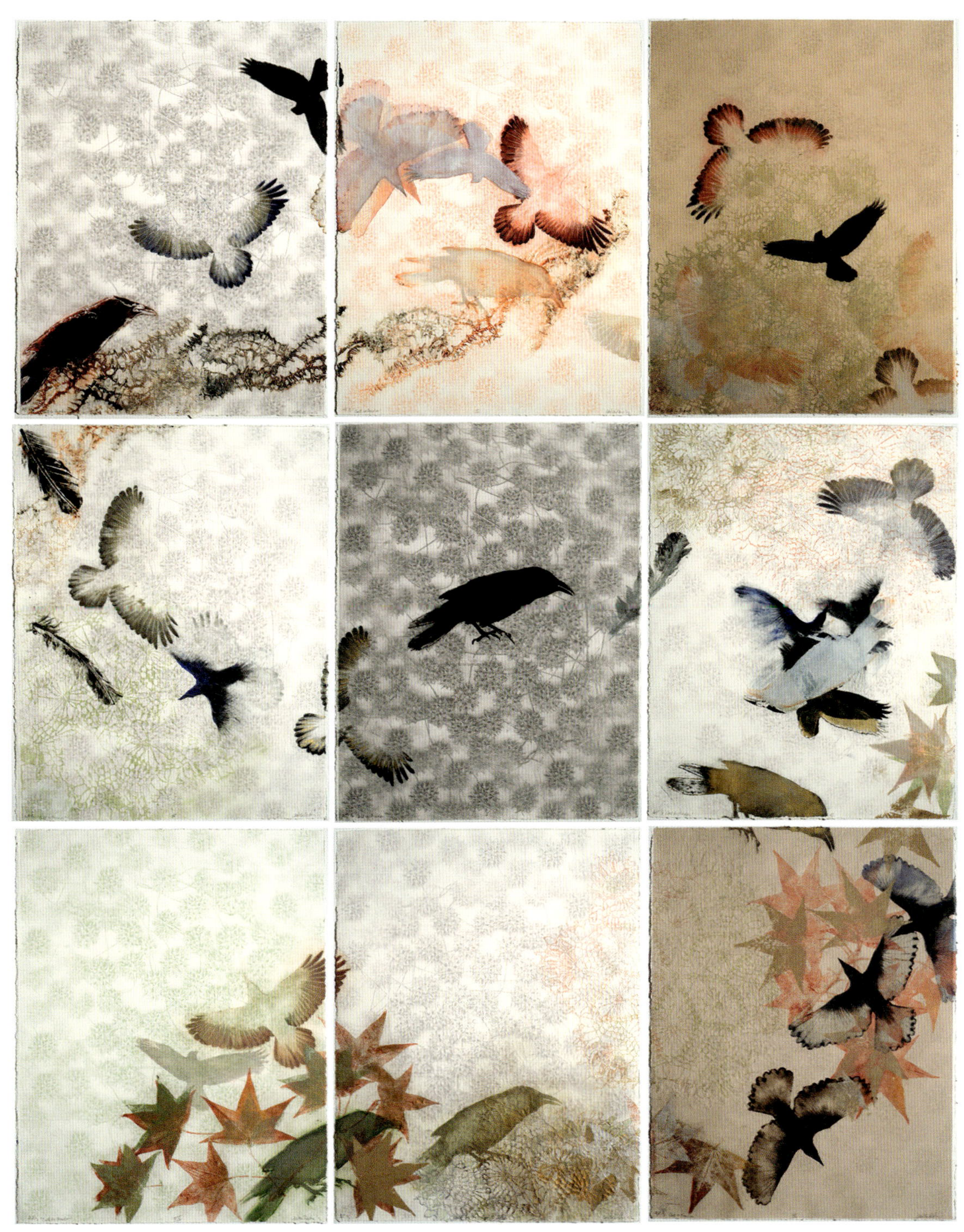

Call to Freedom, 2012,
9 screen prints

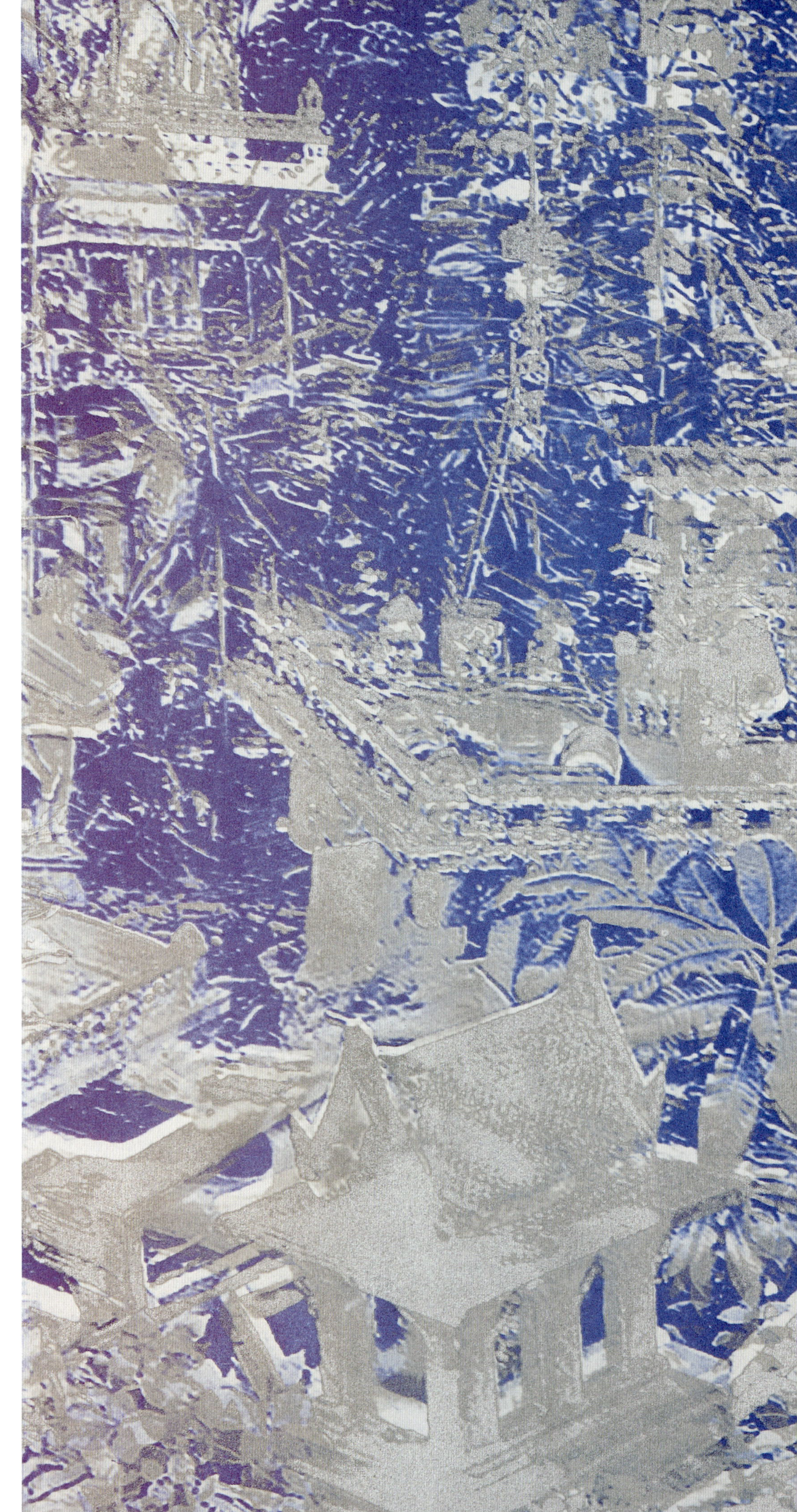

Thai Spirit House, 2013,
solar etching

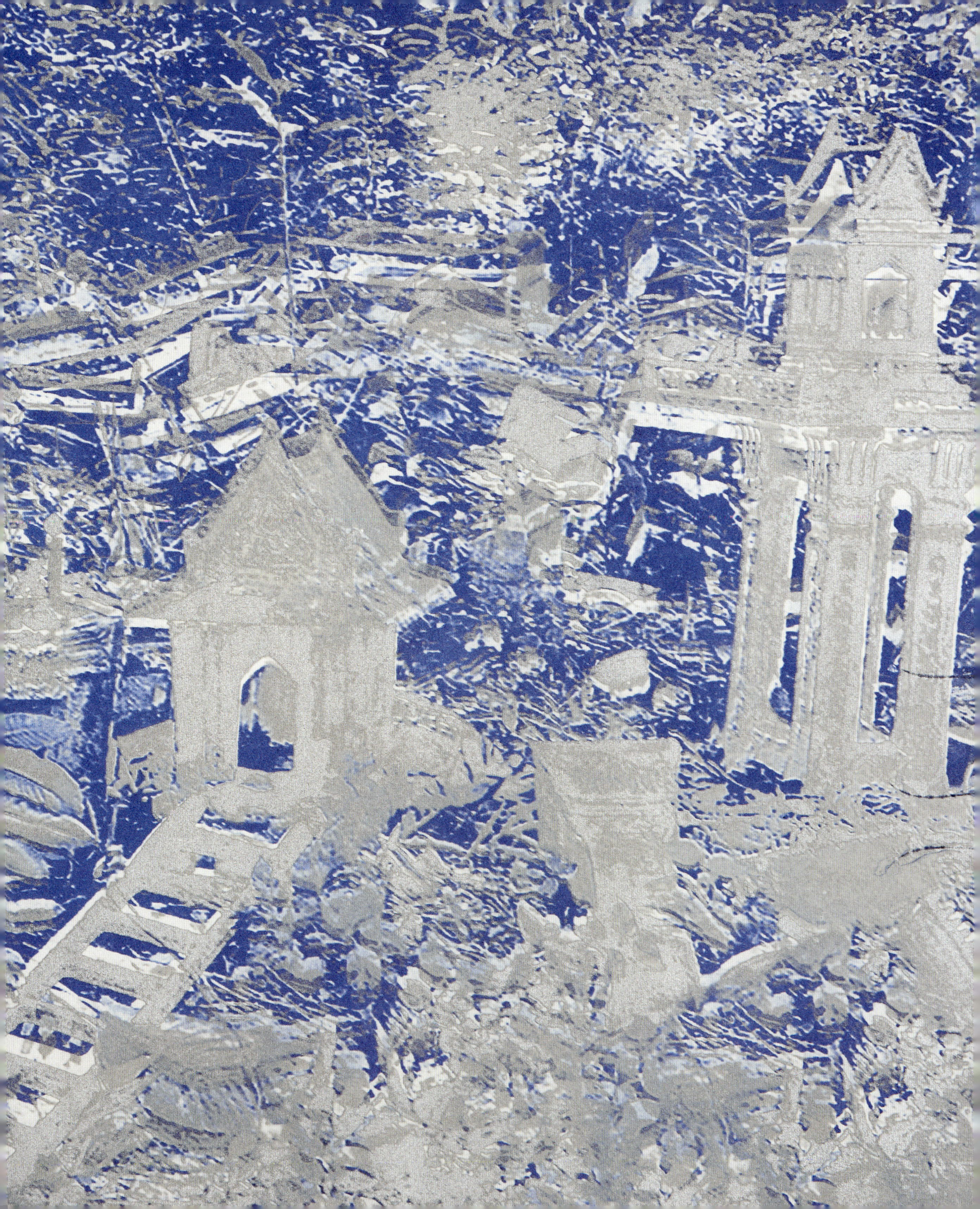

Garden, 2015, encaustic

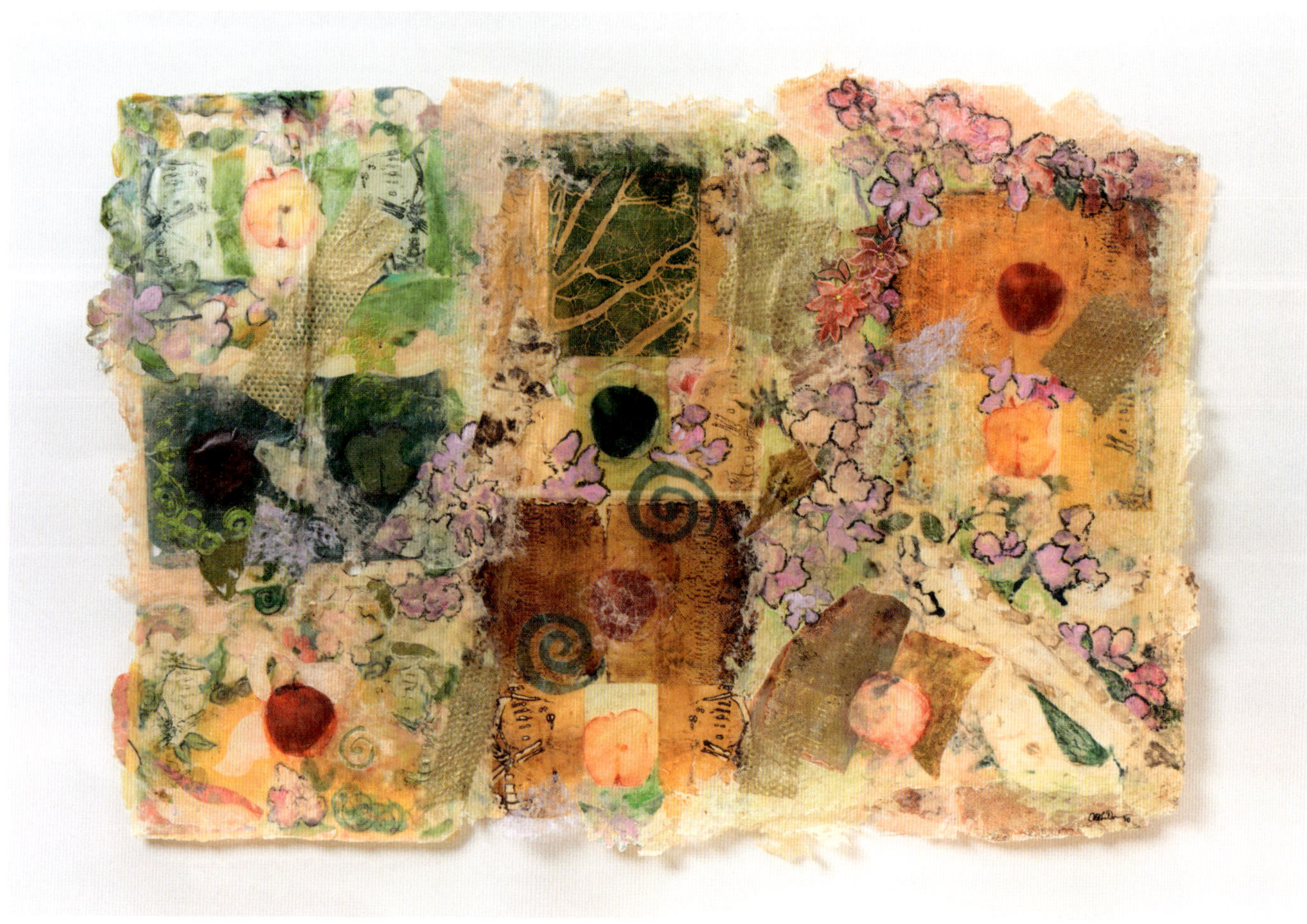

Dion'e: Searching for Self,
2016, video, 6 minutes,
33 seconds

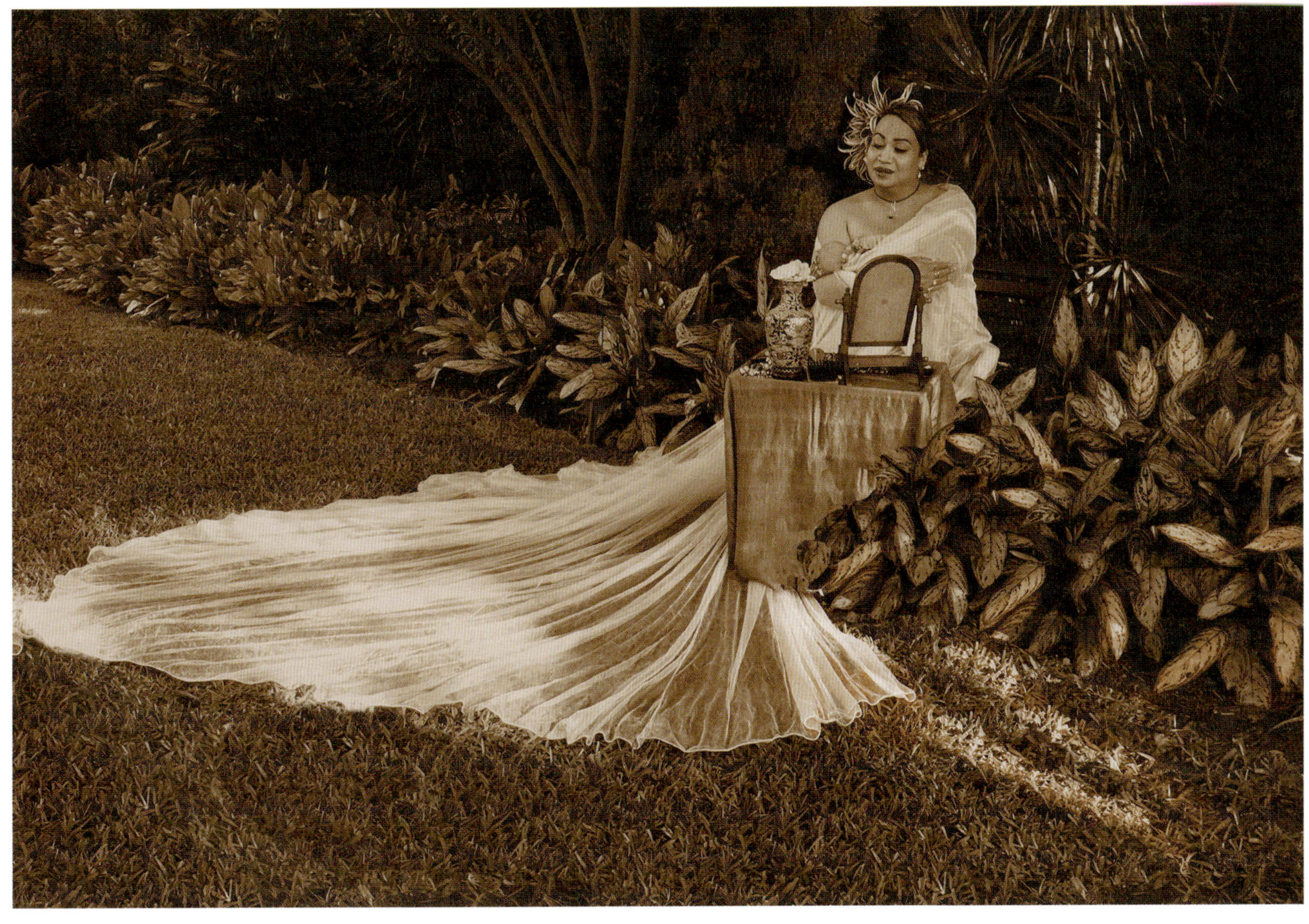

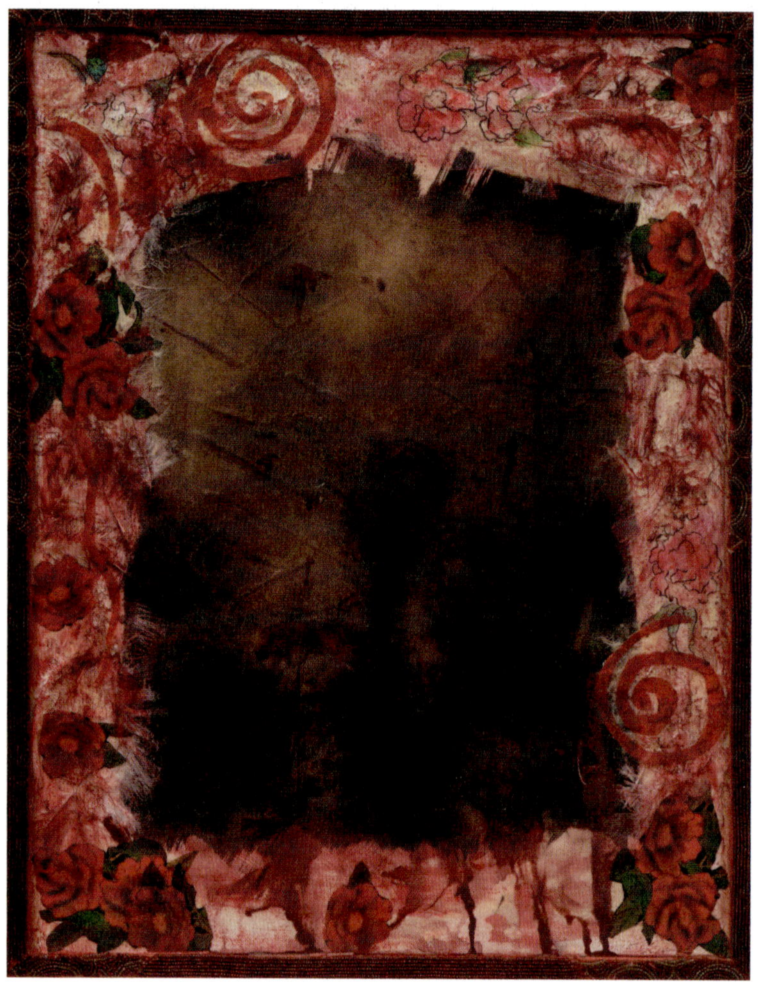 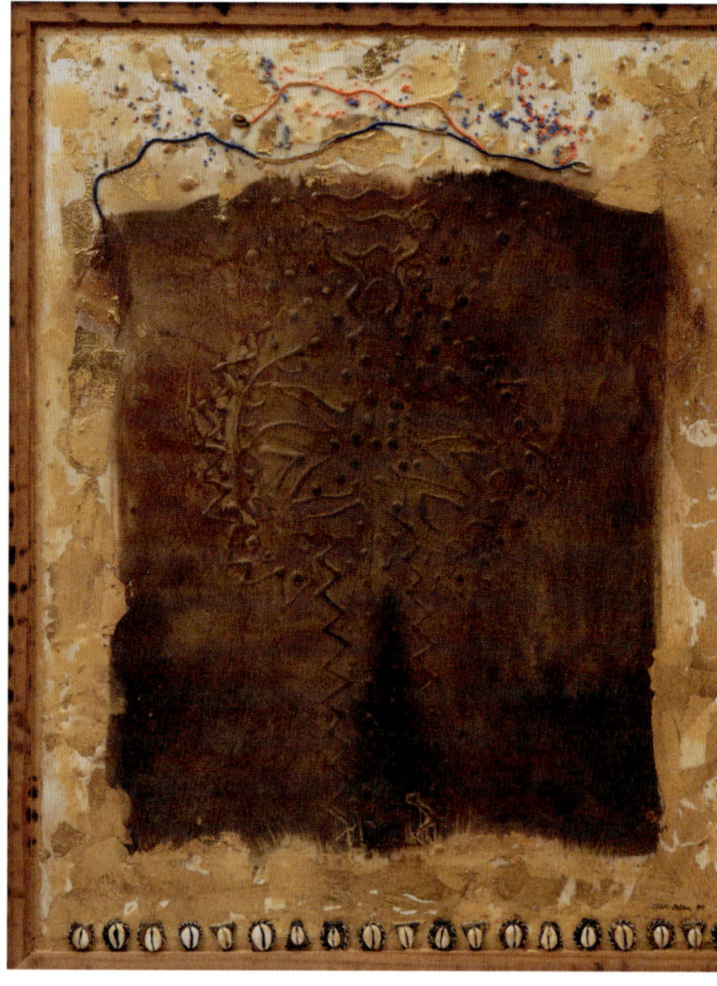

Martyr (Scarification Series),
2009, encaustic on paper

**Out of Africa (Scarification
Series)**, 2009, encaustic
and Van Dyke process on
Rives paper, with cowrie
shells, beads

**Star Map (Harriet Tubman
Series)**, 2010, Van Dyke
process and burnt marks
on Rives paper

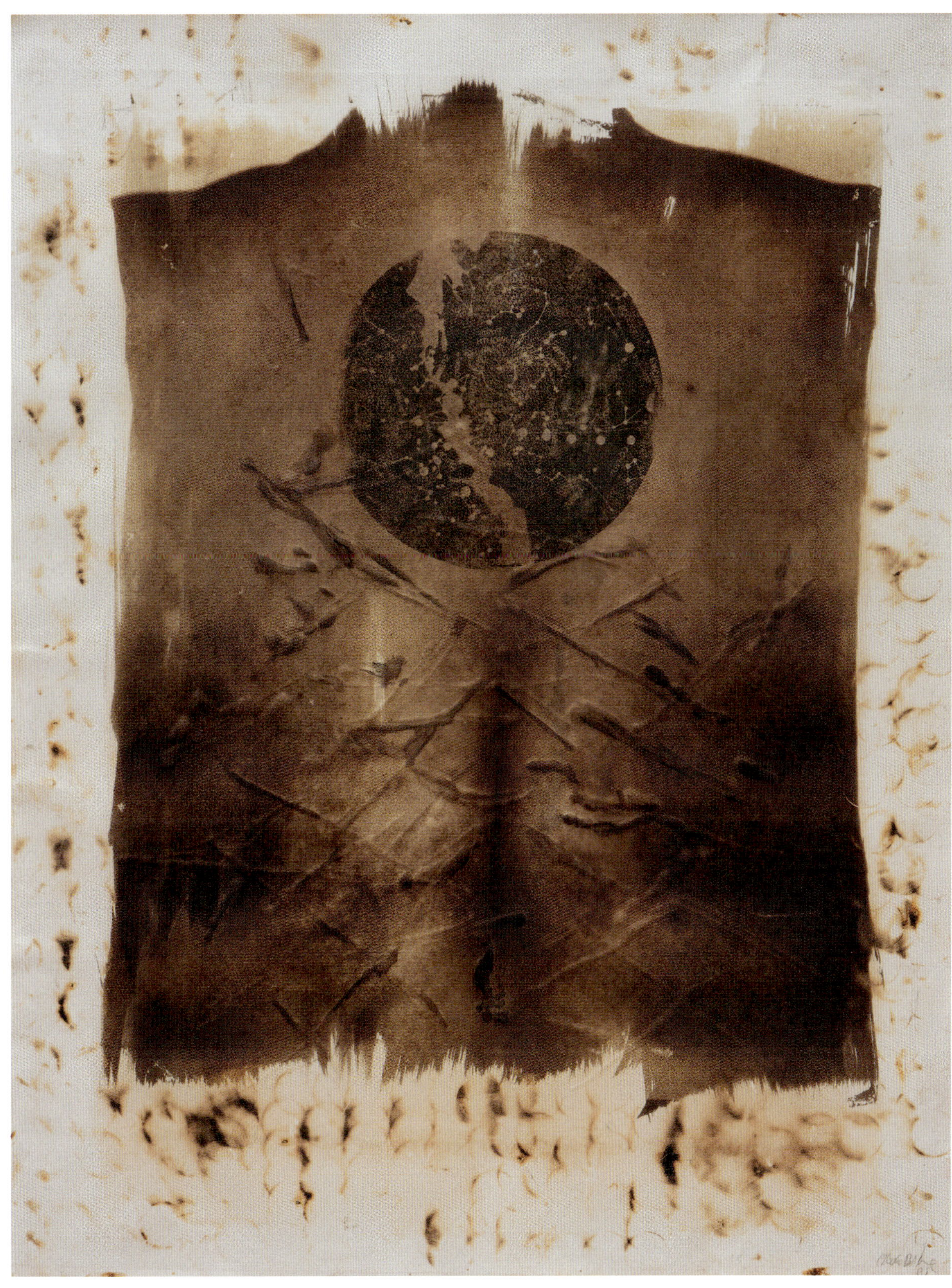

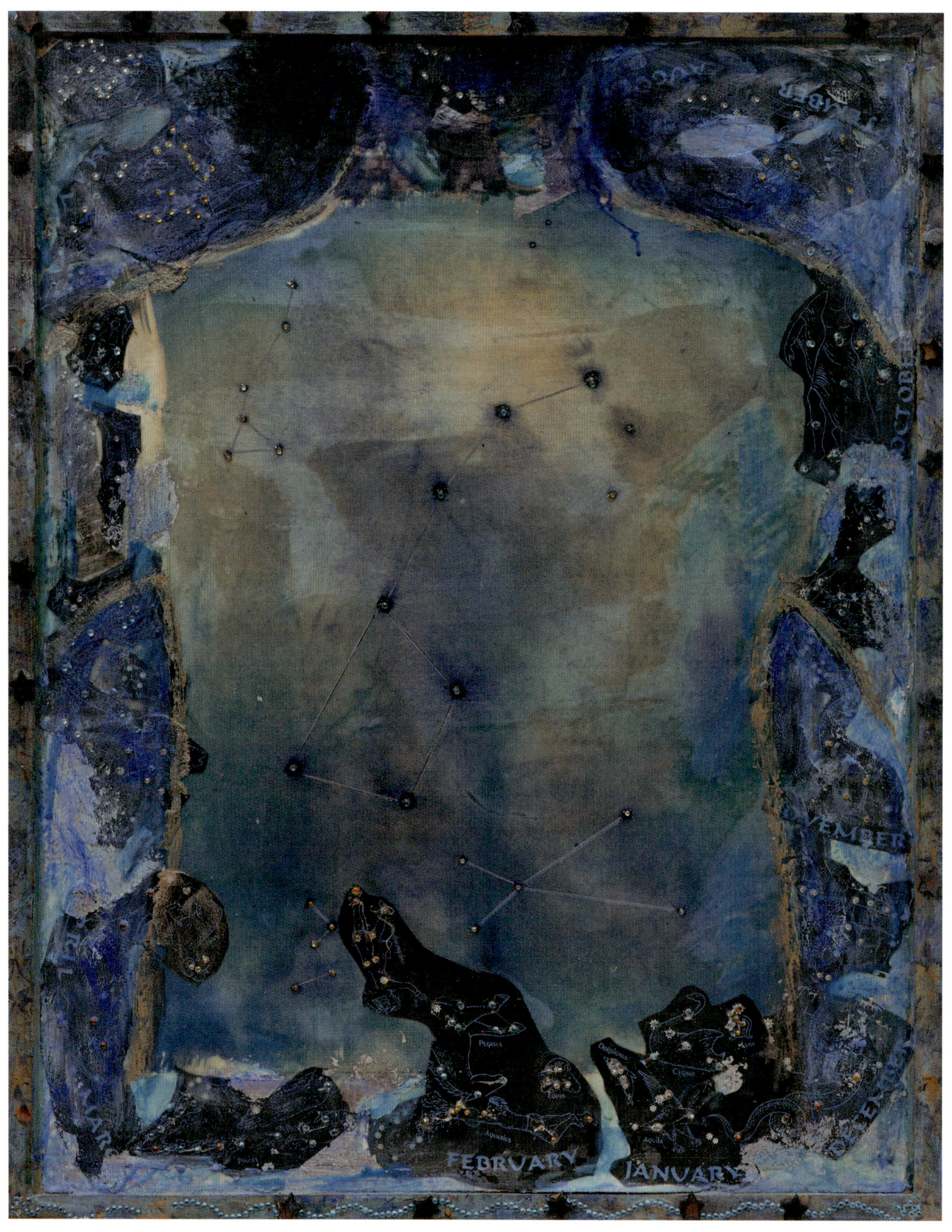
AUGUST
SEPTEMBER
OCTOBER
NOVEMBER
DECEMBER
Pegasus
Delphinus
Equuleus
Aquarius
Aquila
FEBRUARY
JANUARY

Drinking Gourd (Harriet Tubman Series), 2010, cyanotype, wood, fabric, sequins, acrylic

Out of Africa: from beauty to pain, 2010, Van Dyke process, acrylic, embossing on Rives paper

Life Pulse, 2010, encaustic, solar etching

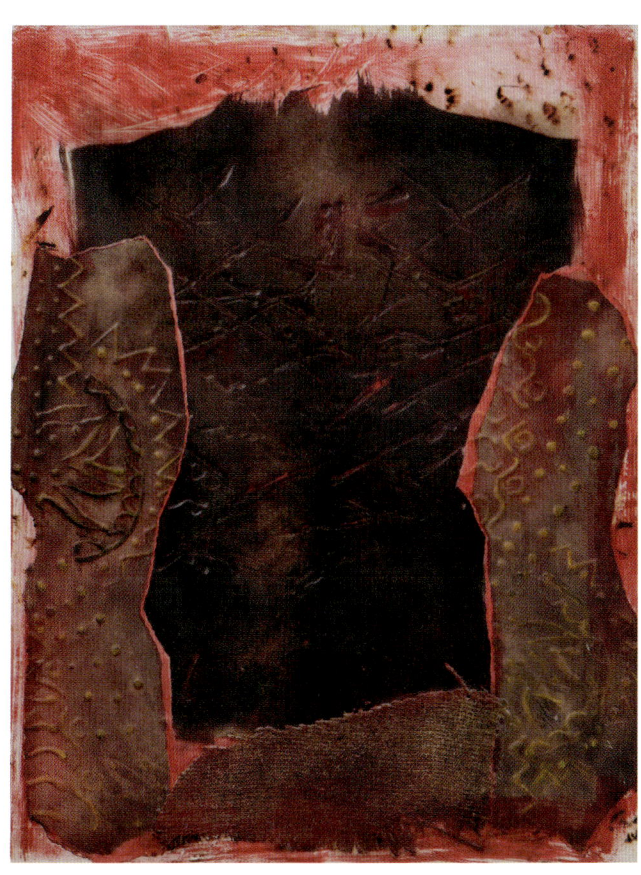

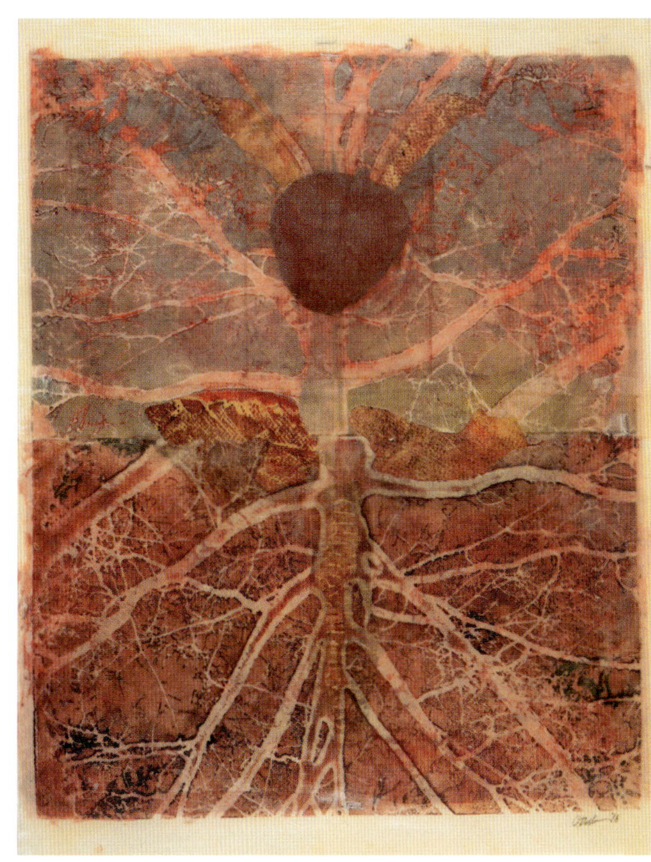

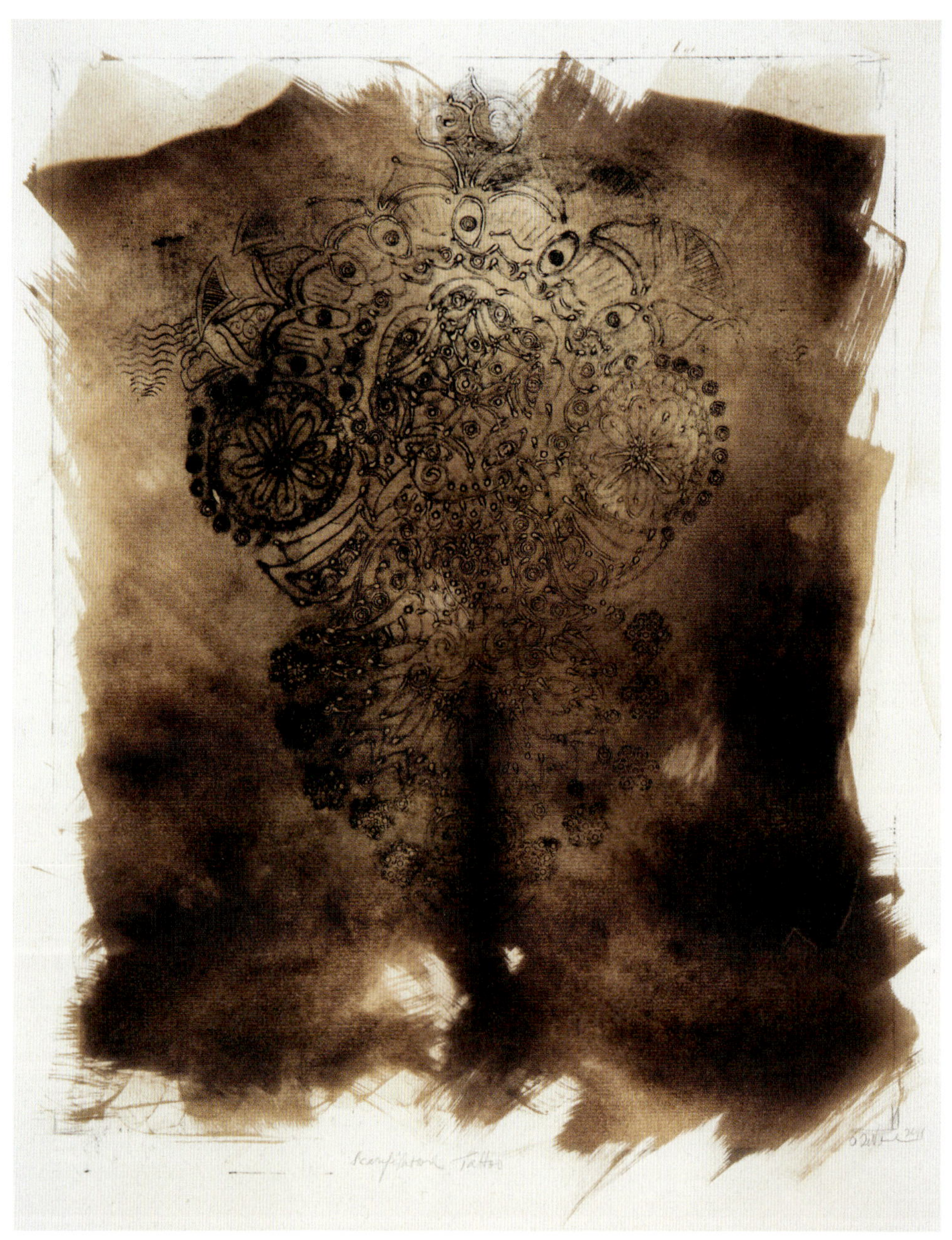

Tattoo (Scarification Series), 2011,
Van Dyke process and
ink on paper

OPPOSITE
An American Story,
2010, solar etching

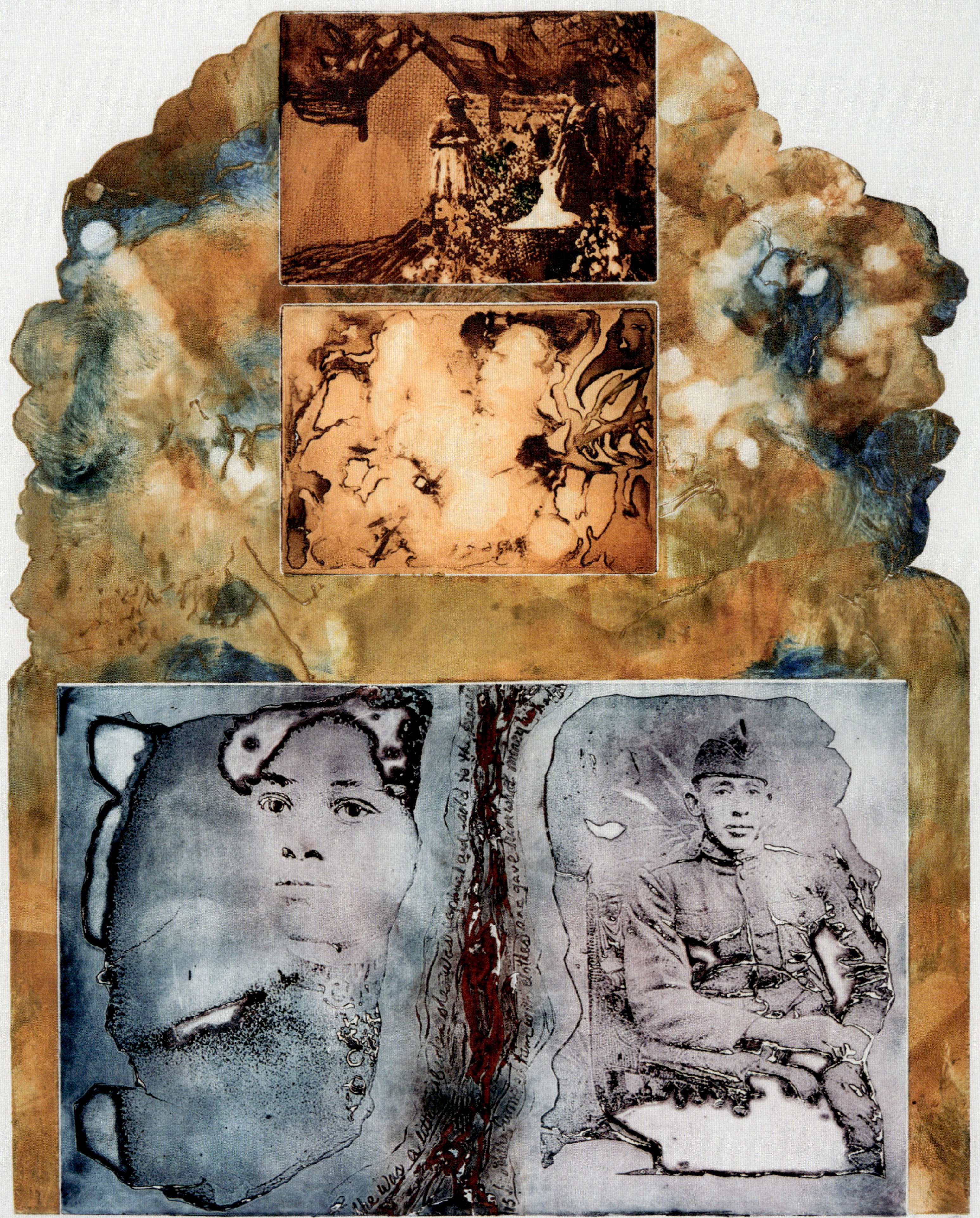

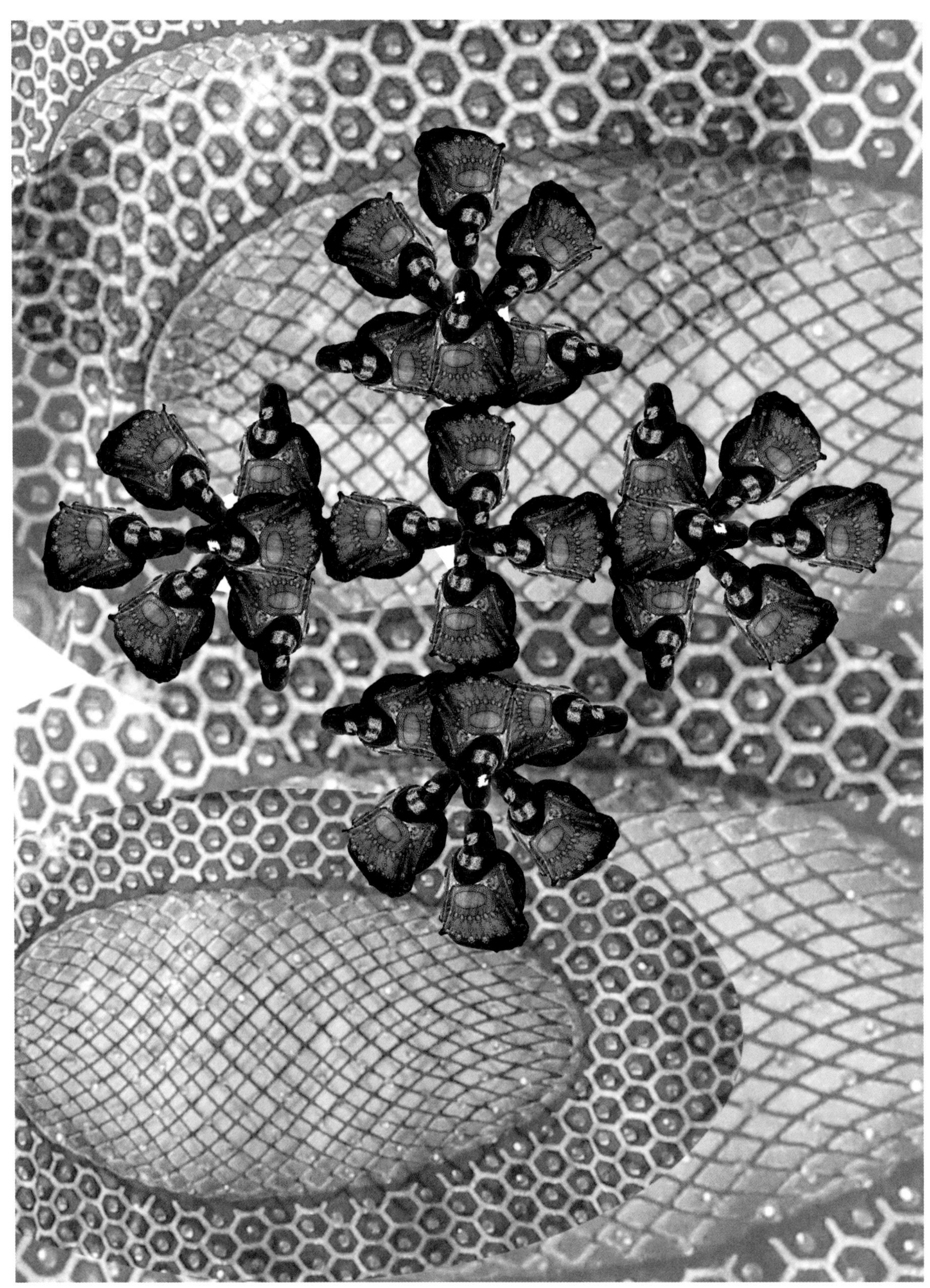

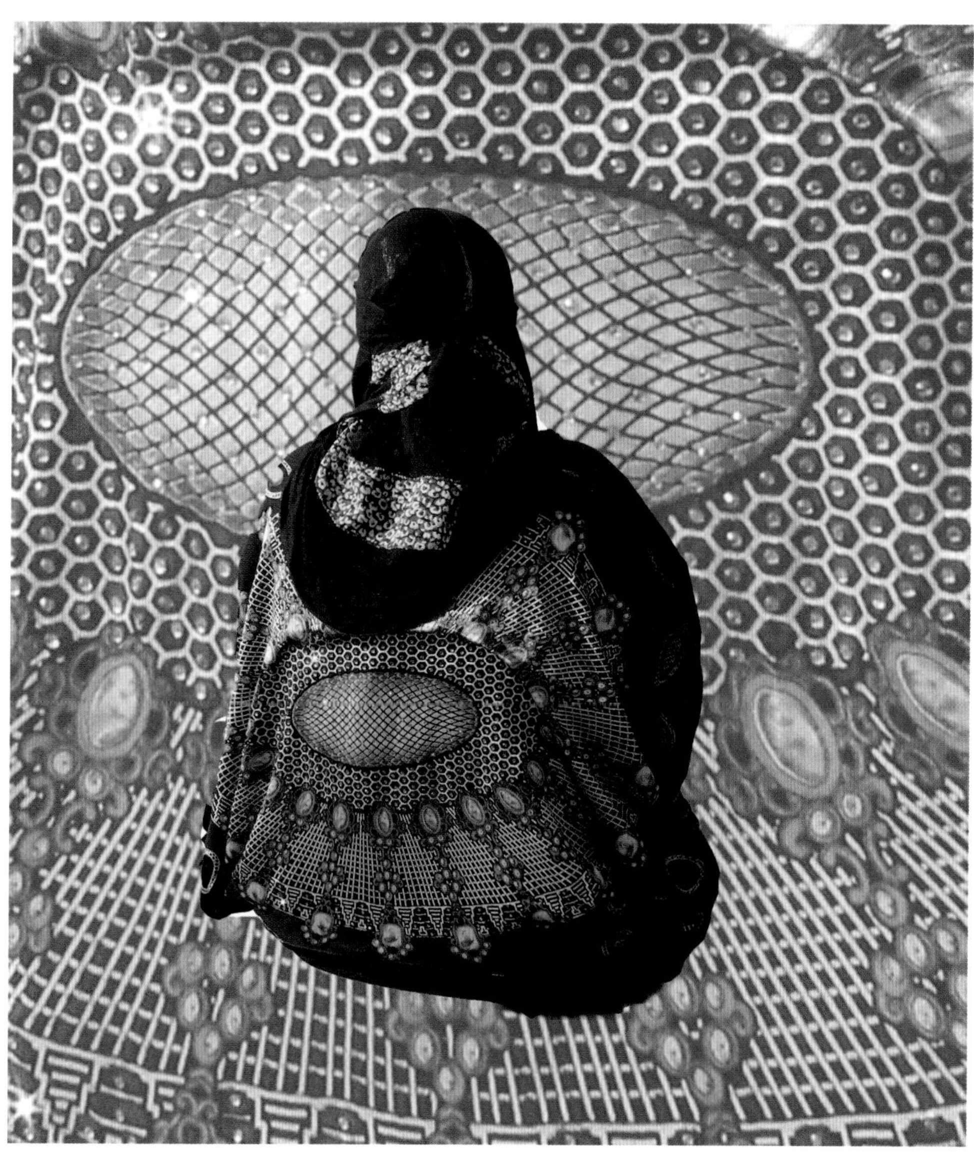

OPPOSITE

Chador Flowers I, 2014, digital print collage

Patterns (Three Women from Dubai), 2015, solar etching

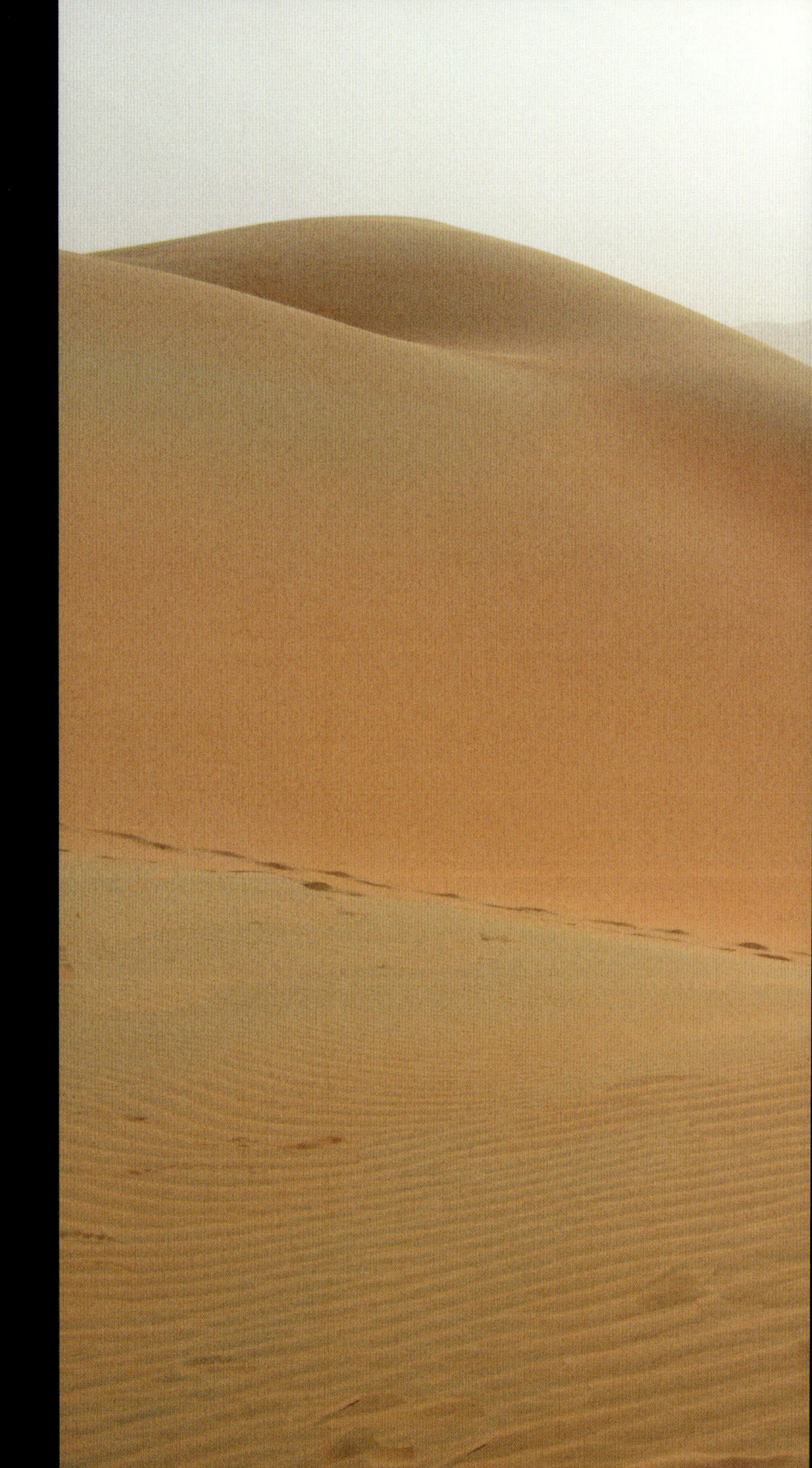

Absence/Presence
[Empty Quarters],
2016, video, 3 minutes,
39 seconds

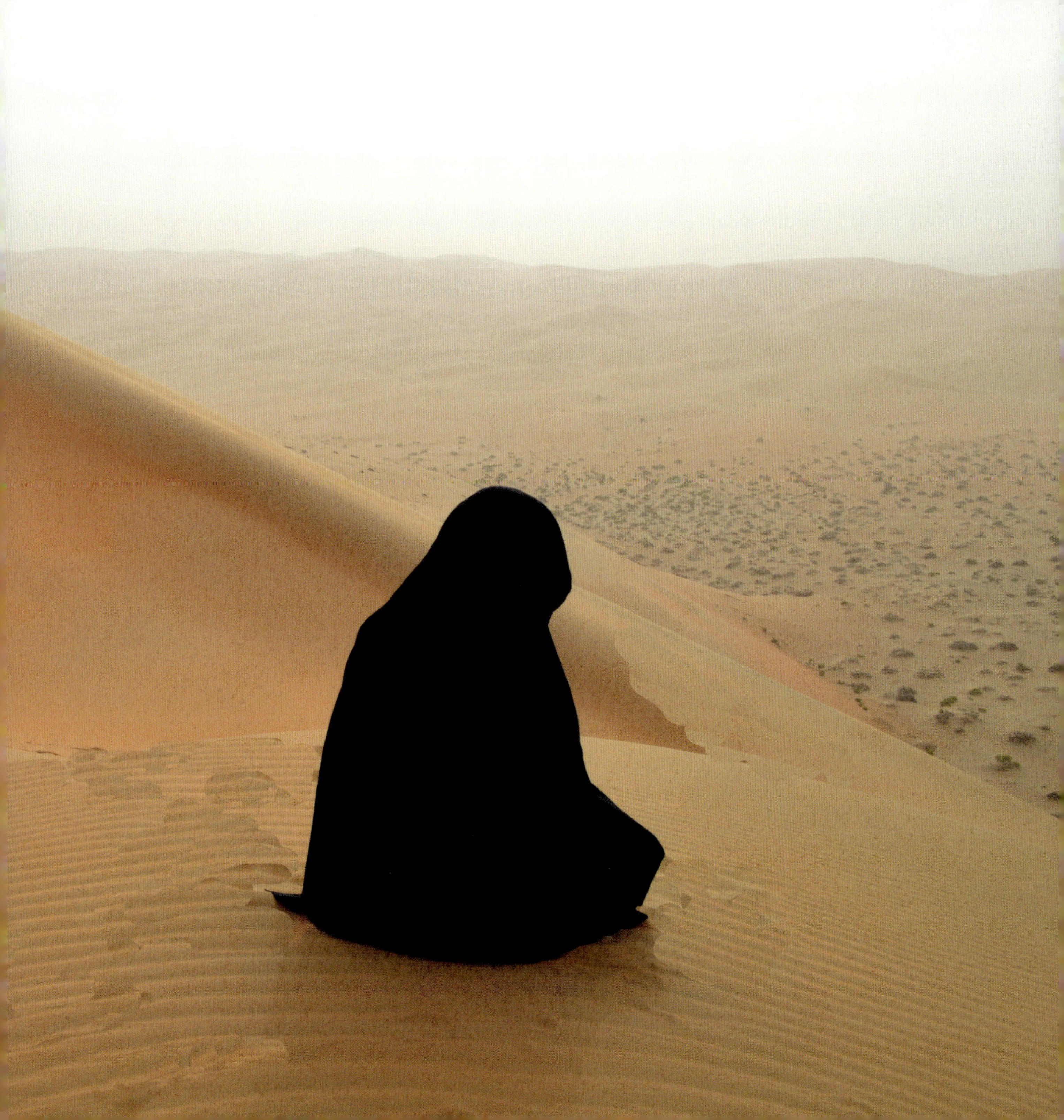

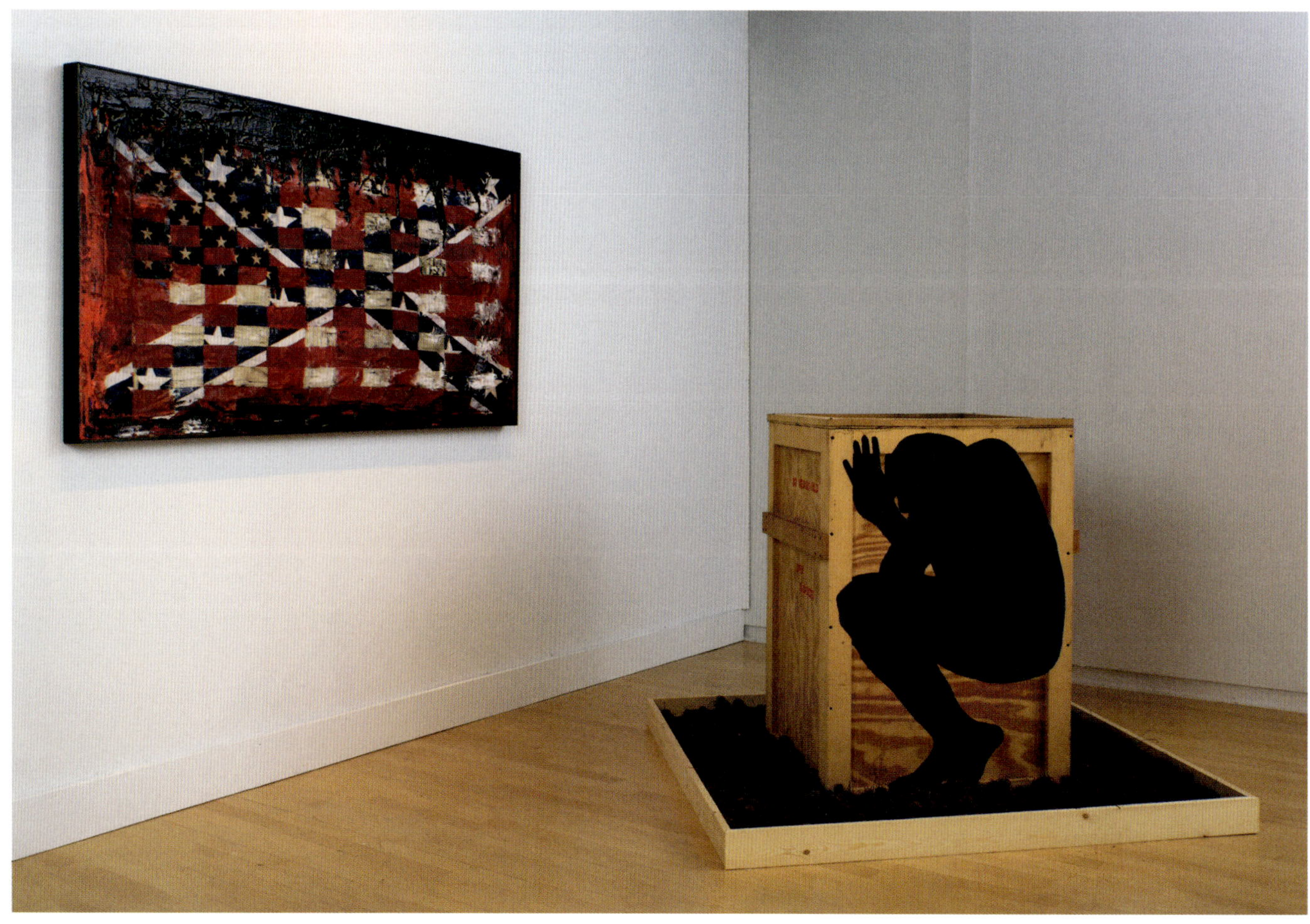

Henry "Box" Brown, 2015,
wood, acrylic, sweet gum balls,
United States of America flag
fabric, Confederate flag fabric,
acrylic on canvas

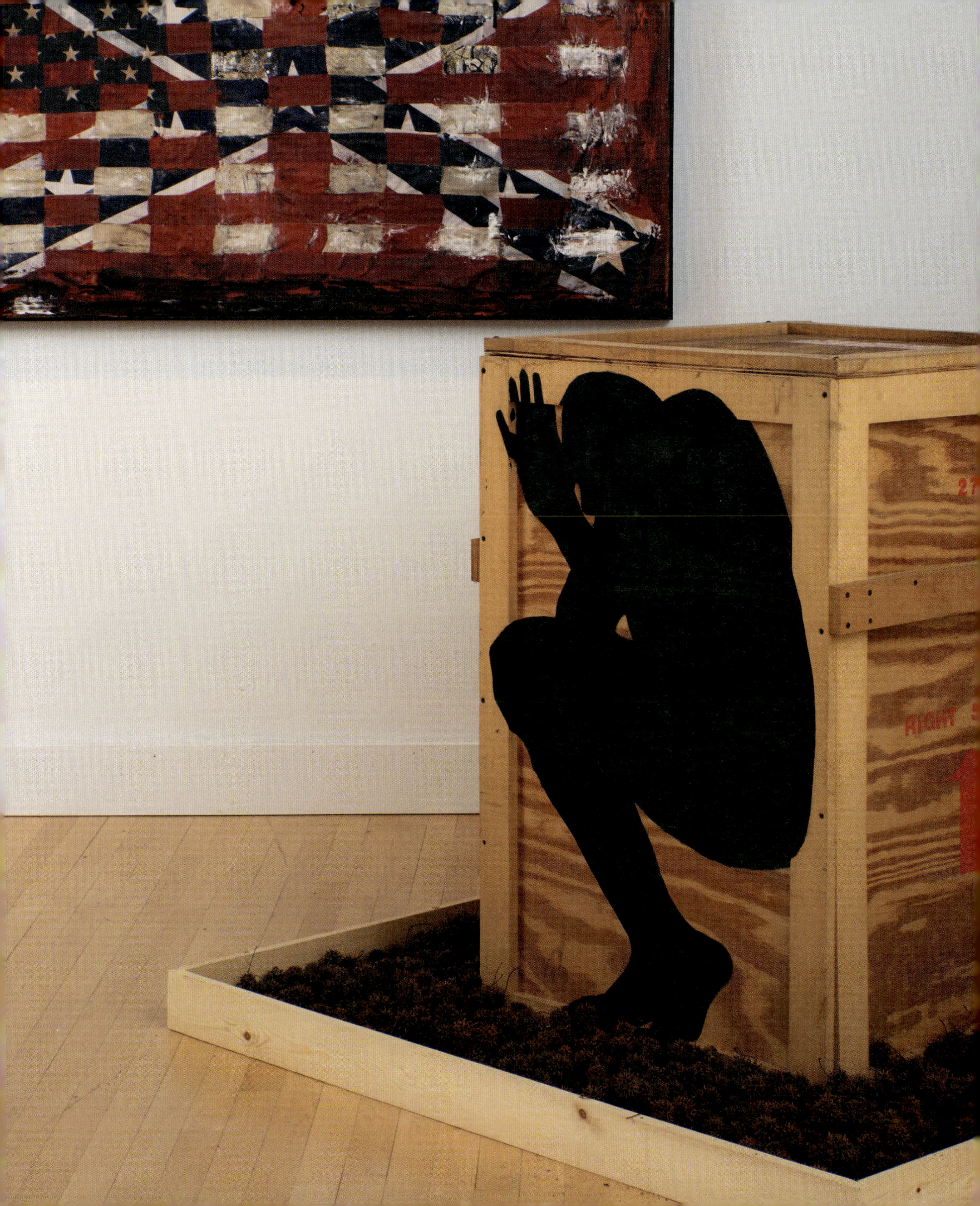

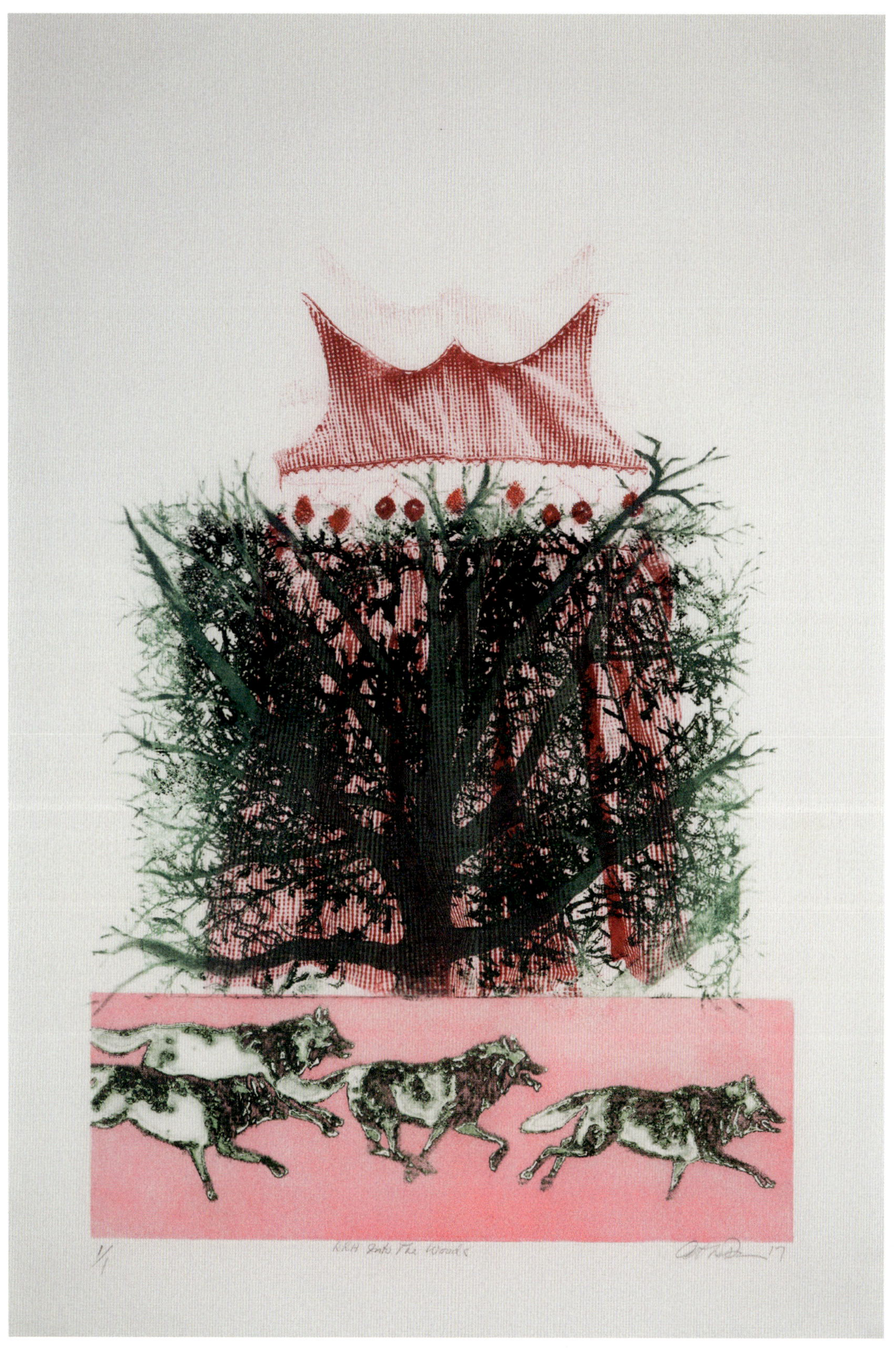

1/1
RRH Into The Woods

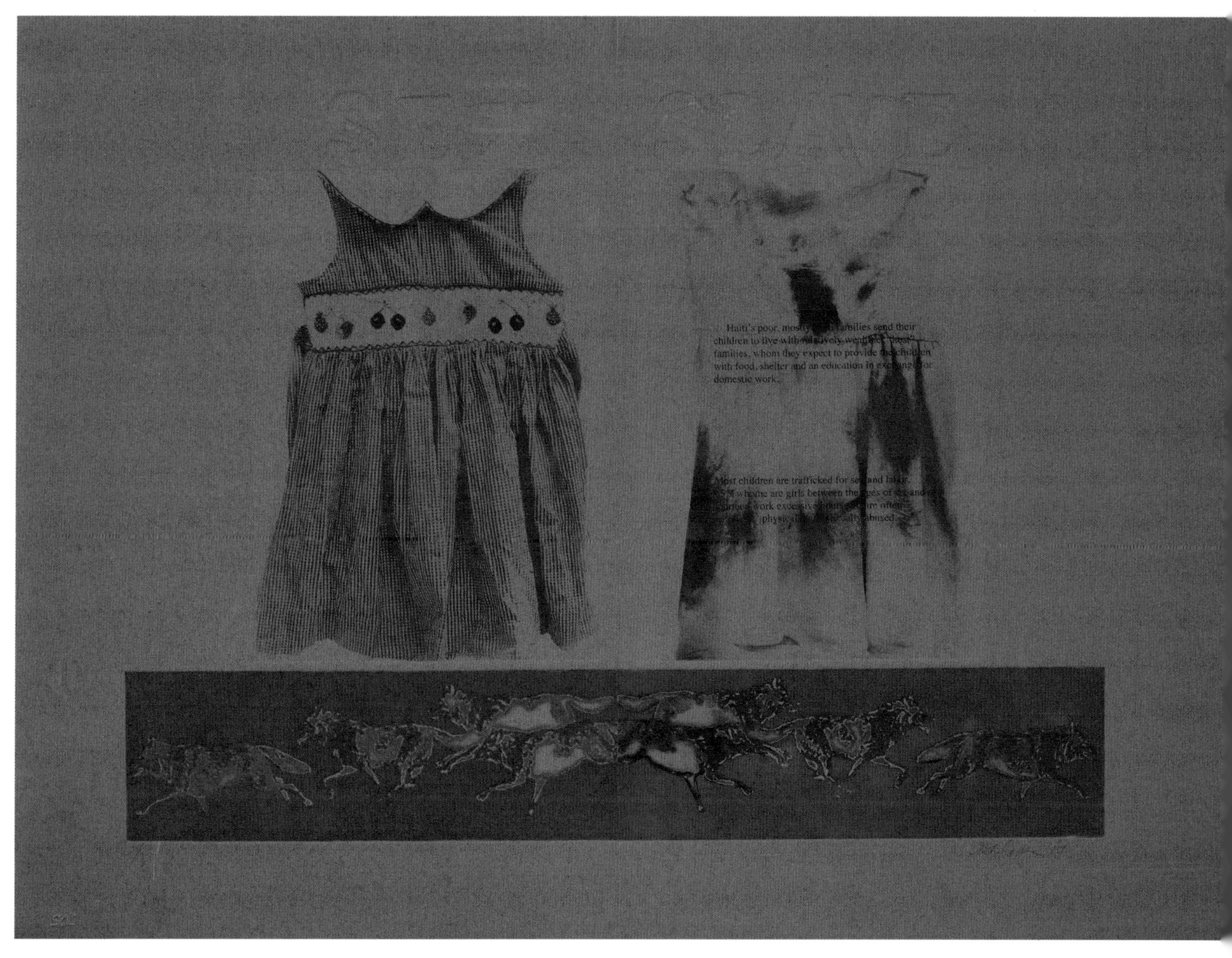

Red Riding Hood, 2016,
solar etching on BFK
Rives paper

Sex Slave, 2016, solar
etching and relief printing

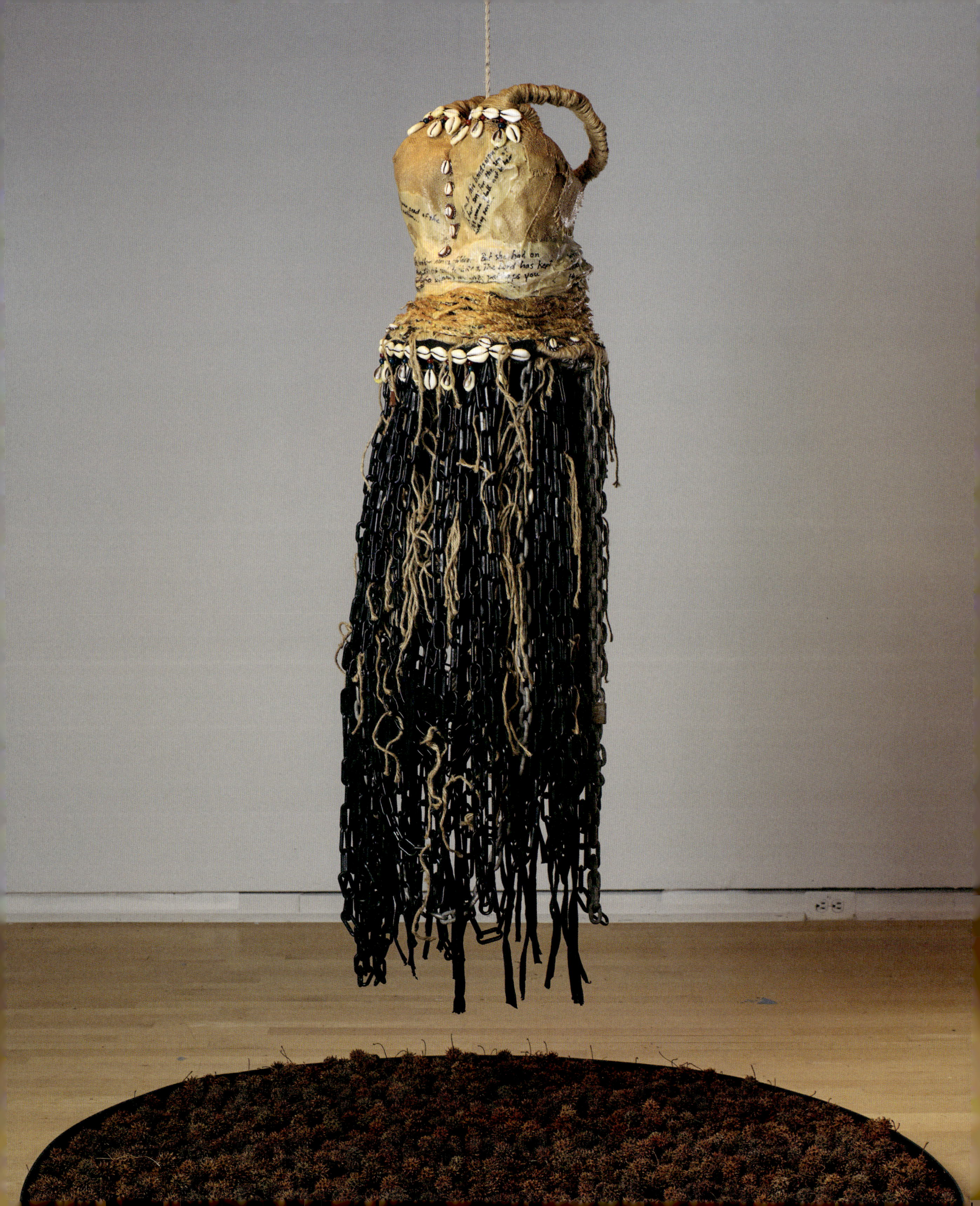

Hagar's Dress in Her Exile,
2012, chains, hemp cord,
fabric, beads, sweet gum
balls, cowrie shells

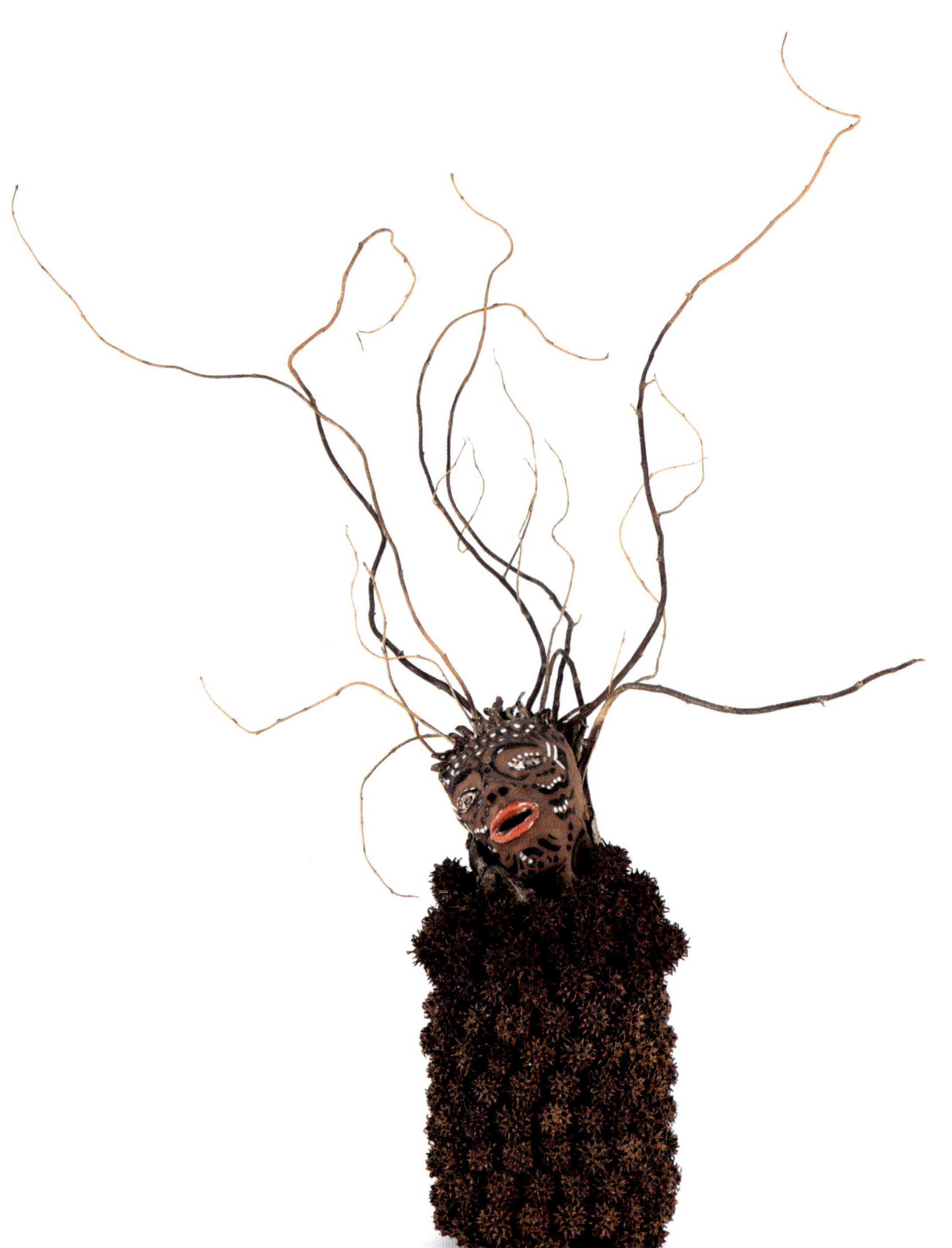

Escape, 2016, wood, clay,
branches, sweet gum balls

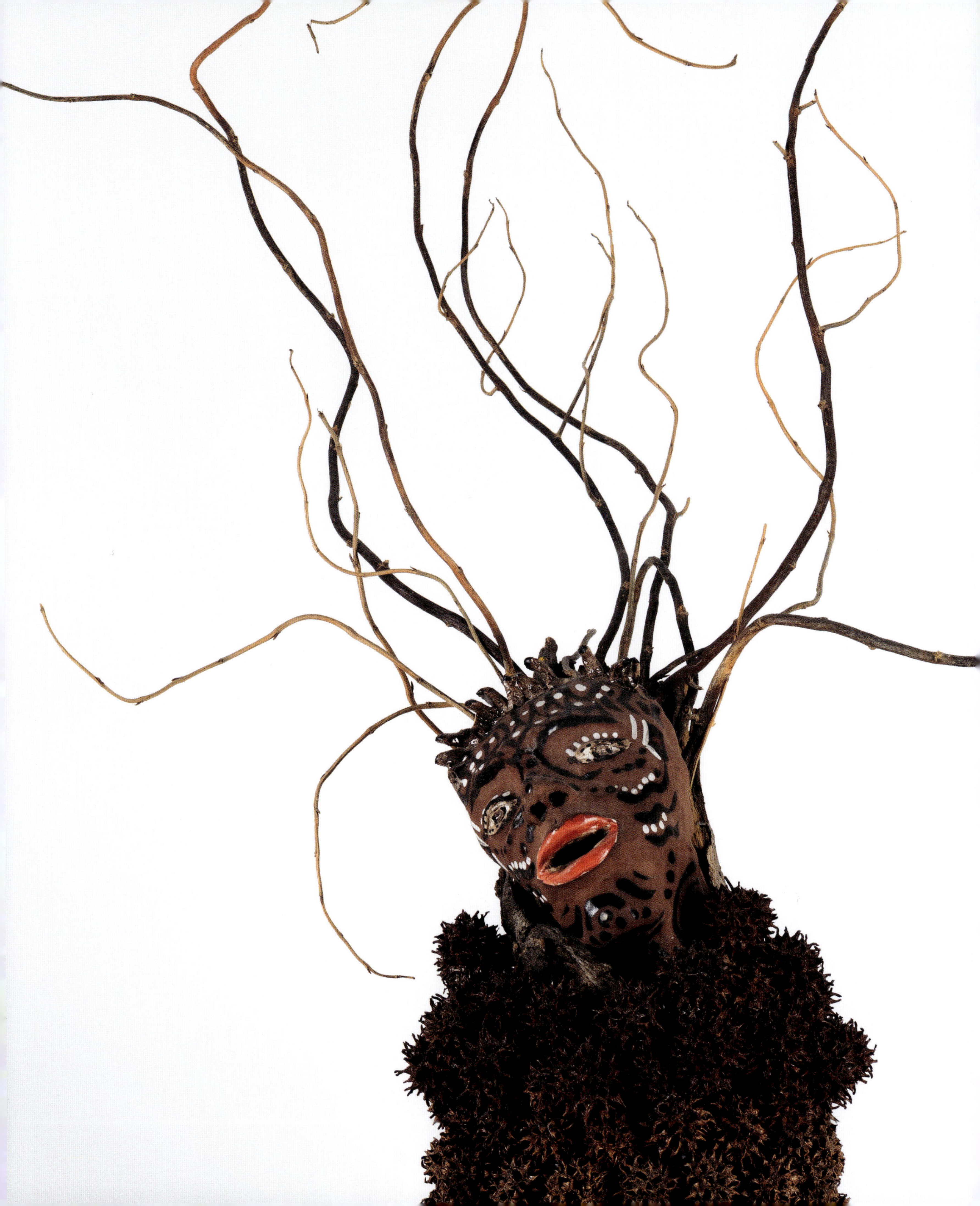

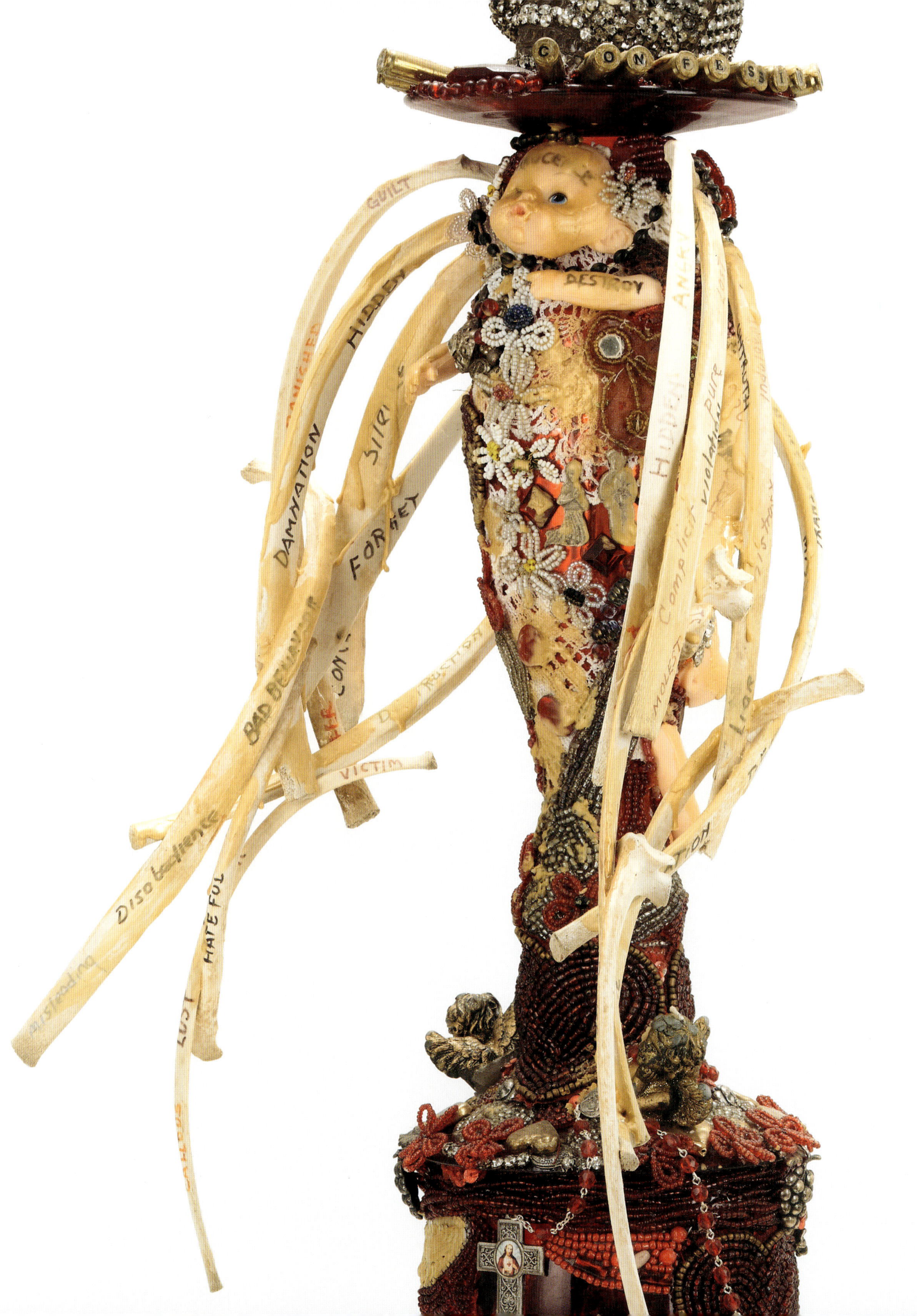

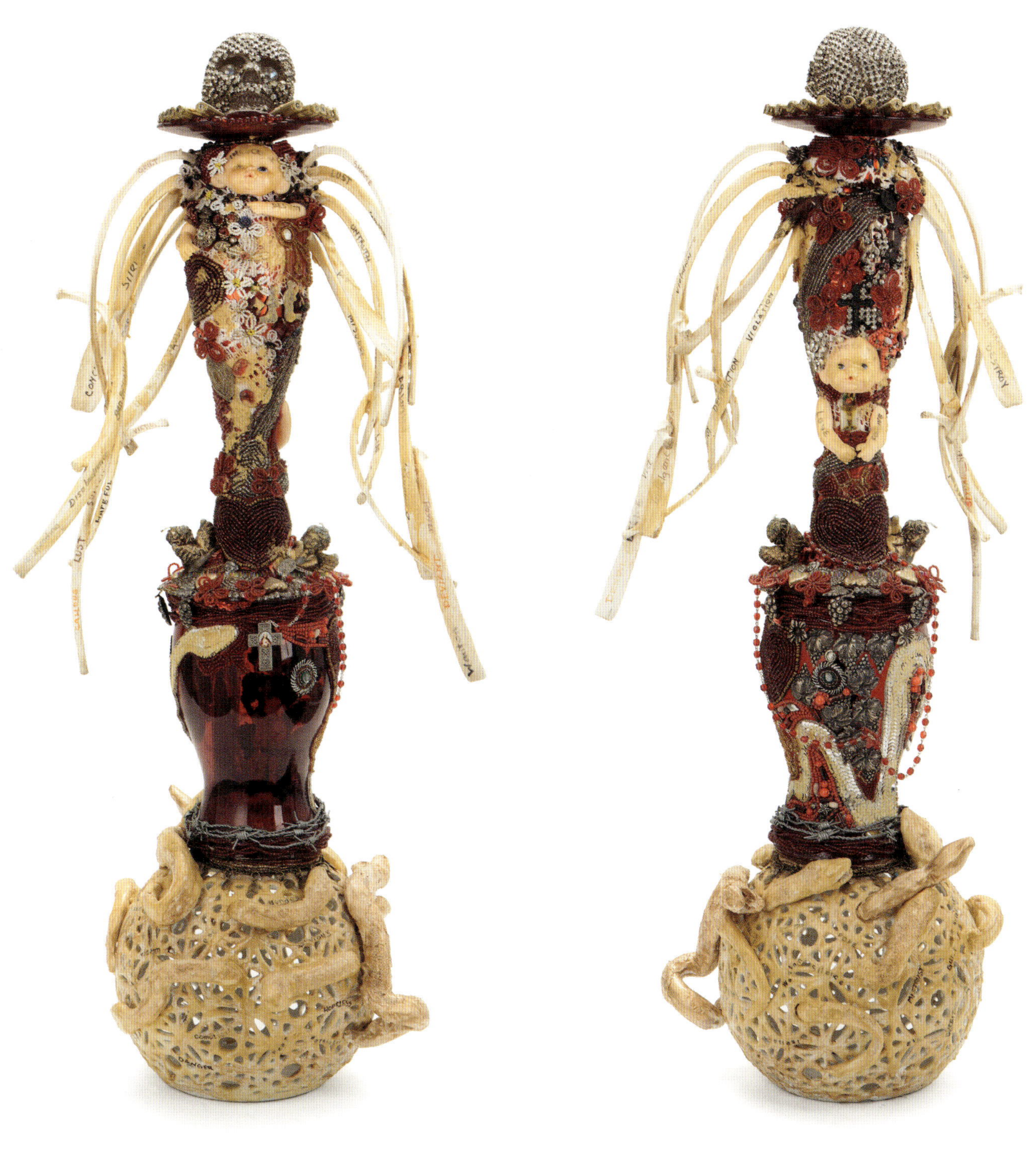

Fall from Grace, 2013, glass,
wax, beads, bones, plastic

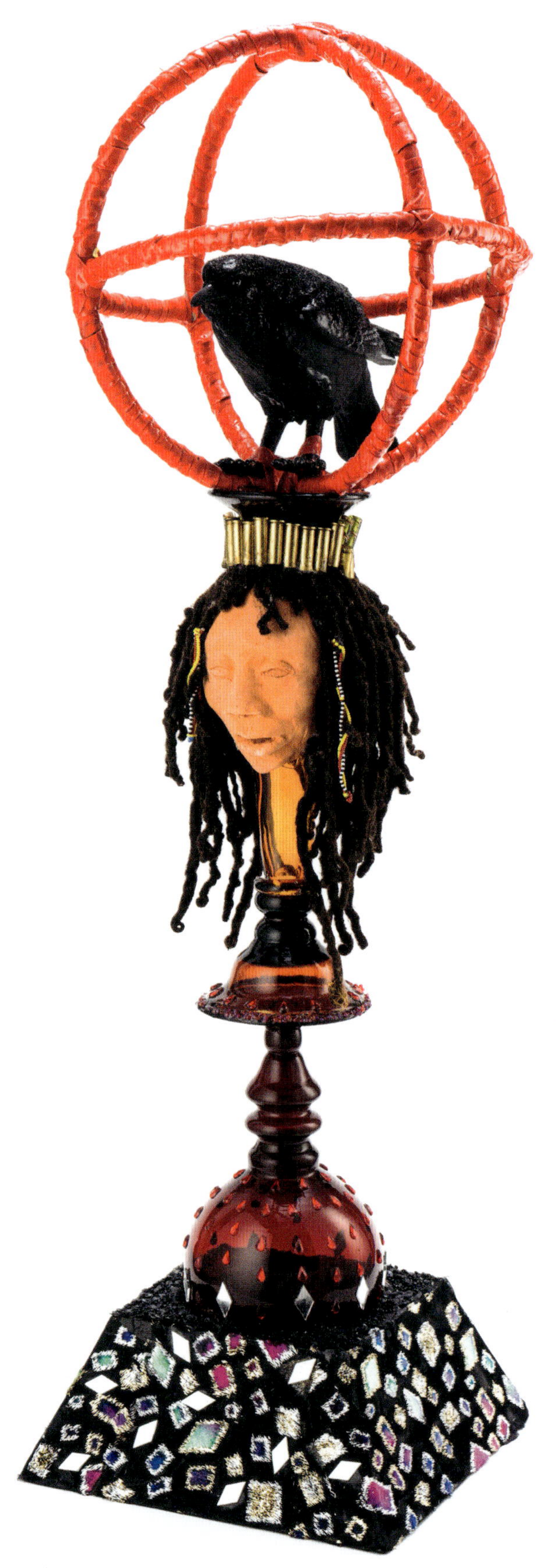

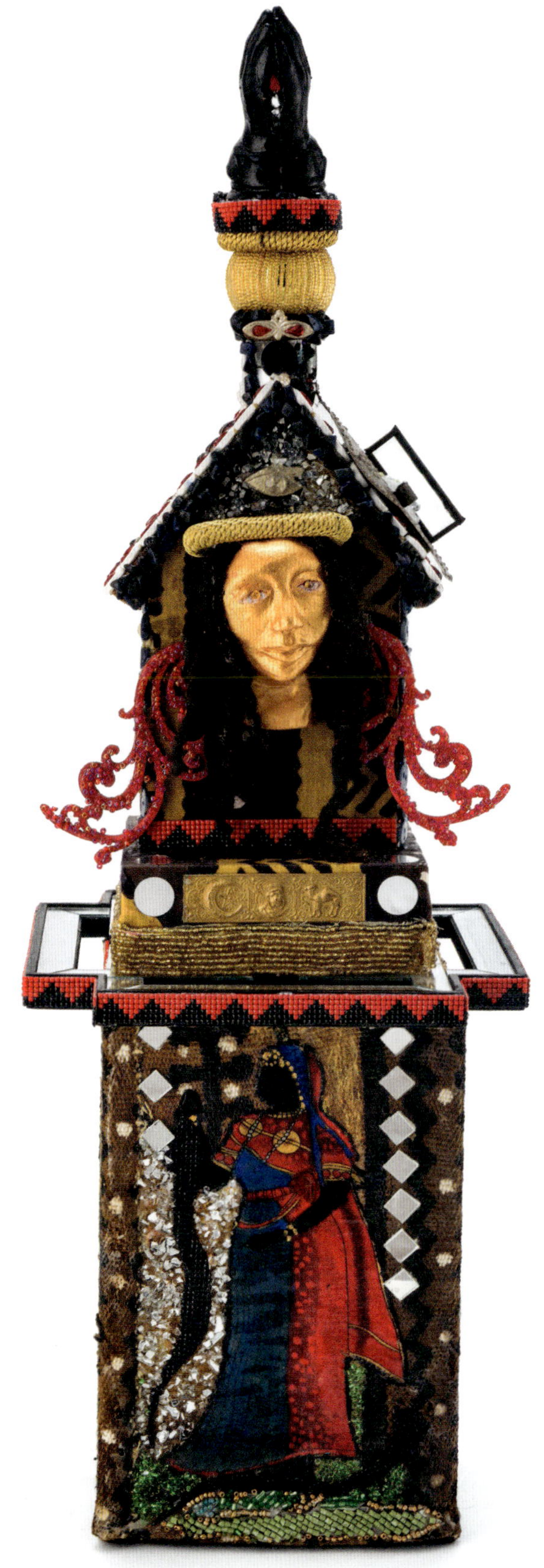

Gemini, 2018, wood, clay, glass, mirrors, bullet casings, wire, fabric, human hair

Healer (Pilgrimage), 2018, wood, fabric, glass, mirror, plastic, beads, clay, acrylic, buttons

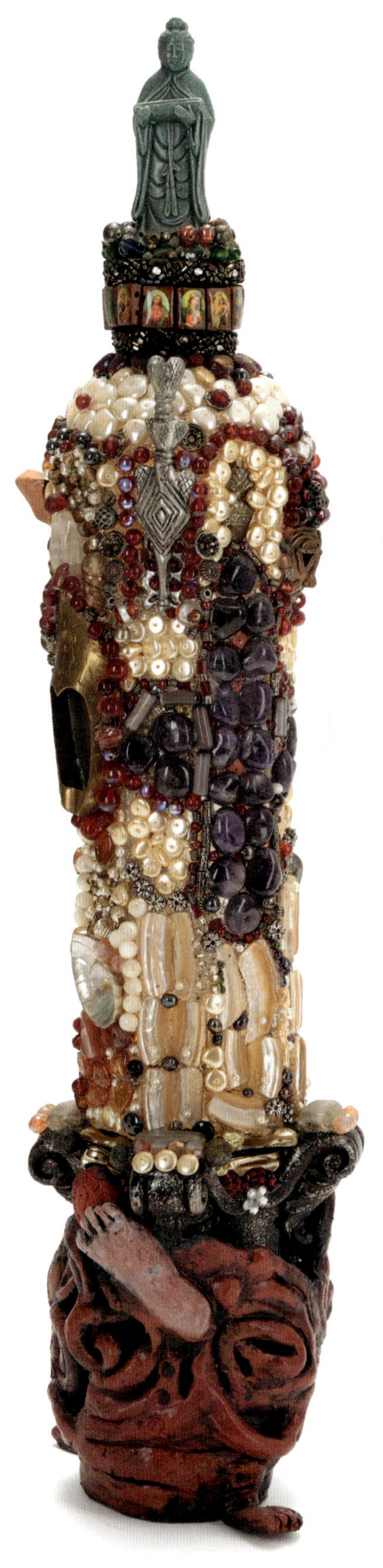

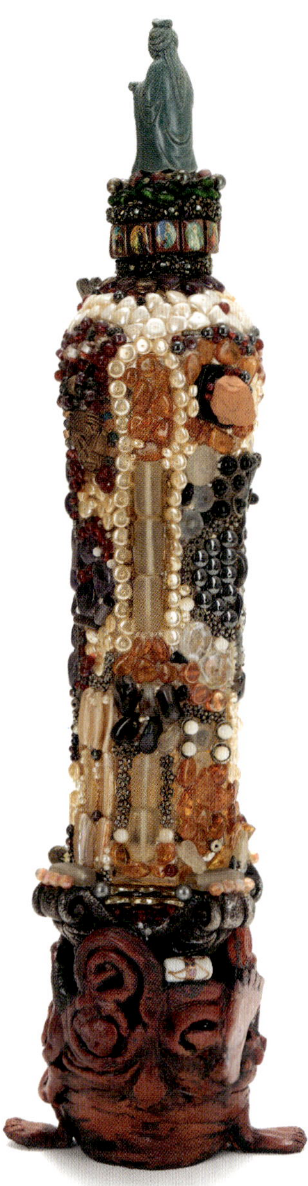

Wedding Gift, 2016, mixed media, Collection of Leslie King-Hammond

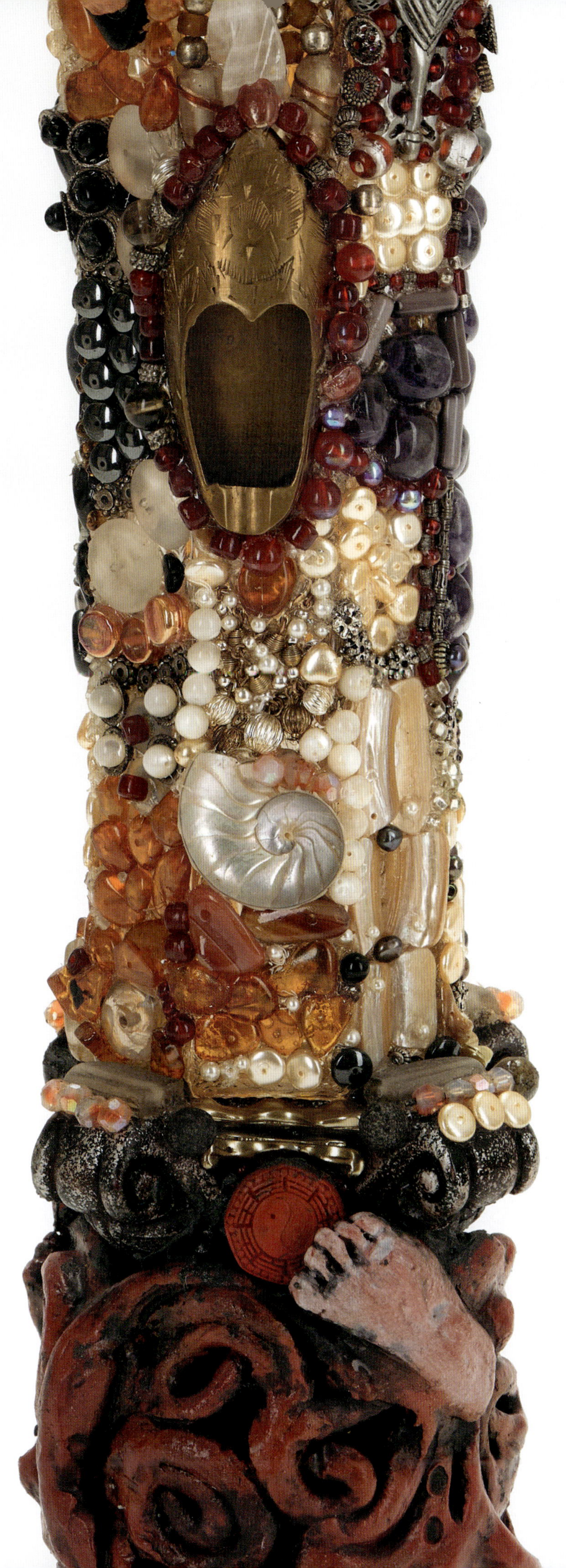

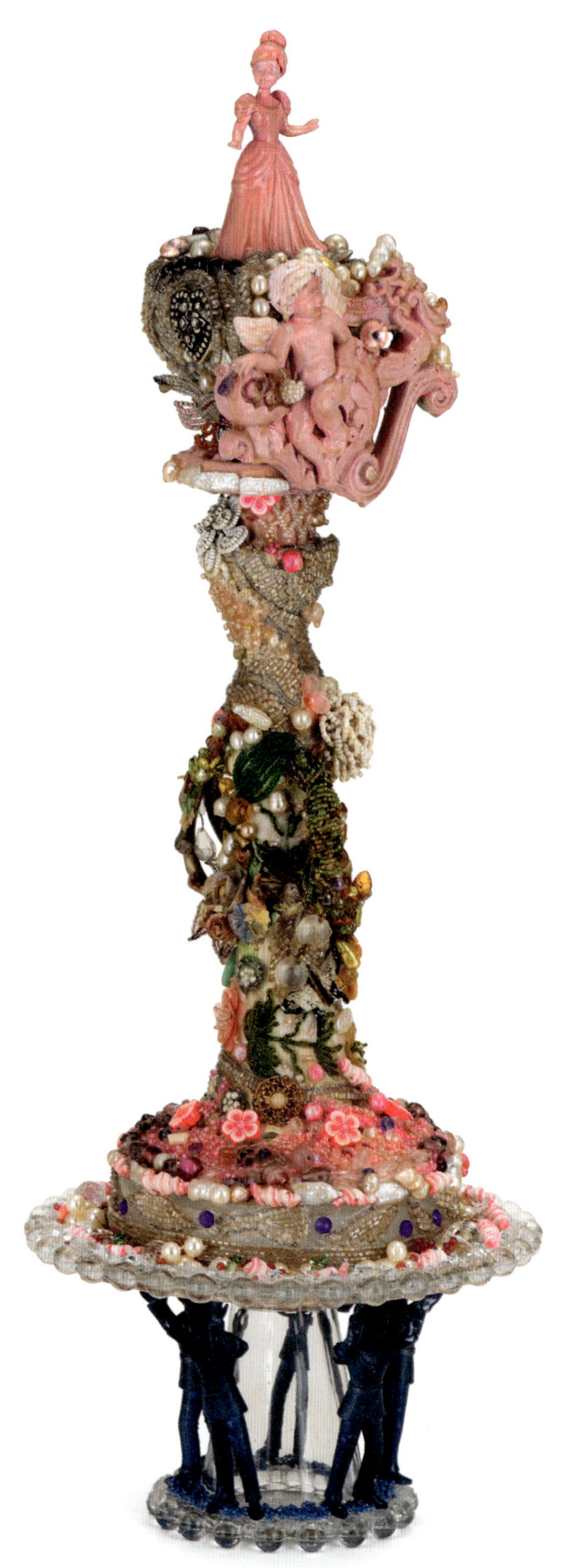

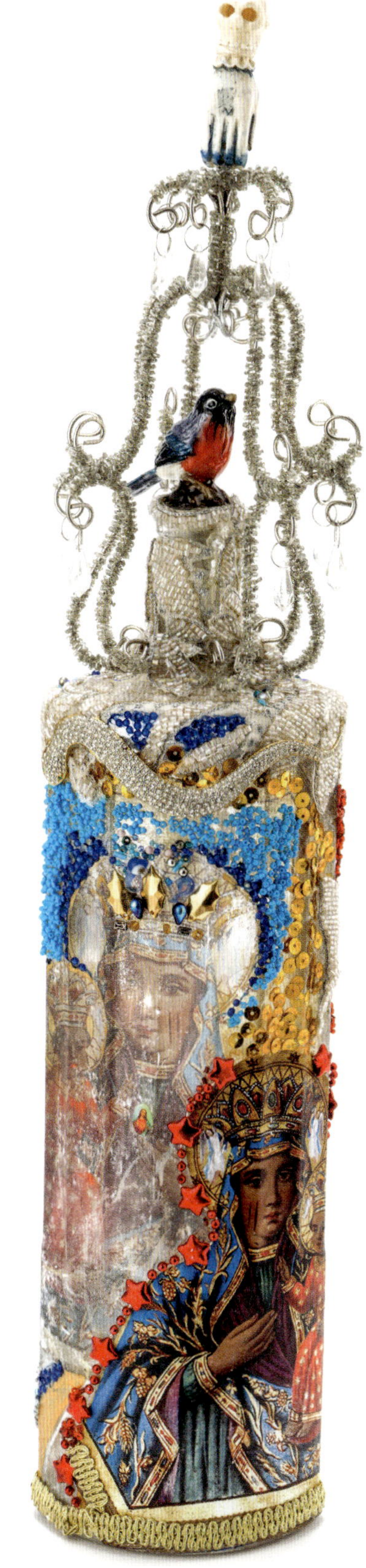

OPPOSITE

Lifeisbutadream, 2015, clay, plastic, beads, metal

Erzulie Dandor, 2017, glass, beads, image transfer, wire, porcelain, fabric

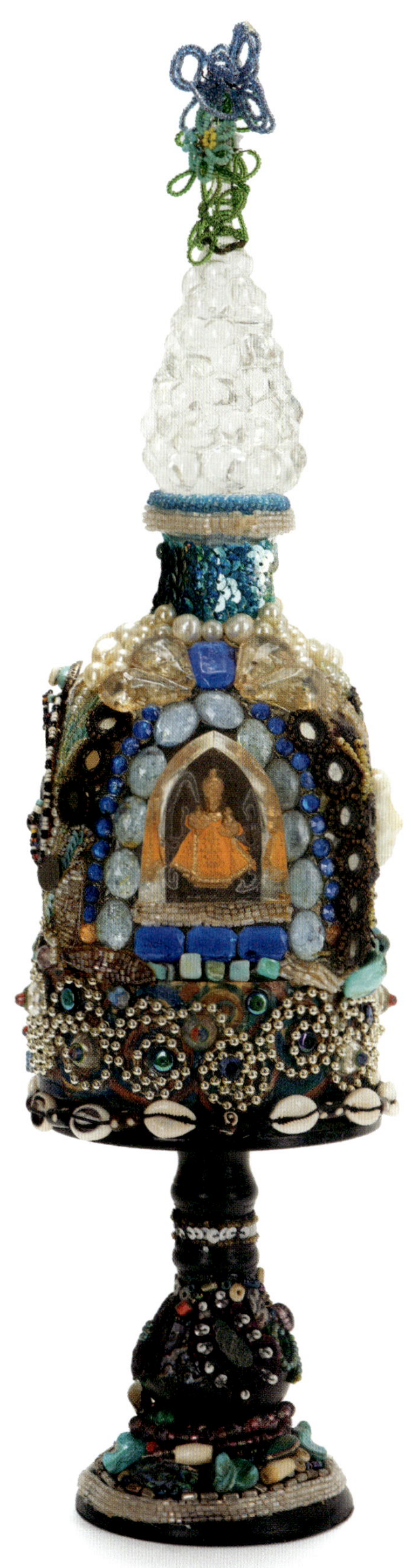

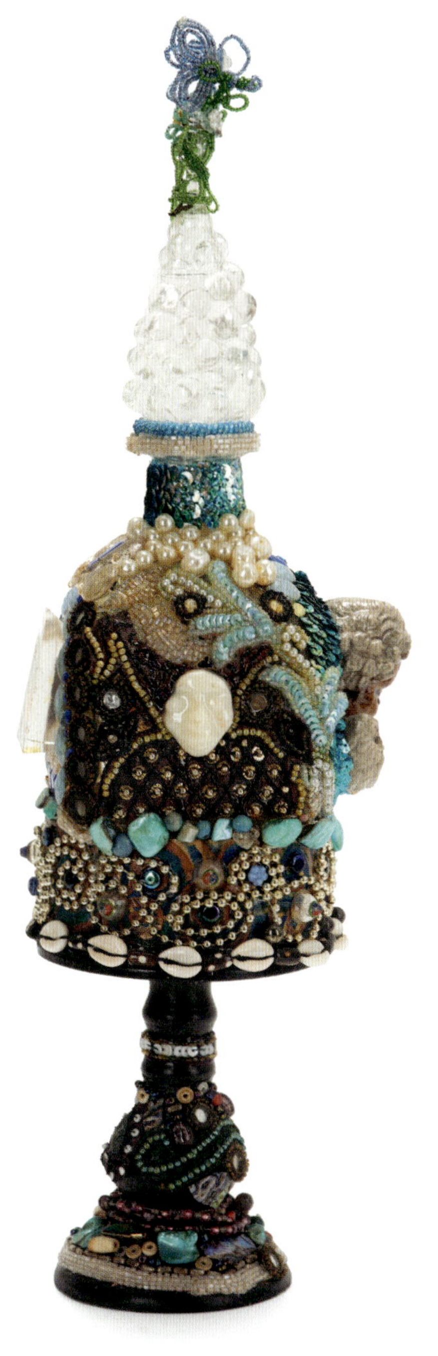

Grappa, 2018, mixed
media, including grappa

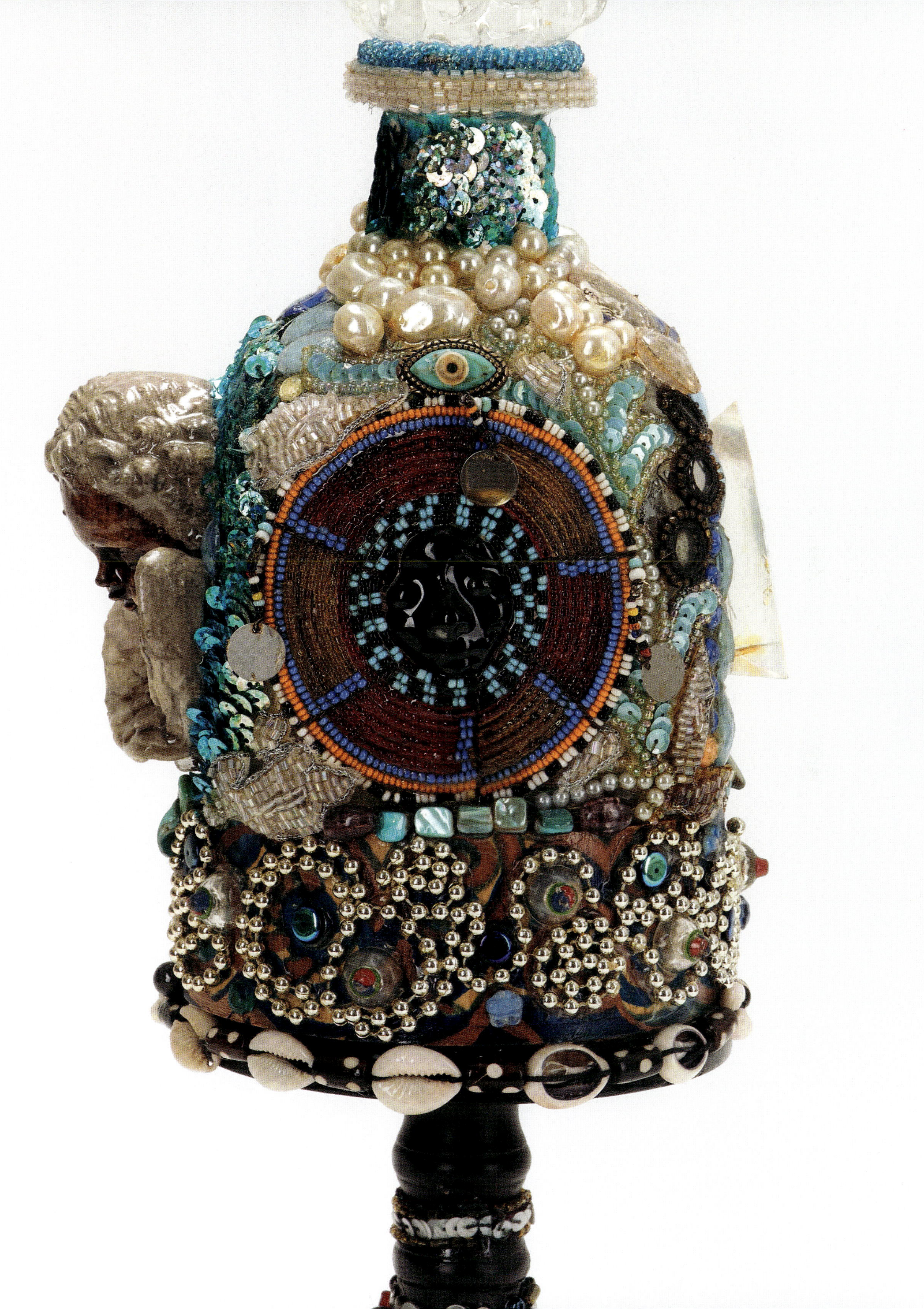

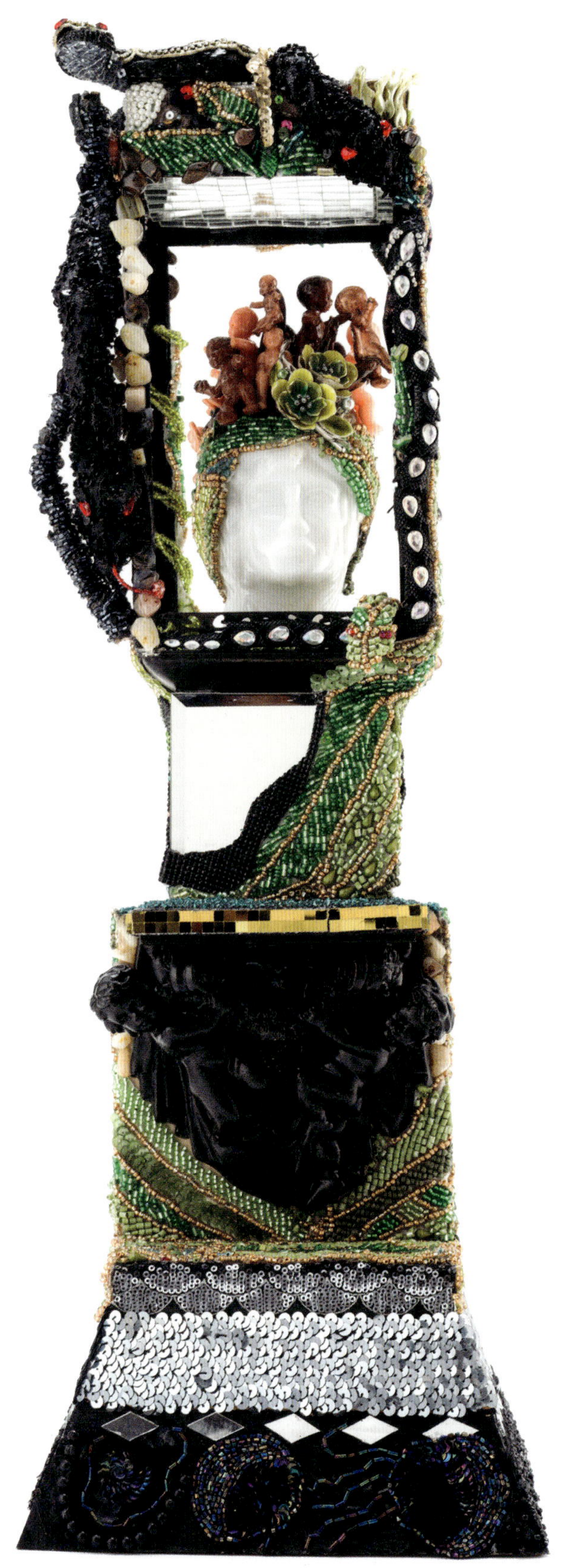

Woman Who Married a Snake, 2017, glass, metal, beads, plastics, mirrors, pebbles

Kronos (Collateral), 2018, glass beads, glass, metal, metal fiber, wood, plastic

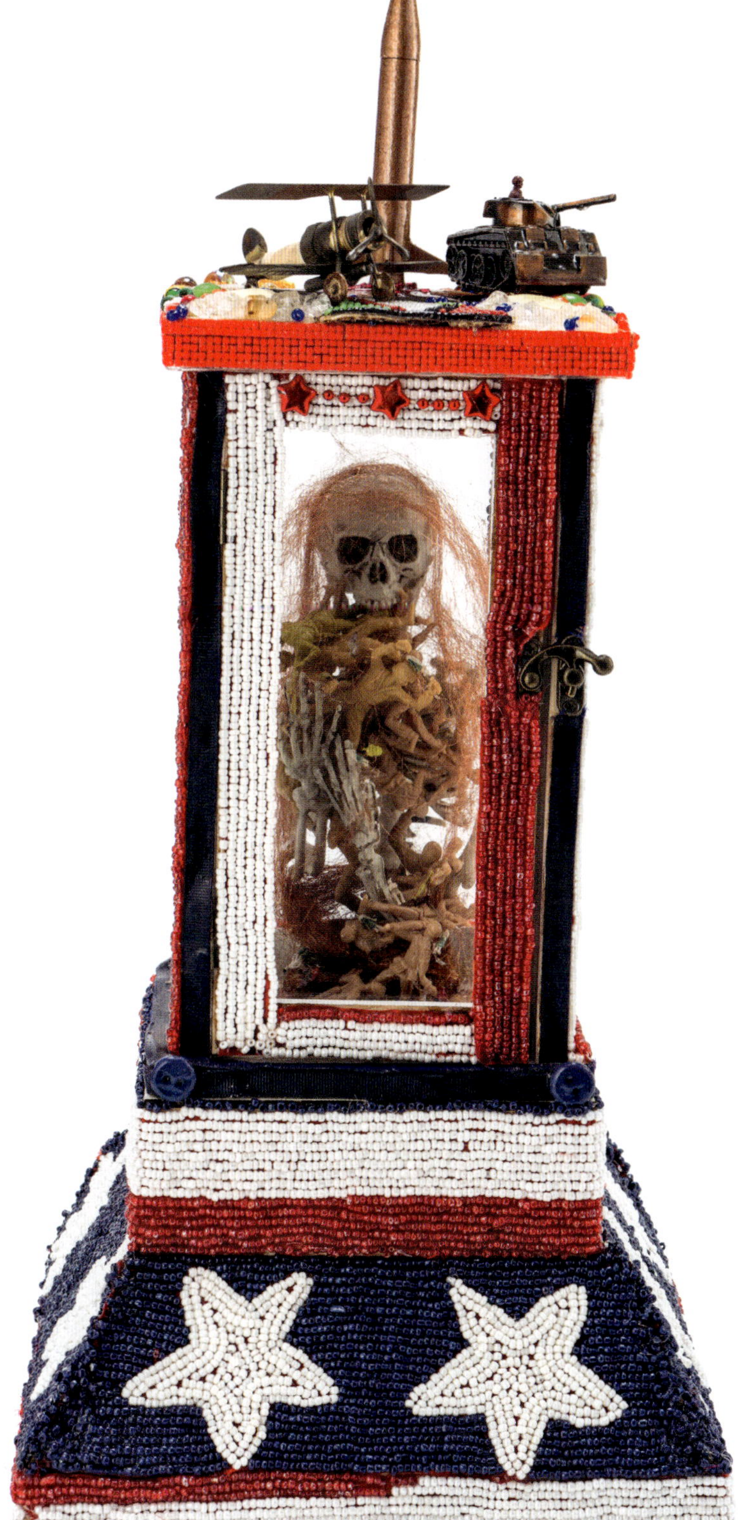

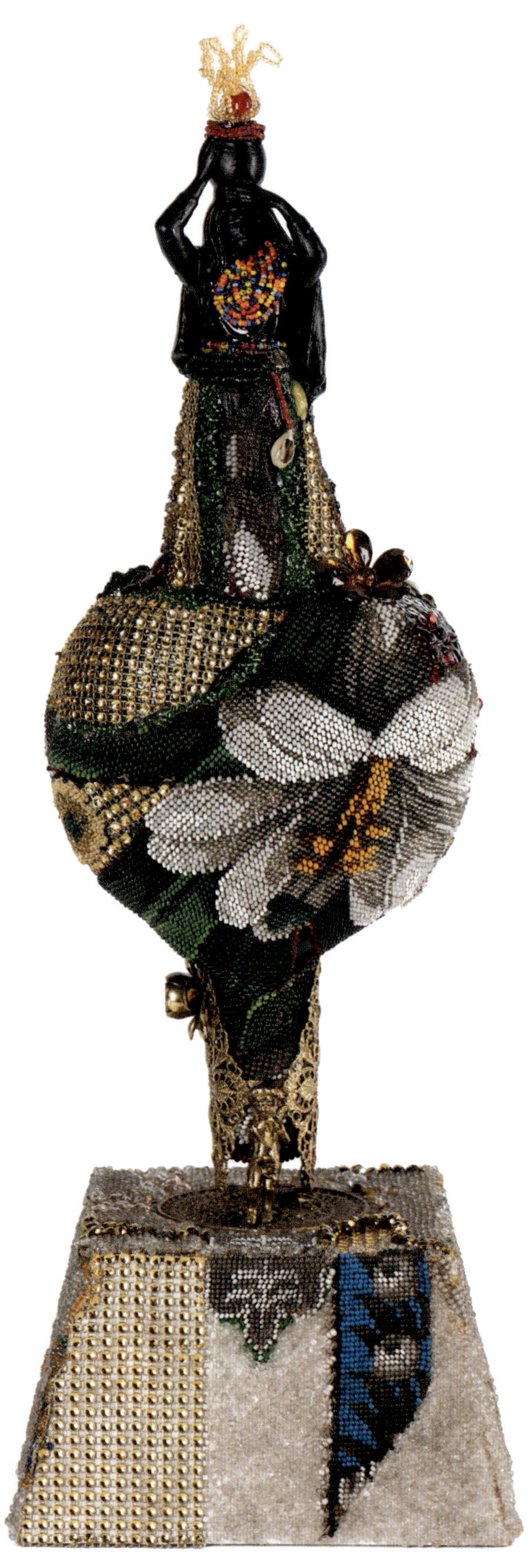

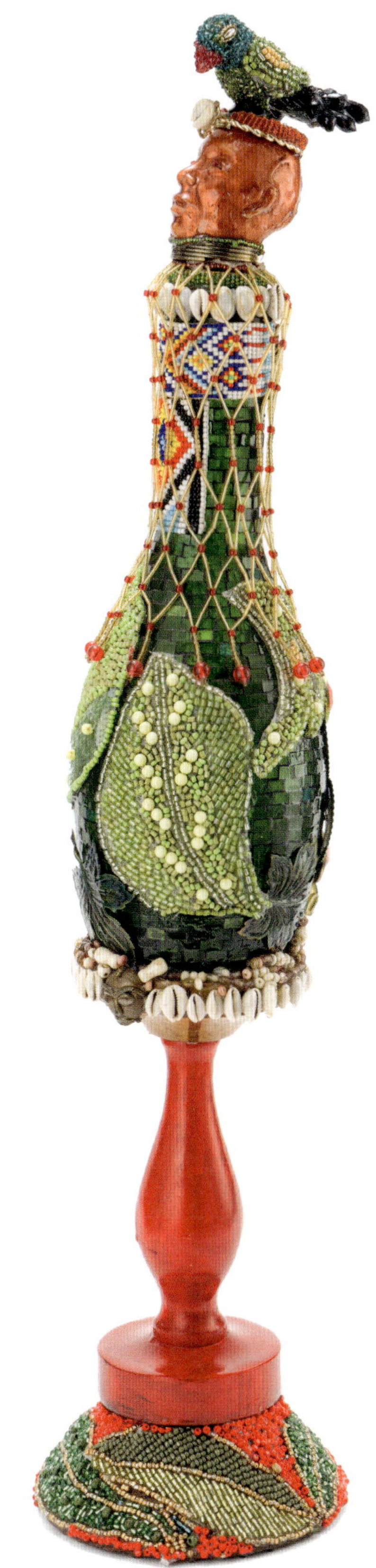

OPPOSITE

Protector of the Flame, 2020,
glass beads, fabric, wood

Orisha, 2008, wood, glass,
clay, glass beads, shells, green
metal

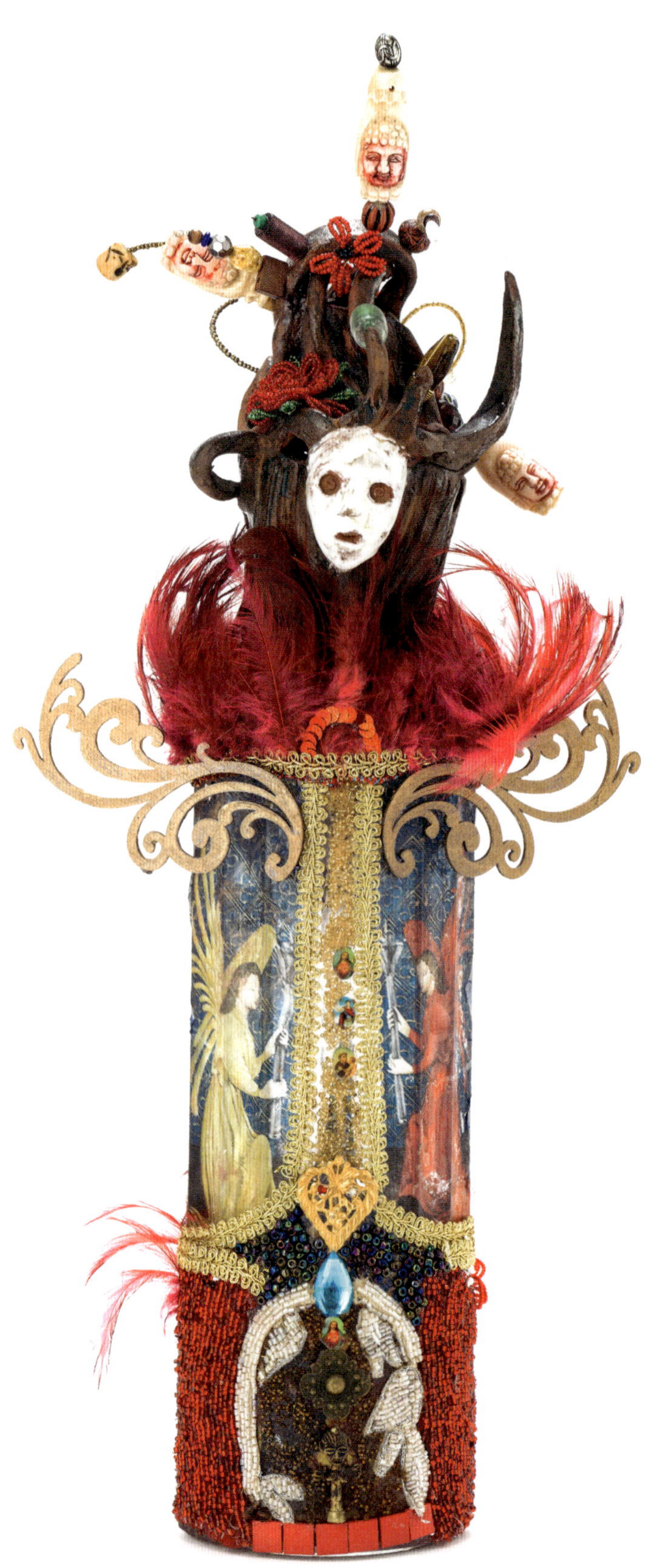

Medieval, 2017, glass, red feathers, wire, fabric, plastic, wood, beads

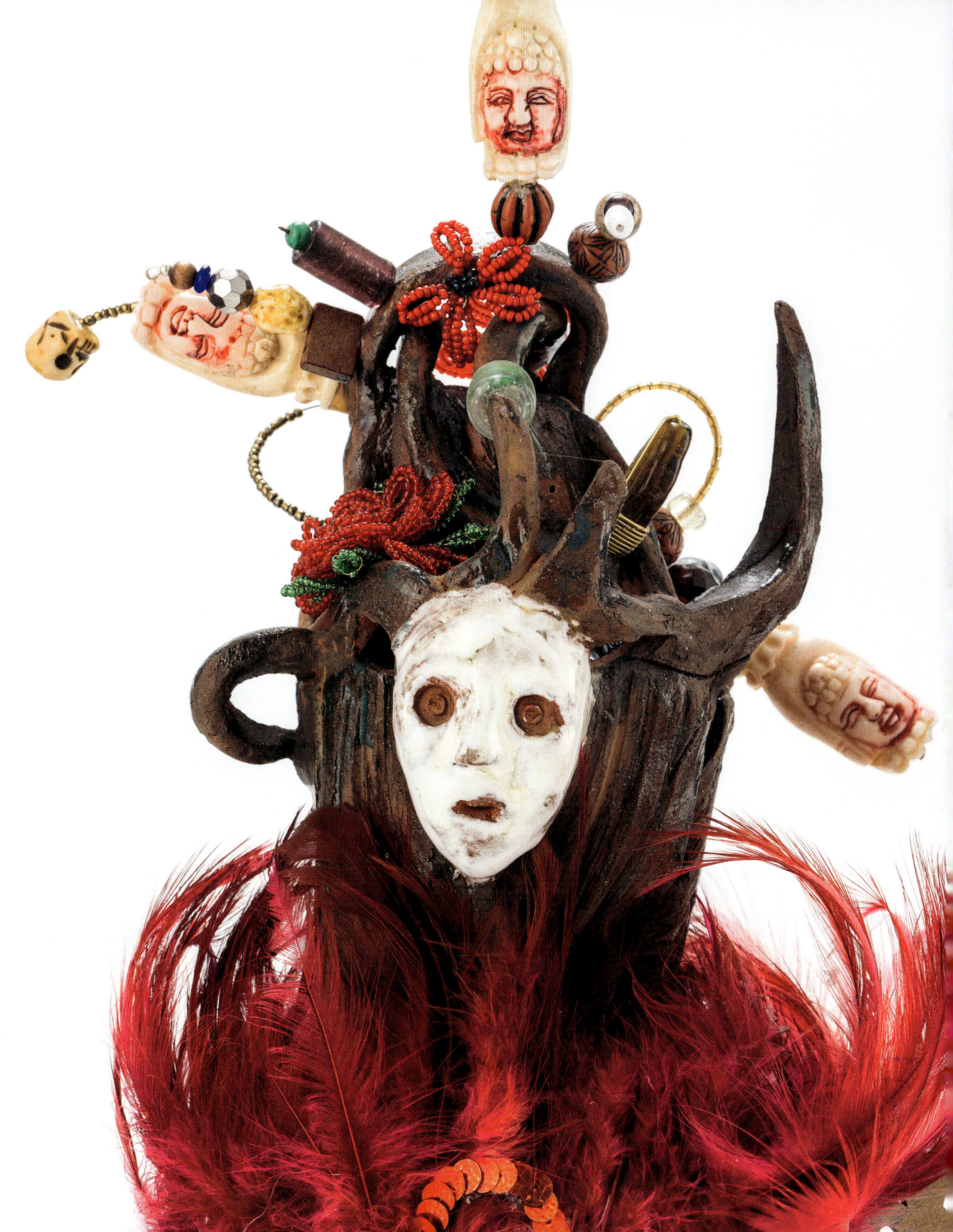

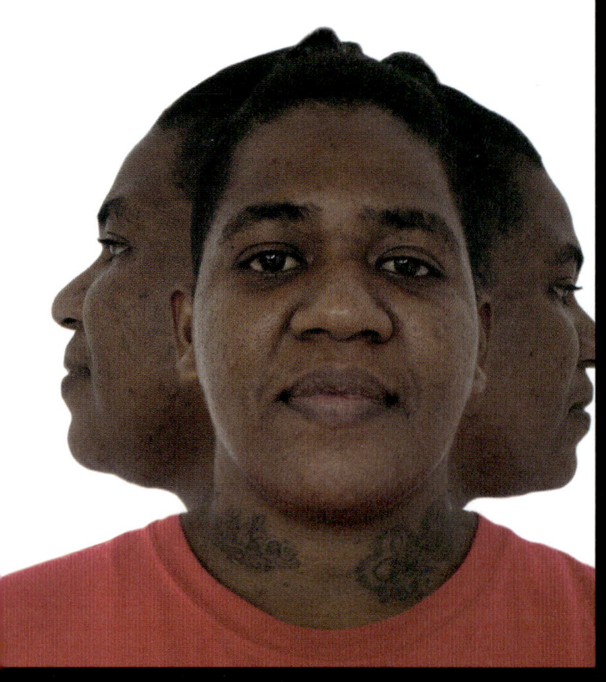

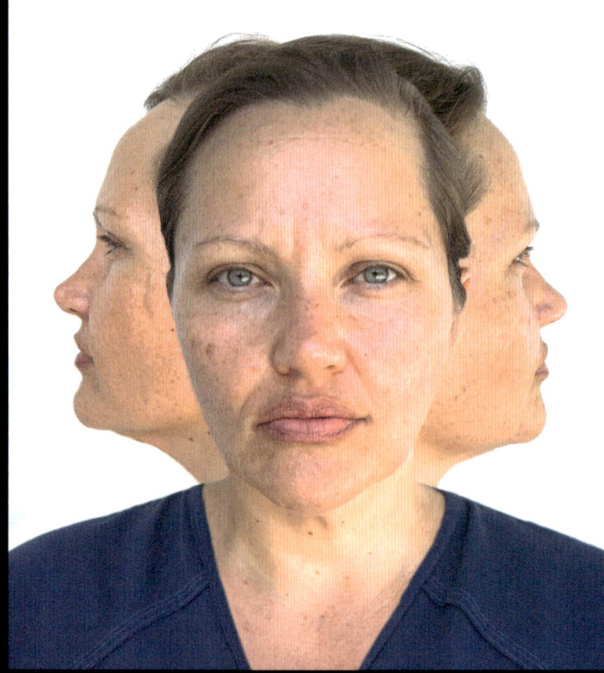

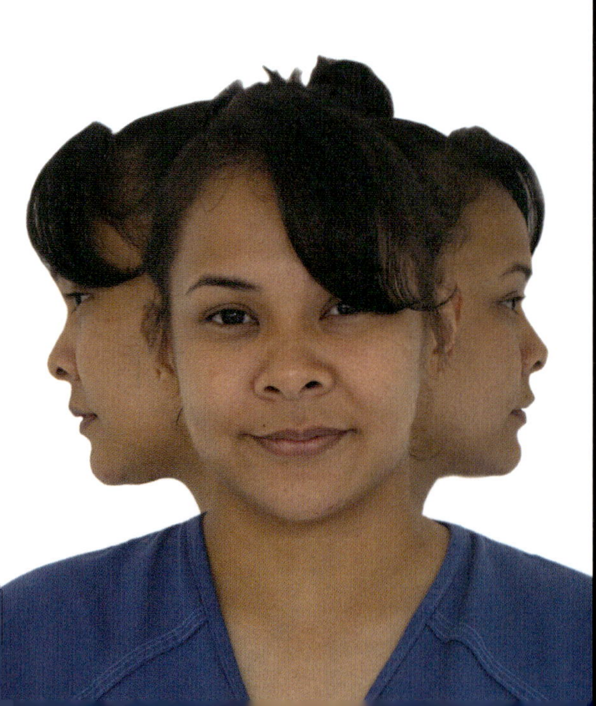

Beyond Bars: Prison Women Speak [collaboration with Tadia Rice], 2018–ongoing, video, 19 minutes, 39 seconds

TOP LEFT
Momi, 2018, photograph

TOP RIGHT
Zoe, 2018, photograph

BOTTOM LEFT
Anjie, 2018, photograph

OPPOSITE
Tiana, 2018, photograph

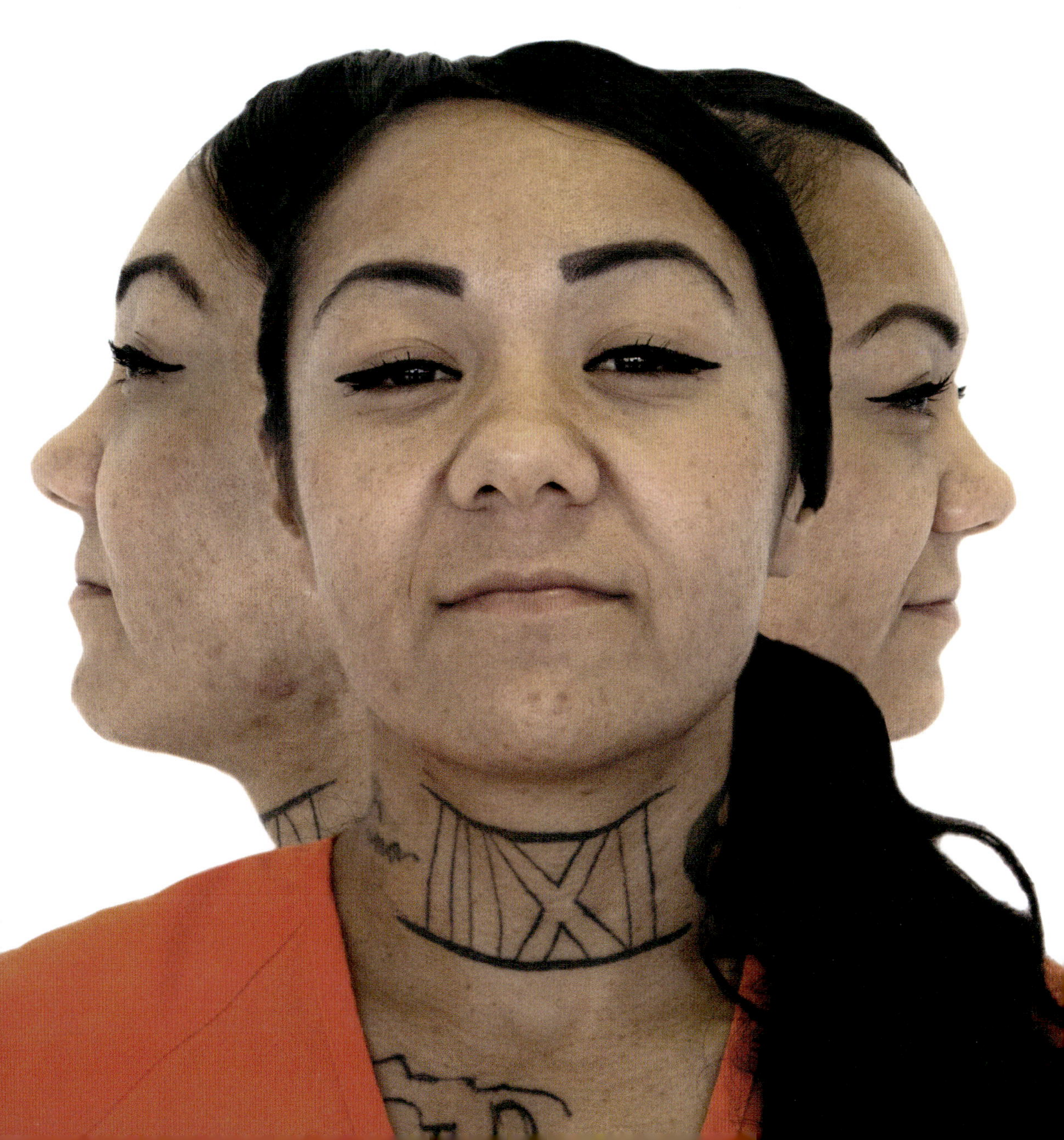

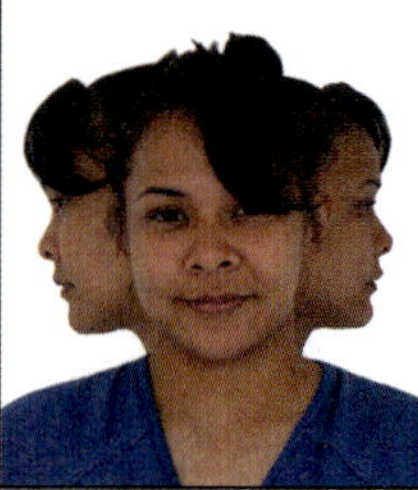

Name: Anjie
Felony: Robbery.
Age at Arrest: 26
Sentence: 20 Years
Date of Incarceration: 2015
Date of release: Late 2022

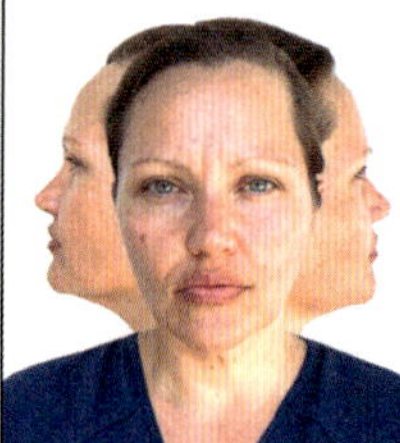
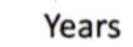

Name: Zoe
Felony: Meth trafficking, promoting dangerous drugs, drug paraphernalia.
Age at Arrest: 34
Sentence: Concurrent 5,10, and 20 Years
Date of Incarceration: 2014
Date of release: 2020

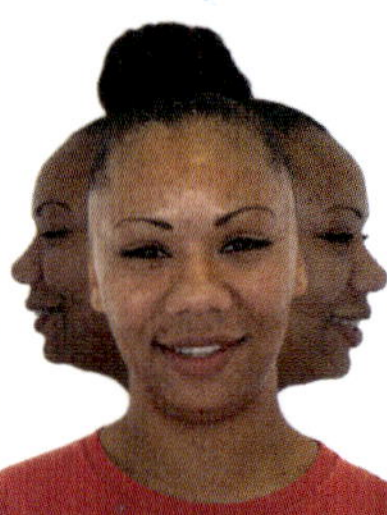

Name: Mae Mae
Felony: Identity Theft.
Age at Arrest: 29
Sentence: 20 Years
Date of Incarceration: 2014 Date of release: 2019

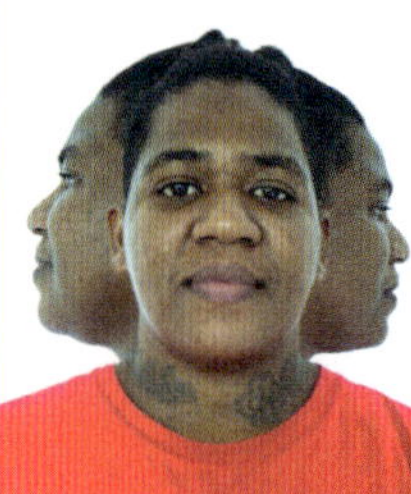

Name: Momi
Felony: Assault, possession of drug paraphernalia.
Age at Arrest: 34
Sentence: 10 Years
Date of Incarceration: 2015 Date of release: Mid-2022

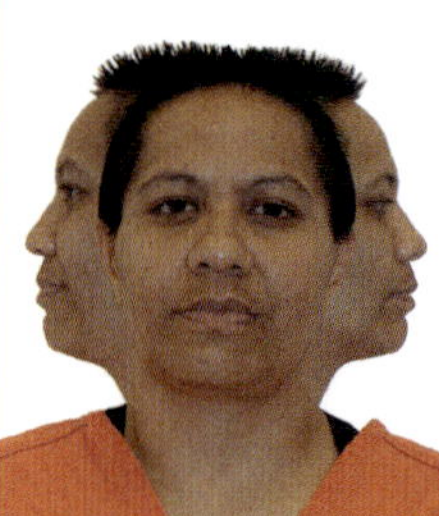

Name: Neko
Felony: Conspiracy to file false claims, Second-degree identity theft, aggravated identity theft, wire fraud, criminal contempt, unauthorized possession of confidential personal information.
Age at Arrest: 27
Sentence: 84 months.
 Pay $193,602 in restitution.
Date of Incarceration: 2014
Date of release: 2022 with 36 months of supervised release.

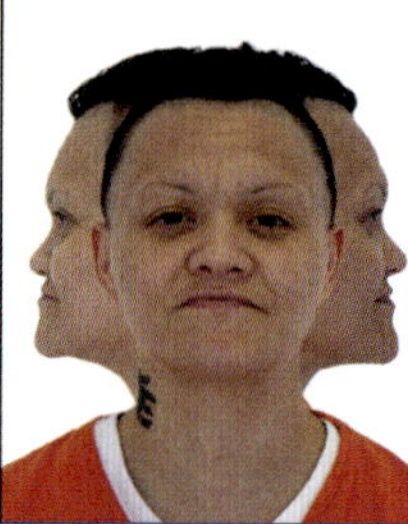
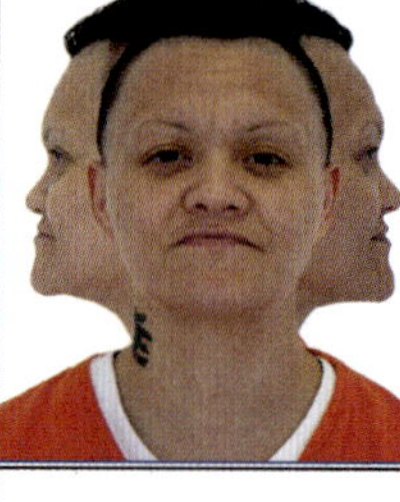

Name: Shay Boy
Felony: First Degree Burglary, First Degree Kidnapping, Second Degree Robbery.
 Age at Arrest: 28
Sentence: 6-10 Years
Date of Incarceration: 2015 Date of release: Mid-2022

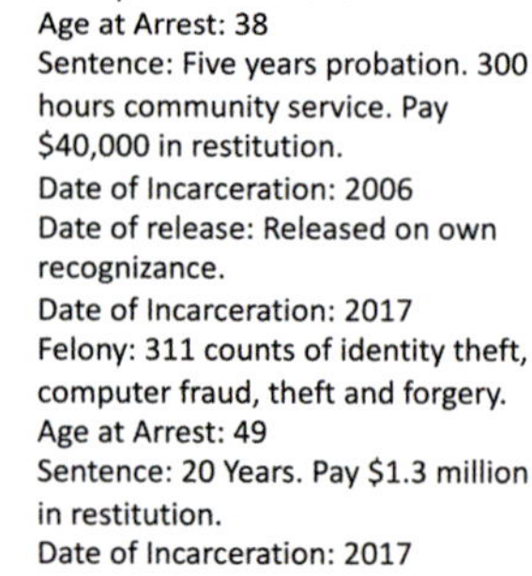

Name: Tammy
Felony: Embezzlement.
Age at Arrest: 38
Sentence: Five years probation. 300 hours community service. Pay $40,000 in restitution.
Date of Incarceration: 2006
Date of release: Released on own recognizance.
Date of Incarceration: 2017
Felony: 311 counts of identity theft, computer fraud, theft and forgery.
Age at Arrest: 49
Sentence: 20 Years. Pay $1.3 million in restitution.
Date of Incarceration: 2017
Date of release: 2037

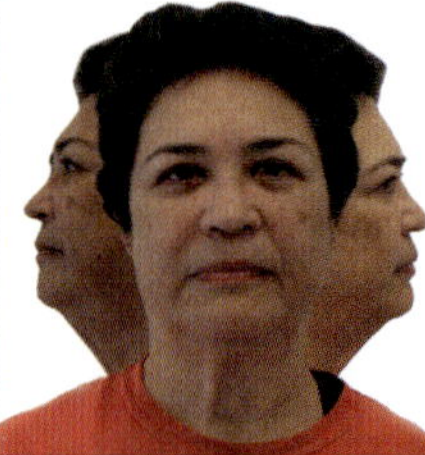

Name: Tiana
Felony/Misdemeanor: Property Damage
Age at Arrest: 12
Sentence: Truancy, Runaway, Contempt of Court, Drug Use, Probation Violation, First Degree Escape.
Date of Incarceration: Youth correctional Facility/Juvenile Detention 1998
Date of release: 2002
Felony: Auto Theft, Second Degree Escape.
Age at Arrest: 18
Sentence: Supervised Release on own recognizance.
Date of Incarceration: 2004
Date of release: Escaped
Felony: Second Degree Escape.
Age at Arrest: 26
Sentence: 10 Years.
Date of Incarceration: 2011

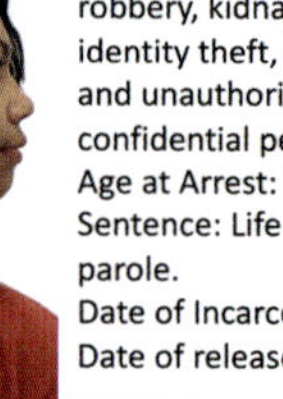

Name: Jess
Felony: Second-degree attempted murder, two counts of first-degree robbery, kidnapping, second-degree identity theft, second-degree theft and unauthorized possession of confidential personal information.
Age at Arrest: 20
Sentence: Life with the possibility of parole.
Date of Incarceration: 2015
Date of release: Life

ARTIST'S STATEMENT

Tadia Rice
Writer. Performer. Recording Artist. Playwright. Poet.

I give voice to women whose words have been quieted, the voices of incarcerated women, locked in, locked out, and locked up in prison cells. Their voices are loud and clear, whether on the inside or outside, all are working to reenter society, to piece together a different and better life for themselves and their children.

Their stories may seem unreal, but they are are poignant reminders that anyone, given certain circumstances, can end up incarcerated. The common thread is childhood trauma, violence, sexual assaults, addiction, and homelessness.

Once you know these women you see how it could have been you. For some it was drunk-driving that killed best friends, or murder of a man from whom she protected herself from beatings, forced prostitution, and rape by other men. The stories are endless. Life-changing circumstances can happen to the best of people, and the worst. What did they do … how did they get there … what happened inside … what will happen when they get out?

For ten years I listened to their voices. I still do. Please hear them.

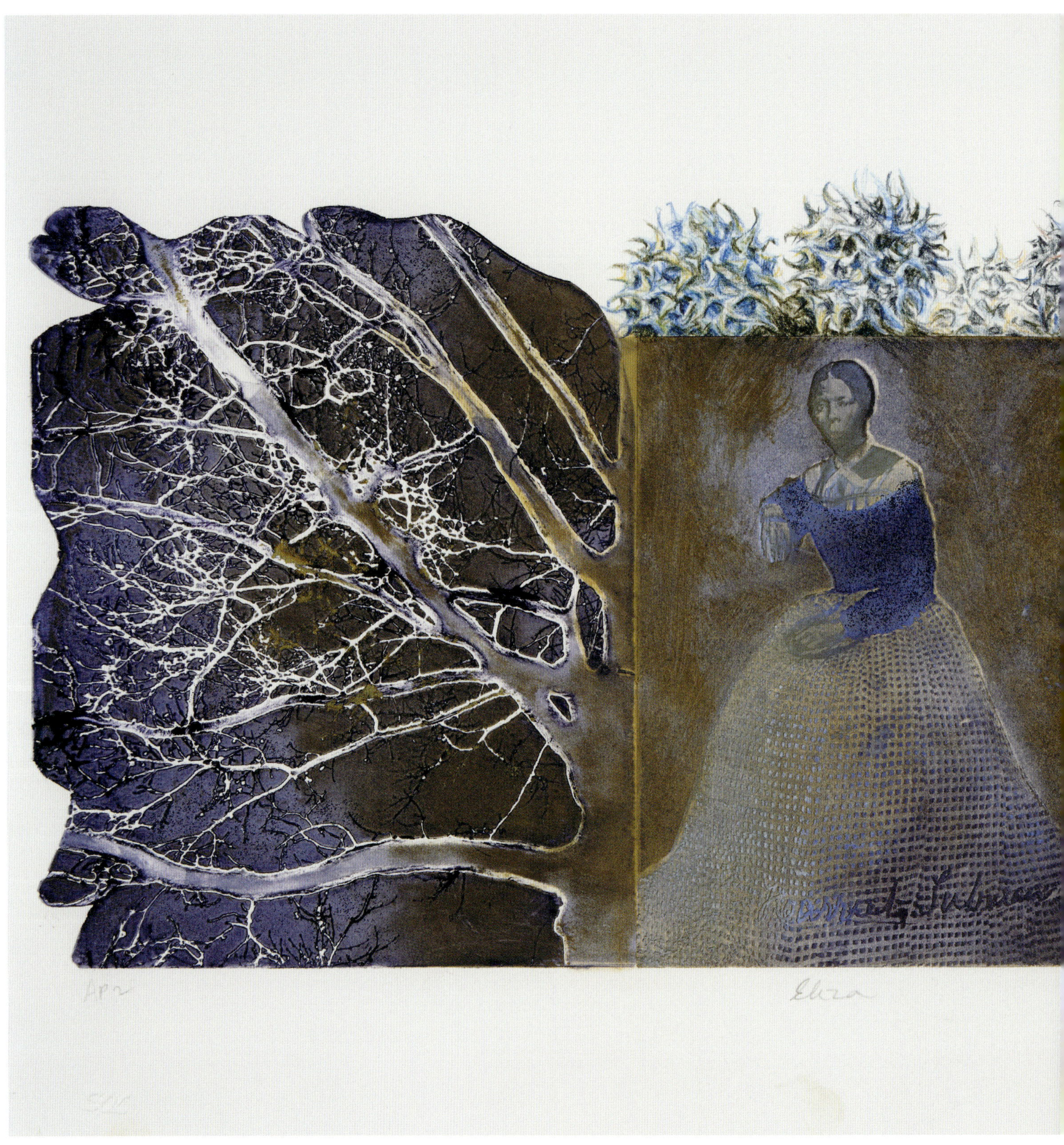

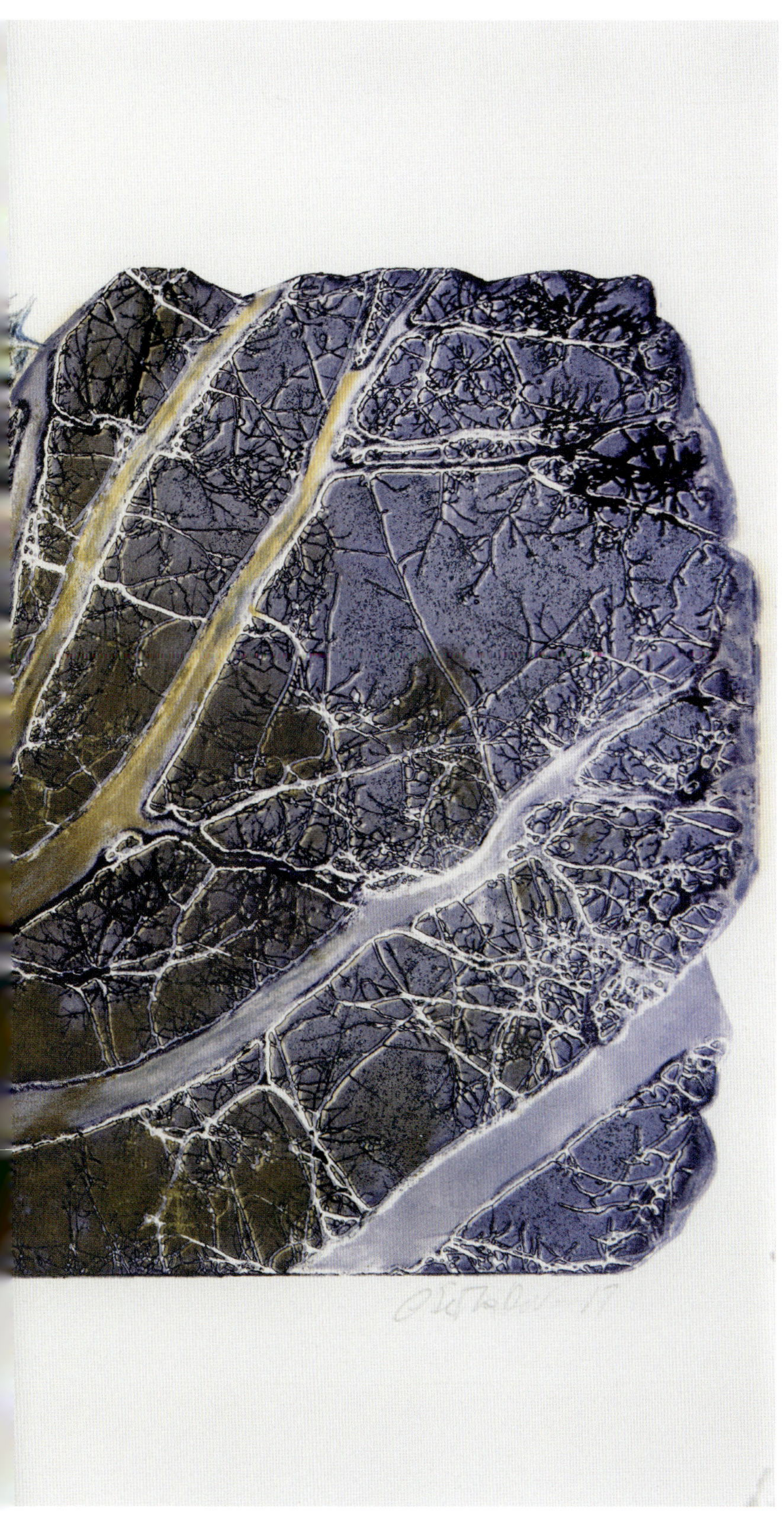

Eliza, 2017, etching, AP/2

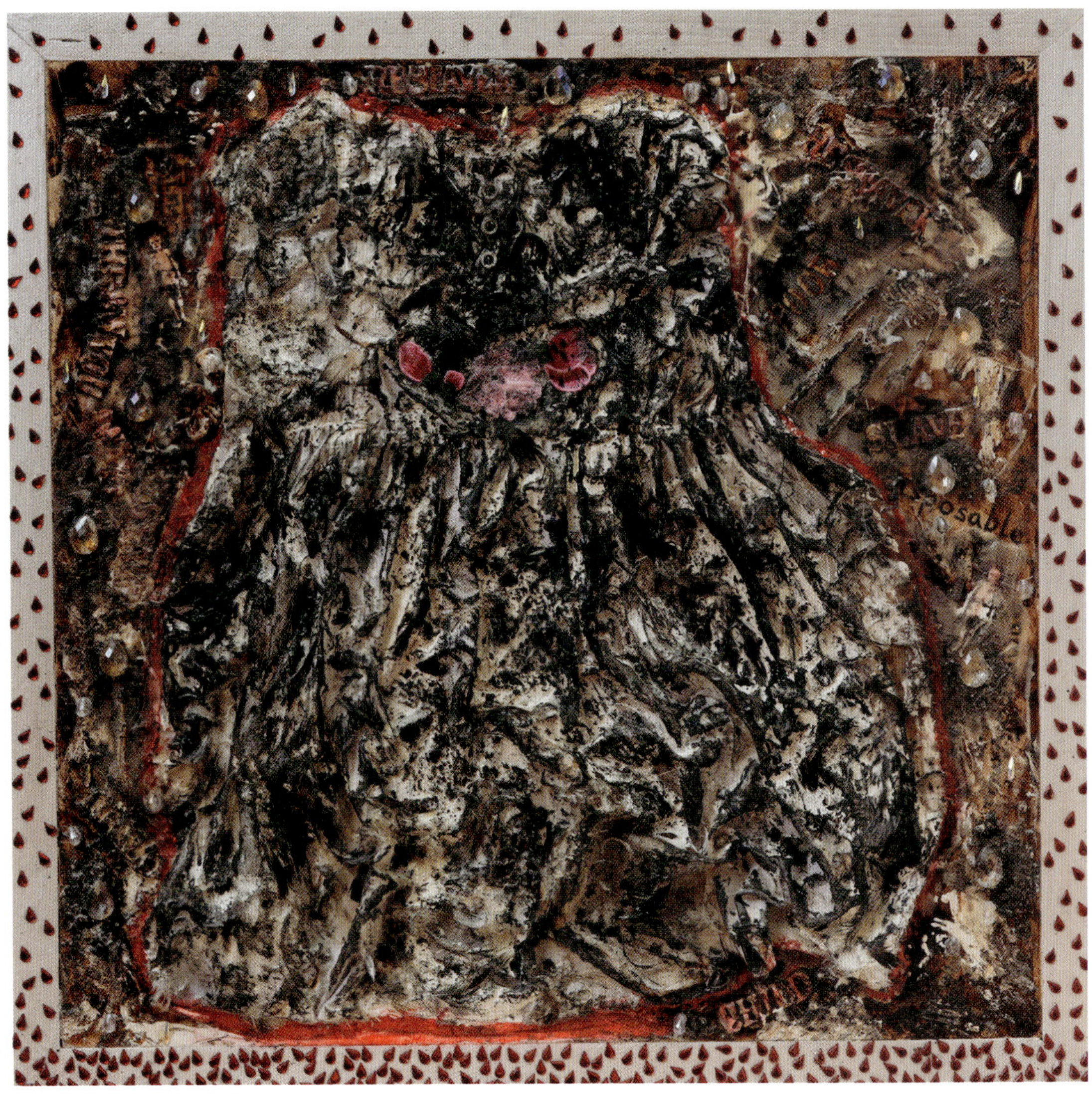

Restavek, 2016, encaustic,
fabric, plastics, glass,
feathers, oil, beads

OPPOSITE
Minty, 2017, solar etching,
Anonymous loan

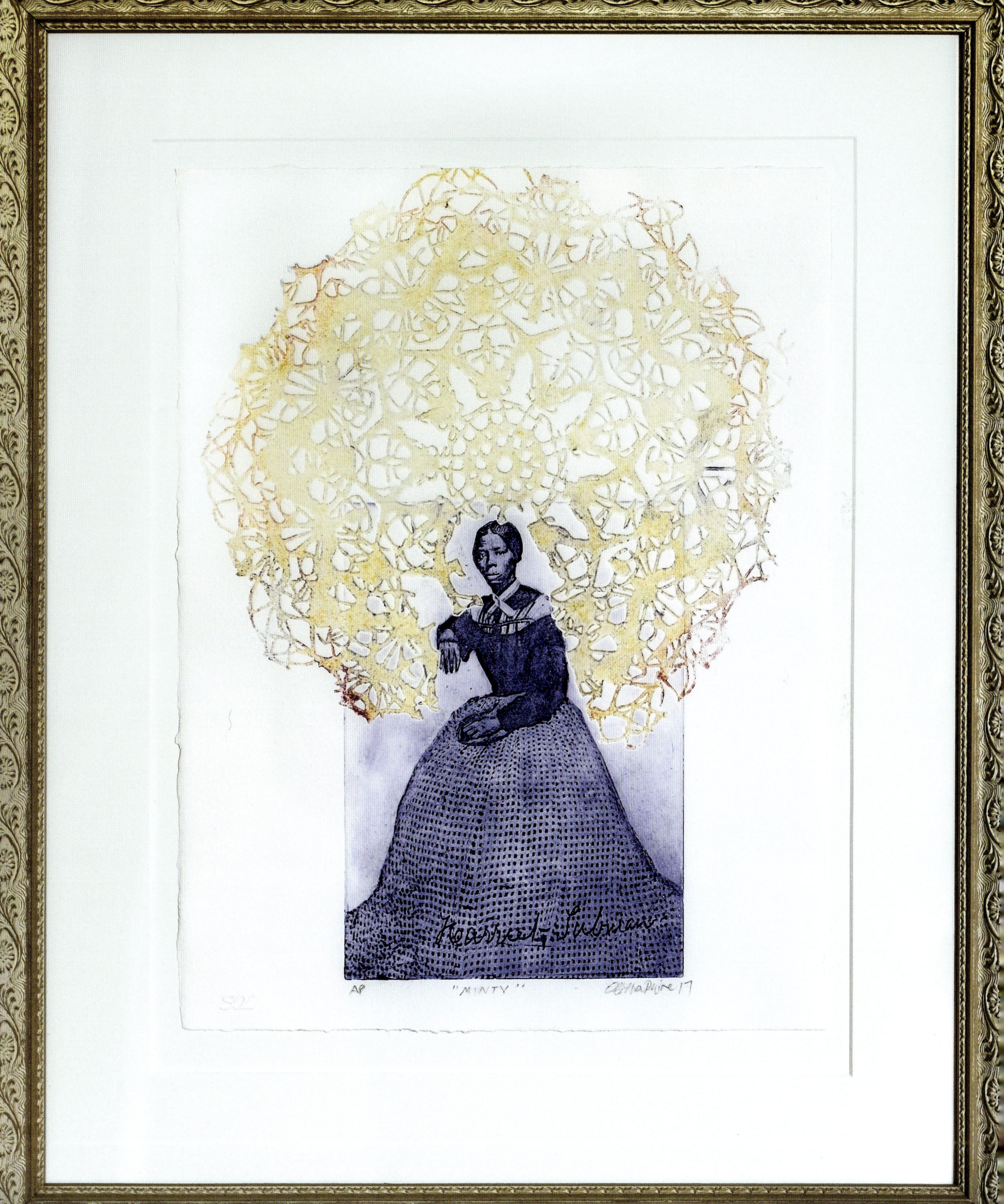

Harriet Tubman
AP
"MINTY"

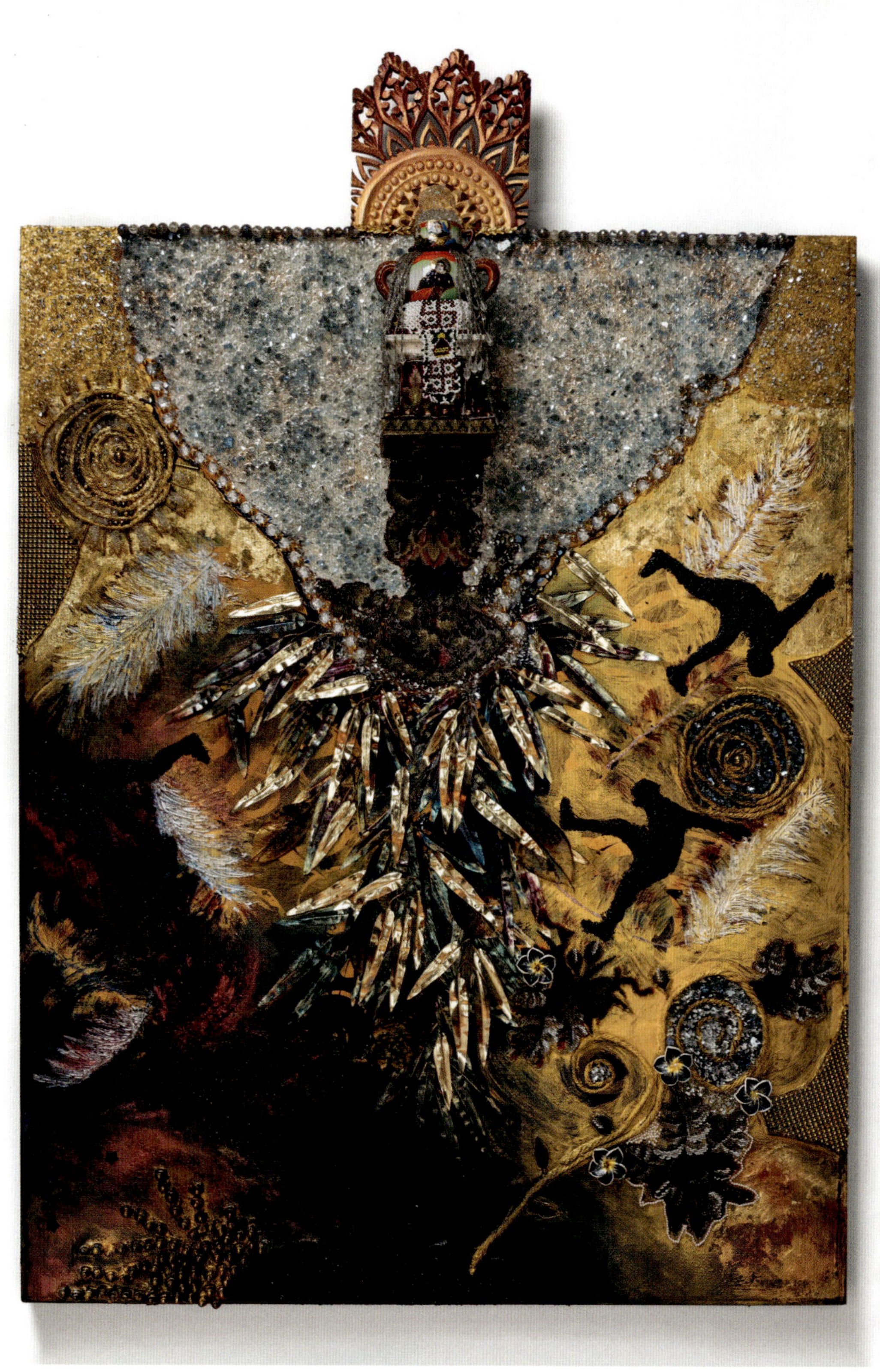

Whatever Happened to Icarus?, 2020, acrylic, glass chips, rope, ceramic, wood, plastics

Tree from Hell, 2021, beads, ceramic, fabric, glass, wood

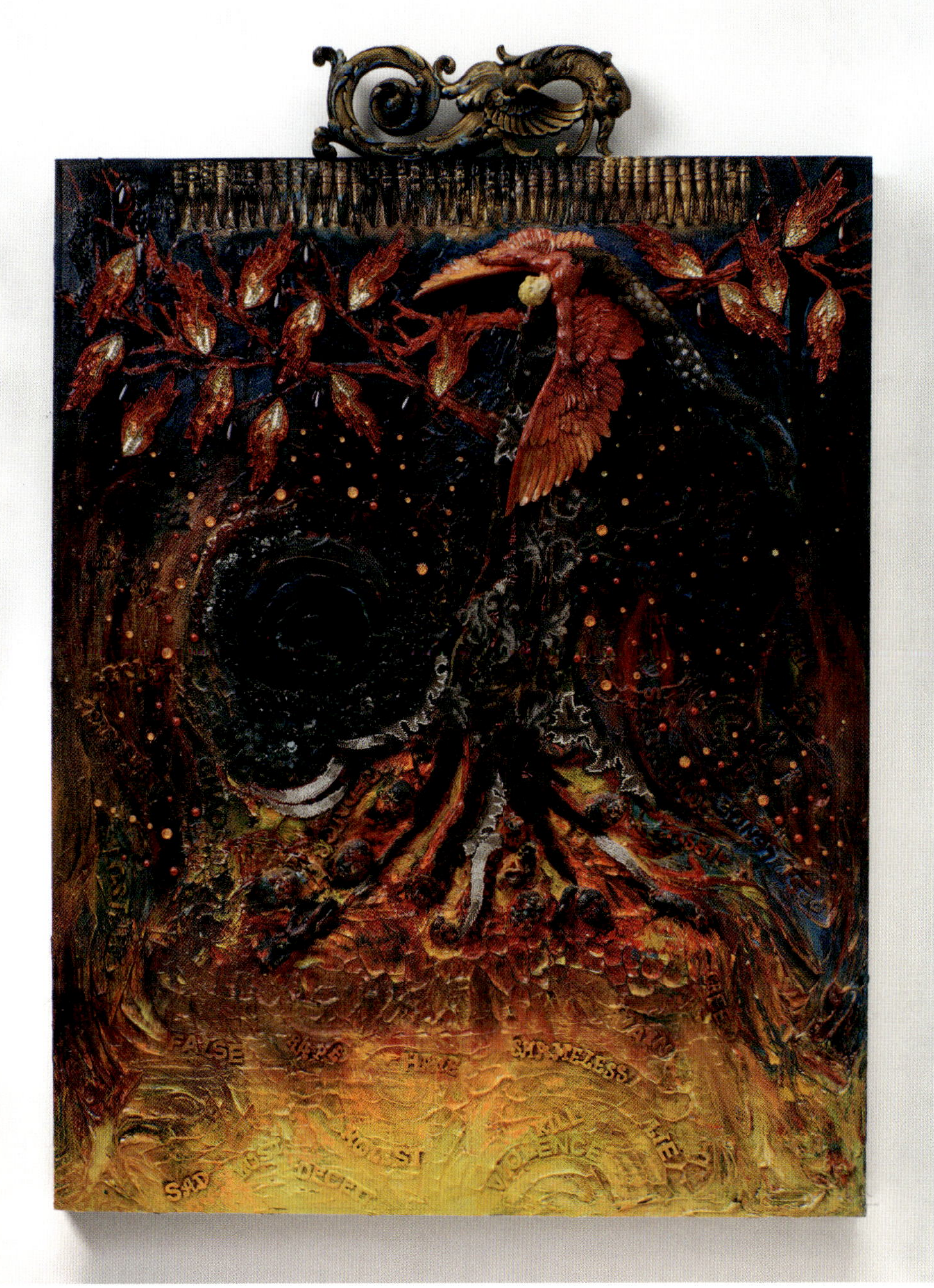

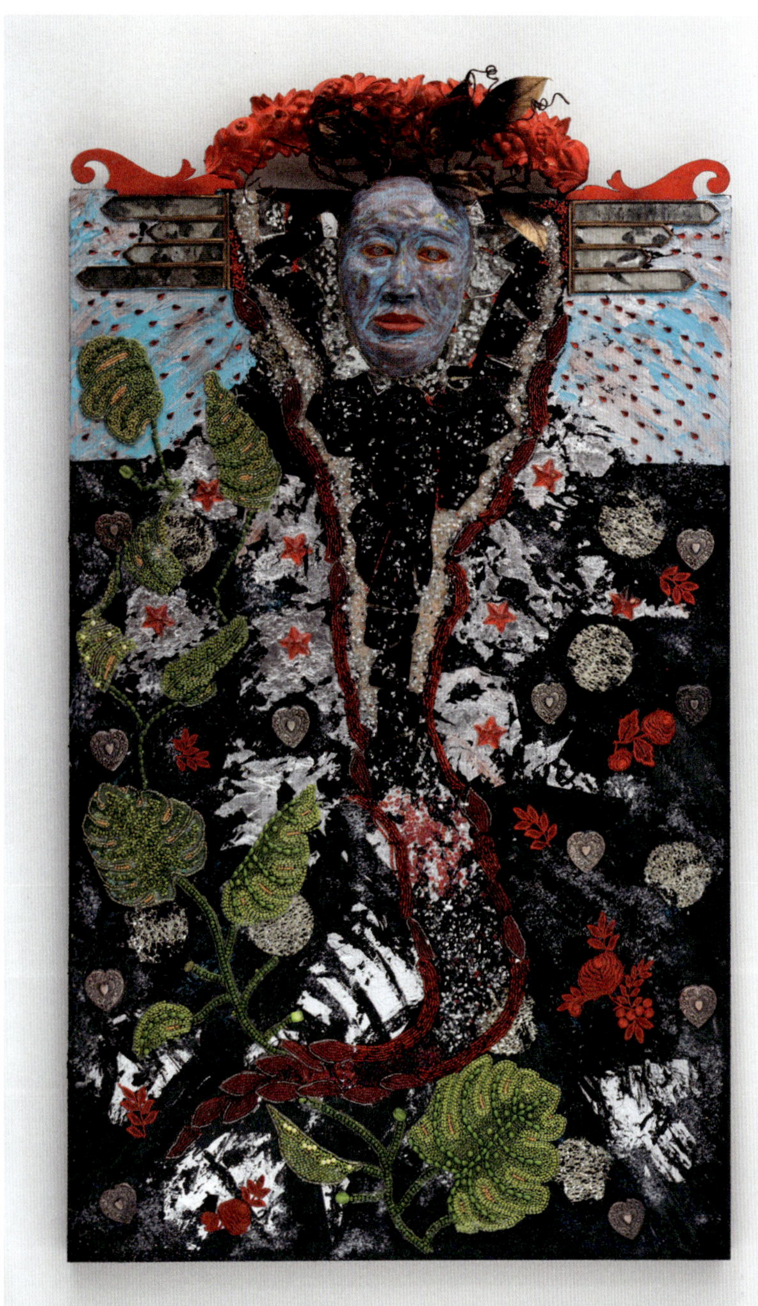

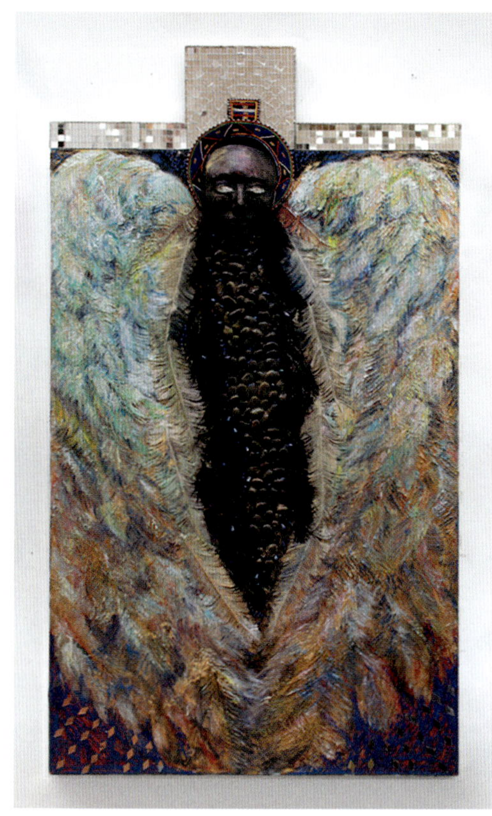

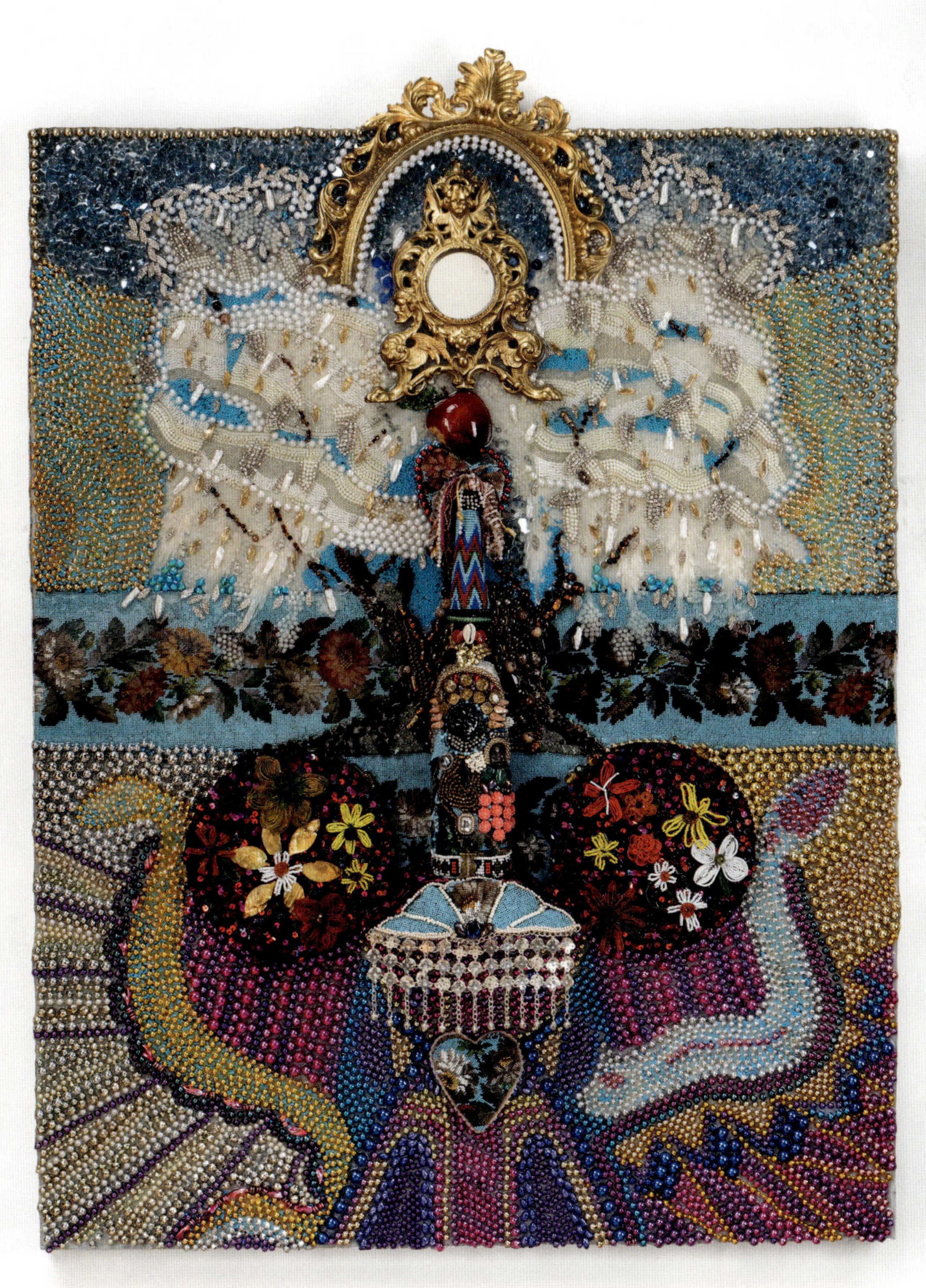

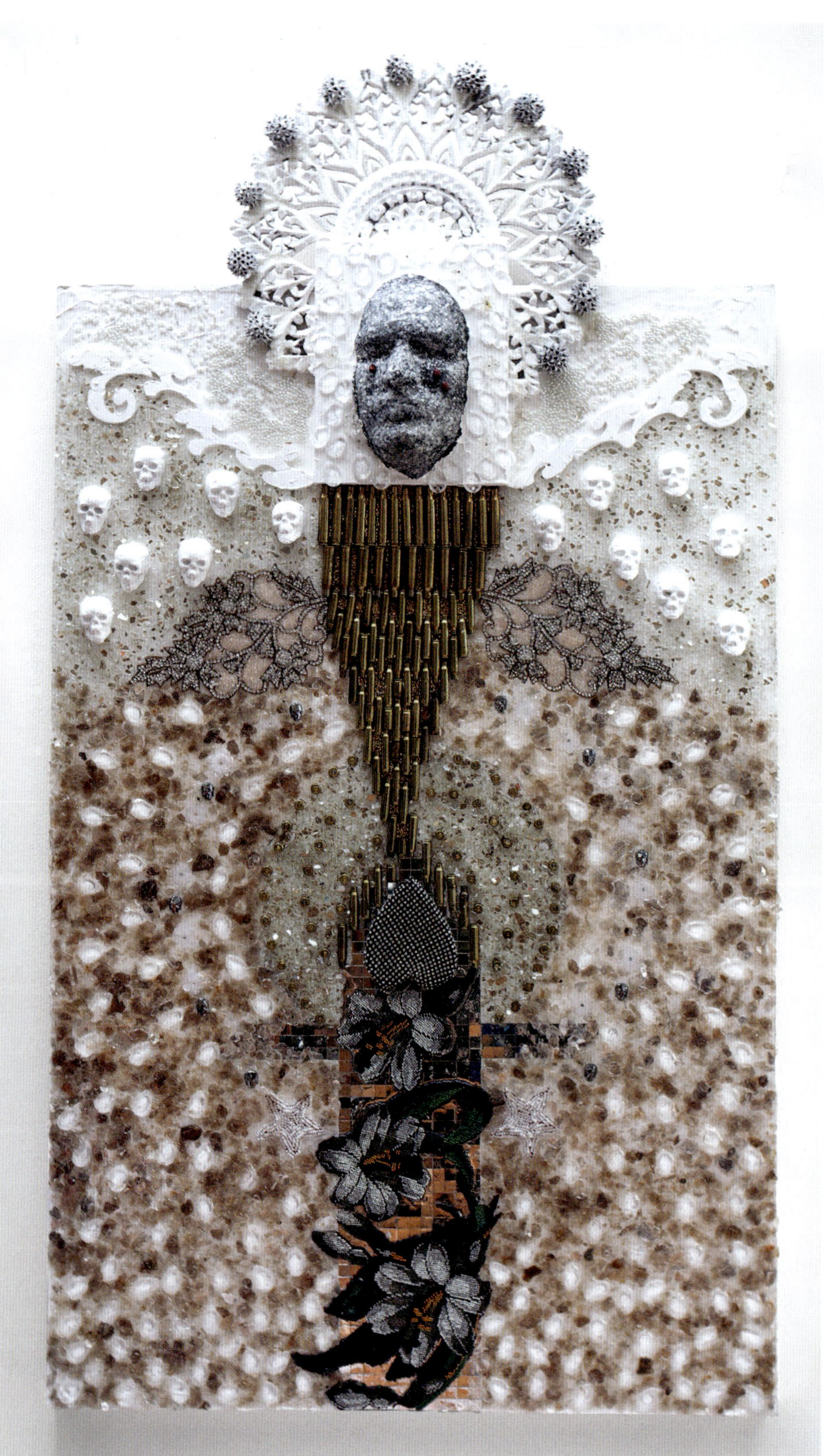

Subsumed by Whiteness,
2020, mixed media

Mamawata's Earth Song,
2019, acrylic, geo stones,
plastic, nails, wood,
rope, clay

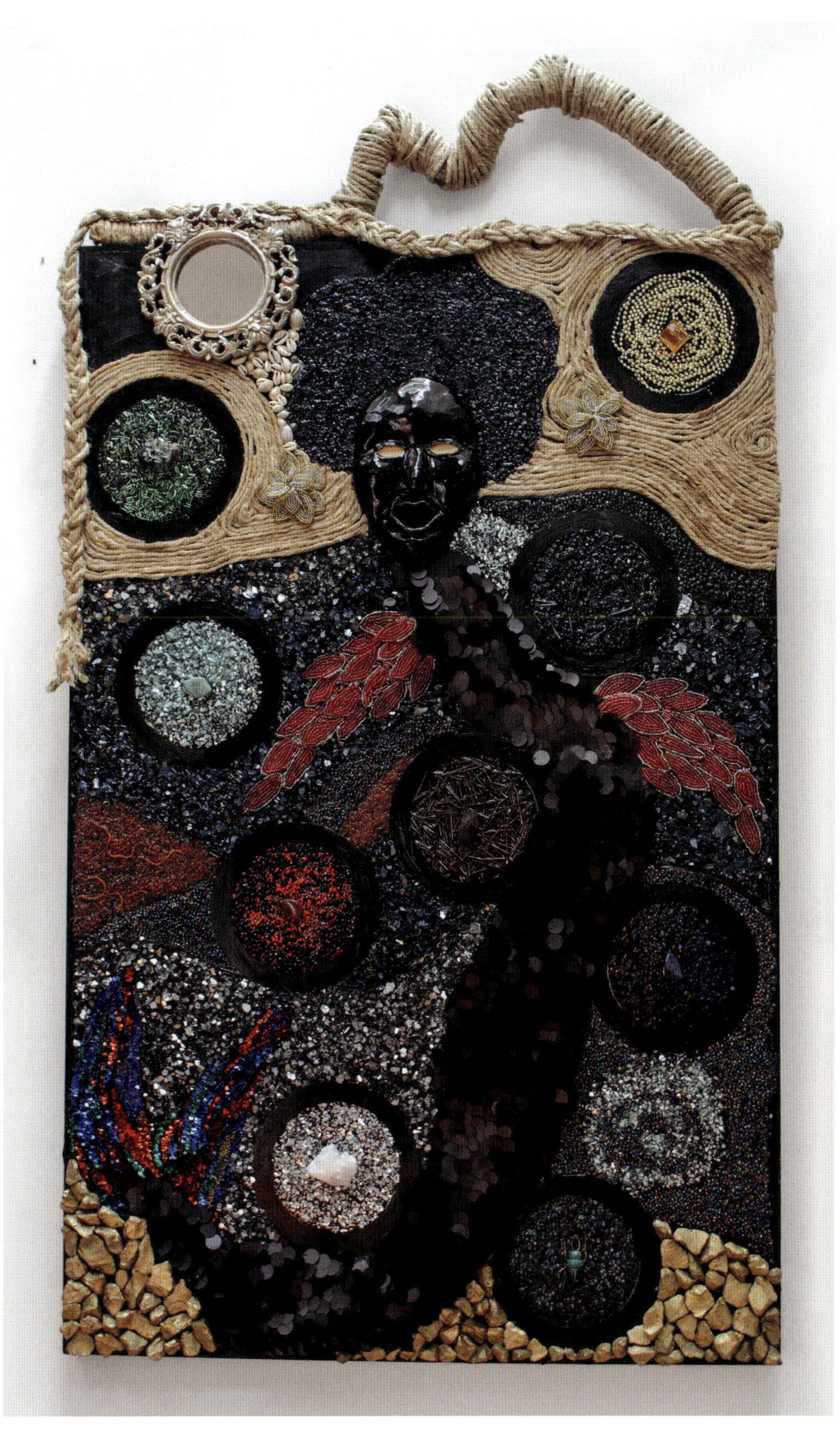

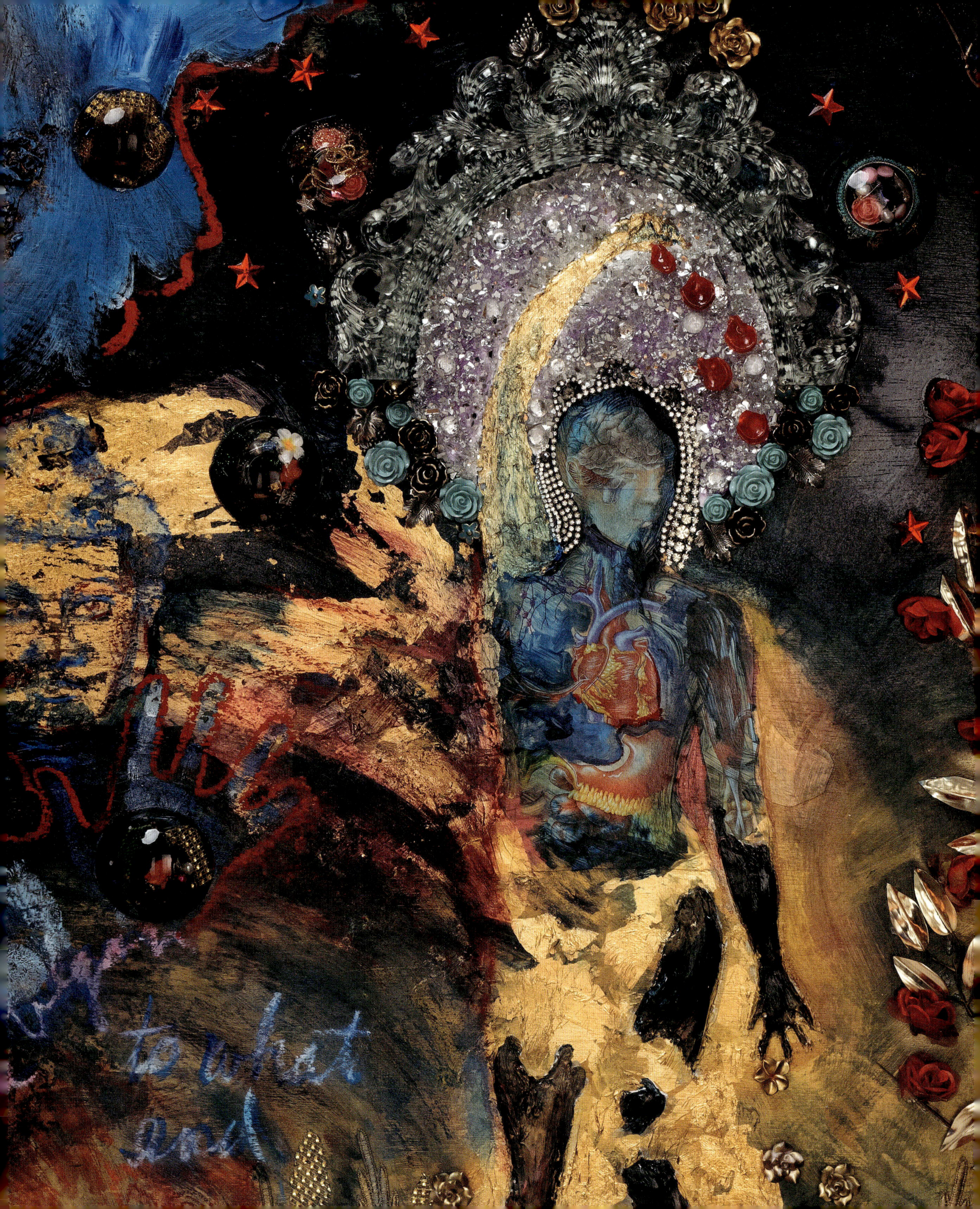

to what
end

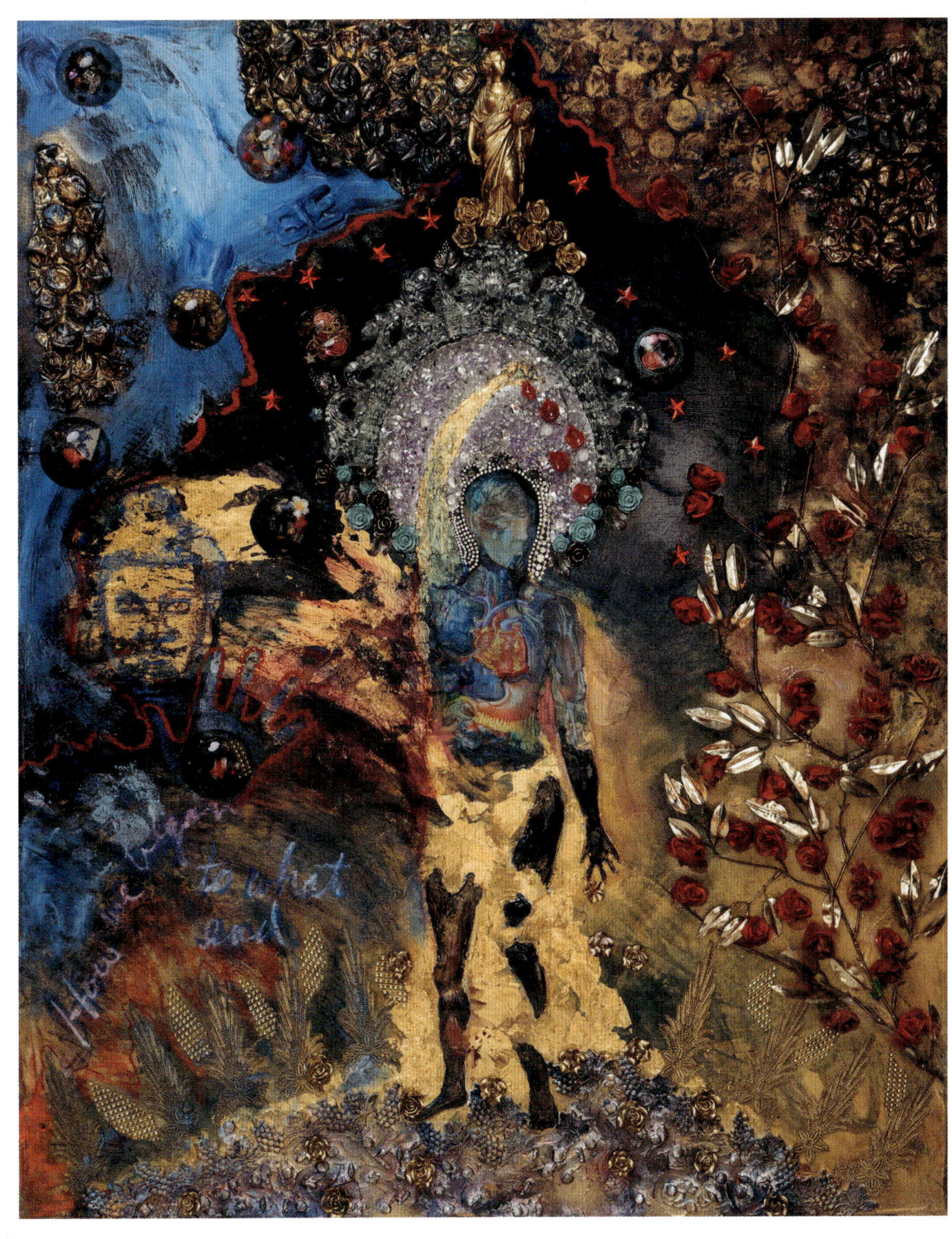

Sirius–Asteria, 2020, glass, fabric, acrylic, wood, paper

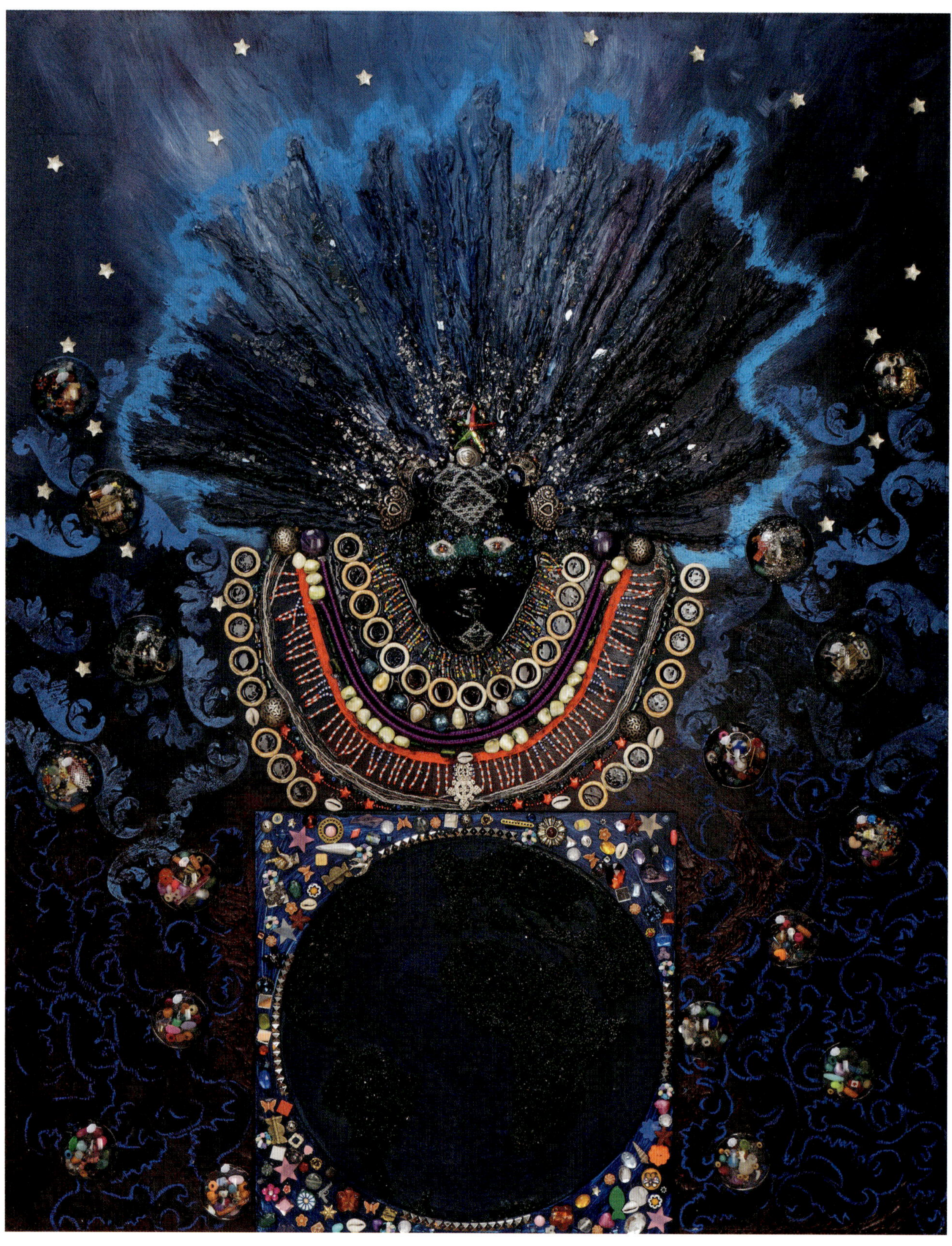

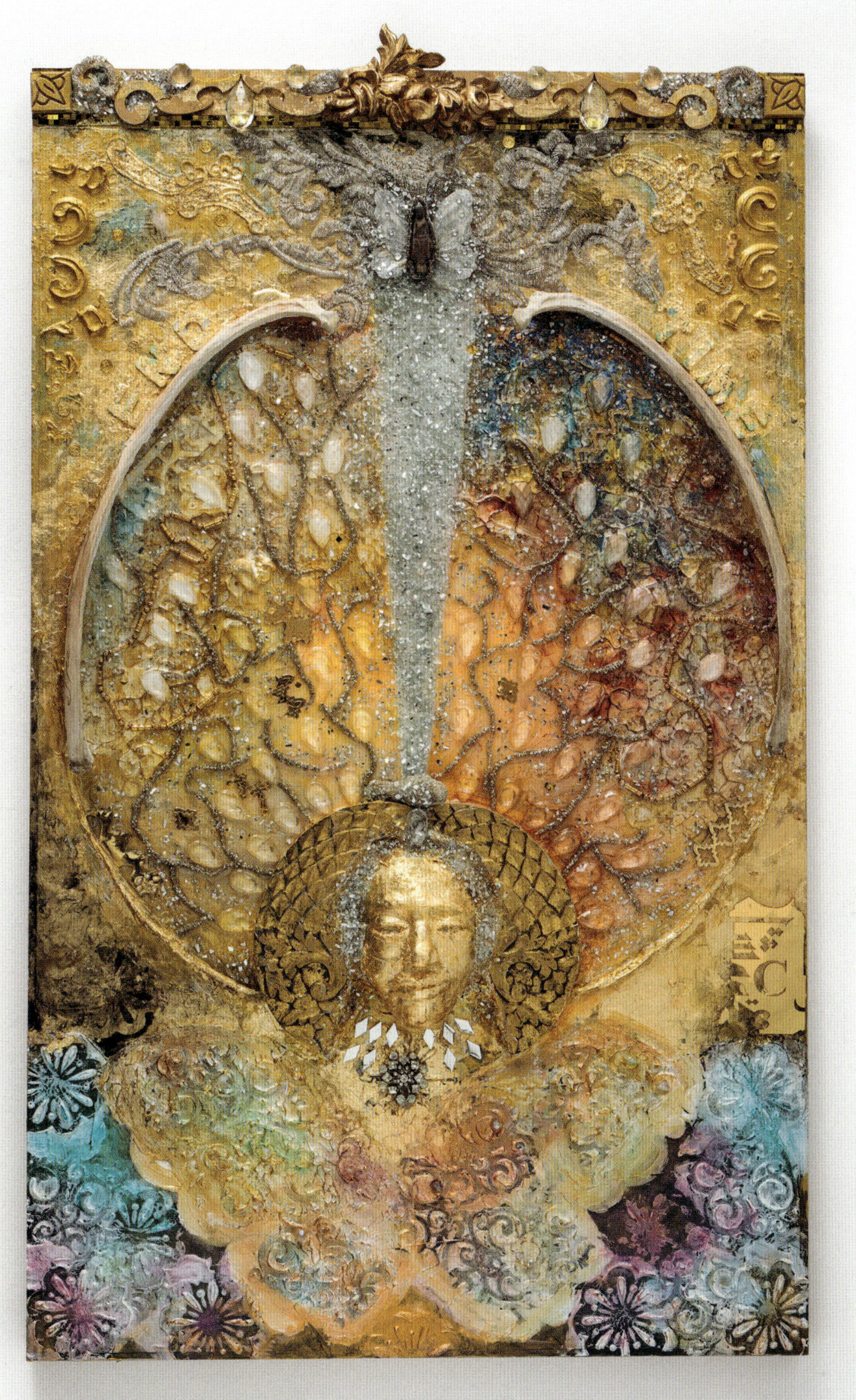

OPPOSITE

Mawumoongoddess, 2019, wood, acrylic, glass, beads, rope, and resin on wood panel

Epiphany, 2018, wood, glass, acrylic, bones, plastic

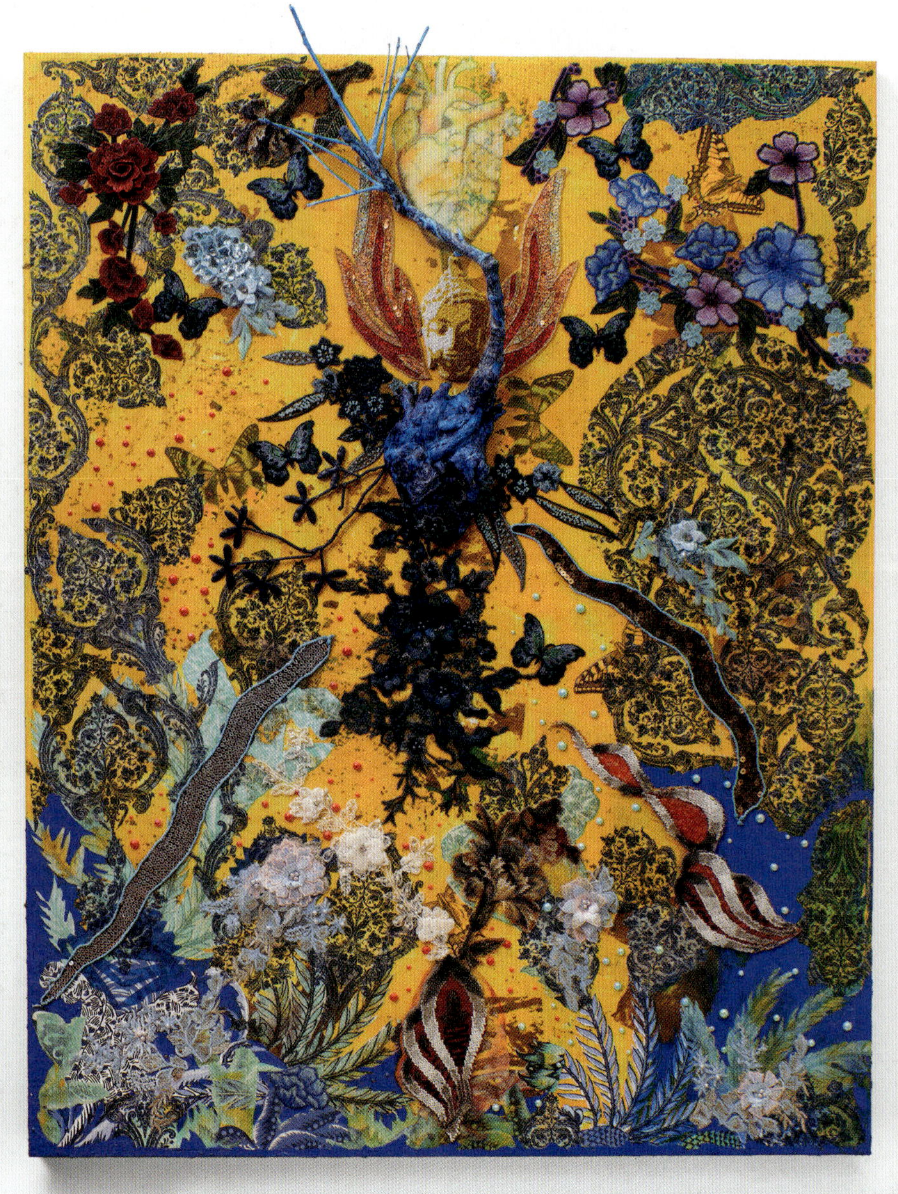

Garden of the Heart,
2021, mixed media

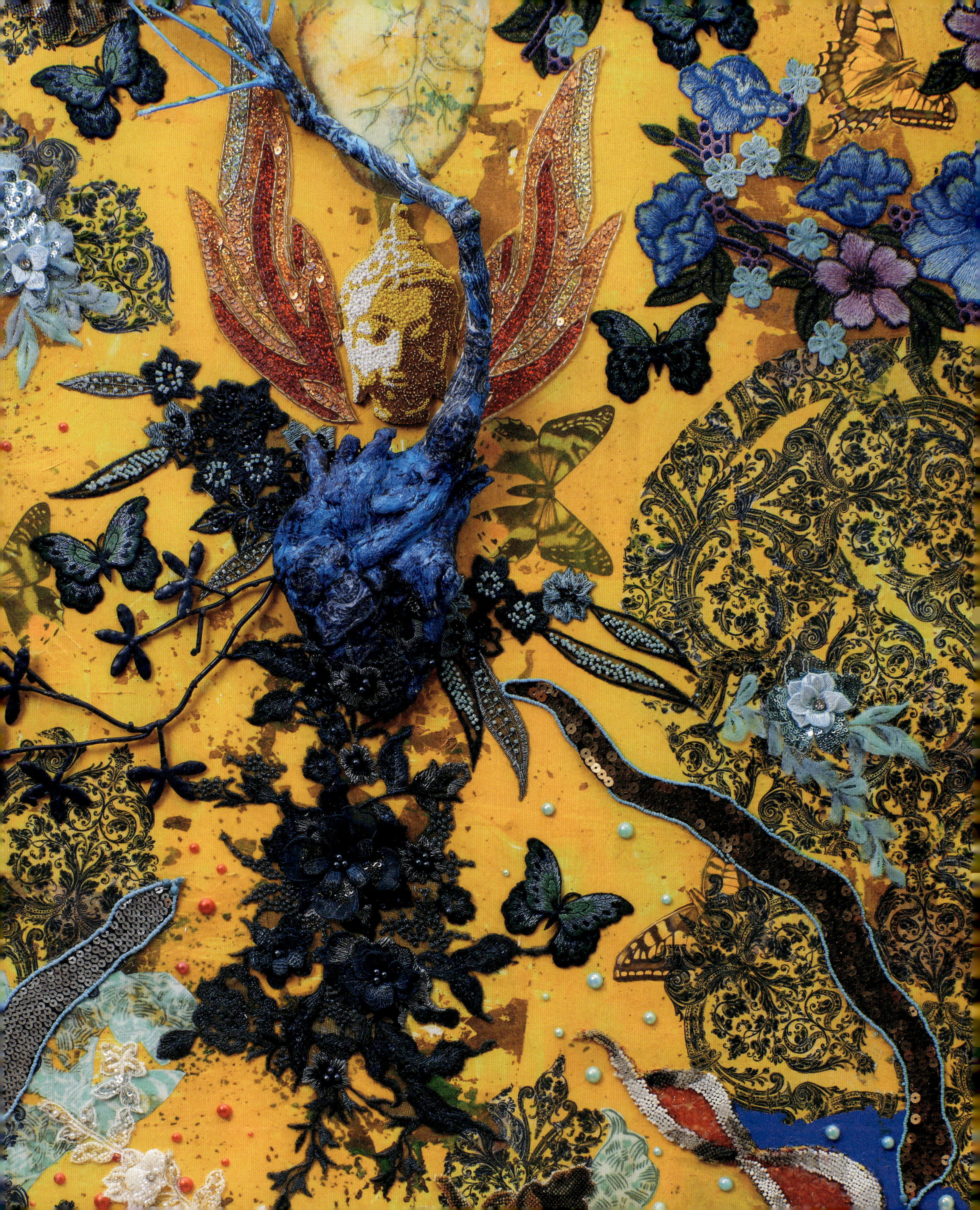

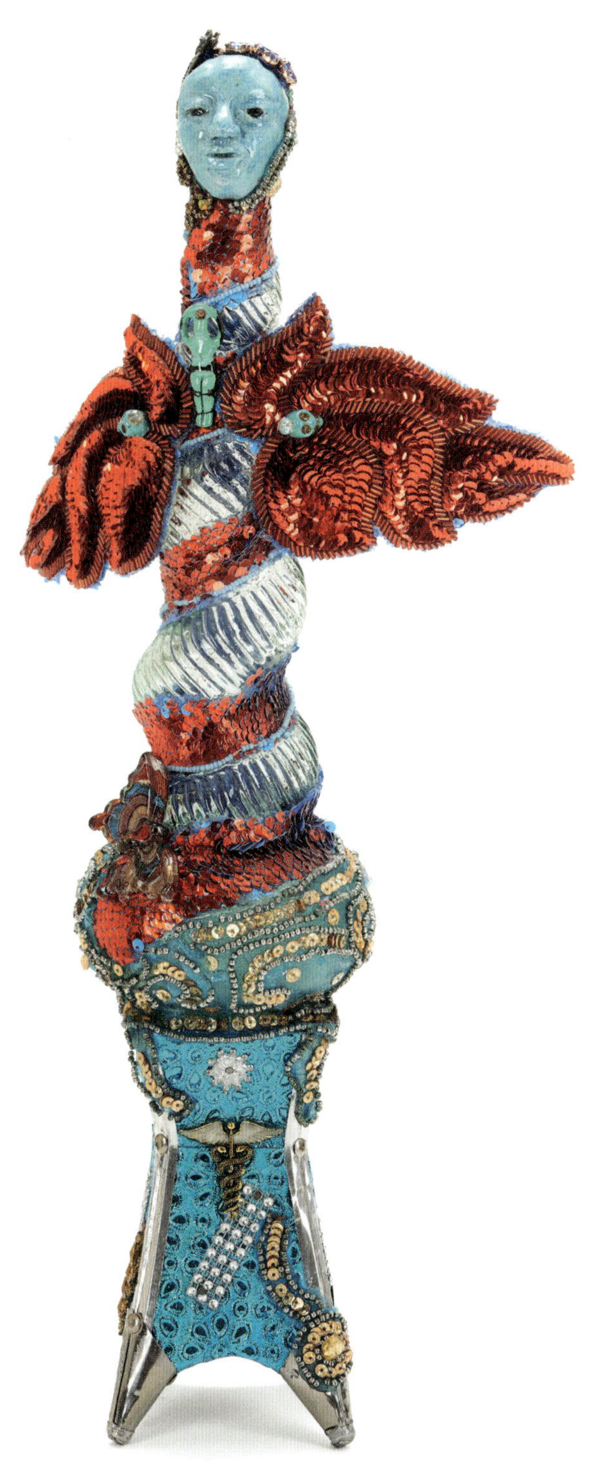
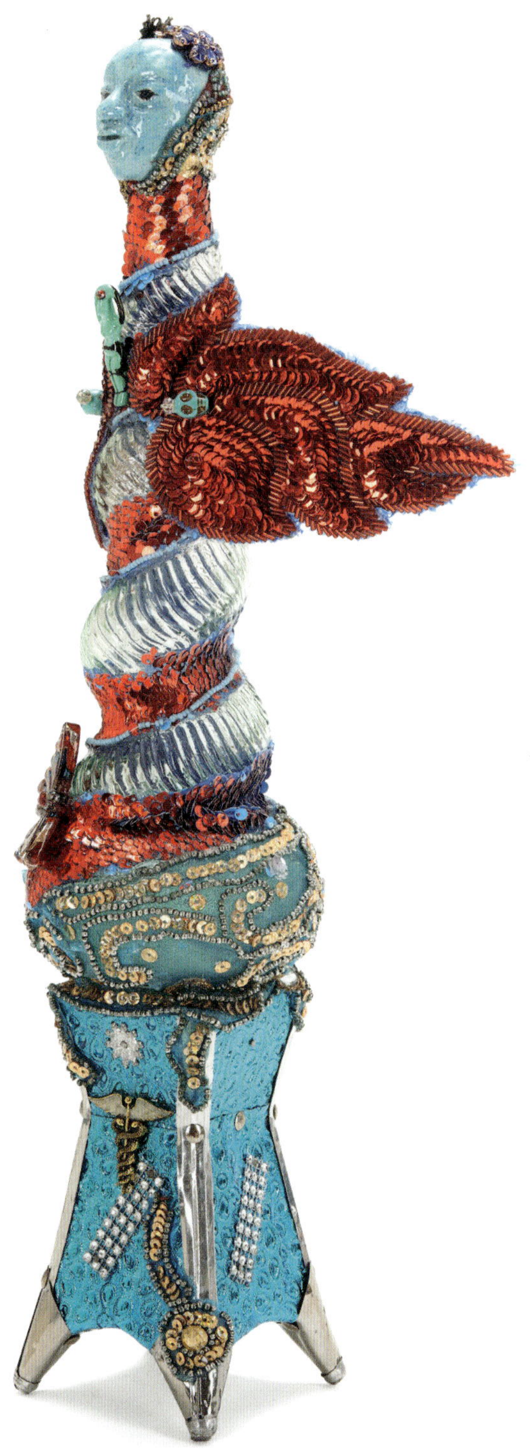

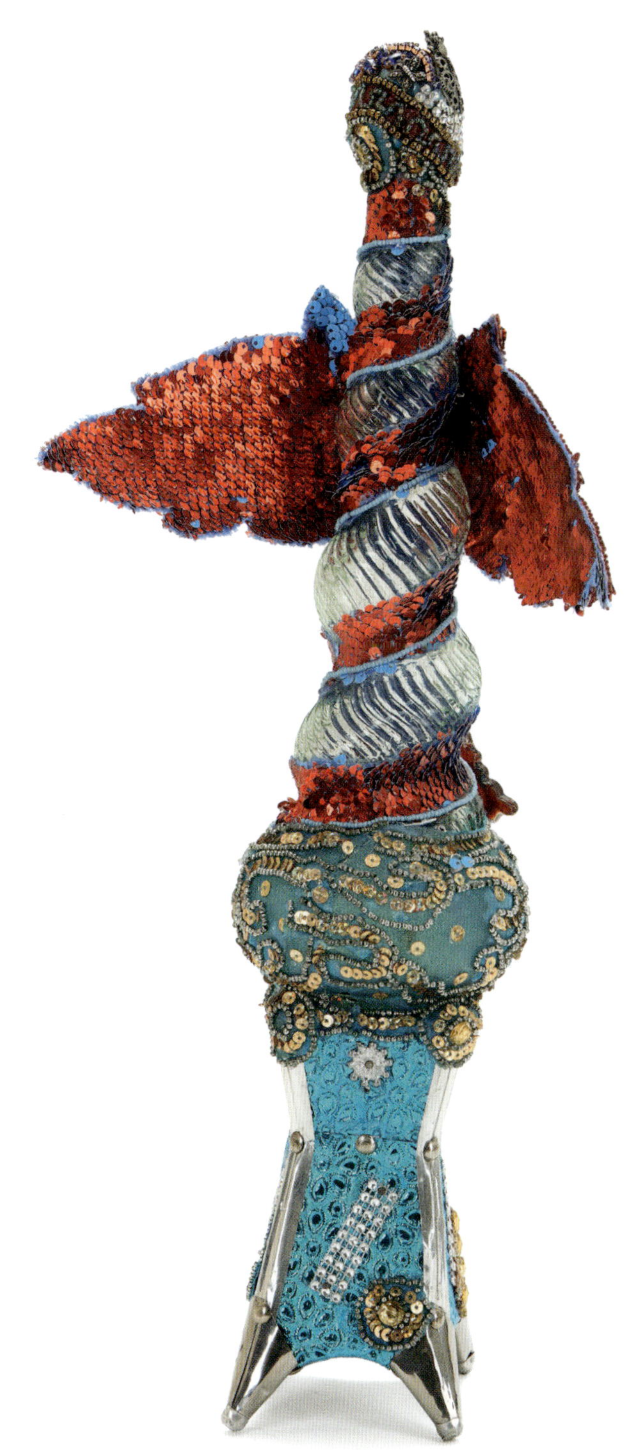

Serpent, 2022, glass, beads, sequins, fabric, clay

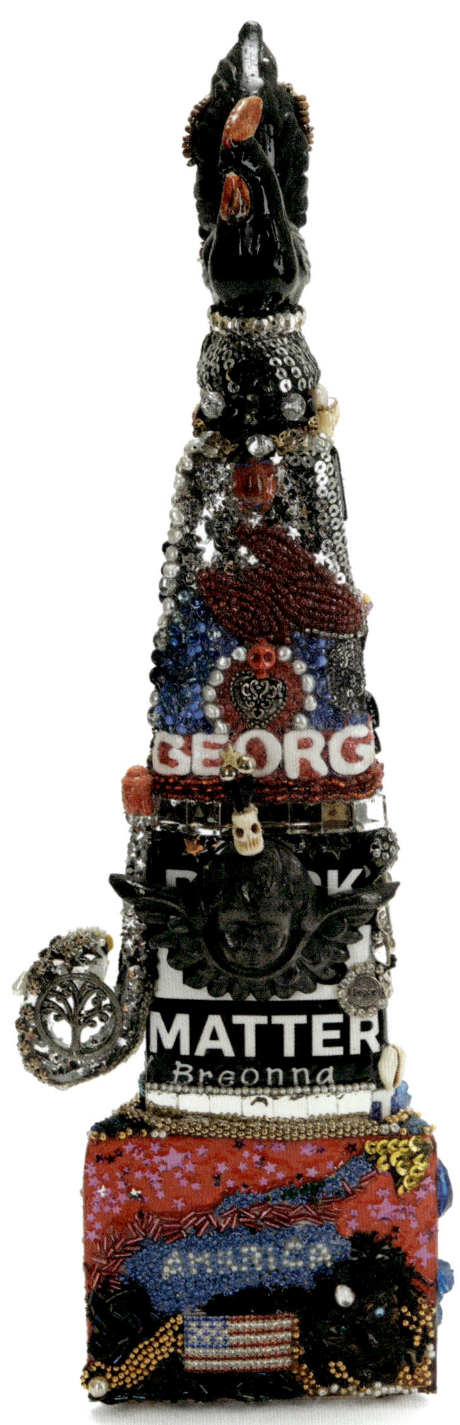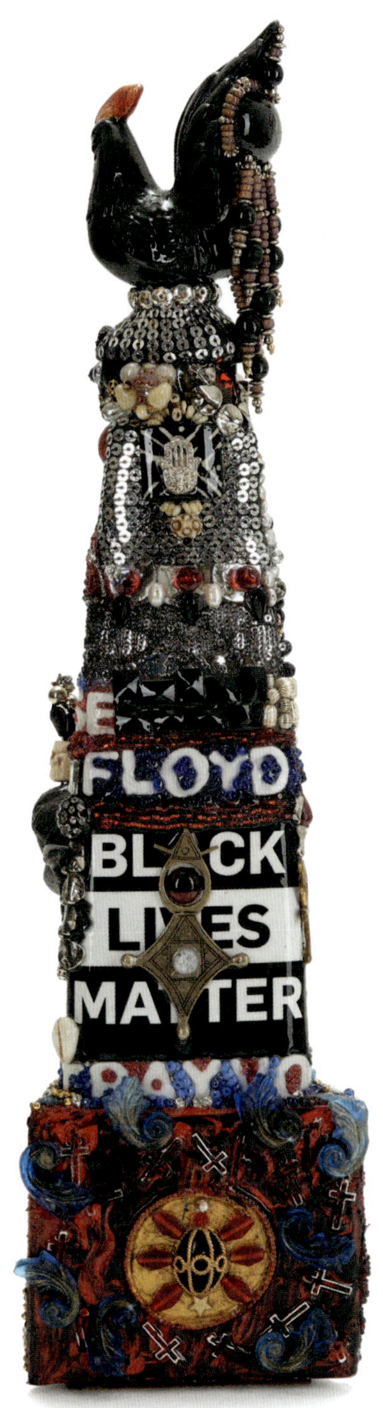

George Floyd (Black Lives Matter), 2021, glass, beads, clay, metal, paper

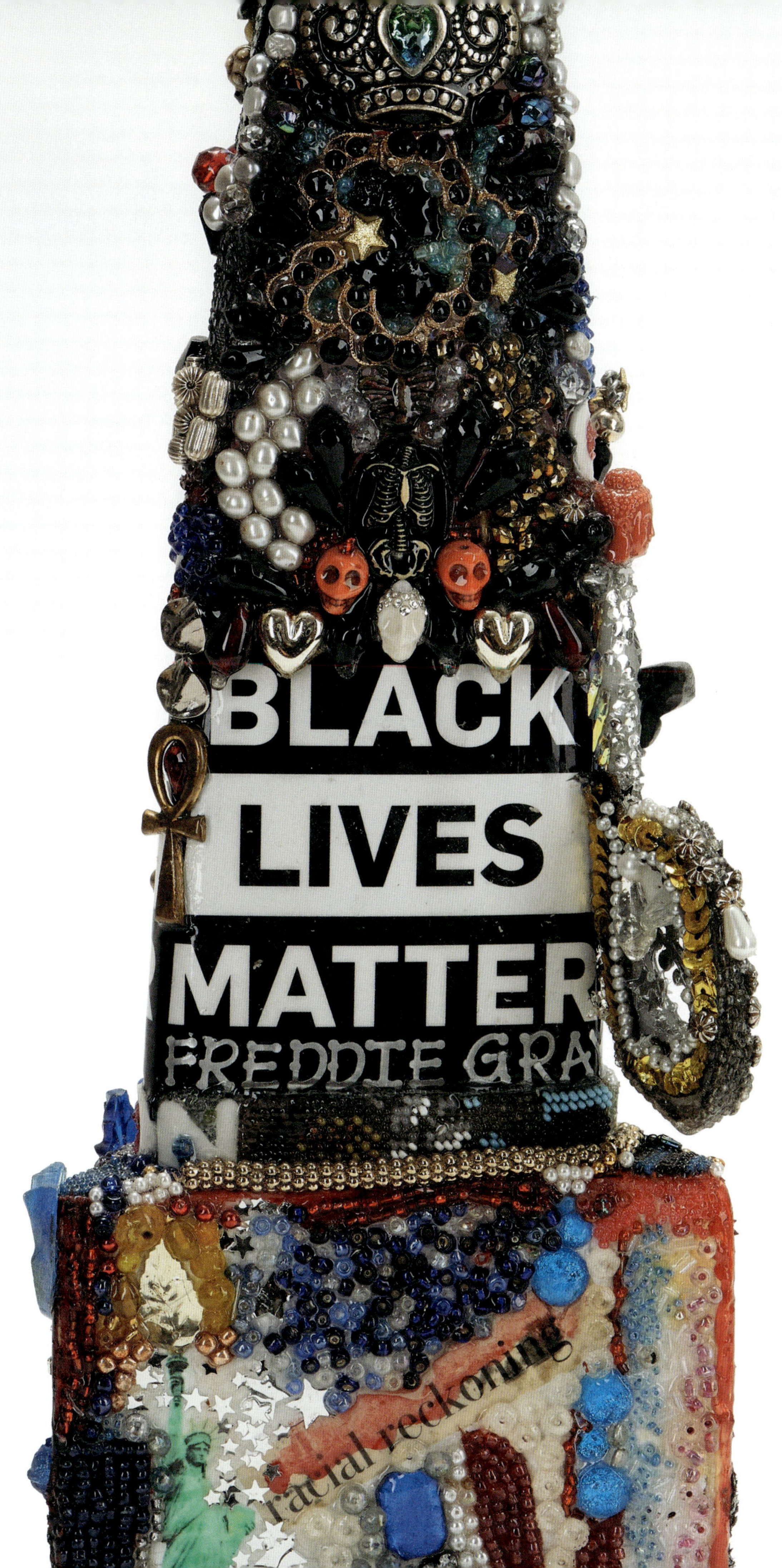

BLACK
LIVES
MATTER
FREDDIE GRAY
racial reckoning

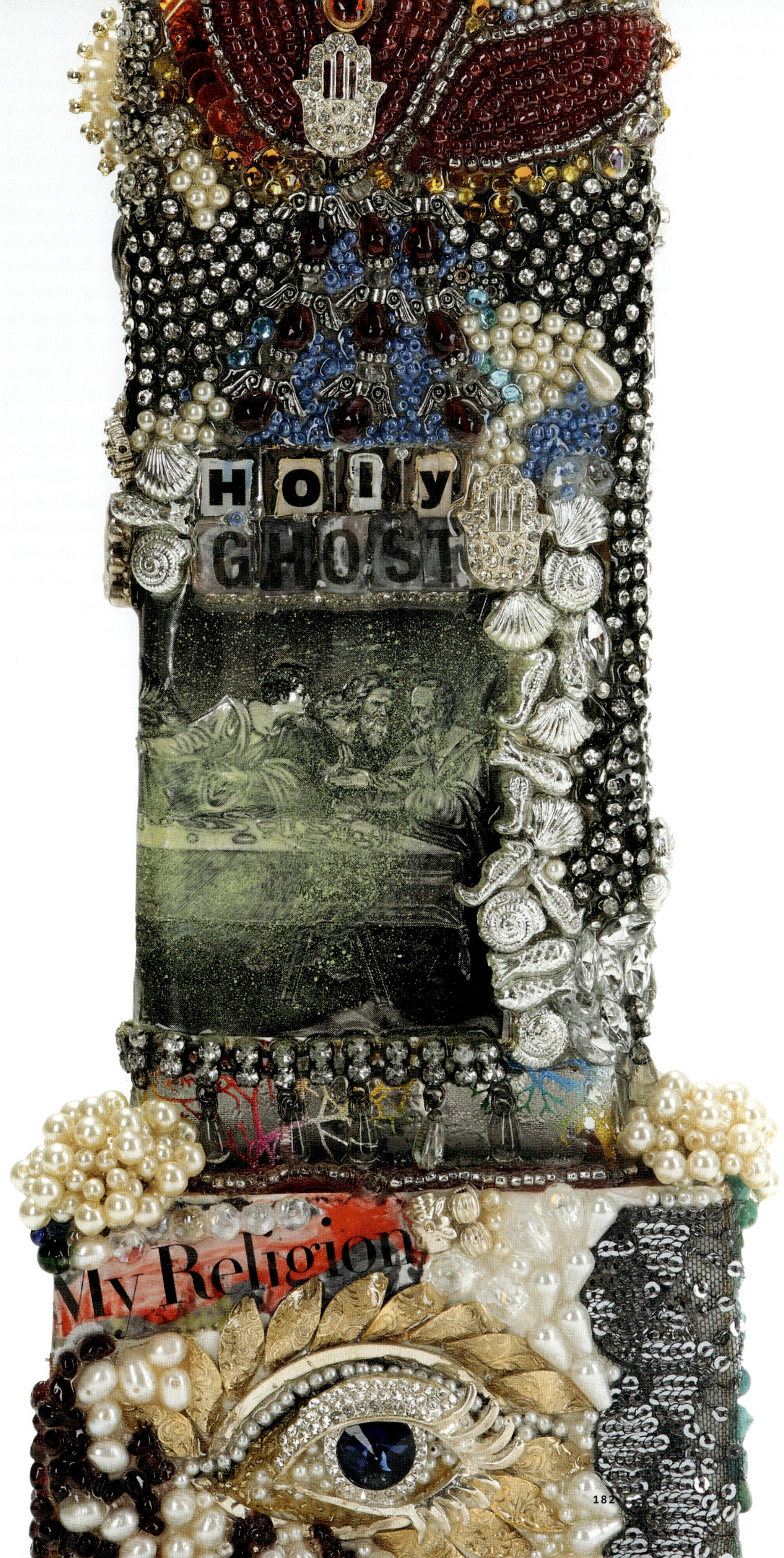

HOLY
GHOST
My Religion

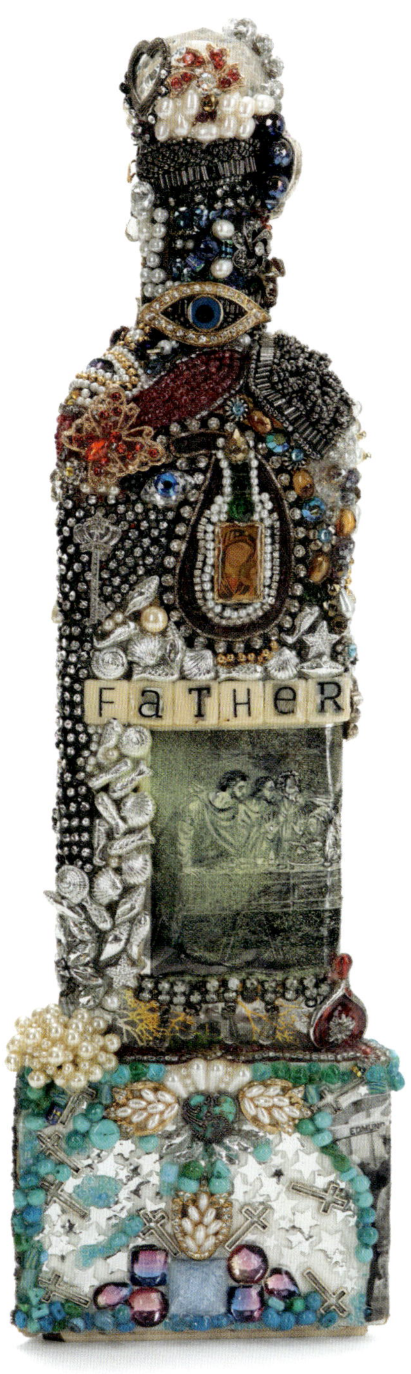

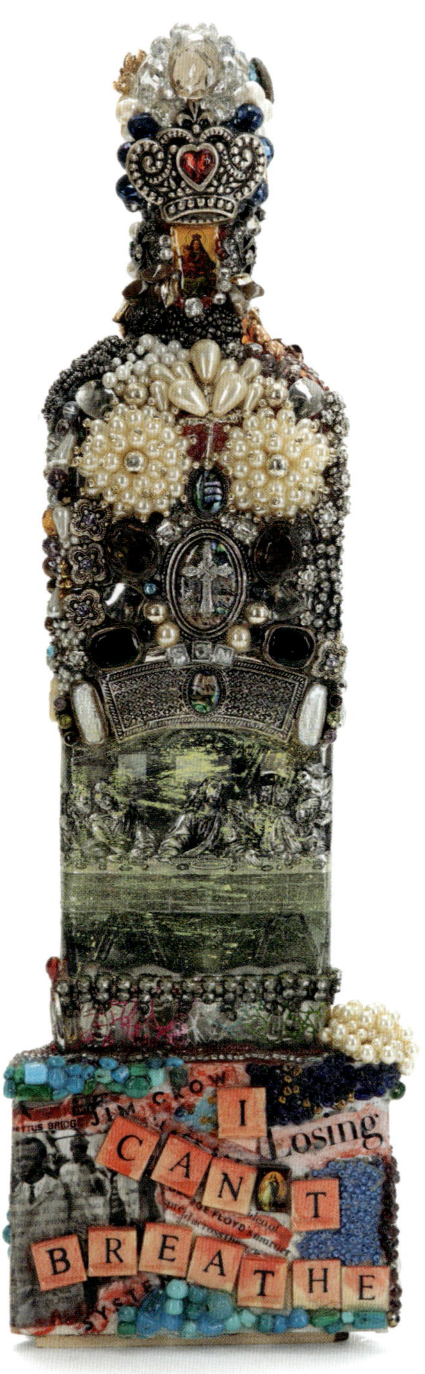

I can't Breathe, 2021, glass, beads, metal, wood, paper, image transfer

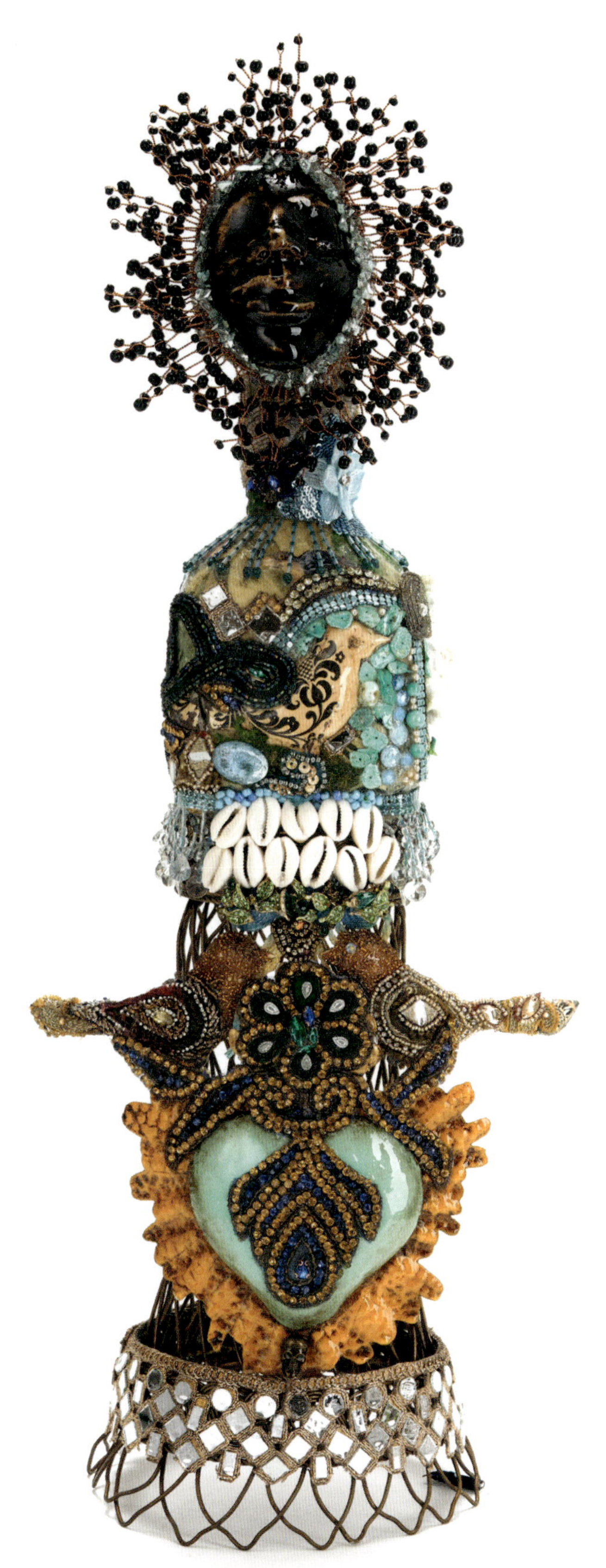

Transcend, 2022, glass, clay, beads, metal, sequins, mirrors, cowrie shells

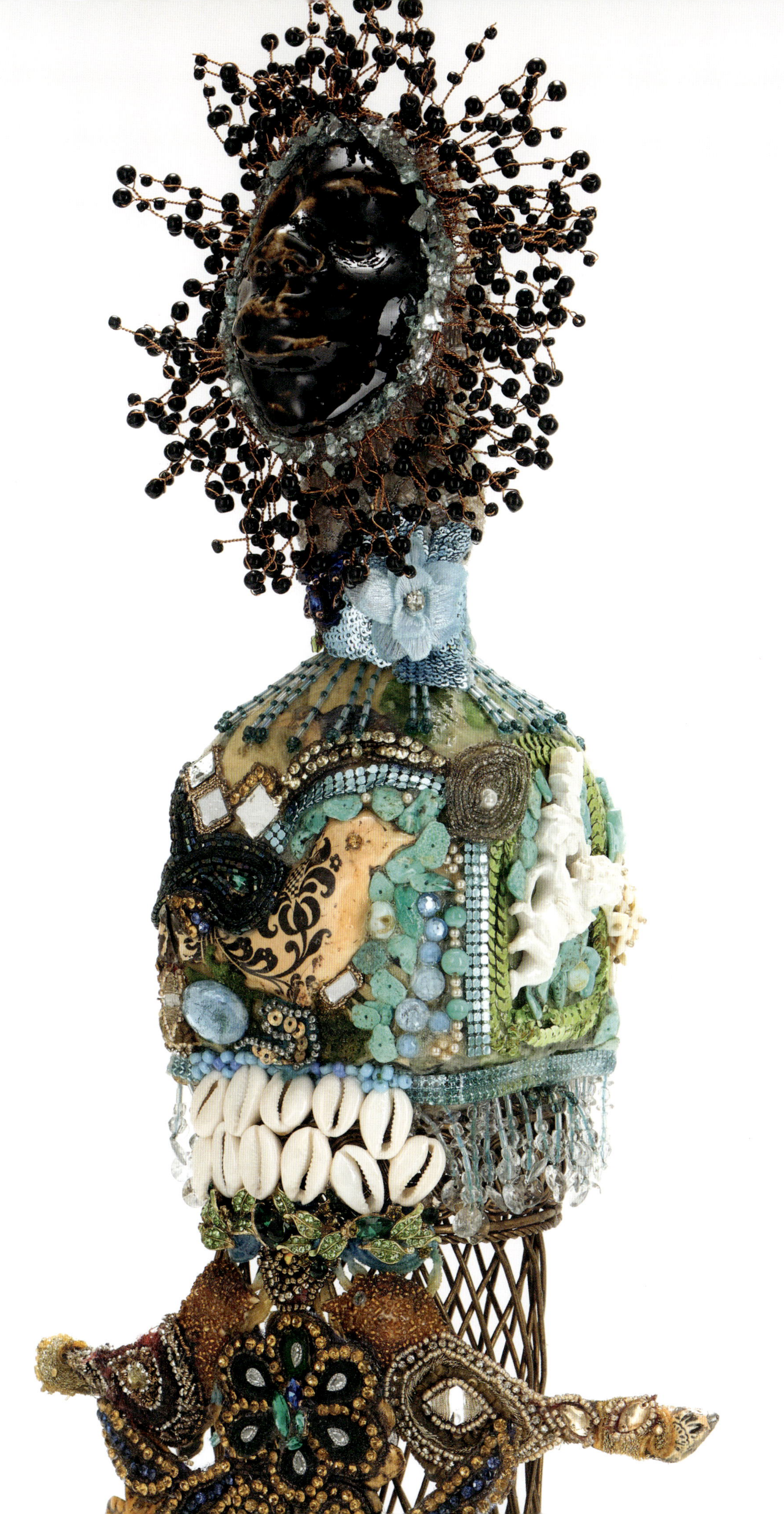

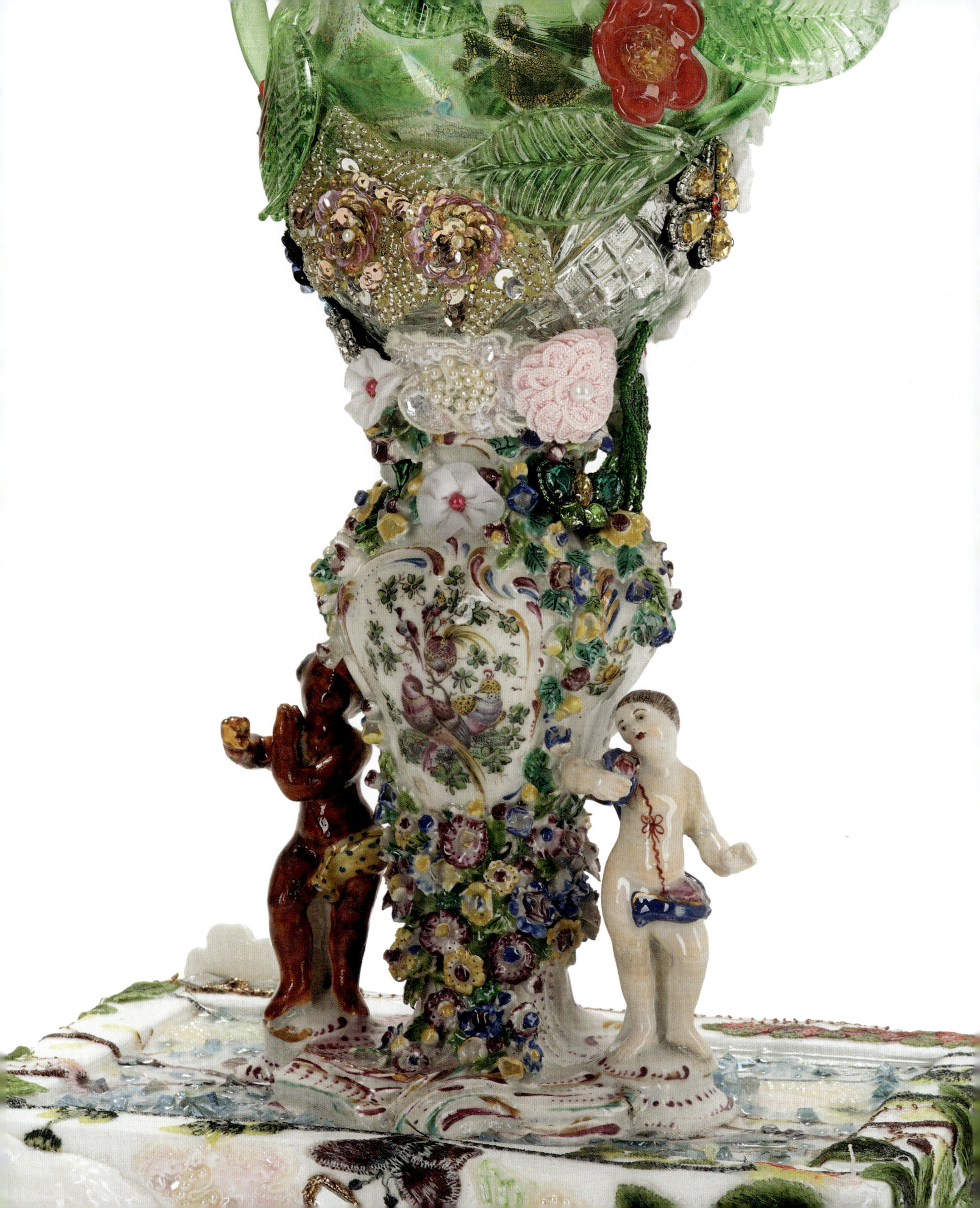

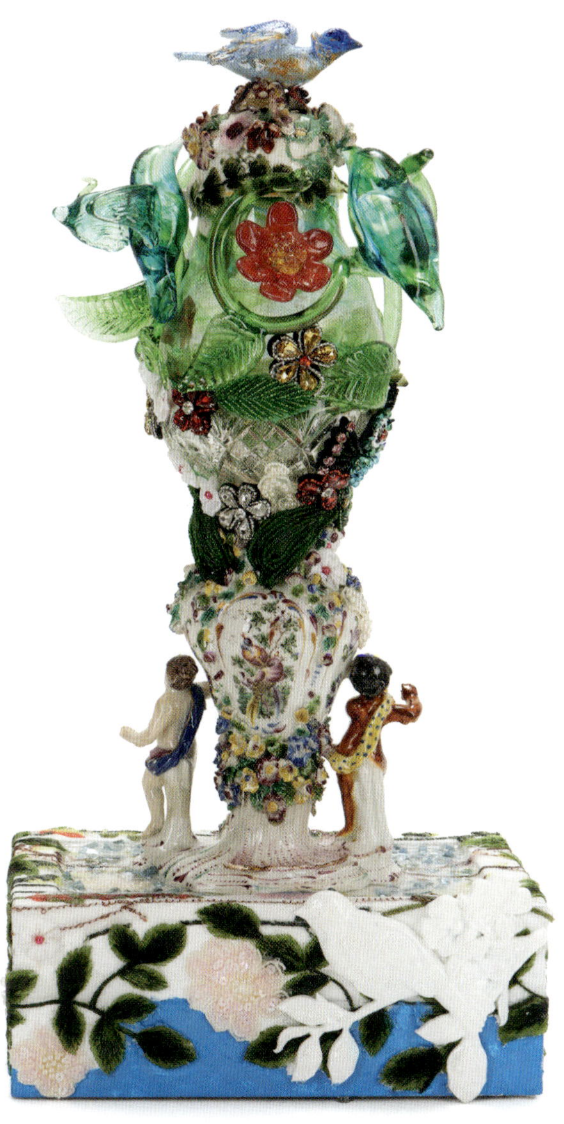 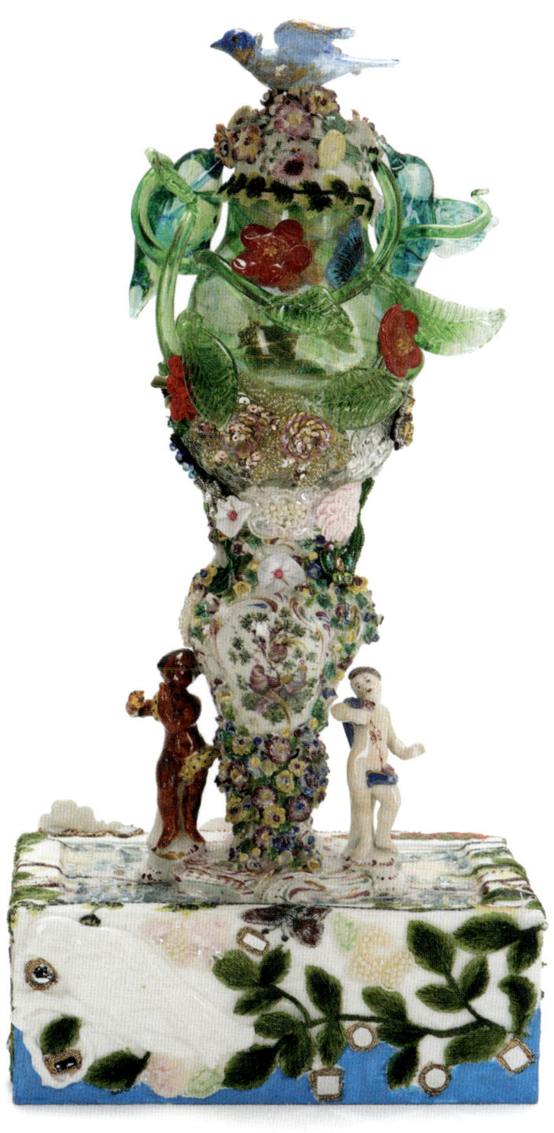

12202021 [collaboration with
Tim McFadden], 2022, glass,
found Meissen porcelain vase,
found Czech bowl

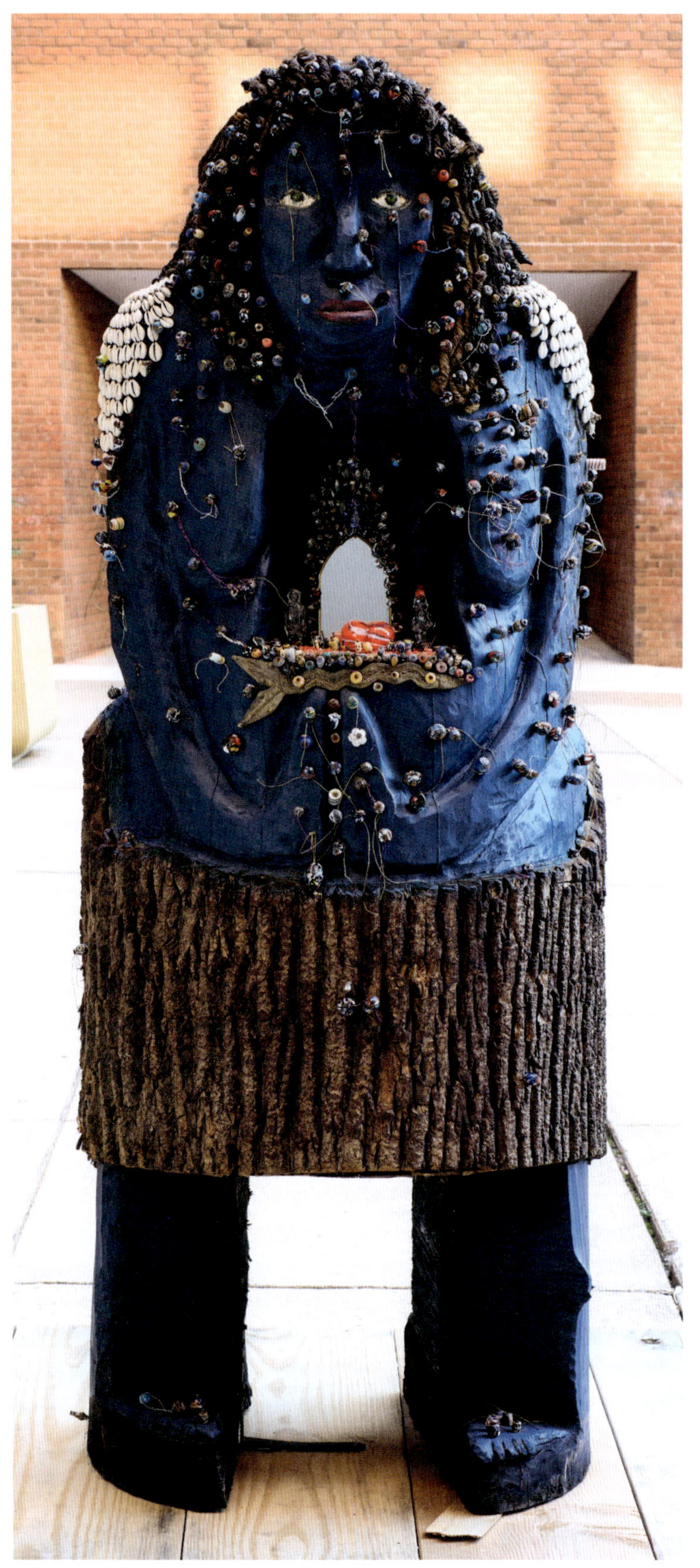
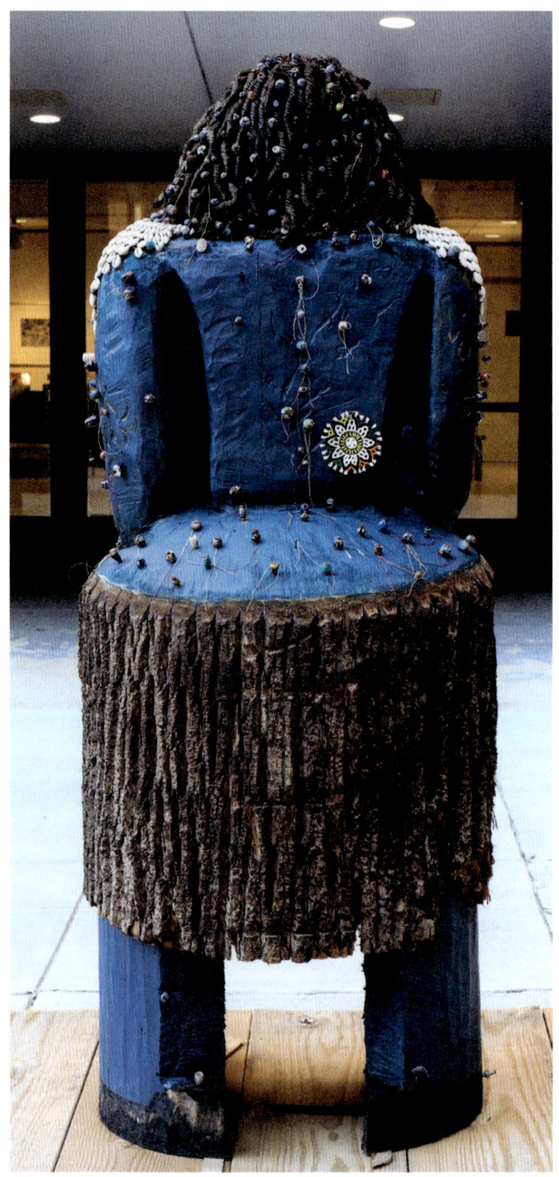

**N'Kisi Woman–Universal
N'Kisi**, 2021–2022, wood,
beads, cowrie shells, paint
Photos: Mitro Hood.

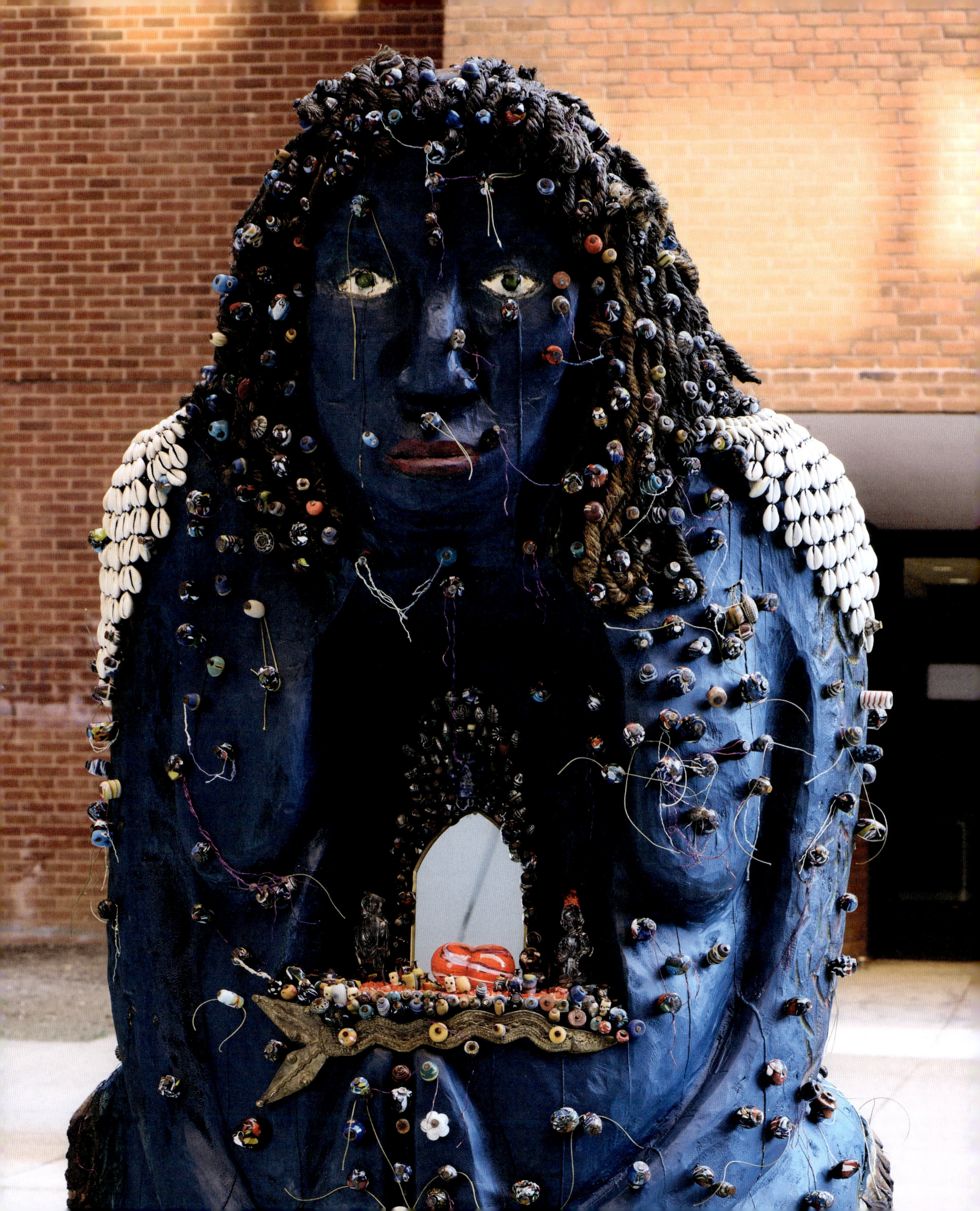

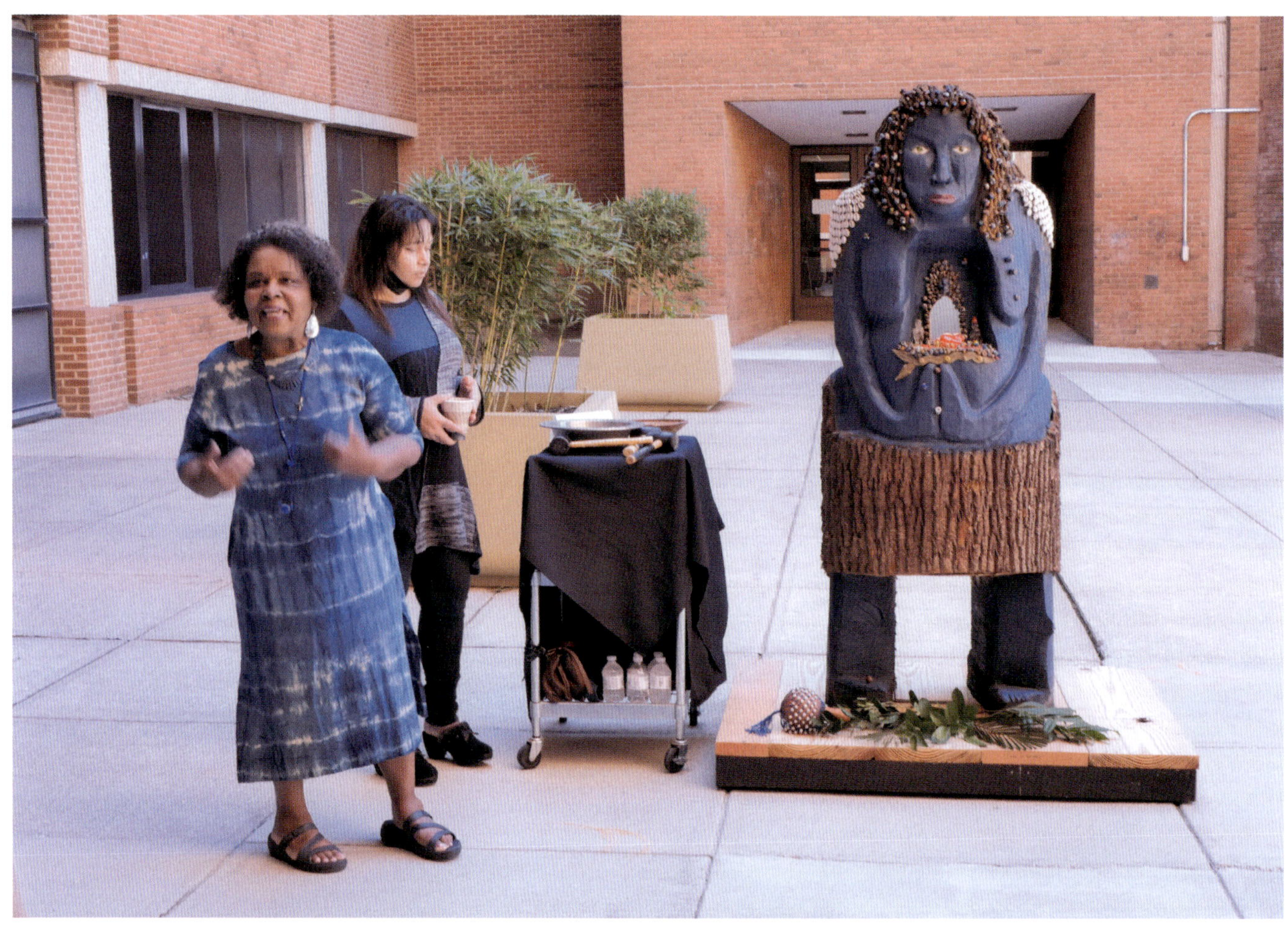

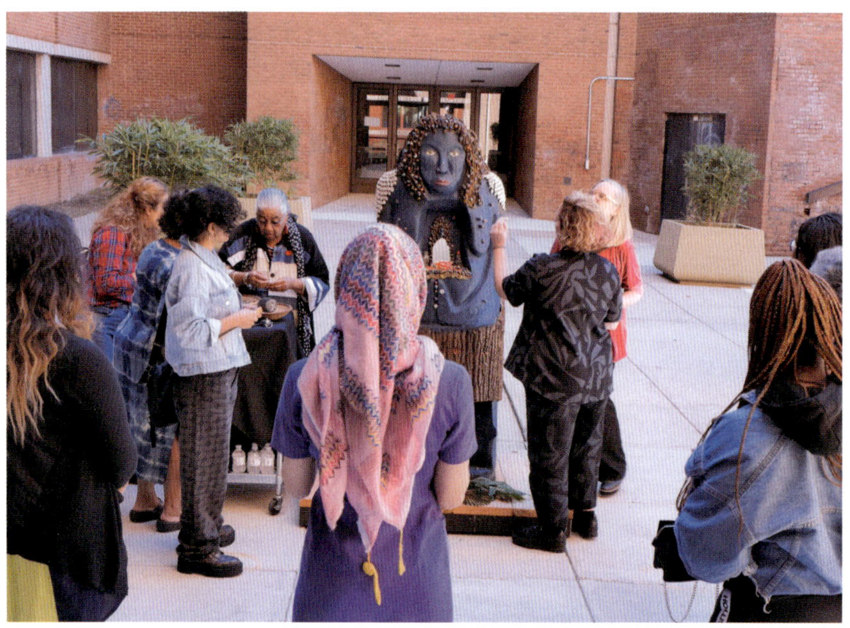

Oletha DeVane and Nichole Kojzar
greet participants at *N'Kisi*
activation, CADVC amphitheatre,
UMBC, October 6, 2022.

Participants engaging with *N'Kisi*
activation event.

Photos: Rassaan Hammond.

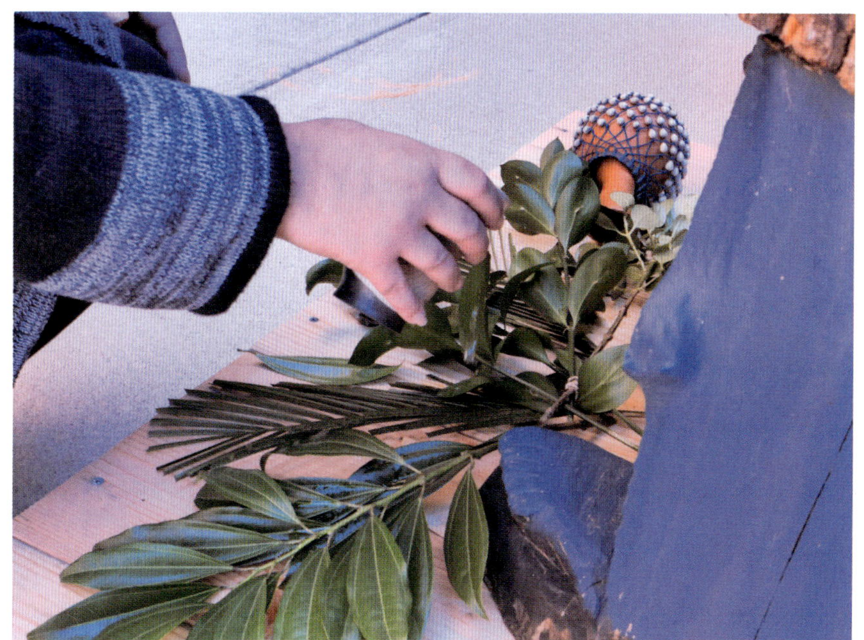

Oletha DeVane performs a
libation with plants and water.
Photos: Rassaan Hammond.

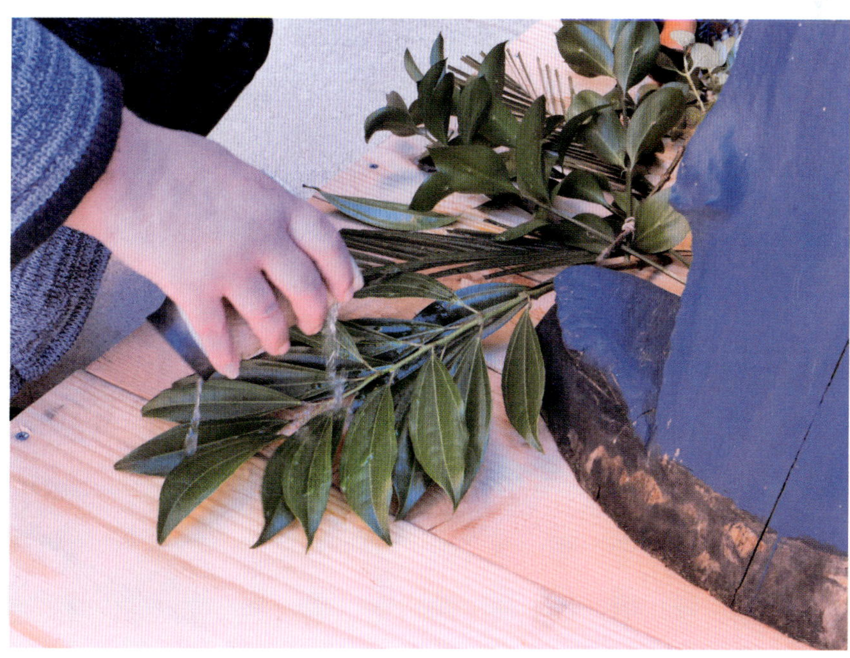

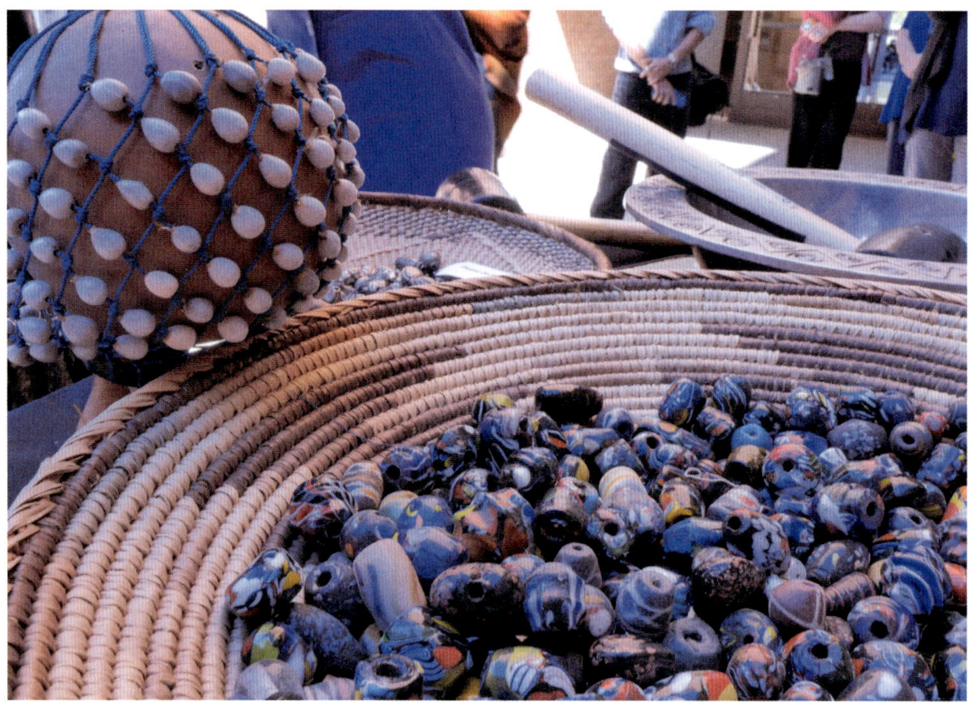

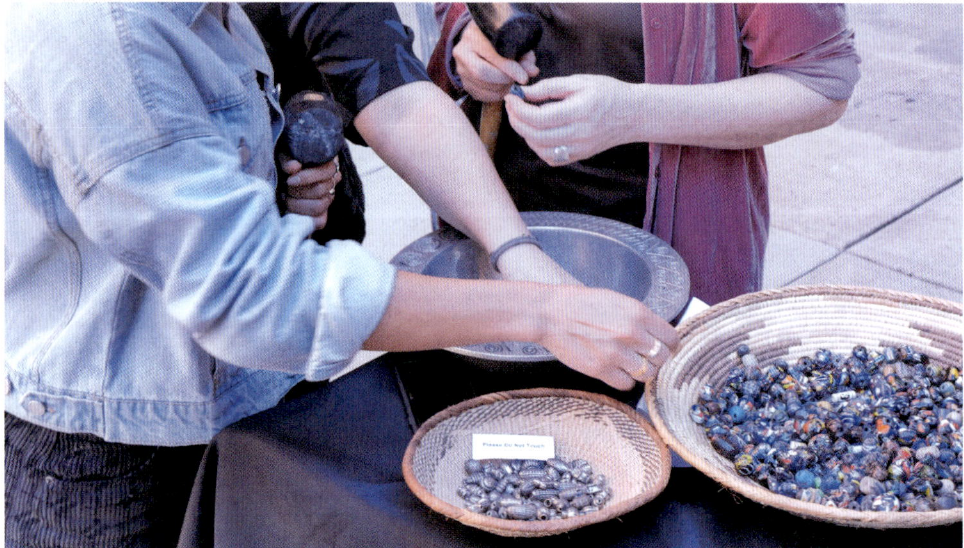

TOP
The beads and nails to be applied to *N'Kisi*.

BOTTOM
Choosing beads to add to *N'Kisi*.

OPPOSITE
Exhibition Curator Lowery Stokes Sims adds a bead to the surface of *N'Kisi*.

Photos: Rassaan Hammond.

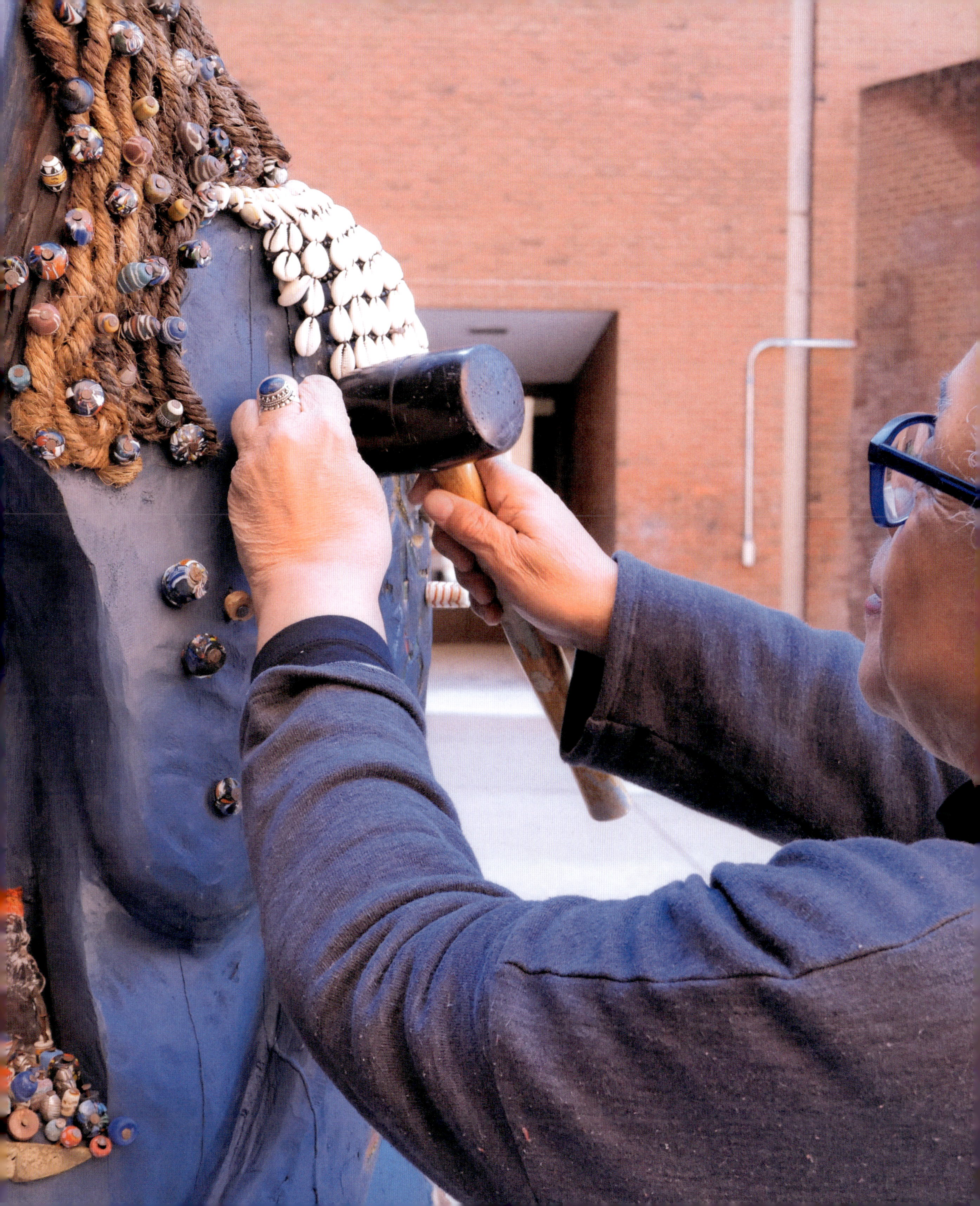

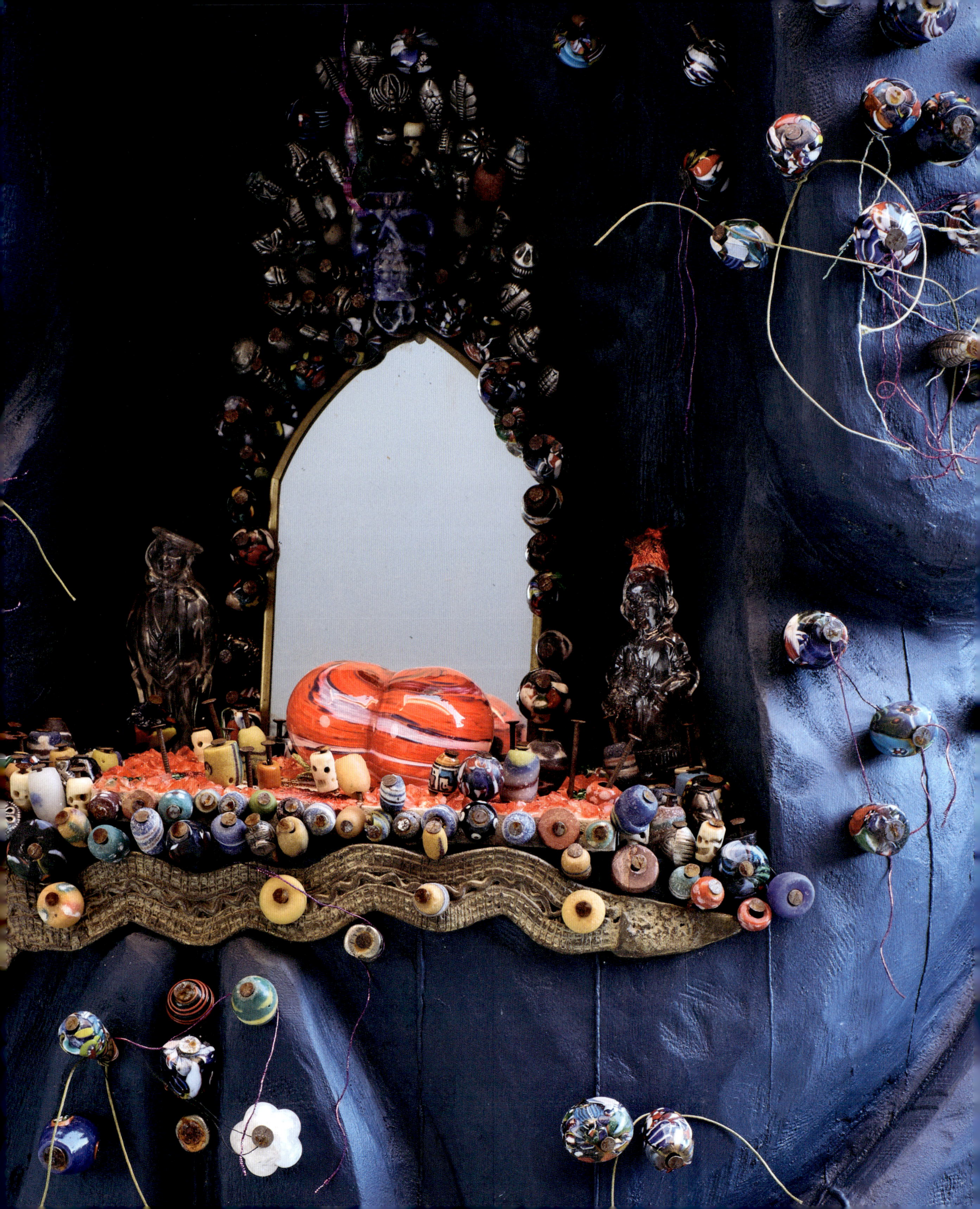

Compiled by Lowery Stokes Sims

NOTE: Unless otherwise noted, all artwork is courtesy of the artist, Oletha DeVane.

Migration
2012
etching and silkscreen
16 × 44.75 inches
photo: Michael Koryta
(p. 45)

Meditation
2019
glass, beads, porcelain, wood
20 × 4 × 6 inches
photo: Mitro Hood
(p. 72)

Spring [Sohappyitsspring]
2018
glass, wood, metal, glass beads, plastic, metal wire, sequins, fabric
26 × 9.25 × 10 inches
photo: Mitro Hood
(p. 75)

Doorway to Nowhere
1980s
acrylic, charcoal on paper
27.5 × 18.5 inches
photo: Mitro Hood
(p. 78)

Ode to Pre-Existence
1998
acrylic, pastels
46 × 31.5 inches
photo: Mitro Hood
(p. 79)

Spirits II
2000
acrylic, feathers, fabric, beads
29 × 29 inches
photo: Mitro Hood
(p. 80)

Roses
2000
acrylic on canvas
64 × 64 inches
Collection of Dorothy DeVane
photo: Mitro Hood
(p. 81)

Veil I
2000
Van Dyke process, fabric, acrylic
24.5 × 24.5 inches
photo: Mitro Hood
(p. 82)

Veil II
2000
Van Dyke process, fabric, acrylic
24.5 × 24.5 inches
photo: Mitro Hood
(p. 82)

Veil III
2000
Van Dyke process, fabric, acrylic
24.5 × 24.5 inches
photo: Mitro Hood
(p. 83)

Veil IV
2000
Van Dyke process, fabric, acrylic
24.5 × 24.5 inches
photo: Mitro Hood
(p. 82)

Witness I
2003
acrylic, watercolor and solar etching
32.5 × 26 inches
photo: Mitro Hood
(p. 84)

Witness II
2003
acrylic, watercolor and
solar etching
32.5 × 26 inches
photo: Mitro Hood
(p. 85)

**Untitled [figure climbing
hill towards fire and
figure with red snake]**
2003
charcoal and pastel on paper
diptych, each panel:
25 × 19 inches
photos: Mitro Hood
(p. 86)

**Through the Gates
of Babylon**
2003
lithograph
29.25 × 24.5 inches
photo: Mitro Hood
(p. 87)

Sacred Geometry
[collaboration
with Donna Denizé]
2001
mixed media
9 double folios, each:
34 × 25 inches closed,
34 × 50 inches open
photo: Dan Meyers
(pp. 88–97)

Zulu
2007
sequins, beads, glass,
clay, acrylic, wood
23 × 7 × 6 inches
photo: Mitro Hood
(pp. 98–99)

Janus
2007
clay, glass, shell, features
and bullet casings
24 × 14 × 5 inches
photo: Mitro Hood
(p. 100)

Absinthe
2009
nails, shells, beads, fish
bones, glass, painted clay,
toy soldiers, wood,
paint, twine, encaustic
29 × 5 × 6 inches
photo: Michael Koryta
(p. 101)

Siren (Mami Wata)
2011
glass, metal, shells, beads,
clay, string, metal wire,
silver fabric
30 × 12 × 13 inches
photo: Michael Koryta
(pp. 102–103)

A Lady of Means
2010
glass, beads, ceramic
24 × 7 × 5 inches
photo: Mitro Hood
(pp. 104–105)

Isis/Virgin
2010
wood, beads, fabric,
glass and metal
20 × 12 × 6 inches
photo: Mitro Hood
(pp. 106–107)

Garden
2019
glass, sequins, beads, clay
16 × 6 × 9 inches
photo: Mitro Hood
(pp. 108–109)

Mourning
2003
acrylic and oil on canvas
30 × 30 × 2.5
photo: Mitro Hood
(p. 110)

On the Hill
2003
acrylic and oil on canvas
30 × 30 inches
photo: Mitro Hood
(p. 111)

**Red Tails
(Tuskegee Airman Series)**
2003
acrylic and oil on canvas
30 × 30 inches
photo: Mitro Hood
(p. 112)

Wish
2003
acrylic and oil on canvas
30 × 30 inches
photo: Mitro Hood
(p. 113)

Love Letter
2004
acrylic, oil and paper
on canvas
63.5 × 63.5 inches
photo: Mitro Hood
(pp. 114–115)

Sugarcane Blues
2020
solar and digital etching
on Rives paper
30.5 × 38 inches
photo: Mitro Hood
(pp. 116–117)

Harriet the Raven
2019
digital media, solar
etching, and graphite
on paper
28 × 34.5 inches
photo: Michael Koryta
(p. 118)

Call to Freedom
2012
9 screen prints
90 × 60 inches overall,
33.5 × 27.25 each
photo: Michael Koryta
(p. 119)

Thai Spirit House
2013
solar etching
26 × 32 inches
photo: Mitro Hood
(pp. 120–121)

Garden
2015
encaustic
51 × 68 inches
photo: Mitro Hood
(p. 122)

Dion'e: Searching for Self
2016
video, 6 minutes, 33 seconds
image: Oletha DeVane

(p. 123)

**Martyr
(Scarification Series)**
2009
encaustic on paper
32 × 25 inches
photo: Mitro Hood

(p. 124)

**Out of Africa
(Scarification Series)**
2009
encaustic and Van Dyke
process on Rives paper,
with cowrie shells, beads
32.5 × 25.5 inches
photo: Mitro Hood

(p. 124)

**Star Map
(Harriet Tubman Series)**
2010
Van Dyke process, and
burnt marks on Rives paper
32 × 24.5 inches
photo: Mitro Hood

(p. 125)

**Drinking Gourd
(Harriet Tubman Series)**
2010
cyanotype, wood, fabric,
sequins, acrylic
31.5 × 24.5 inches
photo: Mitro Hood

(p. 126)

**Out of Africa: from beauty
to pain**
2010
Van Dyke process, acrylic,
embossing on Rives paper
32 × 24.5 inches
photo: Mitro Hood

(p. 127)

Life Pulse
2010
encaustic, solar etching
31 × 25 inches
photo: Mitro Hood

(p. 127)

**Tattoo
(Scarification Series)**
2011
Van Dyke process and
ink on paper
34.25 × 26.75 inches
photo: Mitro Hood

(p. 128)

An American Story
2010
solar etching
34.5 × 28.25 inches
photo: Mitro Hood

(p. 129)

Chador Flowers I
2014
digital print collage
38.5 × 31.5 inches
photo: Michael Koryta

(p. 130)

**Patterns (Three Women
from Dubai)**
2015
solar etching
38.5 × 31.5 inches
photo: Michael Koryta

(p. 131)

**Absence/Presence
[Empty Quarters]**
2016
video, 3 minutes,
39 seconds
image: Oletha DeVane

(pp. 132–133)

Henry "Box" Brown
2015
wood, acrylic, sweet
gum balls, United States
of America flag fabric,
Confederate flag fabric,
acrylic on canvas
dimensions variable
photo: Mitro Hood

(pp. 134–135)

Red Riding Hood
2016
solar etching on BFK
Rives paper
31 × 23.5 inches
photo: Mitro Hood

(p. 136)

Sex Slave
2016
solar etching and relief
printing
31 × 38.5 inches
photo: Mitro Hood

(p. 137)

Hagar's Dress in Her Exile
2012
chains, hemp cord, fabric,
beads, sweet gum balls,
cowrie shells
58 × 16 × 16 inches
photo: Mitro Hood

(p. 138)

Escape
2016
wood, clay, branches
and sweet gum balls
38 × 24 × 8 inches
photo: Mitro Hood

(pp. 140–141)

Fall from Grace
2013
glass, wax, beads, bones
and plastic
38 × 13 × 9 inches
photo: Mitro Hood

(pp. 142–143)

Gemini
2018
wood, clay, glass, mirrors,
bullet casings, wire, fabric,
human hair
38 × 10 × 11 inches
photo: Mitro Hood

(p. 144)

Healer (Pilgrimage)
2018
wood, fabric, glass, mirror,
plastic, beads, clay, acrylic,
buttons
30 × 10 × 10 inches
photo: Mitro Hood

(p. 145)

Wedding Gift
2016
mixed media
22 × 5 × 6 inches
Collection of Leslie King-
Hammond
photo: Mitro Hood
(pp. 146–147)

Lifeisbutadream
2015
clay, plastic, beads, metal
24 × 8.5 × 4 inches
photo: Mitro Hood
(p. 148)

Erzulie Dandor
2017
glass, beads, image transfer,
wire, porcelain, fabric
25 × 6 × 5 inches
photo: Mitro Hood
(p. 149)

Grappa
2018
mixed media, including
grappa
22 × 8 × 3 inches
photo: Mitro Hood
(pp. 150–151)

**Woman Who Married
a Snake**
2017
glass, metal, beads, plastics,
mirrors, pebbles
28 × 9 × 8 inches
photo: Mitro Hood
(p. 152)

Kronos (Collateral)
2018
glass beads, glass,
metal, metal fiber,
wood, plastic
29 × 10 × 10 inches
photo: Mitro Hood
(p. 153)

Protector of the Flame
2020
glass beads, fabric,
wood
21 × 8 × 7 inches
photo: Mitro Hood
(p. 154)

Orisha
2008
wood, glass, clay, glass
beads, shells, green
metal
28.75 × 6.5 × 6 inches
photo: Mitro Hood
(p. 155)

Medieval
2017
glass, red feathers, wire,
fabric, plastic, wood,
beads
23 × 10 × 6 inches
photo: Mitro Hood
(pp. 156–157)

**Beyond Bars:
Prison Women Speak**
[collaboration
with Tadia Rice]
2018–ongoing
video, 19 minutes,
39 seconds
(pp. 158–160)

Anjie
2018
photograph
27 × 21 inches
photo: Oletha DeVane
(p. 158)

Mae Mae
2018
photograph
27 × 21 inches
photo: Oletha DeVane

Momi
2018
photograph
27 × 21 inches
photo: Oletha DeVane
(p. 158)

Shay Boy
2018
photograph
27 × 21 inches
photo: Oletha DeVane

Tammy
2018
photograph
27 × 21 inches
photo: Oletha DeVane

Tiana
2018
photograph
27 × 21 inches
photo: Oletha DeVane
(p. 159)

Jess
2018
photograph
27 × 21 inches
photo: Oletha DeVane

Neko
2018
photograph
27 × 21 inches
photo: Oletha DeVane

Zoe
2022
photograph
27 × 21 inches
photo: Tadia Rice
(p. 158)

Eliza
2017
etching, AP/2
23 × 29 inches
photo: Mitro Hood
(pp. 162–163)

Restavek
2016
encaustic, fabric,
plastics, glass, feathers,
oil, beads
27 × 27 × 3 inches
photo: Mitro Hood
(p. 164)

Minty
2017
solar etching
22 × 17.5 inches
anonymous loan
photo: Mitro Hood
(p. 165)

Whatever Happened to Icarus?
2020
acrylic, glass chips, rope, ceramic, wood, plastics
54 × 36 × 7 inches
photo: Mitro Hood
(p. 166)

Tree from Hell
2021
beads, ceramic, fabric, glass, wood
52.5 × 36 × 3 inches
photo: Mitro Hood
(p. 167)

Dumballa
2018
acrylic on panel, glass, beads, resin, crystals, clay, wood, fabric, metal
54 × 30.5 × 4 inches
photo: Mitro Hood
(p. 168)

Erzulie
2018
encaustic on canvas, clay, beads, stones, mirrors, plastic
57 × 30.25 × 4 inches
photo: Mitro Hood
(p. 168)

The Lote-Tree
2020
beads, ceramic, fabric, glass, wood,
49 × 37 × 6 inches
photo: Mitro Hood
(p. 169)

Subsumed by Whiteness
2020
mixed media
56.5 × 30 × 4.5 inches
photo: Mitro Hood
(p. 170)

Mamawata's Earth Song
2019
acrylic, geo stones, plastic, nails, wood, rope, clay
57 × 30 × 3.5 inches
photo: Mitro Hood
(p. 171)

Sirius–Asteria
2020
glass, fabric, acrylic, wood, paper
46 × 36 × 3 inches
photo: Mitro Hood
(pp. 172–173)

Mawumoongoddess
2019
wood, acrylic, glass, beads, rope, and resin on wood panel
47 × 36 × 4 inches
photo: Mitro Hood
(p. 174)

Epiphany
2018
wood, glass, acrylic, bones, plastic
50.25 × 30 × 3.5 inches
photo: Mitro Hood
(p. 175)

Garden of the Heart
2021
mixed media
49 × 36 × 4.5 inches
photo: Mitro Hood
(pp. 176–177)

Serpent
2022
glass, beads, sequins, fabric, clay
22 × 10 × 5 inches
photo: Mitro Hood
(pp. 178–179)

George Floyd (Black Lives Matter)
2021
glass, beads, clay, metal, paper
24 × 5 × 6 inches
photo: Mitro Hood
(pp. 180–181)

I can't Breathe
2021
glass, beads, metal, wood, paper, image transfer
20 × 4 × 6 inches
photo: Mitro Hood
(pp. 182–183)

Transcend
2022
glass, clay, beads, metal, sequins, mirrors, cowrie shells
26 × 10 × 7 inches
photo: Mitro Hood
(pp. 184–185)

12202021
[collaboration with Tim McFadden]
2022
glass, found Meissen porcelain vase, found Czech bowl
20 × 10 × 7 inches
photo: Mitro Hood
(pp. 186–187)

N'Kisi Woman–Universal N'Kisi
2021–2022
wood, beads, paint
72 × 36 × 24 inches
photo: Mitro Hood
(pp. 4, 188–189, 194)

Icarus
2013
solar print with sequins
29 × 22 inches

Witness
2005
video, 2 minutes, 31 seconds

Lowery Stokes Sims

For the last four decades DeVane has been a prominent presence in the Balti-more area art scene as an arts administrator, curator, educator, and artist. She began her undergraduate studies in 1968at the Maryland Institute College of Art (MICA), where she studied with poet-artists David Franks and Joe Cardarelli, who in her words "fed" her "curiosity in poetry and language as it relate to visual art." Paul Sharits inspired her with his lectures and films, and Albert Sangiamo with his draftsmanship. Her work with women artists such as Lois Hennessey, Sharon Yates, and Leslie King-Hammond was significant in the context of the emergence of the feminist art movement in the late 1960s and early 1970s. DeVane also singles out Raoul Middleman, known in the Baltimore area for his aggressively expressionistic work, from whom she learned about the quality of painting. The noted anthropologist Margaret Mead was another inspiration when she came to lecture at MICA.

In 1973 DeVane went to the University of Massachusetts Amherst to pursue her graduate degree, where her advisor was the painter Nelson Stevens, a key figure in the AfriCobra group. She also took advantage of a course on Black women and African studies offered by Johnnetta Cole and Esther Terry, which provided her with "a wealth of knowledge and challenge in thinking about the role of women and claiming self-determination." DeVane's career was incubated in the hothouse of postmodernism which brought the rubrics of identity to art discourses in the 1980s. Deploying a number of media—prints, paintings, assemblaged wall works, installations, and videos—she has explored realms of the human experience in terms of cultural identity, traditions, and rituals, including the history and heroes and (s)heroes of African Americans, the richness of cultural expression from that community, and the richness of ritual and materiality in Haitian art and culture.

After receiving her MA, DeVane taught and worked as an administrator for the Maryland State Arts Council from 1979 to 1992 before taking a position in 1993 at the McDonogh School in Owings Mills, Maryland, where she was Director of the Tuttle Gallery and head of visual arts in the Upper Level until her retirement in 2019. In 2007 she was the recipient of the Rollins/ Luetkemeyer Chair for Distinguish Teaching. DeVane was a Sondheim Semi-Finalist in 2011, and received a Rubys Artist Grant and an Art Matters Fellowship in 2017 in recognition of her work involving communities for social change. These endeavors include her work in Haiti, where in collaboration with the Build Haiti Foundation she initiated a public mural in mosaic with local artisans and students at Camp Coq, Haiti, with funding from the Ruby Foundation. DeVane and performance artist poet Tadia Rice produced the Cannes International Film Festival award-winning film, *Beyond Bars: Prison Women Speak*, that featured women at the Women's Community Correctional Center, the only prison for women in Hawai`i.

She received the Trawick Prize in 2019, an "Anonymous Was A Woman" Grant in 2021, and was a Baker Award Finalist in 2023.

DeVane has had solo exhibitions at the Howard Community College Gallery, Columbia, Maryland; the Catonsville Community College Gallery; Western Maryland College, Westminster, Maryland; McDaniel College [Western Maryland College], Westminster, Maryland; Project 1628, Baltimore; and the Baltimore Museum of Art. In addition to her 2016 residency in Abu Dhabi, UAE, she has also been an artist in residence in Banff, Canada, and in Lecce, Italy. Her work has been collected by the Hilton Hotel, Baltimore; Sheppard Pratt Hospital; The Baltimore Museum of Art; and the Museums of Johns Hopkins University; and is the private collections of Dr. Thomas and Cindy Kelly, Leslie King-Hammond, Dorothy DeVane, and Soledad Salamé. Recent public commissions include *Memorial to Those Enslaved and Freed* at McDonogh School, Owings Mills, and *Robert and Rosetta* at Lexington Market, Baltimore.

DeVane counts among the artistic cohort she has formed over the years the art historian/artist Leslie King-Hammond, former Graduate Dean at MICA; the bead and glass artist Joyce J. Scott; the poet/writer Charles Fox; and a women's artistic collaborative known as the Girls of Baltimore, which includes King-Hammond, Scott, Patti Tronolone, Ellen Burchenal, and Linda DePalma.

Compiled by Lowery Stokes Sims

1976

Ten Abstract Painters, Springfield Museum of Fine Arts, Springfield, MA

1979

Impact 79: Afro-American Women in Art, Foster Tanner Fine Arts Gallery, FAMU, Tallahassee, FL

1980

One Person Exhibition, Catonsville Community College Gallery, Baltimore, MD

1984

Group Exhibition, Maryland Art Place, Baltimore, MD

Joyce Scott & Oletha DeVane, Ohio State University Gallery, Wilberforce, OH

Group Exhibition, Meredith Art Gallery, Baltimore, MD

1990

Visual AIDS (curator: George Ciscle), Museum for Contemporary Arts, Baltimore, MD

1991

Passages (curators: Faith Ringgold and Clarissa Sligh), School 33 Art Center, Baltimore, MD

MAP Benefit Exhibition (curator: Susan Badder), Maryland Art Place, Baltimore, MD

Coast to Coast: A Women of Color National Artists' Book Project, Flossie Martin Gallery, Radford University, Radford, VA (traveling exhibition: Eubie Black National Jazz Institute and Cultural Center, Baltimore, MD; Artemisia Gallery, Chicago, IL)

1992

One Person Exhibition, McDaniel College [Western Maryland College], Westminster, MD

Group Show, Marketplace, National Black Arts Festival, Atlanta, GA

1993

Five Baltimore Artists, Maryland Art Place, Baltimore, MD

God Bless the Child: Tribute to Billie Holiday, Eubie Blake National Museum and Cultural Center, Baltimore, MD

Women Image Women, Baltimore Life Gallery, Owings Mills, MD

Shades/Hues: Variations in Black, Ruby Blakeney Gallery, Historic Savage Mill, Savage, MD

1994–95

What We Need To Know About Art: Schroeder Cherry, Oletha DeVane, Angela Franklin, Maryland Art Place, Baltimore, MD (traveling exhibition)

1996

Free to Be: African American Artists in a Postmodern Era, Howard County Center for the Arts, Ellicott City, MD

1999

DeVane, Ford, Jones, Moore, Pierleoni, Chesapeake Gallery, Harford, MD

Inside/Outside, Howard County Center of the Arts, Ellicott City, MD

Through the Fire to the Limits: African American Artists in Maryland, Government House, Annapolis, MD

Maryland Women (selected by Doreen Bolger), Government House, Annapolis, MD

Kromah Gallery Revisited, Artscape Festival '98, Meyerhoff Gallery, MICA, Baltimore, MD

Works by Oletha DeVane (solo exhibition), Howard Community College Gallery, Columbia, MD

Unfolding Cycle (garden installation with students), West Friendship Elementary, West Friendship, MD

2000

Women's History Exhibition, James E. Lewis Museum, Morgan State University, Baltimore, MD

Artafexus, Pinkard Galleries, MICA, Baltimore, MD

2001

Kings, Hummingbirds & Monsters: Artist's Books at Evergreen, Evergreen House, Johns Hopkins University, Baltimore, MD

2002

Arts Maryland, Howard County Center for the Arts, Ellicott City, MD

Masks, Villa Julie College [now Stevenson University], Baltimore County, MD

2003

Charmopolis, Maryland Art Place, Baltimore, MD

Select 2003 Auction Exhibition, WPA/Corcoran Gallery, Washington, DC

2004

Phenomenology, Meyerhoff Gallery, MICA, Baltimore, MD

2005

Witness (permanent video installation), Reginald F. Lewis Museum of African American History and Culture, Baltimore, MD

2006

Riffs/Rhythms: Abstract Forms/Lived Realities, James E. Lewis Museum, Morgan State University, Baltimore, MD

COLLABORATION, Maryland Art Place, Baltimore, MD, and Pyramid Atlantic Art Center, Silver Spring, MD

2007

Conflict/Peace: Finding Common Ground, Columbia Art Center, Columbia, MD

Mirror Me: Self-Portraits by Women, The Gallery, Community College of Baltimore County, Baltimore, MD

2008

Tracks/Trails/Tarmac, Thurgood Marshall Airport, Anne Arundel County, MD

2009

Our Common Bond: Mother, Daughters, Sisters, Self, Galerie Myrtis, Baltimore, MD

Nu Voo Doo, WESTNORTH Studio Gallery, Baltimore, MD

Life's Hardest Things, James E. Lewis Museum, Morgan State University, Baltimore, MD

2010

Sondheim Artscape Prize Semi-Finalist Exhibition, Meyerhoff Gallery, MICA, Baltimore, MD

Nineth National Juried Exhibition, Ceres Gallery, New York, NY

21st National Drawing and Print Competitive Exhibition (purchase award), Gomley Gallery, Notre Dame of Maryland University, Baltimore, MD

The Wine Dark Sea: Works by Joyce J. Scott & Friends, Mitchell Gallery, St. John's College, Annapolis, MD

2011

Corridor: Baltimore, Maryland/Washington, DC, Art Museum of the Americas, Organization of American States, Washington, DC

Altered Truths, Fractured Myths, City Arts Gallery, Baltimore, MD

Select 2011 Auction Exhibition, Washington Project for the Arts, Washington, DC

Femme Fatale, Galleries at Community College Baltimore County, MD

Miami Basel/Global Africa Project, The Betsy Hotel, Miami, FL

2012

Four Artists—Sondheim, Top of the World Observation Level Gallery, Baltimore, MD

2013

Ashe to Amen: African Americans and Biblical Imagery, The Museum of the Bible, New York, NY (traveling exhibition: The Dixon Gallery, Memphis, TN; Reginald F. Lewis Museum, Baltimore, MD)

Noetics, The Cosmos Club, Washington, DC

Miami Basel: Gurlz of Baltimore, The Betsy Hotel, Miami, FL

M/I/C/A: Then/Now, Ethan Cohen Fine Arts/Kunst-halle, Beacon, NY

2014

Ordinary Woman, Howard County Center of the Arts, Ellicott City, MD

2015

African American History Art Month, Abu Dhabi Art Hub, United Arab Emirates

Breathe in Gold Light, New Door Creative Gallery, Baltimore, MD

Inside/Outside: Christopher Kojzar & Oletha DeVane, Creative Alliance, Baltimore, MD

breathe in gold light, New Door Creative Gallery, Baltimore, MD

2016

To Be Black in White America, Galerie Myrtis, Baltimore, MD

International Juried Photographic Solarplate Exhibit, Alex Ferrone Gallery, New York, NY

2017

Human Trafficking, Watergate Gallery, Washington, DC

The Other Side of Darkness (solo exhibition), Project 1628 Gallery, Baltimore, MD

35th Anniversary Exhibition, Maryland Art Place, Baltimore, MD.

2018

Elixir: Artists Respond to Making and Healing, Hisaoka Healing Arts Gallery, Washington, DC

Relics and Prospects, Montpelier Art Center, Laurel, MD

In Her Own Words: Art, Blackness and Womanhood, James E. Lewis Museum, Morgan State University, Baltimore, MD

Collaboration & Innovation, The American Craft Center, Los Angeles, CA

The Circuitry of Joyce Jane Scott: A Group Exhibition of Collaboration & Innovation, American Craft Center, Los Angeles, CA

2019

Traces of the Spirit (solo exhibition), Baltimore Museum of Art, Baltimore, MD

Trawick Prize Finalists, Gallery B, Bethesda, MD

Love from Baltimore (curator: Schroeder Cherry), Brentwood Arts Exchange, Brentwood, MD

2020

Women Heal through Rite and Ritual, Galerie Mrytis, Baltimore, MD

2022

Exploring Presence: African American Artists In the Upper South, James E. Lewis Museum of Art, Morgan State University, Baltimore, MD

Oletha DeVane: Spectrum of Light and Spirit (solo exhibition, curator: Lowery Stokes Sims), Center for Art, Design, and Visual Culture, UMBC, Baltimore, MD

Fired Up! (curators: Howard L. Cohen, Amy Eva Raehse, Linda Day Clark), Cryor Art Gallery, Coppin State University, Baltimore, MD

The Radical Voices of Blackness, (curator: Myrtis Bedolla), Banneker Douglas Museum, Annapolis, MD

Compiled by Lowery Stokes Sims

Publications

Anderson, Virginia. "Artist Oletha DeVane on Materials and the Meanings They Hold." *BMA/Stories*, May 17, 2019, https://stories.artbma.org/oletha-devane/.

———, ed. *Oletha DeVane: Traces of the Spirit*. Exh. cat., essays by Leslie King-Hammond and Lowery Stokes Sims. Baltimore: Baltimore Museum of Art, 2019.

Bayehe, Simone Ebongo. "Baltimore Artists Bring Life to the City." *Baltimore Watchdog*, December 4, 2016, http://baltimorewatchdog.com/2016/12/04/baltimore-artists-bring-life-to-the-city/.

Benitez, Sylvia. "On Oletha DeVane." *Gentileschi Aegis Gallery Association*, https://gentileschiaegis.wordpress.com.

Carroll, Angela N. "Dark Things Matter: Oletha DeVane's The Other Side of Darkness at Project 1628." *Bmore Art*, May 10, 2017, http://www.bmoreart.com/2017/05/dark-things-matter.html.

———. "Oletha DeVane Showcases Sculptural Works in 'Traces of the Spirit' at the BMA." *Baltimore*, August 12, 2019, https://www.baltimoremagazine.com/section/artsentertainment/oletha-devane-showcases-sculptural-works-in-bma-exhibit-traces-of-spirit/.

Cascone, Sarah. "The Anonymous Was a Woman Grant Has Selected Its Largest-Ever Cohort of Female Artists Over 40." *Artnet*, November 9, 2021, https://news.artnet.com/art-world/anonymous-was-a-woman-expands-grant-program-2032181.

Copeland, Oswald S. "Baltimore Needs a Black High Priestess." *Theculturepagedotcom*, July 9, 2019, https://theculturepage.com/2019/07/09/baltimore-needs-a-black-high-priestess/.

"A Critical Look at the BMA's Year of Acquiring Art Only by Women." *Baltimore Brew*, January 23, 2021. https://baltimorebrew.com/2021/01/23/a-critical-look-at-the-bmas-year-of-acquiring-art-only-by-women/.

Guntz, Ed. "Local Artists Selected for Lexington Market." *Baltimore Fishbowl*, November 16, 2021, https://baltimorefishbowl.com/stories/local-artists-selected-for-lexington-market/.

McNatt, Glenn. "Works by Contemporary Artists, in a Range of Style, On View." *Baltimore Sun*, March 29, 2006, https://www.baltimoresun.com/news/bs-xpm-2006-03-29-0603290049-story.html.

Michaels, Leah Clare. "The Divinity of Water: An Interview with Artist Oletha DeVane." *The Debutante: The Feminist-Surrealist Arts Journal*, October 29, 2020, https://www.thedebutante.online/post/the-divinity-of-water-an-interview-with-artist-oletha-devane-by-leah-clare-michaels.

Ober, Cara. "Scene See: Inside Outside: Christopher Kojzar & Oletha DeVane at the Creative Alliance." *Bmore Art*, October 24, 2015, https://bmoreart.com/2015/10/scene-seen-inside-outside-christopher-kojzar-oletha-devane-at-creative-alliance.html.

Reed, Lillian. "'Complex Legacy': A Baltimore County Private School Considers How to Remember Those Enslaved by Its Founder." *Baltimore Sun*, April 19, 2022, https://www.baltimoresun.com/education/bs-md-mcdonogh-slavery-20220412-20220419-epoygntognguvfcgzjdkfmnjwu-story.html.

Roulet, Laura, and Irene Hoffman. *Corridor: Baltimore, Maryland–Washington, DC*. Exh. cat. Washington, DC: Art Museum of the Americas, Organization of American States, 2011, http://museum.oas.org/img/exhibitions/2011corridor/CorridorExhibitionCat_AMA.pdf.

Tooten, Tim. "'It Just Really Touches Me': New Memorial at McDonough School Honors Enslaved People." *WBAL-TV*, April 19, 2022, https://www.wbaltv.com/article/mcdonogh-school-memorial-honors-slaves/39764928#.

Websites

http://www.olethadevane.com/.

https://www.instagram.com/devanekojzar.

Oletha DeVane, Baker Artist Portfolio website: https://bakerartist.org/portfolios/oletha-devane.

Oletha DeVane, Artist Registry, Maryland State Arts Council website: https://msac.org/directory/artists/oletha-devane.

Oletha DeVane, *Craft in America* website: https://www.craftinamerica.org/artist/oletha-devane.

Oletha DeVane, *Art Matters Foundation* website: https://www.artmattersfoundation.org/grantees/oletha-devane.

Oletha DeVane, M/I/C/A Community Arts MFA: https://www.mica.edu/graduate-programs/community-arts-mfa/oletha-devane/.

Oletha DeVane, *Africanah.org*: https://africanah.org/oletha-devane/.

Oletha DeVane, *Exploring Presence*: https://vimeo.com/646653357.

Oletha DeVane, *Peter Bruun Gallery*: https://bruunstudios.com/oletha/.

McDonogh School website, page on DeVane: https://www.mcdonogh.org/about/news-photos/news/stories/2008/an-artist-s-invitation-to-closing-reception-at-evergreen-house.

"Women Heal Through Rite and Ritual," Galerie Myrtis Fine Art & Advisory: http://galeriemyrtis.net/women-heal-through-rite-and-ritual-oletha-devane/.

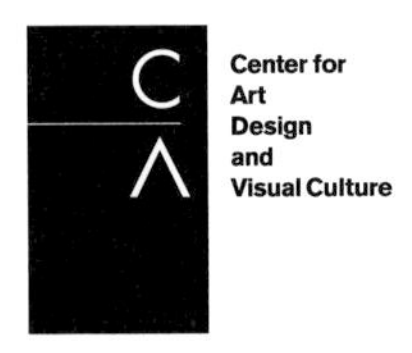

Center for Art Design and Visual Culture

Published by the

Center for Art, Design, and Visual Culture

University of Maryland, Baltimore County

Fine Arts Building
1000 Hilltop Circle
Baltimore, MD 21250
cadvc.umbc.edu

Available through

Artbook | D.A.P.

75 Broad Street, Suite 630
New York, NY 10004
www.artbook.com

Library of Congress Control Number:
2022949285

ISBN:
978-0-9600885-4-6

Published in conjunction with the exhibition *Oletha DeVane: Spectrum of Light and Spirit*, the first career retrospective of the Maryland-based artist, organized by Curator Lowery Stokes Sims. September 22 – December 17, 2022.

Center for Art, Design, and Visual Culture, UMBC

Rebecca Uchill, *Director*
Sandra Abbott, *Curator of Collections & Outreach*
Janet Magruder, *Business Manager*
Mitchell Noah, *Exhibition Coordinator*

Volume edited by Lowery Stokes Sims and Symmes Gardner

Designed by A. Mattson Gallagher

Copyeditor: James Gibbons
Proofreader: Amy Teschner

Typeset in Signifier and Fira Sans. The paper is 150 gsm Arctic Volume White.

Printed and bound by Oddi Sales in Slovenia.

Exhibition photography: Mitro Hood, Michael Koryta, Dan Meyers, Rassaan Hammond (Greeneye Media), Linda Day Clark, Tadia Rice, Marlayna Demond, and Oletha DeVane

The presentation of *Oletha DeVane: Spectrum of Light and Spirit* at the University of Maryland, Baltimore County, and the publication of this volume were made possible by generous support from the Maryland State Arts Council, funded by the State of Maryland, and the National Endowment for the Arts; and the Baltimore County Commission on Arts and Sciences.

Generous support for the publication was also provided by Joyce J. Scott, Dave Farace, and anonymous donors.

This publication is hosted digitally under a Creative Commons Attribution-NonCommercial-NoDerivatives 4.0 International (CC BY-NC-ND 4.0) license. The work can be copied and redistributed with appropriate credit, without modification, and not for commercial use.

This publication and all of the work contained within it © 2023 Center for Art, Design, and Visual Culture, with the exception of the following:

Texts:

"An Artist's Statement" © 2022 Oletha DeVane
"The Essence of Being Lies Within Ordinary, Useful/less Stuff, and Tangible Things" © 2019 Leslie King-Hammond, courtesy of the Baltimore Museum of Art, Baltimore, MD
"Artist's Statement" © 2022 Tadia Rice

Images:

Exhibition photography by Marlayna Demond © UMBC
Images of *N'Kisi* activation event at UMBC © Rassaan Hammond
Process image of *N'Kisi* sculpture © Camille Olliviere
Peter (formerly identified as "Gordon"), William D. McPherson and Mr. Oliver
Portrait of Harriet Tubman, Benjamin F. Powelson
Oletha DeVane artwork documentation © Michael Koryta
Documentation images © Christopher Kojzar
View of *Memorial to Those Enslaved and Freed*, 2022 © Dave Radford
Oletha DeVane artwork documentation © Mitro Hood
Sacred Geometry documentation © Dan Meyers

All Oletha DeVane original artworks © the artist and, where applicable, her collaborators.